STUDY GUIDE

PRINCIPLES OF OPERATIONS MANAGEMENT
Fifth Edition

OPERATIONS MANAGEMENT
Seventh Edition

STUDY GUIDE
Robert Woosley
Louisiana State University

PRINCIPLES OF OPERATIONS MANAGEMENT
Fifth Edition

OPERATIONS MANAGEMENT
Seventh Edition

Jay Heizer
Barry Render

Prentice
Hall

Upper Saddle River, New Jersey 07458

Editor-in-Chief: PJ Boardman
Acquisitions Editor: Tom Tucker
Assistant Editor: Erika Rusnak
Manager, Print Production: Christy Mahon
Production Editor & Buyer: Carol O'Rourke
Printer/Binder: VonHoffman Graphics, Inc., MD

Pearson Prentice Hall™ is a trademark of Pearson Education, Inc.

10 9 8 7 6 5 4 3 2 1
ISBN 0-13-101942-2

Contents

MODULES

Overview of Study Guide

This book is written for students. It is to help their understanding of the concepts and quantitative methods of Production and Operations Management. This book is meant to be a comprehensive collection of fundamental ideas while also utilizing a step-by-step format to illustrate the problem solving and analysis skills.

The chapters of this book have four basic components.

1. Lecture Notes
2. Key Lecture Points
3. Example Solved Problems
4. Supplemental Example Problems

The lecture notes are the outline form of the text chapters, with the bulk of the material in the text highlighted. The Key Lecture Points are elements that may need special emphasis. The Example Solved Problems are step-by-step solutions to the techniques within the chapter. The Supplemental Example Problems are extra problems that are separated into the various techniques for easier navigation to supplemental work. Since students may not need to practice large numbers of some techniques, they can easily skip around to the topics of interest.

*This book is written in loving tribute
to my wife, Janelle, and my daughter, Madilyn.
Without your support, understanding, and sacrifice,
this project would not have been completed.
Special thanks to my family and friends
during this project as well.*

1

Operations and Productivity

I. **Operations and Productivity**

   A. Operations Management (OM) – a discipline that applies to restaurants like Hard Rock Cafe as well as factories like Sony, Ford, and Maytag.

   B. The production of goods and services requires operations management.

II. **What is Operations Management?**

   A. Production – the creation of goods and services.

   B. Operations Management – a set of activities that create value in the form of goods and services by transforming inputs into outputs.

   C. Transformation can take many forms:
      1. In manufacturing, production activities create tangible products such as a Sony TV.
      2. In organizations such as banks, hospitals, airline offices, or colleges, production is in the form of a service where the process may not be visible.

Lecture Key: The transformation process is based on adding value for the customer by transforming the inputs into outputs.

III. **Organizing to Produce Goods and Services**

   A. Requires 3 functions:
      1. Marketing – generates the demand, or at least takes the order for a product or service.
      2. Production/Operation – creates the products.
      3. Finance/Accounting – tracks how well the organization is doing, pays the bills, and collects the money.

   B. These functions are also crucial for the organization's survival.

Lecture Key: Operations is one of the basic functions of any business. Without operations, there is no reason to be in business. Pressures come from many environments and managers must be aware of the impact on all parties.

IV. **Why Study OM?**

   A. OM is one of the 3 major functions. Studying how people organize themselves for productive enterprise.

   B. Want to know how goods and service are produced.

   C. Want to know what operations managers do. This will help develop the skills necessary to become a manager.

   D. It is a very costly part of an organization.

Fisher Technologies is a small firm that must double its dollar contribution to fixed cost and profit in order to be profitable enough to purchase the next generation of production equipment. Management has determined that if the firm fails to increase contribution, its bank will not make the loan and the equipment cannot be purchased. If the firm cannot purchase the equipment, the limitations of the old equipment will force Fisher to go out of business and, in doing so, put its employees out of work and discontinue producing goods and services for its customers.

The table below shows a simple profit-and-loss statement and three strategic options for the firm. The first option is a marketing option where good marketing management may increase sales by 50%. By increasing sales by 50%, contribution will in turn increase 71%, but increasing sales by 50% may be difficult; it may even be impossible.

The second option is a finance/accounting option where finance costs are cut in half through good financial management. But even a reduction of 50% is still inadequate for generating the necessary increase in contribution. Contribution is increased by only 21%.

The third option is an OM option where management reduces production costs by 20% and increases contribution by 114%. Given the conditions of our brief example, Fisher Technologies has increased contribution from $10,500 to $22,500 and will now have a bank willing to lend it additional funds.

OPTIONS FOR INCREASING CONTRIBUTION				
		Marketing Option	**Finance/Acct. Option**	**OM Option**
	Current	**Increase Sales Revenue 50%**	**Reduce Finance Costs 50%**	**Reduce Production Costs 20%**
Sales	$100,000	$150,000	$100,000	$100,000
Costs of goods	-80,000	-120,000	-80,000	-64,000
Gross margin	20,000	30,000	20,000	36,000
Finance costs	-6,000	-6,000	-3,000	-6,000
Subtotal	14,000	24,000	17,000	30,000
Taxes at 25%	-3,500	-6,000	-4,250	-7,500
Contribution	$10,500	$18,000	$12,750	$22,500

V. What Operations Managers Do

A. Management process consists of:
   1. Planning
   2. Organizing
   3. Staffing
   4. Leading
   5. Controlling
B. Managers use the management process to aid in decisions in the following areas:
   1. Service and product design
   2. Quality management
   3. Process and capacity design
   4. Location
   5. Layout design
   6. Human resources and job design
   7. Supply-chain management
   8. Inventory, material requirements planning, and JIT
   9. Intermediate and short-term scheduling
   10. Maintenance

VI.   The Heritage of Operations Management

A. Eli Whitney (1800) – credited for the early popularization of interchangeable parts. It was achieved through standardization and quality control.

B. Frederick Taylor (1881) – known as the father of scientific management.
1. Contributed to personnel selection, planning and scheduling, motion study, and ergonomics.
2. Believed that management should be much more resourceful and aggressive in the improvement of work methods. Also, believed that management should assume more responsibility for:
   a. Matching employees to the right job.
   b. Providing the proper training.
   c. Providing proper work methods and tools.
   d. Establishing legitimate incentives for work to be accomplished.

C. Henry Ford & Charles Sorensen (1913) – combined what they knew about standardized parts with the quasi-assembly lines of the meat packing and mail-order industries and added the revolutionary concept of the assembly line.

D. Walter Shewhart (1924) – combined his knowledge of statistics with the need for quality control and provided the foundations for statistical sampling in quality control.

E. W. Edwards Deming (1950) – believed that management must do more to improve the work environment and processes so that quality can be improved.

F. OM has also received contributions from the areas of industrial engineering and management science.

G. Information sciences have made some important contributions recently. Information science is the systematic processing of data to yield information.

VII.   Operations in the Service Sector

A. Services – include repair and maintenance, government, food and lodging, transportation, insurance, trade, financial, real estate, education, legal, medical, and entertainment.

B. Difference between goods and services. Services are:
1. Usually intangible.
2. Often produced and consumed simultaneously; there is not stored inventory.
3. Often unique.
4. Have high customer interaction.
5. Have inconsistent product definition.
6. Often knowledge based.
7. Frequently dispersed.

C. Operations for goods and services are very similar.

D. Most services are a mixture of a service and a tangible product.

VIII.   Exciting New Trends in OM

A. OM is facing an ever-changing world.

B. Some of the new challenges include:
1. Global focus.
2. Just-in-time performance.
3. Supply-chain partnering.
4. Rapid product development.
5. Mass customization.
6. Empowered employees.
7. Environmentally sensitive production.

IX. The Productivity Challenge

A. The creation of goods and services requires changing resources into goods and services.

B. The more efficient the conversion, the more productive we are and the more value is added to the good or service provided.

C. Productivity – the ratio of outputs (goods and services) divided by the inputs (resources such as labor and capital).

Productivity = Output / Input

D. Improvements can be made by:
1. Reducing inputs while outputs remain constant.
2. Increasing outputs while inputs remain constant.

E. Measurement of productivity is an excellent way to evaluate a country's ability to provide an improving standard of living for its people.

F. Productivity Measurement
1. Can be measured in a direct form such as labor-hours per ton of steel, known as single factor productivity.

Productivity = Units produced / Labor-hours used

2. A broader view known as multifactor productivity can also be used.

Productivity = Output / Labor + Material + Energy + Capital + Misc.

3. Using measures of productivity aids managers in determining how well they are doing.

4. Multifactor provides better information about the trade-offs among factors, but measurement problems remain.
a. Quality may change while the quality of inputs and outputs remains constant.
b. External elements may cause an increase or decrease in productivity for which the system under study may not be directly responsible.
c. Precise units of measure may be lacking.

5. Particularly difficult to measure service productivity.

Lecture Key: There are obviously several ways to measure competitiveness and productivity. The important key is to measure on a constant basis to determine the validity of the information.

Example: Productivity

Collins Title Company has a staff of 4, each working 8 hours per day (for a payroll cost of $640 / day) and overhead expenses of $400 per day. Collins processes and closes on 8 titles each day. The company recently purchased a computerized title-search system that will allow the processing of 14 titles per day. Although the staff, their work hours, and pay will be the same, the overhead expenses are now $800 per day.

Solution:

Labor productivity with the old system	= 8 titles per day / 32 labor-hrs.
	= .25 titles per labor-hr.
Labor productivity with the new system	= 14 titles per day / 32 labor-hrs.
	= .4375 titles per labor-hr.
Multifactor productivity with the old system	= 8 titles per day / $640 + 400
	= .0077 titles per dollar
Multifactor productivity with the new system	= 14 titles per day / $640 + 400
	= .0097 titles per dollar

4

Labor productivity has increased from .25 to .4375. The change is .4375 / .25 = 1.75, or a 75% increase in labor productivity. Multifactor productivity has increased from .0077 to .0097. This change is .0097 / .0077 = 1.259, or 25.9% increase in multifactor productivity.

   G. Product Variables
      1. Labor
         a. Contributes about 10% of the annual increase.
         b. Three key variables for improved labor productivity:
            i.   Basic education appropriate for an effective labor force.
            ii. Diet of the labor force.
            iii. Social overhead that makes labor available, such as transportation and sanitation.
      2. Capital
         a. Contributes about 38% of the annual increase.
         b. Capital investment has increased in the U.S. every year except during a few very severe recession periods.
         c. U.S. has increased annual capital investment by 1.5% annually.
         d. Inflation and taxes increase the cost of capital investment.
      3. Management
         a. Contributes about 52% of the annual increase.
         b. A factor of production and an economic resource.
         c. Responsible for ensuring that labor and capital are effectively used to increase productivity.
         d. Includes improvements made through the application of technology and the utilization of knowledge.
   H. Productivity and the Service Sector
      1. Services pose special challenges and problems when attempting to measure productivity and productivity improvement.
      2. Reasons for service-sector work being difficult:
         a. Typically labor-intensive (for example, counseling, teaching).
         b. Frequently individually processed (for example, investment counseling).
         c. Often an intellectual task performed by professionals (for example, medical diagnosis).
         d. Often difficult to mechanize and automate (for example, a haircut).
         e. Often difficult to evaluate for quality (for example, performance of a law firm).

2
Operations Strategy in a Global Environment

I. Operations Strategy in a Global Environment

    A. OM must take on a global view.

    B. Emerging economies have required companies to extend OM globally.

    C. New standards of global competitiveness have been developed that include:

        1. Quality

        2. Variety

        3. Customization

        4. Convenience

        5. Timeliness

        6. Cost

    D. Companies are responding to the global environment with new strategies and speeds.

II. A Global View of Operations

    A. Reduced costs in the form of cheaper labor, lower taxes and tariffs are available by shifting operations internationally.

    B. Improved supply-chain can be achieved by locating facilities in countries where unique resources are available.

    C. Provide better goods and services that can be customized to fit different cultures.

    D. Attracts firms to new markets, products, and services.

    E. Companies can learn to improve operations by remaining open to ideas from international operations.

    F. Companies can attract and retain global talent in the form of better employees.

III. Developing Missions and Strategies

    A. Effective OM must have a mission and strategy.

    B. Missions are used to:

        1. Identify how to satisfy a customer's needs and wants.

        2. An organization's purpose – what it will contribute to society.

        3. Provide boundaries and focus for organizations.

        4. State why an organization exists.

    C. Strategy

        1. An organization's action plan to achieve the mission.

        2. Developed and implemented after mission is established.

        3. Each functional area develops a strategy for achieving its mission and the overall mission of the organization.

4. Firms achieve missions in 3 conceptual ways:
   a. Differentiation
   b. Cost leadership
   c. Quick response

Lecture Key: *The mission statement has to be used as a management tool to provide direction to management, employees, and customers.*

IV. Achieving Competitive Advantage Through Operations

A. Competitive Advantage – the creation of a system that has a unique advantage over competitors.

B. Trying to create customer value in an efficient and sustainable way.

C. Three ways to compete:
   1. Competing on differentiation –
      a. Concerned with providing uniqueness, which can arise in everything a firm does.
      b. Differentiation should go beyond both physical characteristics and service attributes to encompass everything about the product or service that influences the value that the customers derive from it.
      c. Experience differentiation is used in services to engage the customer. Want people to use their 5 senses so they become immersed and perhaps even an active participant in the product.
   2. Competing on cost (low-cost leadership) –
      a. Entails achieving maximum value as defined by your customer.
      b. Requires examining each of the 10 OM decisions in a relentless effort to drive down costs while meeting customer expectations of value.
      c. Does not imply low value or low quality.
   3. Competing on response –
      a. Response – the entire range of values related to timely product development and delivery, as well as reliable scheduling and flexible performance.
      b. Flexible response – the ability to match changes in a marketplace where design innovations and volumes fluctuate substantially.
         i. Reliability of scheduling and quickness are other aspects of response.
   4. The concepts are implemented through six specific strategies:
      a. Flexibility in design and volume
      b. Low price
      c. Delivery
      d. Quality
      e. After-sale service
      f. Broad product line

V. Ten Strategic OM Decisions

A. Goods and service design – defines much of the transformation process.
   1. Costs, quality, and human resource decisions are often determined by design decisions.
   2. Designs determine the lower limits of cost.
   3. Designs determine the upper limits of quality.

B. Quality – customer's quality expectations must be determined and policies and procedures established to identify and achieve that quality.

C. Process and capacity design

D. Location selection – may determine the firm's ultimate success.

E. Layout design – material flows, capacity needs, personnel levels, technology decisions, and inventory requirements influence layout.
F. Human resources and job design – it is important to determine the quality of work life provided, the talent and skills required, and their costs must be determined.
G. Supply-chain management – determine what is to be made and what is to be purchased.
H. Inventory – can be optimized only when customer satisfaction, suppliers, production schedules, and human resource planning are controlled.
I. Maintenance – made regarding desired levels of reliability and stability, and systems must be established to maintain that reliability and stability.

VI.   Issues In Operations Strategy

A. Research
   1. Research of high ROI firms found the characteristics that impact strategic OM decisions are:
      a. High product quality (relative to the competition).
      b. High capacity utilization.
      c. High operating efficiency (the ratio of expected to actual employee productivity).
      d. Low investment intensity (the amount of capital required to produce a dollar of sales).
      e. Low direct cost per unit (relative to the competition).
   2. These characteristics should be considered as an organization develops a strategy.
B. Preconditions
   1. Many factors influence strategy development and execution, and they must be considered before establishing a strategy.
   2. Some of the factors to consider include:
      a. Strengths and weaknesses of competitors, as well as possible new entrants into the market, substitute products, and commitment of suppliers and distributors.
      b. Current and prospective environmental, technological, legal, and economic issues.
      c. Product life cycle, which may dictate the limitations of operations strategy.
      d. Resources available within the firm and within the OM function.
      e. Integration of the OM strategy with the company's strategy and other functional areas.
C. Dynamics
   1. Strategies change due to changes within the organization. Changes may occur in a variety of areas including:
      a. Personnel
      b. Finance
      c. Technology
      d. Product life
   2. Strategies change due to changes in the environment.

VII.   Strategy Development and Implementation

A. After evaluating the issues in effective strategy development, the company performs a SWOT analysis (Strength, Weakness, Opportunities, and Threats)
B. Successful strategy implementation requires identifying those tasks that are critical success factors.
   1. Critical success factors (CSFs) – those relatively few activities that make a difference between having and not having a competitive advantage.
   2. Successful organizations identify and use critical success factors to develop a unique and distinct competence.

3. The CSFs have to be supported by related activities. An activity map is a tool used to help identify these related activities by links between the competitive advantage, CSFs, and supporting activities.
C. Building and staffing the organization with personnel who will get the job done is critical.
D. The operations function is most successful when the operations strategy integrates with the firm's other functional area.

Strategy Development Process

> **Environmental Analysis**
> Identify the strengths, weakness, opportunities, and threats.
> Understand the environment, customers, industry, and competitors.

> **Determine Corporate Mission**
> State the reason for the firm's existence and identify the value it wishes to create.

> **Form a Strategy**
> Build a competitive advantage, such as low price, design or volume flexibility, quality, quick delivery, dependability, after-the-sale services, broad product lines.

VIII. Global Operations Strategy Options

A. International business – any firm that engages in international trade or investment.
B. Multinational corporation (MNC) – a firm with extensive international business involvement. MNCs buy resources, create goods and services, and sell goods or services in a variety of countries.
C. Four strategies that international businesses and multinational corporations use to approach global opportunities.
   1. International strategy – Uses exports and licenses to penetrate the global arena. This is a very limited strategy.
   2. Multidomestic strategy – Uses a decentralized organization, which provides substantial autonomy through the forms of subsidiaries, franchises, or joint ventures with substantial independence. The advantage is maximizing a competitive response for the local market.
   3. Global strategy – Uses a high degree of centralization, with headquarters coordinating the organization to seek out standardization and learning between plants, thus generating economies of scale. This is the best strategy if the focus is cost reduction.
   4. Transnational strategy – Exploits the economies of scale and learning, as well as pressure for responsiveness, by recognizing that core competence does not reside in just the "home" country, but can exist anywhere in the organization.

3

Project Management

I. The Importance of Project Management

A. Scheduling projects is a difficult challenge to operations managers. The stakes in project management are high. Cost overruns and unnecessary delays occur due to poor scheduling and poor controls.

B. The management of projects involves three phases (see Figure 3.1 below):

1. Planning: This phase includes goal setting, defining the project, and team organization.

2. Scheduling: This phase relates people, money, and supplies to specific activities and relates activities to each other.

3. Controlling: Here the firm monitors resources, costs, quality, and budgets. It also revises or changes the plans and shifts resources to meet time and cost demands.

FIGURE 3.1 ■

Project Planning, Scheduling, and Controlling

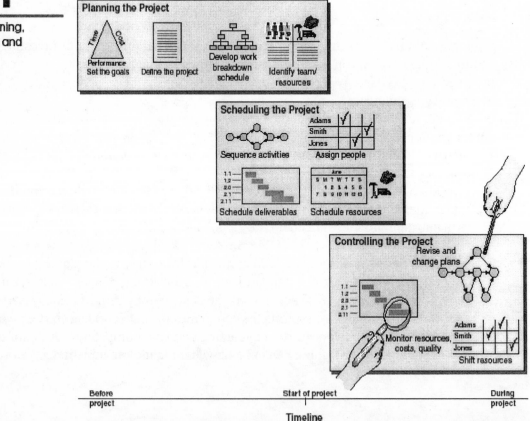

Lecture Key: All projects require the manager to focus on planning, scheduling, and controlling of the projects. Most companies are placing great emphasis on improving their current project management processes due to project complexity and collapsing product/service life cycles.

10

II.   Project Planning

A. Projects can be defined as a series of related tasks directed toward a major output.
B. The project organization works best when (see figure on next page):
1. Work can be defined with a specific goal and deadline.
2. The job is unique or somewhat unfamiliar to the existing organization.
3. The work contains complex interrelated tasks requiring specialized skills.
4. The project is temporary but critical to the organization.
5. The project cuts across organizational lines.

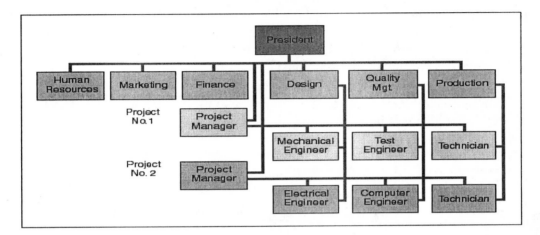

C. Project managers receive high visibility in a firm and are responsible for making sure that:
1. All necessary activities are finished in proper sequence and on time.
2. The project comes in within budget.
3. The project meets its quality goals.
4. The people assigned to the project receive the motivation, direction, and information needed to do their jobs.
D. The work breakdown structure typically decreases in size from top to bottom and is indented like this:

Level	Level ID Number	Activity
1	1.0	Develop/launch Windows XP Operating System
2	1.1	Development of GUIs
2	1.2	Ensure compatibility with earlier Windows versions
3	1.21	Compatibility with Windows 98
3	1.22	Compatibility with Windows NT
3	1.23	Compatibility with Windows 2000
4	1.231	Ability to import files

Lecture Key: *The manager heading the project coordinates activities with other departments and reports directly to top management. The manager defines the project with the work breakdown structure. This divides it into its major subcomponents (or tasks), which are then subdivided into more detailed components, and finally into a set of activities and their related costs.*

III. Project Scheduling

   A. Project scheduling involves sequencing and allotting time to all project activities.

   B. One popular project scheduling approach is the Gantt chart (see Figure 3.4 on next page). Gantt charts are a low-cost means of helping managers make sure that:

      1. All activities are planned for.

      2. Their order of performance is accounted for.

      3. The activity time estimates are recorded.

      4. The overall project time is developed.

   C. To summarize, whatever the approach taken by a project manager, project scheduling serves several purposes:

      1. It shows the relationship of each activity to others and to the whole project.

      2. It identifies the precedence relationships among activities.

      3. It encourages the setting of realistic time and cost estimates for each activity.

      4. It helps make better use of people, money, and material resources by identifying critical bottlenecks in the project.

FIGURE 3.4 ■

Gantt Chart of Service Activities for a Delta Jet during a 60-Minute Layover

		Time, minutes
Passengers	Deplaning	
	Baggage claim	
Baggage	Container offload	
Fueling	Pumping	
	Engine injection water	
Cargo and mail	Container offload	
Galley servicing	Main cabin door	
	Aft cabin door	
Lavatory servicing	Aft, center, forward	
Drinking water	Loading	
Cabin cleaning	First-class section	
	Economy section	
Cargo and mail	Container/bulk loading	
Flight service	Galley/cabin check	
	Receive passengers	
Operating crew	Aircraft check	
Baggage	Loading	
Passengers	Boarding	

0   15   30   45   60
Time, minutes

Lecture Key: Managers have to decide how long each activity will take and compute how many people and materials will be needed at each stage of production. Managers also chart personnel needs by type of skill (management, engineering, or pouring concrete). Charts (such as the Gantt chart above) also can be developed for scheduling materials.

IV. Project Controlling

   A. The control of large projects, like the control of any management system, involves close monitoring of resources, costs, quality, and budgets.

   B. Computer programs produce a broad variety of reports, including:

      1. Detailed cost breakdowns for each task.

      2. Total program labor curves.

      3. Cost distribution tables.

      4. Functional cost and hour summaries.

      5. Raw material and expenditure forecasts.

      6. Variance reports.

      7. Time analysis reports.

      8. Work status reports.

Lecture Key: *Control also means using a feedback loop to revise the project plan and having the ability to shift resources to where they are needed most.*

V.   Project Management Techniques: PERT and CPM

A. Program evaluation and review technique (PERT) and the critical path method (CPM) were both developed to help managers schedule, monitor, and control large and complex projects.

B. The objectives and analysis of both techniques are similar, but PERT employs three time estimates for each activity, while CPM uses only one time estimate.

C. PERT and CPM both follow six basic steps:
1. Define the project and prepare the work breakdown structure.
2. Develop the relationships among the activities. Decide which activities must precede and which must follow others.
3. Draw the network connecting all of the activities.
4. Assign time and/or cost estimates to each activity.
5. Compute the longest time path through the network (called critical path).
6. Use the network to help plan, schedule, monitor, and control the project.

D. There are two approaches for drawing a project network: activity on node (AON) and activity on arrow (AOA). Under the AON convention, nodes designate activities. Under AOA, arrows represent activities.

E. Dummy activities have no time but are inserted into the network to maintain the logic of the network.

F. See the figure on the following page for an explanation on how to properly draw a project network.

Activity on Node (AON)	Activity Meaning	Activity on Arrow (AOA)
A → B → C	A comes before B, which comes before C.	A → B → C
A, B → C	A and B must both be completed before C can start.	A, B → C
A → B, C	B and C cannot begin until A is completed.	A → B, C
A, B → C, D	C and D cannot begin until A and B have both been completed.	A, B → C, D
A, B → C; B → D	C cannot begin until both A and B are completed; D cannot begin until B is completed. A dummy activity is introduced in AOA.	A → C; B → D (Dummy activity)
A → B → D; A → C → D	B and C cannot begin until A is completed. D cannot begin until both B and C are completed. A dummy activity is again introduced in AOA.	A → B → D; C → (Dummy activity)

Lecture Key: Program evaluation and review technique (PERT) and the critical path method (CPM) both help the manager schedule, monitor, and control large and complex projects. The processes are similar, differing only in the number of time estimates used. Using a system of nodes and arrows, projects can be drawn to give a helpful visual representation of a project.

Given the following information, develop a table showing activity precedence relationships.

Milwaukee General Hospital, located in downtown Milwaukee, has long been trying to avoid the expense of installing air pollution control equipment in its extensive laundry/cleaning operations facility. The Environmental Protection Agency has recently given the hospital 16 weeks to install a complex air filter system. Milwaukee General has been warned that it may be forced to close the laundry facility unless the device is installed in the allotted period. Dr. Joni Steinberg, the hospital administrator, wants to make sure that installation of the filtering system progresses smoothly and on time.

Milwaukee General has identified the eight activities that need to be performed in order for the project to be completed. When the project begins, two activities can be simultaneously started: building the internal components for the device (activity A) and the modifications necessary for the floor and roof (activity B). The construction of the collection stack (activity C) can begin when the internal components are completed. Pouring the concrete floor and installation of the frame (activity D) can be started as soon as the internal components are completed and the roof and floor have been modified.

After the collection stack has been constructed, two activities can begin: building the high-temperature burner (activity E) and installing the pollution control system (activity F). The air pollution device can be installed (activity G) after the concrete floor has been poured, the frame has been installed, and the high temperature burner has been built. Finally, after the control system and pollution device have been installed, the system can be inspected and tested (activity H).

Activities and precedence relationships may seem rather confusing when they are presented in this descriptive form. It is therefore convenient to list all the activity information in a table, as shown below. We see in the table that activity A is listed as an immediate predecessor of activity C. Likewise, both activities D and E must be performed prior to starting activity G.

Activity	Description	Immediate Predecessors
A	Build internal components	---
B	Modify roof and floor	---
C	Construct collection stack	A
D	Pour concrete and install frame	A, B
E	Build high-temperature burner	C
F	Install pollution control system	C
G	Install air pollution device	D, E
H	Inspect and test	F, G

Solution:

Step 1: Draw the AON network for Milwaukee General Hospital. Recall that in the AON approach, we denote each activity by a node. The lines represent the precedence relationships between the activities. In this example, there are two activities (A and B) that do not have any predecessors. We draw separate nodes for each of these activities, as shown below. Although not required, it is usually convenient to have a unique starting activity for a project. We have therefore included a dummy activity called a Start. This dummy activity does not really exist and takes up zero time and resources. Activity Start is an immediate predecessor for both activities A and B, and serves as the unique starting activity for the entire project.

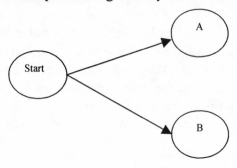

We now show the precedence relationships using lines with arrow symbols. For example, an arrow from activity Start to activity A indicates that Start is a predecessor for activity A. In a similar fashion, we draw an arrow from Start to B.

Step 2: Next, we add a new node for activity C. Since activity A precedes activity C, we draw an arc from node A to node C. Likewise, we first draw a node to represent activity D. Then, since activities A and B both precede activity D, we draw arrows from A to D, and B to D.

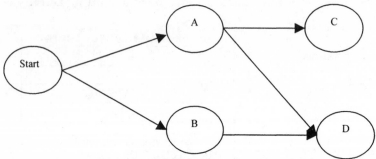

Step 3: We proceed in this fashion, adding a separate node for each activity and a separate line for each precedence relationship that exists. The complete AON project network for the Milwaukee General Hospital project is shown below.

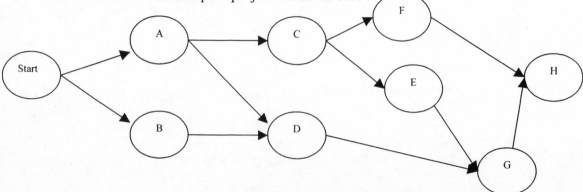

Draw the complete AOA project network for Milwaukee General Hospital's problem.

Solution:

Using the data from the table in the previous problem, we see that activity A starts at event 1 and ends at event 2. Likewise, activity B starts at event 1 and ends at event 3. Activity C, whose only immediate predecessor is activity A, starts at node 2 and ends at node 4. Activity D, however, has two predecessors (i.e., A and B). Hence, we need both activities A and B to end at event 3, so that activity D can start at that event. However, we cannot have multiple activities with common starting and ending nodes in an AOA network. To overcome this difficulty, in such cases, we may need to add a dummy line (activity) to enforce the precedence relationship. The dummy activity, shown in the figure below as a dashed line, is inserted between events 2 and 3 to make the diagram reflect the precedence between A and D. Recall that the dummy activity does not really exist in the project and takes up zero time. The remainder of the AOA project network for Milwaukee General Hospital's example is also shown.

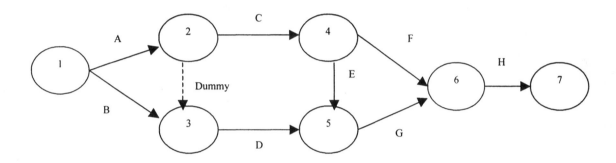

VI.   Determining the Project Schedule

 A. To find the critical path, we calculate two distinct starting and ending times for each activity. These are defined as follows:
   1. Earliest start (ES) = earliest time at which an activity can start, assuming all predecessors have been completed
        ES = Max {EF of all immediate predecessors}
   2. Earliest finish (EF) = earliest time at which an activity can be finished
        EF = ES + Activity time
   3. Latest start (LS) = latest time at which an activity can start so as to not delay the completion time of the entire project
        LF = Min {LS of all immediate following activities}
   4. Latest finish (LF) = latest time by which an activity has to finish so as to not delay the completion time of the entire project
        LS = LF – Activity time

B. To clearly show the activity schedules on the project network, we use the notation below.

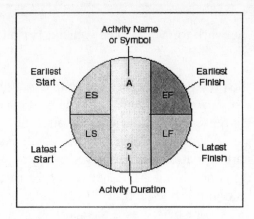

C. The early start and finish times (ES & EF) are determined during the forward pass. The forward pass through the nodes allows us to determine the earliest project completion time.
D. The late start and finish times (LS & LF) are determined during the backward pass.
E. After all early and late times have been determined, the free time of an activity, slack, can be found. Slack = LS – ES or Slack = LF – EF.
F. The activities with zero slack are called critical activities and are said to be on the critical path.

Lecture Key: *First, find all of the earliest times that an activity can start and finish. This determines the expected completion time of a project. Then, determine all of the latest times that an activity can start and finish. This evaluates the slack that each activity is allowed, as well as the critical path of the project.*

Example: Network Diagram Using AON (continued from previous example)

Activity	Description	Time (weeks)	Immediate Predecessors
A	Build internal components	2	---
B	Modify roof and floor	3	---
C	Construct collection stack	2	A
D	Pour concrete and install frame	4	A, B
E	Build high-temperature burner	4	C
F	Install pollution control system	3	C
G	Install air pollution device	5	D, E
H	Inspect and test	2	F, G
		25	

Calculate the earliest start and finish times for the activities in the Milwaukee General Hospital project. The table above has the activity times.

Solution:

Step 1: Draw the precedence diagram (completed in an earlier example) & compute the early start and finish times with a forward pass through the diagram. The forward pass tells you the expected completion time of your project.

$$ES = Max\ (EF)\ \&\ EF = ES + t$$

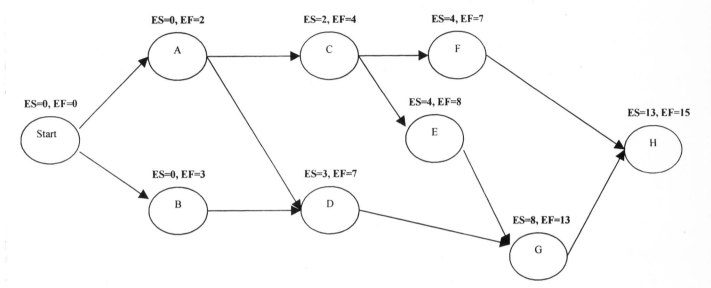

Since activity Start has no predecessors, we begin by setting its ES to 0. That is, activity Start can begin at the end of week 0, which is the same as the beginning of week 1. If activity Start has an ES of 0, its EF is also 0, since its activity time is 0.

Next, we consider activities A and B, both of which have only Start as an immediate predecessor. Using the earliest start time rule, the ES for both activities A and B equals zero, which is the EF of activity Start. Now, using the earliest finish time rule, the EF for A is 2 (= 0 + 2), and the EF for B is 3 (= 0 + 3).

Since activity A precedes activity C, the ES of C equals the EF of A (= 2). The EF of C is therefore 4 (= 2 + 2).

We now come to activity D. Both activities A and B are immediate predecessors for B. Whereas A has an EF of 2, activity B has an EF of 3. Using the earliest finish time rule, we compute the ES of activity D as follows:

ES of D = Max (EF of A, EF of B) = Max (2, 3) = 3

The EF of D equals 7 (= 3 + 4). Next, both activities E and F have activity C as their only immediate predecessor. Therefore, the ES for both E and F equals 4 (= EF of C). The EF of E is 8 (= 4 + 4), and the EF of F is 7 (= 4 + 3).

Activity G has both activities D and E as predecessors. Using the earliest start time rule, its ES is therefore the maximum of EF of D and EF of E. Hence, the ES of activity G equals 8 (= maximum of 7 and 8), and its EF equals 13 (= 8 + 5).

Finally, we come to activity H. Since it also has two predecessors, F and G, the ES of H is the maximum EF of these two activities. That is, the ES of H equals 13 (= maximum of 13 and 7). This implies that the EF of H is 15 (= 13 + 2). Since H is the last activity in the project, this also implies that the earliest time in which the entire project can be completed is 15 weeks (the expected completion time of the project).

Calculate the latest start and finish times for each activity in Milwaukee General's pollution project.

Step 2: Compute the late start and finish times with a backward pass through the diagram. The backward pass tells you the acceptable delays (slack) of your project. It also identifies your critical path.

$$LS = LF - t \ \& \ LF = Min\,(LS)$$

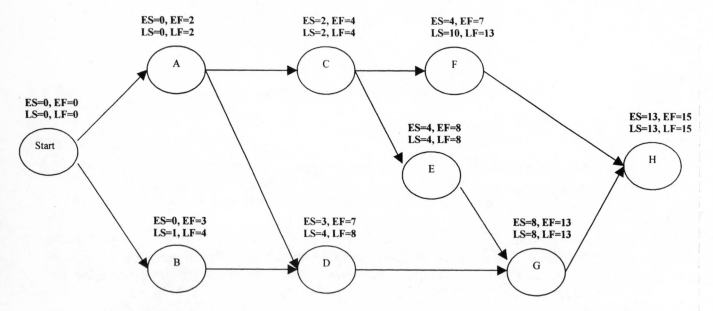

We begin by assigning an LF value to 15 weeks for activity H. That is, we specify that the latest finish time for the entire project is the same as its earliest finish time. Using the latest start time rule, the LS of activity H is equal to 13 (= 15 − 2).

Since activity H is the lone succeeding activity for both activities F and G, the LF for both F and G equals 13. This implies that the LS of G is 8 (= 13 − 5), and the LS of F is 10 (= 13 − 3).

Proceeding in this fashion, the LF of E is 8 (= LS of G), and its LS is 4 (= 8 − 4). Likewise, the LF of D is 8 (= LS of G), and its LS is 4 (= 8 − 4).

We now consider activity C, which is an immediate predecessor to two activities: E and F. Using the latest finish time rule, we compute the LF of activity C as follows:

LF of C = Min (LS of E, LS of F) = Min (4, 10) = 4

The LS of C is computed as 2 (= 4 − 2). Next, we compute the LF of B as 4 (= LS of D), and its LS as 1 (= 4 − 3).

We now consider activity A. We compute LF as 2 (minimum of LS of C and LS of D). Hence, the LS of activity A is 0 (= 2 – 2). Finally, both the LF and LS of activity Start are equal to 0.

Calculate the slack for the activities in the Milwaukee General Hospital project and identify the critical path of the project.

Step 3: Compute the slack of your project activities. This identifies your critical activities.

$$S = LF - EF \text{ or } LS - ES$$

Activity	t	ES	EF	LS	LF	Slack
A	2	0	2	0	2	0
B	3	0	3	1	4	1
C	2	2	4	2	4	0
D	4	3	7	4	8	1
E	4	4	8	4	8	0
F	3	4	7	10	13	6
G	5	8	13	8	13	0
H	2	13	15	13	15	0

Step 4: Identify the critical activities and the critical path.

Path: A-C-E-G-H are all critical activities since they all have slacks of 0, so the sequence of activities A-C-E-G-H determine the critical path or shortest time to complete this project.

VII.   Variability in Activity Times

A. In practice, it is likely that activity completion times vary depending on various factors, and therefore, we cannot ignore the impact of variability in activity times when deciding the schedule for a project.
B. In PERT, we employ a probability distribution based on three time estimates for each activity, as follows:
   a. Optimistic time (a) – time an activity will take if everything goes as planned.
   b. Pessimistic time (b) – time an activity will take assuming very unfavorable conditions.
   c. Most likely time (m) – most realistic estimate of the time required to complete an activity.
C. To find the expected activity time, we use:
   $$t_e = (a + 4m + b)/6$$
D. To find the variance of activity completion time, we use:
   $$\text{Variance } (\sigma^2) = [(b - a) / 6]^2$$
E. Project variance equals the sum of variances of activities on critical path.
F. The probability of completing the project by a certain date can be found by:
   (Due date – expected date of completion) / standard deviation
      or
   $$z = (x - \mu) / \sigma$$

Suppose Dr. Steinberg and the project management team at Milwaukee General Hospital developed the following time estimates for Activity F (Installing the Pollution Control System):

$$a = 1 \text{ week}, \quad m = 2 \text{ weeks}, \quad b = 9 \text{ weeks}$$

a. Find the expected time and variance for Activity F.
b. Then compute the expected time and variance for all of the other activities in the pollution control project. Use the time estimates in previous example.

Solution:
a. The expected time for Activity F is:

$$t_e = (a + 4m + b)/6 = (1 + 4(2) + 9)/6 = 3 \text{ weeks}$$

The variance for Activity F is:

$$\sigma^2 = [(b - a)/6]^2 = [(9 - 1)/6]^2 = 1.78 \text{ weeks}$$

b. The rest of the calculations follow in the table.

Activity	Optimistic (a)	Most Likely (m)	Pessimistic (b)	Expected Time $t_e = (a+4m+b)/6$	Variance $\sigma^2 = [(b-a)/6]^2$
A	1	2	3	2	$= [(3-1)/6]^2 = .11$
B	2	3	4	3	$= [(4-2)/6]^2 = .11$
C	1	2	3	2	$= [(3-1)/6]^2 = .11$
D	2	4	6	4	$= [(6-2)/6]^2 = .44$
E	1	4	7	4	$= [(7-1)/6]^2 = 1.00$
F	1	2	9	3	$= [(9-1)/6]^2 = 1.78$
G	3	4	11	5	$= [(11-3)/6]^2 = 1.78$
H	1	2	3	2	$= [(3-1)/6]^2 = .11$

The expected times in this table are, in fact, the activity times we used in our earlier computation and identification of the critical path.

We know that the variance of activity A is 0.11, variance of activity C is 0.11, variance of activity E is 1.00, variance of activity G is 1.78, and variance of activity H is 0.11. Compute the total project variance and project standard deviation.

Solution:
Project Variance $(\sigma_p^2) = 0.11 + 0.11 + 1.00 + 1.78 + 0.11 = 3.11$

Where: Project standard deviation $(\sigma_p) = \sqrt{3.11} = 1.76 \text{ weeks}$

Dr. Joni Steinberg would like to find the probability that her project will be finished on or before the 16 week deadline. Calculate the probability.

Solution:

To do so, she needs to determine the appropriate area under the normal curve. The standard normal equation can be applied as follows:

$$z = \text{(due date} - \text{expected date of completion)} / \sigma_p$$
$$= (16 \text{ weeks} - 15 \text{ weeks}) / 1.76 \text{ weeks} = 0.57$$

Where z is the number of standard deviations, the due or target date lies from the mean or expected date.

Referring to the Normal Table (Appendix I of text), we find a probability of 0.7157. Thus, there is a 71.57% chance that the pollution control equipment can be put in place in 16 weeks or less.

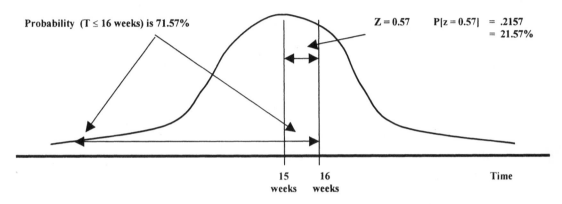

Dr. Steinberg wants to find the due date under which her hospital's project has a 99% chance of completion. She first needs to compute the z-value corresponding to 99%. Calculate the completion date.

Solution:

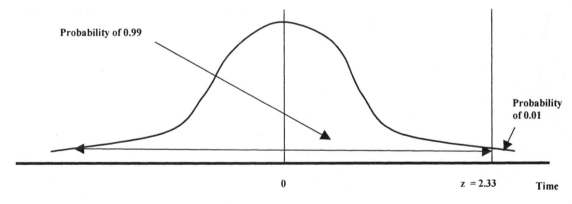

Referring again to the Normal Table (Appendix I of text), we identify a z value of 2.33 as being closest to the probability of 0.99. That is, Dr. Steinberg's due date should be 2.33 standard deviations above the mean project completion time. Starting with the standard normal equation, we can solve for the due date and rewrite the equation as:

$$\text{Due date} = \text{Expected completion time} + \text{z-value} \times \sigma_p$$
$$= 15 \text{ weeks} + 2.33 \times 1.76 \text{ weeks} = 19.1 \text{ weeks}$$

Hence, if Steinberg can get the environmental group to agree to give her a new deadline of 19.1 weeks (or more), she can be 99% sure of finishing the project on time.

Lecture Key: *In reality, factors such as shortage of materials or work absences can cause variability in the completion of activities. These factors are inputs that must be considered and the variability that they contribute to the project when creating a schedule. Using equations for variances, it is possible to estimate the probability of a project's completion by a certain date.*

VIII.   Cost-Time Trade-Offs and Project Crashing

A. It is not uncommon for a project manager to be faced with either (or both) of the following situations:
  1. The project is behind schedule.
  2. The scheduled project completion time has been moved forward.
B. Crashing – shortening activity time in a network to reduce time on the critical path so total completion time is reduced.
C. Crashing a project involves four steps, as follows:
  1. Compute the crash cost per week. If crash costs are linear over time, the following formula can be used:

$$\text{Crash cost per period} = \frac{(\text{Crash cost} - \text{Normal cost})}{(\text{Normal time} - \text{Crash time})}$$

  2. Find the critical path.
  3. Depends on the number of critical paths:
    a. One critical path – crash the activity that has the smallest crash cost per period.
    b. More than one critical path – select one activity from each path to crash.
  4. Update all activities. If due date is reached stop. If not return to step 2.

Lecture Key: *Crashing is especially important when contracts for projects include bonuses or penalties for early or late finishes.*

Example: Project Crashing

Suppose that Milwaukee General Hospital has been given only 13 weeks (instead of 16 weeks) to install the new pollution control equipment or face a court-ordered shutdown. As you recall, the length of Joni Steinberg's critical path was 15 weeks. Which activities should Steinberg crash, and by how much, in order to meet this 13-week due date? Naturally, Steinberg is interested in speeding up the project by 2 weeks, at the least additional cost.

Solution:
The hospital's normal and crash times, and normal and crash costs, are shown in table below. Note, for example, activity B's normal time is 3 weeks (the estimate used in computing the critical path), and its crash time is 1 week. This means that activity B can be shortened by up to 2 weeks if extra resources are provided. The cost of these additional resources is $4,000 (= the difference between the crash cost of $34,000 and the normal cost of $30,000). If we assume that the crashing cost is linear over time (i.e., the cost is the same each week), activity B's crash cost per week is $2,000 (= $4,000 / 2).

	TIME (wks)		COST ($)			
Activity	Normal	Crash	Normal	Crash	Crash Cost per Wk ($)	Critical Path?
A	2	1	22,000	22,750	750	Yes
B	3	1	30,000	34,000	2,000	No
C	2	1	26,000	27,000	1,000	Yes
D	4	3	48,000	49,000	1,000	No
E	4	2	56,000	58,000	1,000	Yes
F	3	2	30,000	30,500	500	No
G	5	2	80,000	84,500	1,500	Yes
H	2	1	16,000	19,000	3,000	Yes

Steps 2, 3, and 4 can now be applied to reduce Milwaukee General's project completion time at a minimum cost.

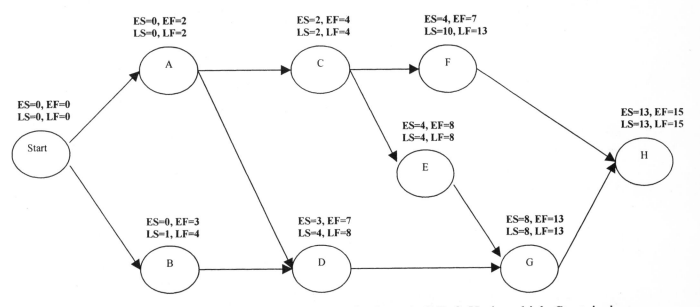

The current critical path (using normal times) is Start-A-C-E-G-H, in which Start is just a dummy starting activity. Of these critical activities, activity A has the lowest crash cost per week of $750. Joni Steinberg should therefore crash activity A by 1 week to reduce the project completion time to 14 weeks. The cost is an additional $750. Note that activity A cannot be crashed any further since it has reached its crash limit of 1 week.

At this stage, the original path Start-A-C-E-G-H remains critical with a completion time of 14 weeks. However, a new path Start-B-D-G-H is also critical now, with a completion time of 14 weeks. Hence, any further crashing must be done to both critical paths.

On each of these critical paths, we need to identify one activity that can still be crashed. We also want the total cost of crashing an activity on each path to be the smallest. We might be tempted to simply pick the activities with the smallest crash cost per period in each path. If we do this, we would select activity C from the first path and activity D from the second path. The total crash cost would then be $2,000 (= $1,000 + $1,000).

But we spot that activity G is common to both paths. That is, by crashing activity G, we will simultaneously reduce the completion time of both paths. Even though the $1,500 crash cost for activity G is higher than that for activities C and D, we would still prefer crashing G since the total cost is now only $1,500 (compared with the $2,000 if we crash C and D).

Hence, to crash the project down to 13 weeks, Dr. Steinberg should crash activity A by 1 week, and activity G by 1 week. The additional cost is $2,250 (= $750 + $1,500).

IX. A Critique of PERT and CPM

A. Advantages
  1. Especially useful when scheduling and controlling large projects.
  2. Straightforward concept and not mathematically complex.
  3. Graphical networks help to perceive relationships among project activities quickly.
  4. Critical path and slack time analyses help pinpoint activities that need to be closely watched.
  5. Project documentation and graphs point out who is responsible for various activities.
  6. Applicable to a wide variety of projects.
  7. Useful in monitoring not only schedules, but costs as well.

B. Limitations
  1. Project activities have to be clearly defined, independent, and stable in their relationships.
  2. Precedence relationships must be specified and networked together.
  3. Time estimates tend to be subjective and are subject to fudging by managers who fear the dangers of being overly optimistic or not pessimistic enough.
  4. There is the inherent danger of too much emphasis being placed on the longest, or critical path. Near-critical paths need to be monitored closely as well.

Lecture Key: *In large projects, there too many activities to monitor closely, but managers can concentrate on the critical activities.*

X. Using Microsoft Project to Manage Projects

A. Microsoft Project is extremely useful in drawing project networks, identifying the project schedule, and managing project costs and other resources. It does not, however, perform PERT probability calculations.

B. Creating a Project Schedule Using MS Project
  1. Entering Activity Information – for each activity (or task, as Microsoft Project calls it), we enter its name and duration. Microsoft Project identifies tasks by numbers (e.g., 1, 2) rather than letters (pg. 78–79 of text).

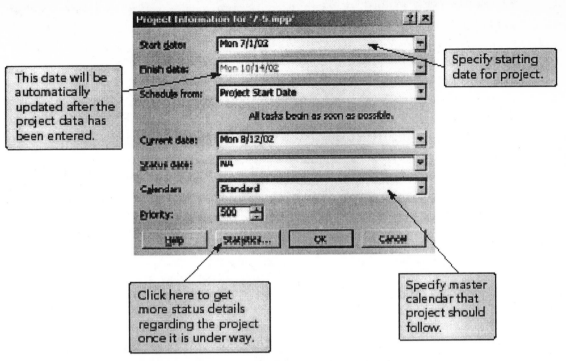

This date will be automatically updated after the project data has been entered.

Specify starting date for project.

Click here to get more status details regarding the project once it is under way.

Specify master calendar that project should follow.

PROGRAM 3.1 ■ Project Summary Information in MS Project

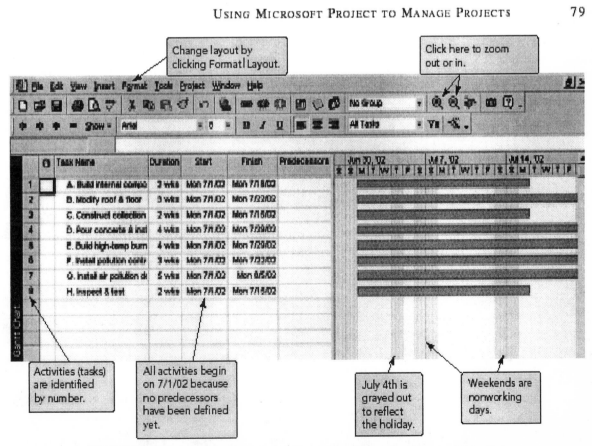

Change layout by clicking Format| Layout.

Click here to zoom out or in.

Activities (tasks) are identified by number.

All activities begin on 7/1/02 because no predecessors have been defined yet.

July 4th is grayed out to reflect the holiday.

Weekends are nonworking days.

PROGRAM 3.2 ■ Activity Entry in MS Project for Milwaukee General Hospital

2. Defining Precedence Relationships – There are two ways of specifying these links. The first is to enter the relevant activity numbers (e.g., 1, 2) in the Predecessor column. The other approach uses the Link icon (pg. 80 of text).

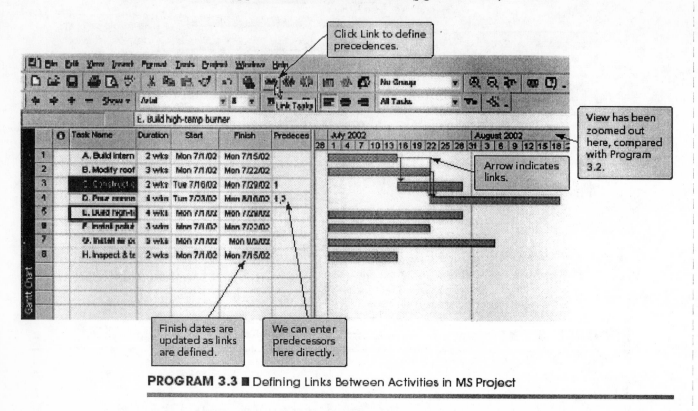

PROGRAM 3.3 ■ Defining Links Between Activities in MS Project

3. Viewing the Project Schedule – project can be viewed as a Gantt chart or, select View|Network Diagram to view the schedule as a project (text pg. 81).

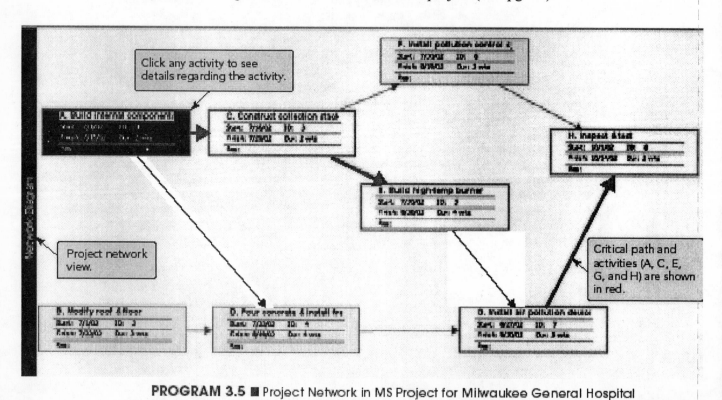

PROGRAM 3.5 ■ Project Network in MS Project for Milwaukee General Hospital

C. Tracking Progress and Managing Costs Using MS Project
  1. Tracking the Time Status of a Project – An easy way to track the time progress of tasks is to enter the percent of work completed for each task (pg. 82 of text).

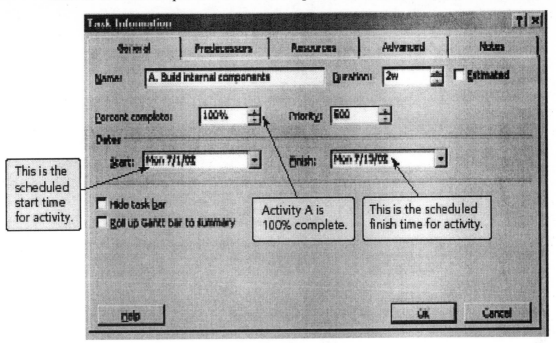

PROGRAM 3.6 ■ Updating Activity Progress in MS Project

  2. In addition to reading this section on MS Project, we encourage you to load the software from your Student CD-ROM and try these procedures (pg. 82 of text).

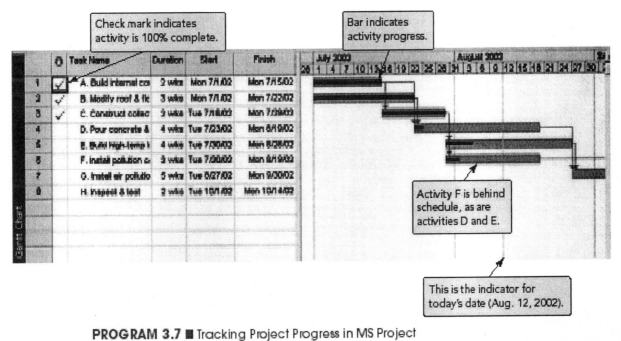

PROGRAM 3.7 ■ Tracking Project Progress in MS Project

Lecture Key: "Poorly managed projects are costly, not only financially, but also in wasted time and demoralized personnel. But failure is almost never the result of poor software." Fujinami and A. Marshal. Failure is often related to human error.

Network Diagramming

S1.   The information in the table pertains to a project that is about to commence. As the project manager, which activities would you be concerned with in terms of timely project completion? Explain.

Activity	Precedes	Time (Days)
A-B	B-D,B-C	5
A-I	I-J	9
B-D	D-J	2
B-C	C-E	4
C-E	E-F	16
E-F	F-G,F-H	15
F-G	G-J	13
F-H	H-J	5
D-J	--	10
G-J	--	5
H-J	--	12
I-J	--	8

Solution:

Step 1:   Draw the precedence diagram using the precedence relationships in the table above.

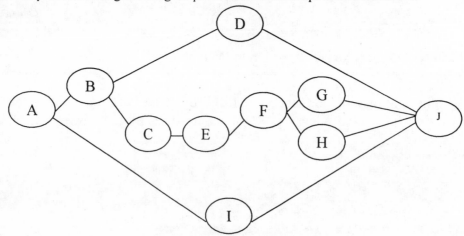

Step 2:   Compute the early start and finish times with a forward pass through the diagram. The forward pass tells you the expected completion time of your project using ES = Max (EF) & EF = ES + t. For example beginning with activity A, the early start (ES) is 0 since activities A-B and A-I are connected to the start of the project. Activities A-B and A-I can begin when the project begins or time 0. The early finish (EF) is equal to ES + activity time (t), so EF = 0 + 5 or during day 5. For activity A-I, ES is 0 and EF is 9. For activities B-C and B-D, the ES is equal to the max (EF), which is the EF for activity A-B since activities B-C and B-D are connected or preceded by activity A-B. So, the ES for activity B-C is 5 and the EF is 5 + 4 or 9.

Step 3: Compute ALL the ES and EF for all activities. This forward pass tells us the earliest finish time or estimated project completion time. The table below shows all the ES and EF.

Activity	Time (Days)	ES	EF
A-B	5	0	5
A-I	9	0	9
B-D	2	5	7
B-C	4	5	9
C-E	16	9	25
E-F	15	25	40
F-G	13	40	43
F-H	5	40	45
D-J	10	7	17
G-J	5	43	48
H-J	12	45	57
I-J	8	9	17

Step 4: Compute the LF and LS for all activities. To do this, work backwards through the diagram using the early completion time that was calculated with the forward pass. Starting with activity G-J, the late finish (LF) is equal to the minimum late start time, which in this case is the early completion time. Then, calculate the late start for the activities using the formula LS = LF – t. For activity G-J, this would be 58 – 5 or during week 53. For activity I-J, this would mean that the LF = 58 and LS = 49. Remember that as you work backwards you would always choose the minimum LS time to become the LF time for the next activity. The table below shows all the LS and LF.

Activity	Time (Days)	LS	LF
A-B	5	0	5
A-I	9	40	49
B-D	2	45	47
B-C	4	5	9
C-E	16	9	25
E-F	15	25	40
F-G	13	40	53
F-H	5	40	45
D-J	10	47	57
G-J	5	53	57
H-J	12	45	57
I-J	8	49	57

Step 5: Calculate slack (acceptable delay) for each activity. This is what the backwards pass determines. To calculate slack you use the formulas: Slack (S) = LF – EF or S = LS – ES. For activity A-B, slack is equal to 5 – 5 (LF – EF) or 0. This means that activity A-B cannot be delayed without delaying the project since the slack is 0. For activity A-I, slack is 50 – 9 (LF – EF) or 41 days. This means that activity D can be delayed up to 41 days without delaying the project.

Activity	Time (Days)	ES	EF	LS	LF	S
A-B	5	0	5	0	5	0
A-I	9	0	9	41	50	41
B-D	2	5	7	46	48	41
B-C	4	5	9	5	9	0
C-E	16	9	25	9	25	0
E-F	15	25	40	25	40	0
F-G	13	40	53	40	53	0
F-H	5	40	45	41	46	1
D-J	10	7	17	48	58	41
G-J	5	53	58	53	58	0
H-J	12	45	57	46	58	1
I-J	8	9	17	50	58	41

31

Step 6:   Analysis: Identify the critical activities and the critical path. Activity Sequence – A-B, B-C, C-E, E-F, F-G, and G-J are the critical activities and path since they all have slacks of 0, so the sequence of activities A-B, B-C, C-E, E-F, F-G, and G-J determines the critical path or shortest time to complete this project. The expected completion time of the project is 58 days. These are the most important activities, so concentrate on managing them the most. They determine the completion time of the project, so reducing those times will reduce the project time.

S2.   Dave, the manager of the local ice cream store, is going to construct a new storage container for its new line of ice cream. The activities, activity descriptions, and estimated durations are given in the following table. Determine the critical path and shortest completion time of the project.

Activity	Activity Description	Predecessor	Time (wks)
A	Excavate	---	2
B	Erect Building	A	6
C	Install AC	A	4
D	Install generator	A	2
E	Install maintenance equipment	B	4
F	Connect AC & generator to building	B, C, D	5
G	Paint on a finish	B	3
H	Check out facility	E, F	2

Solution:

Step 1:   Draw the precedence diagram using the precedence relationships in the table above.

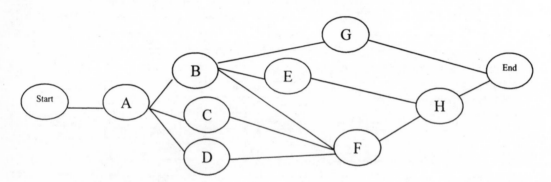

Step 2:   Compute the early start and finish times with a forward pass through the diagram. The forward pass tells you the expected completion time of your project using ES = Max (EF) & EF = ES + t. For example, beginning with activity 1, the early start (ES) is 0 since activity 1 is connected to the Start node (or beginning of the project). Activity A can begin when the project begins or time 0. The early finish (EF) is equal to ES + activity time (t), so EF = 0 + 2 or during week 2. For activity B, the ES is equal to the max (EF), which is the EF for activity A since activity B is connected or preceded by activity A. So, the ES for activity B is 2 and the EF is 2 + 6 or 8. For activity F, a decision has to be made between three EF times (8, 6, and 4). The ES is equal to the max (EF), which is the EF for activity B since activity F is connected or preceded by activity B. So, the ES for activity F is 8 and the EF is 8 + 5 or 13.

Step 3:   Compute ALL the ES and EF for all activities. This forward pass tells us the earliest finish time or estimated project completion time. The table below shows all the ES and EF.

Activity	t (weeks)	ES	EF
A	2	0	2
B	6	2	8
C	4	2	6
D	2	2	4
E	4	8	12
F	5	8	13
G	3	8	11
H	2	13	15

32

Step 4: Compute the LF and LS for all activities. To do this, work backwards through the diagram using the early completion time that was calculated with the forward pass. Starting with activity H, the late finish (LF) is equal to the minimum late start time, which in this case is the early completion time of the project (15 weeks). Then, calculate the late start for the activities using the formula $LS = LF - t$. For activity H, this would be $15 - 2$ or during week 13. As you work backwards toward activity B, you have a decision to make since three activities (E, F, and G) all work into B. In this case, you want to still pick the minimum LS of the three, which is 8 or the LS of activity F. The table below shows all the LS and LF.

Activity	t (weeks)	LS	LF
A	2	0	2
B	6	2	8
C	4	4	8
D	2	6	8
E	4	9	13
F	5	8	13
G	3	12	15
H	2	13	15

Step 5: Calculate slack (acceptable delay) for each activity. This is what the backwards pass determines. To calculate slack you use the formulas: Slack $(S) = LF - EF$ or $S = LS - ES$. For activity A, slack is equal to $2 - 2$ $(LF - EF)$ or 0. This means that activity 1 cannot be delayed without delaying the project since the slack is 0. For activity C, slack is $8 - 6$ $(LF - EF)$ or 2 weeks. This means that activity C can be delayed up to 2 weeks without delaying the project.

Activity	t (weeks)	ES	EF	LS	LF	S
A	2	0	2	0	2	0
B	6	2	8	2	8	0
C	4	2	6	4	8	2
D	2	2	4	6	8	4
E	4	8	12	9	13	1
F	5	8	13	8	13	0
G	3	8	11	12	15	4
H	2	13	15	13	15	0

Step 6: Analysis: Identify the critical activities and the critical path. Activity Sequence – A-B-F-H are the critical activities and path, since they all have slacks of 0, so the sequence of activities A-B-F-H determines the critical path or shortest time to complete this project. The expected completion time of the project is 15 weeks.

S3. The airport must build a new aircraft hangar and maintenance shop to service a company that is beginning service with the airport. The sooner the project is completed, the sooner the company comes to the airport, and the sooner the airport can start collecting fees. The airport director would like to know what different paths the construction could take and what the estimated, longest time period the construction could take (critical path). The activities are in weeks and are as follows:

Activity	Precedence	t (weeks)
Start	--	--
1-2	Start	2
2-5	1-2	4
1-3	Start	3
1-4	Start	8
3-5	1-3	6
5-6	2-5,3-5	7
4-6	1-4	9
6-7	5-6,4-6	3
End	6-7	--

Solution:

Step 1: Draw the precedence diagram using the precedence relationships in the previous table.

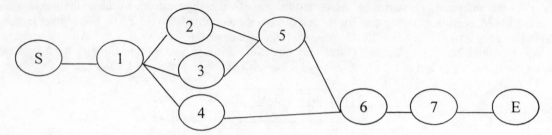

Step 2: Compute the early start and finish times with a forward pass through the diagram. The forward pass tells you the expected completion time of your project using ES = Max (EF) and EF = ES + t. For example, beginning with activity 1-2, the early start (ES) is 0 since activity 1-2 is connected to the Start node (or beginning of the project). Activity 1-2 can begin when the project begins or time 0. The early finish (EF) is equal to ES + activity time (t), so EF = 0 + 2 or during week 2.

Step 3: Compute ALL the ES and EF for all activities. This forward pass tells us the earliest finish time or estimated project completion time. The table below shows all the ES and EF.

Activity	t (weeks)	ES	EF
1-2	2	0	2
2-5	4	2	6
1-3	3	0	3
1-4	8	0	8
3-5	6	3	9
5-6	9	9	18
4-6	7	8	15
6-7	3	18	21

Step 4: Compute the LF and LS for all activities. To do this, work backwards through the diagram using the early completion time that was calculated with the forward pass. Starting with activity 6-7, the late finish (LF) is equal to the minimum late start time, which in this case is the early completion time. Then, calculate the late start for the activities using the formula LS = LF − t. For activity 6-7, this would be 21 − 3 or during week 18. The table below shows all the LS and LF.

Activity	t (weeks)	LS	LF
1-2	2	3	5
2-5	4	5	9
1-3	3	0	3
1-4	8	3	11
3-5	6	3	9
5-6	9	9	18
4-6	7	11	18
6-7	3	18	21

Step 5: Calculate slack (acceptable delay) for each activity. This is what the backwards pass determines. To calculate slack you use the formulas: Slack (S) = LF – EF or S = LS – ES. For activity 1-2, slack is equal to 5 – 2 (LF – EF) or 3. This means that activity 1-2 can be delayed up to 3 weeks without delaying the project since the slack is 3. For activity 1-3, slack is 3 – 3 (LF – EF) or 0 weeks. This means that activity 1-3 cannot be delayed without delaying the project since the slack is 0.

Activity	t (weeks)	ES	EF	LS	LF	S
1-2	2	0	2	3	5	3
2-5	4	2	6	5	9	3
1-3	3	0	3	0	3	0
1-4	8	0	8	3	11	3
3-5	6	3	9	3	9	0
5-6	9	9	18	9	18	0
4-6	7	8	15	11	18	3
6-7	3	18	21	18	21	0

Step 6: Analysis: The paths for construction are:

Path 1: Activity Sequence – 1-3, 3-5, 5-6, and 6-7
Path 2: Activity Sequence – 1-2, 2-5, 5-6, and 6-7
Path 3: Activity Sequence – 1-4, 4-6, and 6-7

Identify the critical activities and the critical path. Path 1 or Activity Sequence – 1-3, 3-5, 5-6, and 6-7 are the critical activities and path since they all have slacks of 0, so the sequence of activities 1-3, 3-5, 5-6, and 6-7 determines the critical path or shortest time to complete this project. The expected completion time of the project is 21 weeks.

S4. With the information provided below, determine: a. the early and late start and finish times as well as slack, b. the critical path, c. the project variance, and d. the probability that this project will be completed within 38 weeks.

Activity	a	m	b
1-2	3	6	9
2-4	2	6	12
2-5			
3-5	1	3	7
4-6	4	9	13
5-6	2	4	8
6-7	5	6	10

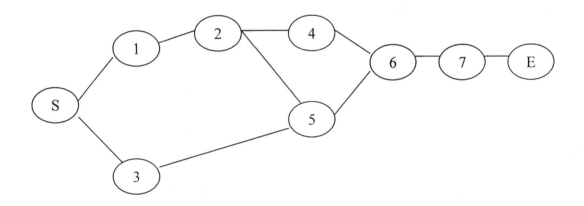

Solution:

Step 1: Compute the activity times given the estimates on the previous page. The mean activity time for the beta distribution can be found using the formula for the expected times (te) for each activity, then calculate the variance.

Expected Time (te) for Activity 1 $= [3 + (4*6) + 9] / 6 = 6$ weeks
Variance for Activity 1 $= [(9 - 3) / 6]2 = 1$ weeks

The table below will give you the remaining activity times and variances for the project.

Activity	T	Variance
1-2	6	1
2-4	6.33	2.78
2-5	1	0
3-5	3.33	1
4-6	8.83	2.25
5-6	6.5	1
6-7	9.75	0.6944

Step 2: Compute the early start and finish times with a forward pass through the diagram. The forward pass tells you the expected completion time of your project using ES = Max (EF) and EF = ES + t. For example beginning with activity 1-2, the early start (ES) is 0 since activity 1 is connected to the Start node (or beginning of the project). Activity 1-2 can begin when the project begins or time 0. The early finish (EF) is equal to ES + activity time (t), so EF = 0 + 6 or during week 6. For activity 2-4, the ES is equal to the max (EF), which is the EF for activity 1-2 since activity 2-4 is connected or preceded by activity 1-2. So, the ES for activity 2-4 is 6 and the EF is 6 + 6.33 or 12.33.

Step 3: Compute ALL the ES and EF for all activities. This forward pass tells us the earliest finish time or estimated project completion time. The table below shows all the ES and EF.

Activity	t_e (weeks)	ES	EF
1-2	6	0	6
2-4	6.33	6	12.33
2-5	1	6	7
3-5	3.33	0	3.33
4-6	12.33	12.33	21.16
5-6	6.5	7	13.5
6-7	9.75	21.16	30.91

Step 4: Compute the LF and LS for all activities. To do this, work backwards through the diagram using the early completion time that was calculated with the forward pass. Starting with activity 6-7, the late finish (LF) is equal to the minimum late start time, which in this case is the early completion time. Then, calculate the late start for the activities using the formula LS = LF – t. For activity 6-7, this would be 30.91 – 9.75 or during week 21.16. The table below shows all the LS and LF.

Activity	t_e (weeks)	LS	LF
1-2	6	0	6
2-4	6.33	6	12.33
2-5	1	13.66	14.66
3-5	3.33	11.33	14.66
4-6	8.83	12.33	21.16
5-6	6.5	14.66	21.16
6-7	9.75	21.16	30.91

Step 5: Calculate slack (acceptable delay) for each activity. This is what the backwards pass determines. To calculate slack you use the formulas: Slack (S) = LF – EF or S = LS – ES. For activity 1-2, slack is equal to 6 – 6 (LF – EF) or 0. This means that activity 1-2 cannot be delayed without delaying the project since the slack is 0. For activity 3-5, slack is 14.66 – 3.33 (LF – EF) or 11.33 weeks. This means that activity 3-5 can be delayed up to 11.33 weeks without delaying the project.

Activity	t (weeks)	ES	EF	LS	LF	S
1-2	6	0	6	0	6	0
2-4	6.33	6	12.33	6	12.33	0
2-5	1	6	7	13.66	14.66	7.66
3-5	3.33	0	3.33	11.33	14.66	11.33
4-6	8.83	12.33	21.16	12.33	21.16	0
5-6	6.5	7	13.5	14.66	21.16	7.66
6-7	9.75	21.16	30.91	21.16	30.91	0

Step 6: Analysis:

For Part b, identify the critical activities and the critical path. Path 1 or Activity Sequence – 1-2, 2-4, 4-6, and 6-7 are the critical activities and path since they all have slacks of 0, so the sequence of activities 1-2, 2-4, 4-6, and 6-7 determines the critical path or shortest time to complete this project. The expected completion time of the project is 30.91 weeks or 31 weeks (it has to rounded up to 31). This is also the expected project time (mean).

For Part c, the project variance is equal to the sum of all critical activity variances.

Project Variance (σ^2) = 1 + 2.78 + 2.25 + 0.694 = 6.724

For Part d, you want to calculate the probability of the project being completed in 38 weeks or less if the mean (μ) time of the project is 31 and the project variance (σ^2) is 6.724. The project standard deviation can be calculated by taking the square root of 6.724. That gives you 2.593.

Then, you can calculate the z score for 38 weeks or less with the following formula:

$P(z \leq 38) = (\chi - \mu) / \sigma = (38 - 31) / (2.593) = 2.699$ (which is the z score)
$P(z = 2.699) = .4965$ (from normal distribution chart with z = 2.7)
$P(z \leq 38) = .5 + .4965 = .9965$ (the 0.50 in this equation is equal to the left side of the distribution curve)

There is a 99.65% chance that the project will be complete within 38 weeks.

Construct the network for this project, identify the critical path, and determine the project duration time.

Identify all the paths in the following network, compute the length of each, and indicate the critical path. Using AON, complete the network diagram. (Activity times are in weeks.)

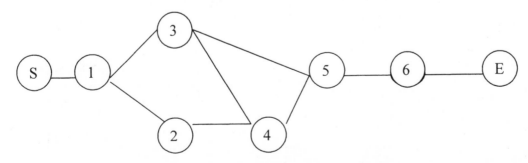

Activity	Predecessor	Time (wks)
Start	---	---
1	Start	6
2	1	4
3	1	2
4	2,3	4
5	4, 5	5
6	5	3
End	6	----

a. Calculate all the early times and expected completion time of the project.
b. Calculate all the late time for the activities and slack.
c. Indicate how the critical path would be determined.

2. Given the following network and activity times in months, create the labeled network diagram. Using AON, complete the network diagram.

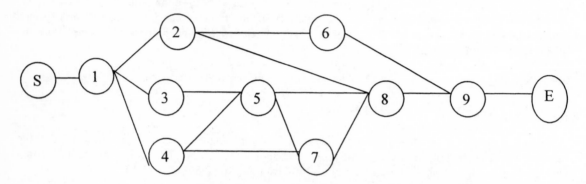

Activity	Predecessor	Time (wks)
Start	---	---
1	Start	10
2	1	8
3	1	5
4	1	9
5	3, 4	12
6	2	2
7	4, 5	4
8	2, 5, 7	7
9	6, 8	15
End	9	---

a. Calculate all the early times and expected completion time of the project.
b. Calculate all the late times for the activities and slack.
c. Indicate how the critical path would be determined.

Activity	ES	EF	LS	LF	Slack
1					
2					
3					
4					
5					
6					
7					
8					
9					

3. A local newspaper is planning to conduct a political survey of a segment of the citizens of the area. The planning process for preparing to conduct the survey consists of six activities with procedure relationships and activity time estimates as follows. Using AON, complete the network diagram.

Activity	Activity Description	Predecessor	Time (wks)
A	Determine survey objectives	---	3
B	Select and hire personnel	A	3
C	Design questionnaire	A	5
D	Train personnel	B, C	4
E	Select target audience	C	3
F	Make personnel assignments	D, E	2

a. Determine all paths through the network from node a to node f and the duration of each, and indicate the critical path.
b. Determine the earliest and latest activity start and finish times.
c. Determine the slack for each activity.

4. A government is planning the next census, which is taken every 10 years to determine the demographic and population shifts. Since this information is very important for funding purposes, especially education, the administration has extensive selection procedures for its interviewers. The planning process for preparing to conduct the survey consists of six activities with procedure relationships and activity time estimates as follows. Using AON, complete the network diagram.

Activity	Activity Description	Predecessor	Time (wks)
A	Determine survey boundaries	---	2
B	Select and hire personnel	A	6
C	Adjust citizen questionnaire	A	2
D	Train personnel	B, C	5
E	Preview areas for interviewers	C	3
F	Make personnel assignments	D, E	1
G	Take interviews	F	8
H	Compile information	G	8

a. Determine all paths through the network from node a to node h and the duration of each, and indicate the critical path.
b. Determine the earliest and latest activity start and finish times.
c. Determine the slack for each activity.
d. If the interviews (activity G) have to begin in January of the Census year, when must the project begin to not be late?

5. A local company has started a Paint Ball Game Area. This game has become very serious to many of its players, to the point where the company has designated Sundays "Hard Core" Days, and only the league teams can participate. Since this league is now organized, the competition has expanded to include planning and strategy sessions. One of the teams has a member that was a history major and has studied military strategy. Tom has made the following plan as part of his preparations for when to attack the enemy. Using critical path analysis, help Tom determine the appropriate times for the game. Suppose that the following project network with activity times in minutes had been available. Determine the earliest start and finish times, latest start and finish times, and activity slack for the network. Indicate the critical path and the time between the Tom's receipt of battle orders and the onset of battle. Using AON, complete the network diagram.

Activity	Activity Description	Predecessor	Time (wks)
Start	----	---	---
1	Explain plan	Start	20
2	Move groups into position	1	20
3	Advance spy team	1	35
4	Flank the other team's positions	1	40
5	Cut retreat routs	3, 4	30
6	Take bridges	2	20
7	Check out facility	5, 6	20
8	Receive supplies	5, 6	15
9	Attack	8	20
End	----	---	---

If the games begin at 9:00 am sharp, what time does Tom think that the battle will be over?

6. Given the following network and probabilistic activity time estimates, determine the expected completion time and standard deviation for each activity and indicate the critical path. Using AON, complete the network diagram.

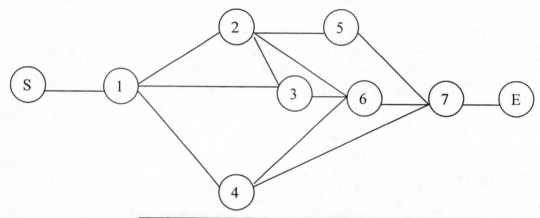

Activity	Time (wks)		
	a	m	b
Start	----	---	---
1	8	10	15
2	2	7	16
3	1	4	9
4	3	10	15
5	8	9	20
6	4	12	15
7	2	5	8
End	----	---	---

7.   The Lower State University is adding a new computerized registration system. University administration has determined the activities required to complete the project, the precedence relationships of activities, and activity time estimates as follows:

Activity	Description	Predecessor	Time (Wks.) a	m	b
A	Bidding Process and Selection	---	5	8	17
B	System Analysis	---	3	12	15
C	Training	A	4	7	10
D	Equipment Installation	A	5	8	23
E	Manual System Test	B, C	1	1	1
F	Preliminary System Changeover	B, C	1	4	13
G	System Interface	D, E	3	6	9
H	Rework	D, E	1	2.5	7
I	Testing	H	1	1	1
J	Debugging and Installation	F, G	2	2	2
K	Online Changeover	G, I	5	8	11

Determine the earliest and latest activity times, the expected completion time and standard deviation, and the probability that the project will be completed in 40 weeks or less. Using AON, complete the network diagram.

8.   Given the following network and probabilistic activity time estimates, determine the expected completion time and standard deviation for each activity and indicate the critical path. Using AON, complete the network diagram.

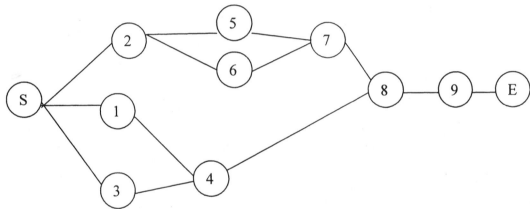

Activity	Time (wks) a	m	b
1	4	8	12
2	3	9	14
3	1	4	9
4	3	10	15
5	8	9	20
6	4	12	15
7	1	3	4
8	2	3	8
9	2	5	8
End	----	---	---

9.   Given the following network and probabilistic activity time estimates, determine the expected completion time and standard deviation for each activity and indicate the critical path. Using AON, complete the network diagram.

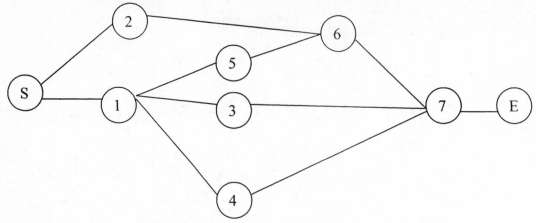

Activity	Time (wks)		
	a	m	b
Start	----	---	---
1	2	4	7
2	4	7	9
3	8	12	20
4	2	7	12
5	5	7	9
6	4	8	11
7	5	9	14
End	----	---	---

10.   Given the following network and probabilistic activity time estimates, determine the expected completion time and standard deviation for each activity and indicate the critical path. Using AON, complete the network diagram.

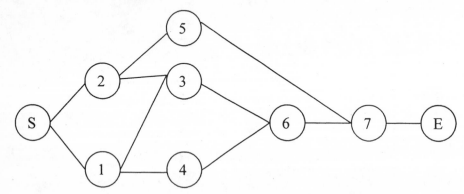

Activity	Time (wks)		
	a	m	b
Start	----	---	---
1	4	10	15
2	3	8	9
3	2	7	16
4	4	10	15
5	4	9	20
6	3	10	15
7	8	15	25
End	----	---	---

11.   Use the following precedence relationships and probabilistic activity time estimates to construct the network diagram. Using AON, complete the network diagram.

Activity	Predecessor	Time (wks)		
		a	m	b
Start	---	----	---	---
1	Start	12	20	30
2	1	10	15	25
3	1	10	14	21
4	1	6	9	18
5	2, 3, 4	4	13	20
6	2	6	18	24
7	4, 5	8	12	20
8	5, 7	15	22	30
9	6, 8	12	21	28
End	9	----	---	---

Determine the following:

a. Expected activity times.
b. Earliest start and finish times, latest start and finish times, and activity slack.
c. Identify the critical path. What is the expected project duration and standard deviation?
d. What is the probability of the project being completed in more than 50 months?
e. What is the probability of the project being completed in less than 56 months?
f. What is the probability of the project being completed in more than 70 months?
g. What is the probability of the project being completed in more than 55 months and less than 63 months?

12.   For the following network diagram, determine both the critical path and the expected project duration. The quantities on the arrows represent expected activity times. Using AON, complete the network diagram.

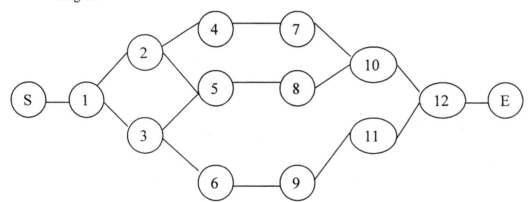

Activity	Time (wks)
Start	---
1	10
2	6
3	8
4	9
5	4
6	5
7	7
8	4
9	2
10	2
11	5
12	4
End	--

15. For the following network diagram, determine both the critical path and the expected project duration. The quantities on the arrows represent expected activity times. Using AON, complete the network diagram.

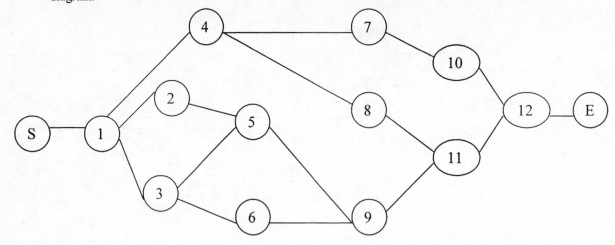

Activity	Time (days)
Start	---
1	15
2	10
3	9
4	11
5	16
6	4
7	18
8	9
9	14
10	2
11	15
12	17
End	--

4

Forecasting

I. **What Is Forecasting?**

    A. Forecasting is the art and science of predicting future events.

        1. Forecasting entails gathering and analyzing historical data and projecting it into the future using some type of mathematical model.

        2. Forecasting can also require the use of these mathematical models in conjunction with a manager's decision and insight (necessary human element).

        3. Although there are many established forecasting techniques that are currently employed, no form of forecasting is deemed "superior" with regards to any other.

            a. Forecasting varies from company to company.

            b. The type of forecasting that is the most effective for one company or department may be quite ineffective for another firm or department, and vice-versa.

        4. Accurate forecasts greatly aid a company by providing a solid basis for short and long run corporate planning.

    B. Forecasting Time Horizons

        1. A forecast is typically classified by the future time horizon that it covers.

        2. These time horizons fall into 3 categories:

            a. Short-Range Forecast

                i. A short-range forecast may have a time span of up to 1 year, but is usually less than 3 months.

                ii. It is used for planning purchasing, job scheduling, workforce levels, job assignments, and production levels.

            b. Medium-Range Forecast

                i. A medium-range forecast (Intermediate Forecast) generally spans from 3 months to 3 years.

                ii. It is used in sales planning, production planning and budgeting, cash budgeting, and analyzing operating plans.

            c. Long-Range Forecast

                i. A long-range forecast usually has a time span of 3 years or more.

                ii. It is used in planning for new products, capital expenditures, facility location or expansion, and research and development.

        2. Medium-range and long-range forecasts differ from short-term forecasts in three ways.

            a. Medium-range and long-range forecasts deal with more comprehensive issues and support management decisions regarding planning and products, plants, and processes.

            b. Short-range forecasting usually employs different methodologies than long-range or medium-range forecasting.

                i. Mathematical techniques (moving averages, exponential smoothing, trend exploration) are typically used with short-run forecasting.

        ii.   Broader, less quantitative methods are used in predicting many issues associated with long-term and short-term forecasting.
      c. Short-range forecasts tend to be more accurate than long-range and medium-range forecasts.
  B. The Influence of Product Life Cycle
    1. The product life cycle must be considered when developing sales forecasts.
    2. The sales rates of products and services tend to fluctuate over time.
    3. There are 4 stages to the product life cycle.
      a. Introduction
      b. Growth
      c. Maturity
      d. Decline
    4. Goods in the first two stages of the product life cycle (introduction and growth) need longer forecasts than those in the final two stages of the product life cycle (maturity and decline).
    5. Product life cycle forecasts are also useful in predicting staffing levels, inventory levels, and factory capacity as the product moves through the cycle.

Lecture Key: *Forecasting can be a very complex, yet useful business tool. It involves the use of historical data, combined with mathematical models and human input, to project future events. Most businesses will use a forecasting technique that uniquely satisfies their individual wants and needs. The three categories of forecasting time horizons are: short-range forecasts, medium-range forecasts, and long-range forecasts. It is also important to be aware of the strong correlation that exists between the product life cycle and forecasting.*

II.   Types of Forecasts

  A. There are 3 main types of forecasts that firms use to plan future operations.
    1. Economic Forecasts predict inflation rates, money supplies, housing starts, and other planning indicators.
    2. Technological Forecasts analyze the rates of technological progress, which can lead to the development of new products, requiring new plants and equipment.
    3. Demand Forecasts (Sales Forecasts) project the demand for a company's goods or services. They control a company's production, capacity, and scheduling systems and serve as inputs to financial, marketing, and personnel planning.
      a. It is important to note that operations management is not responsible for economic and technical forecasting.
      b. Rather, operations management is primarily concerned with demand forecasting.

III.   The Strategic Importance of Forecasting

  A. Forecasts are extremely important to all aspects of a company because the forecast is the only estimate of demand until actual demand becomes known.
  B. Therefore, forecasts of demand drive decisions in several areas, particularly human resources, capacity, and supply-chain management.
    1. Forecasts and Human Resources
      a. Hiring, training, and firing employees all depend on anticipated demand.
      b. For example, if the human resources department must hire additional workers without prior notification, the amount of training declines and the quality of the workforce suffers.
    2. Forecasts and Capacity
      a. Inadequate capacity (shortages of goods or services) can result in undependable delivery, loss of customers, and loss of market share.

        b. It must also be taken into consideration that when excess capacity develops, costs can dramatically increase.
    3. Forecasts and Supply-Chain Management
        a. Accurate forecasts support good customer-supplier relationships.
        b. They also help ensure price advantages for materials and parts (discounts based on order quantity, etc.).

Lecture Key: *As mentioned in this section as well as others, forecasts are necessary elements of nearly all business functions. Forecasts of demand, in particular, directly influence decisions concerning human resources, capacity, and supply-chain management.*

IV. Seven Steps in the Forecasting System

A. There are 7 basic steps in nearly every forecasting technique.
    1. Determine the use of the forecast.
    2. Select the items to be forecasted.
    3. Determine the time horizon of the forecast (short-, medium-, or long-term).
    4. Select the forecasting model(s) (moving averages, exponential smoothing, and regression analysis).
    5. Gather the data needed to make the forecast.
    6. Make the forecast.
    7. Validate and implement the results.
B. By using these 7 steps, operations management can systematically initiate, design, and implement a forecasting system.
C. However, there are unavoidable realities associated with all forecasting systems.
    1. Forecasts are not always perfect.
        a. Unpredictable and uncontrollable outside factors can influence the forecast.
        b. Businesses (particularly operations management) must consider these factors.
    2. Forecasts automatically assume that the overall system is constant.
    3. Product family and aggregated forecasts are more accurate than single product forecasts.

V. Forecasting Approaches

A. Two of the general approaches to forecasting are Quantitative Forecasts and Qualitative Forecasts.
    1. Quantitative forecasts employ one or more mathematical models that rely on historical data and/or casual variables to forecast demand.
    2. Qualitative forecasts incorporate such factors as the decision maker's intuition, emotions, personal experiences, and value system.
B. Overview of Qualitative Methods
    1. There are 4 qualitative forecasting techniques:
        a. The Jury of Executive Opinion method combines the opinion of a small group of high-level managers with statistical models to determine a group estimate of demand.
        b. The Delphi method involves using a group process that allows experts to make forecasts. There are 3 different groups of participants in the Delphi method.
            i. Decision Makers are a group of 5-10 experts who actually make the forecast.
            ii. Staff Personnel assist decision makers by preparing, distributing, collecting, and summarizing questionnaires and survey results.
            iii. Respondents are a group of people whose judgments are valued. They provide inputs to decision makers before the forecast is made.

c. The Sales Force Composite method combines each salesperson's estimates of what sales will occur in his or her region with the estimated district and national levels to create an overall forecast.

d. The Consumer Market Survey method solicits input from customers or potential customers regarding future purchasing plans.

    i. This method also aids in improving product design and planning for new products.

    ii. Both this method and the consumer market survey method can be negatively impacted from overly optimistic forecasts generated by computer output.

C. Overview of Quantitative Methods

1. There are 5 quantitative forecasting methods (all use historical data):

    a. Naïve Approach

    b. Moving Averages

    c. Exponential Smoothing

    d. Trend Projection

    e. Linear Regression

2. Each of these forecasting methods fall into 1 of 2 general categories.

    a. Time Series models include the naïve approach, moving averages, exponential smoothing, and trend projection. They use a series of past data points to make a forecast.

    b. Associative (Causal) models include linear regression. They consider the factors that might influence the quantity being forecasted.

VI. Time-Series Forecasting

A. A time series forecast is based on a sequence of evenly spaced data points (weekly, monthly, quarterly, etc.).

B. Time-series forecasting considers past values only, and ignores all other information.

C. Decomposition of a Time Series – A time series analysis involves breaking down past data and projecting the components forward. There are four components of a time series.

1. Trend is the gradual upward or downward movement of data over time. Trend fluctuations may result from changes in income, population, age distribution, or cultural views.

2. Seasonality repeats itself after a period of days, weeks, months, or quarters. The following table illustrates the six common seasonality patterns.

Period of Pattern	"Season" Length	# of "Seasons" in Pattern
Week	Day	7
Month	Week	4 – 4.5
Month	Day	28 – 31
Year	Quarter	4
Year	Month	12
Year	Week	52

3. Cycles are patterns in the data that occur every several years.

4. Random Variations are "blips" in the data caused by chance and unusual situations.

D. The following figure shows a demand over a 4-year period, including the previously mentioned time series components. The average demand is the sum of the demand for each period divided by the number of data periods.

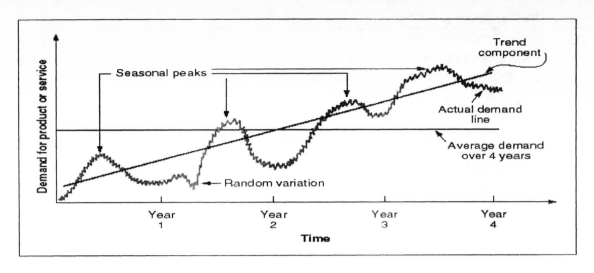

E. Naïve Approach
1. The naïve approach is a forecasting technique that assumes demand in the next period is equal to demand in the most recent period.
2. This approach may be the most cost-effective and efficient objective forecasting model for some product lines.
3. It provides a starting point against which subsequent, more detailed models can be compared.

F. Moving Averages
1. A moving-average forecast uses an average of the *n* most recent periods of data to forecast the next period.
   a. A moving-average forecast is based entirely on historical actual data values.
   b. Furthermore, it is useful only if it can be assumed that the market demands will stay fairly steady over time.
2. The formula for a Simple Moving Average = $\sum$ demand in previous *n* periods / *n*, where *n* is the number of periods in the moving average.
   a. For example, a 4-month simple moving average is calculated by summing the demand during the past 4 months and dividing by 4.
   b. The following example also gives a more detailed illustration of how simple moving averages are calculated.

Example: Moving Averages

Storage shed sales at Donna's Garden Supply are shown in the middle column of the table below. A 3-month moving average appears on the right.

Month	Actual Shed Sales	Solution: 3-Month Moving Average
January	10	
February	12	
March	13	
April	16	= (10 + 12 + 13) / 3 = 11.66
May	19	= (12 + 13 + 16) / 3 = 13.66
June	23	= (13 + 16 + 19) / 3 = 16
July	26	= (16 + 19 + 23) / 3 = 19.33
August	30	= (19 + 23 + 26) / 3 = 22.66
September	28	= (23 + 26 + 30) / 3 = 26.33
October	18	= (26 + 30 + 28) / 3 = 28
November	16	= (30 + 28 + 18) / 3 = 25.33
December	14	= (28 + 18 + 16) / 3 = 20.66

Thus we see that the forecast for December is 20.66. To project the demand for sheds in the coming January, we sum the October, November, and December sales and divide by 3: January forecast = (18 + 16 + 14) / 3 = 16.

3. Weights can be used to place increased emphasis on recent values if a detectable trend or pattern is present.
   a. This allows forecasting techniques to be more responsive to changes because more recent periods may be more heavily weighted.
   b. Since there is no formula used to calculate weights, determining them requires some experience.
   c. The formula for a Weighted Moving Average:
      $WMA_n = \sum$ (weight for period n) (demand in period n) / $\sum$ weights
   d. The following example gives a detailed illustration of how weighted moving averages are calculated.

Example: Weighted Moving Average

Donna's Garden Supply decides to forecast storage-shed sales by weighting the past 3 months as follows:

Weights Applied	Period
3	Last month
2	Two months ago
1	Three months ago
6	Sum of the weights

Solution:

Calculation for the forecast this month:

$$\text{WMAn} = \frac{(3 \times \text{sales last month}) + (2 \times \text{sales 2 mos. Ago}) + (1 \times \text{sales 3 mos. Ago})}{\text{Sum of the weights}}$$

The results of this weighted-average forecast are as follows:

Month	Actual Shed Sales	Solution: 3-month Moving Average
January	10	
February	12	
March	13	
April	16	$= [(3 \times 13) + (2 \times 12) + (10)] / 6 = 12.25$
May	19	$= [(3 \times 16) + (2 \times 13) + (12)] / 6 = 14.33$
June	23	$= [(3 \times 19) + (2 \times 16) + (13)] / 6 = 17$
July	26	$= [(3 \times 23) + (2 \times 19) + (16)] / 6 = 20.5$
August	30	$= [(3 \times 26) + (2 \times 23) + (19)] / 6 = 23.83$
September	28	$= [(3 \times 30) + (2 \times 26) + (23)] / 6 = 27.5$
October	18	$= [(3 \times 28) + (2 \times 30) + (26)] / 6 = 28.33$
November	16	$= [(3 \times 18) + (2 \times 28) + (30)] / 6 = 23.33$
December	14	$= [(3 \times 16) + (2 \times 18) + (28)] / 6 = 18.66$

In this particular forecasting situation, you can see that more heavily weighting the latest month provides a much more accurate projection.

4. Simple and weighted moving averages provide stable forecasts by smoothing out sudden fluctuations in the demand pattern.
5. Nevertheless, there are 3 problems associated with weighted moving averages.
   a. Increasing the size of n smoothes out fluctuations, but it makes the method less sensitive to real data changes.
   b. They do not pick up trends very well. Since they are averages, they always stay within past levels and do not predict changes to higher or lower levels -- they lag the actual values.
   c. They require a great deal of historical data.

G. Exponential Smoothing
   1. Exponential Smoothing is a weighted moving average forecasting technique in which data points are weighted by an exponential function.
   2. The basic exponential smoothing formula is as follows:
      New forecast =
      Last period's forecast + α (last period's actual demand – last period's forecast)
      Where: α = a weight, or smoothing constant. A smoothing constant is defined as the weighing factor used in an exponential smoothing forecast, a number between 0 and 1, chosen by the forecaster.
   3. The previously mentioned basic exponential smoothing formula can also be derived mathematically as follows: $F_t = F_{t-1} + \alpha (A_{t-1} - F_{t-1})$, where F_t = new forecast, F_{t-1} = previous forecast, α = smoothing (weighing) constant ($0 \leq \alpha \leq 1$), and A_{t-1} = previous period's actual demand.
   4. This formula simply states that the latest estimate of demand is equal to the old estimate adjusted by a fraction of the difference between the last period's actual demand and the old estimate. The following example illustrates how to use exponential smoothing to derive a forecast using this formula.

In January, a car dealer predicted February demand for 142 Ford Mustangs. Actual February demand was 153 autos. Using a smoothing constant chosen by management of $\alpha = 0.20$, we can forecast March demand using the exponential smoothing model. Substituting our sample data into the formula, we obtain:

Solution:

New forecast (for March demand) = $142 + .2(153 - 142) = 142 + 2.2$
= 144.2

Thus, the March demand forecast for Ford Mustangs is rounded to 144.

5. The previously mentioned smoothing constant (α) usually ranges from .05 to .50 for business applications.
   a. The smoothing constant can be adjusted to give more weight to recent data (α is high) or more weight to past data (α is low).
   b. The following table illustrates this concept.

Smoothing Constant	Weight Assigned To				
	Most Recent Period (α)	2nd Most Recent Period $\alpha(1 - \alpha)$	3rd Most Recent Period $\alpha(1 - \alpha)^2$	4th Most Recent Period $\alpha(1 - \alpha)^3$	5th Most Recent Period $\alpha(1 - \alpha)^4$
$\alpha = .1$	.1	.09	.081	.073	.066
$\alpha = .5$	.5	.25	.125	.063	.031

   c. High values of α are used when the underlying average is likely to change. Low values of α are used when the underlying average is stable.
H. Measuring Forecast Error
   1. Determining the accuracy of a forecast is accomplished by comparing the forecasted values with the actual (observed) values. In other words, it tells us how well the model performed against itself using past data.
   2. The Forecast Error (Deviation) = $A_t - F_t$, where A_t is the actual demand in period t, and F_t is the forecast in period t.
   3. There are 3 techniques that are frequently used to determine the overall forecast error.
      a. The Mean Absolute Deviation (MAD) is a measure of the overall forecast error for a model.
      b. The MAD is computed by dividing the sum of the absolute values of the individual forecast errors by the number of data periods (n). Mathematically, the $MAD = \sum |actual - forecast| / n$.
      c. The following example illustrates how to compute the MAD using this formula.

Example: Measuring Forecast Error

During the past 8 quarters, the Port of Baltimore has unloaded large quantities of grain from ships. The port's operations manager wants to test the use of exponential smoothing to see how well the technique works in predicting tonnage unloaded. He guesses that the forecast of grain unloaded in the first quarter was 175 tons. Two values of α are examined: $\alpha = .10$ and $\alpha = .50$. The following table shows the detailed calculations for α .10 only:

Solution:

Quarter	Actual Tonnage Unloaded	Rounded Forecast with $\alpha = .10$	Rounded Forecast with $\alpha = .50$
1	180	175	175
2	168	$176 = 175.0 + .10(180 - 175)$	178
3	159	$175 = 175.5 + .10(168 - 175.5)$	173
4	175	$173 = 174.75 + .10(159 - 174.75)$	166
5	190	$173 = 173.18 + .10(175 - 173.18)$	170
6	205	$175 = 173.36 + .10(190 - 173.36)$	180
7	180	$178 = 175.02 + .10(205 - 175.02)$	193
8	182	$178 = 178.02 + .10(182 - 178.22)$	184
9	?	$179 = 178.22 + .10(182 - 178.22)$	184

To evaluate the accuracy of each smoothing constant, we can compute forecast errors in terms of absolute deviations and MADs.

Quarter	Actual Tonnage Unloaded	Rounded Forecast with $\alpha=.10$	Abs. Dev. for $\alpha=.10$	Rounded Forecast with $\alpha=.50$	Abs. Dev. for $\alpha=.50$
1	180	175	5	175	5
2	168	176	8	178	10
3	159	175	16	173	14
4	175	173	2	166	9
5	190	173	17	170	20
6	205	175	30	180	25
7	180	178	2	193	13
8	182	178	4	184	4
	Σ of absolute deviations:		84		100

$$\text{MAD} = \Sigma \,|\text{deviations}| \,/\, n$$
$$\text{MAD}_{\alpha=.10} = 84 \,/\, 8 = 10.50$$
$$\text{MAD}_{\alpha=.50} = 100 \,/\, 8 = 12.50$$

On the basis of this analysis, a smoothing constant of $\alpha=.10$ is preferred to $\alpha=.50$ because its MAD is smaller.

    d. The Mean Squared Error (MSE) is the average of the squared differences between the forecasted and observed values.
       i. Mathematically, the MSE $= \Sigma$ (forecast errors) $/\, n$.
       ii. The following example illustrates how to compute the MSE using this formula.
      iii. One disadvantage of using the MSE is that it emphasizes large deviations.

Example: Mean Squared Error (MSE)

Compute the MSE for the Port of Baltimore.

Solution:

Quarter	Actual Tonnage Unloaded	Rounded Forecast w/ α = .10	(Error)^2
1	180	175	$= (180 - 175) = 5^2 = 25$
2	168	176	$= (168 - 176) = -8^2 = 64$
3	159	175	$-16^2 = 256$
4	175	173	$2^2 = 4$
5	190	173	$17^2 = 289$
6	205	175	$30^2 = 900$
7	180	178	$2^2 = 4$
8	182	178	$4^2 = 16$
		$\sum$ of errors squared:	1,558

$$MSE = \sum (\text{forecast errors}) / n$$
$$= 1{,}558 / 8 = 194.75$$

Is this MSE good or bad? It all depends on the MSEs for other values of α. As a practice exercise, find the MSE for α = .50. (You should get MSE = 201.5.) The result indicates that α = .10 is a better choice because we want to minimize MSE. Coincidentally, this confirms the conclusion we reached using MAD in the previous example.

    e. The Mean Absolute Percent Error (MAPE) is the average of the differences between the forecast and actual values, expressed as a percent of actual values.
        i. The MAPE is used to overcome the problem experienced with both the MAD and MSE – that their values depend on the magnitude of the item being forecasted.
        ii. The MAPE is computed as the average of the absolute difference between the forecasted and actual values, expressed as a percentage of the actual values.
        iii. Mathematically, the MAPE is expressed as follows:

$$MAPE = \frac{100 \sum |\text{actual} - \text{forecast}| / \text{actual}}{n}$$

Compute the MAPE for the Port of Baltimore.

Solution:

Quarter	Actual Tonnage Unloaded	Rounded Forecast w/ α = .10	Abs. % Error
1	180	175	= 100 (5 / 180) = 2.77%
2	168	176	= 100 (8 / 168) = 4.76%
3	159	175	10.06%
4	175	173	1.14%
5	190	173	8.95%
6	205	175	14.63%
7	180	178	1.11%
8	182	178	2.20%
		$\sum$ of % errors:	45.62%

MAPE   = $\sum$ absolute percent errors / n
            =   45.62% / 8   =   5.70%

    I.   Exponential Smoothing with Trend Adjustments
       1.   Simple exponential smoothing is like any moving average technique: It fails to respond to trends. Exponential smoothing must be modified when a trend is present.
       2.   To improve the forecast, a more complex model should be used, one that adjusts for trends.
       3.   The two smoothing constants are α for the average and β for the trend.
       4.   There are three steps to compute a trend-adjusted forecast.
            Step 1:   Compute F_t, the exponentially smoothed forecast for period t, using the formula $F_t = \alpha (A_{t-1}) + (1 - \alpha)(F_{t-1} + T_{t-1})$, where F_t = exponentially smoothed forecast of the data series in period t, α = smoothing constant for the average $(0 \leq \alpha \leq 1)$, A_t = actual demand in period t, and T_t = exponentially smoothed trend in period t.
            Step 2:   Compute the smoothed trend, T_t, using the formula:
                     $T_t = \beta (F_t - F_{t-1}) + (1 - \beta) T_{t-1}$
                     Where: β = smoothing constant for the trend $(0 \leq \beta \leq 1)$.
            Step 3:   Calculate the forecast including trend, FIT_t, using the formula:
                     FIT_t = exponentially smoothed forecast (F_t) + exponentially smoothed trend (T_t).

A large Portland manufacturer uses exponential smoothing to forecast demand for a piece of pollution control equipment. It appears that an increasing trend is present.

Month (t)	Actual Demand (A_t)	Month (t)	Actual Demand (A_t)
1	12	6	21
2	17	7	31
3	20	8	28
4	19	9	36
5	24	10	?

Smoothing constants are assigned the values of $\alpha = .20$ and $\beta = .4$. Assume the initial forecast for month 1 (F_t) was 11 units and the trend over that period (T_1) was 2 units.

Solutions:

Step 1: Forecast for month 2:

$$F_2 = \alpha (A_1) + (1- \alpha)(F_1 + T_1)$$
$$F_2 = (.2)(12) + (1 - .2)(11 + 2) \quad = \quad 12.8 \text{ units}$$

Step 2: Compute the trend in period 2:

$$T_2 = \beta (F_2 - F_1) + (1 - \beta) T_1$$
$$T_2 = .4 (12.8 - 11) + (1 - .4)(2) \quad = \quad 1.92$$

Step 3: Compute the forecast including trend (FIT_t):

$$FIT_2 = F_2 + T_2$$
$$FIT_2 = 12.8 + 1.92 \quad = \quad 14.72 \text{ units}$$

We will also do the same calculations for the third month.

Step 1: Forecast for month 2:

$$F_3 = \alpha (A_2) + (1- \alpha)(F_2 + T_2)$$
$$F_3 = (.2)(17) + (1 - .2)(12.8 + 1.92) \quad = \quad 15.18 \text{ units}$$

Step 2: Compute the trend in period 2:

$$T_3 = \beta (F_3 - F_2) + (1 - \beta) T_2$$
$$T_3 = .4 (15.18 - 12.8) + (1 - .4)(1.92) \quad = \quad 2.10$$

Step 3: Compute the forecast including trend (FIT_t):

$$FIT_2 = F_2 + T_2$$
$$FIT_2 = 15.18 + 2.10 = \quad 17.28 \text{ units}$$

The table below completes the forecasts for the 10-month period.

Month	Actual Demand	Smoothed Forecast, F_t	Smoothed Trend, T_t	Forecast Including Trend FIT_t
1	12	11	2	13.00
2	17	12.80	1.92	14.72
3	20	15.18	2.10	17.28
4	19	17.82	2.32	20.14
5	24	19.91	2.23	22.14
6	21	22.51	2.38	24.89
7	31	24.11	2.07	26.18
8	28	29.28	2.45	29.59
9	36	32.48	2.32	31.60
10	--	32.48	2.68	35.16

     5. The value of the trend smoothing constant, β, resembles the α constant because a high β is more responsive to recent changes in trend.

J. Trend Projections
     1. A Trend Projection is a time-series forecasting method that fits a trend line to a series of historical data points and then projects the line into the future for medium-to-long-range forecasts. It can use exponential, quadratic, or linear mathematical trend equations.
     2. The least squares method can be used to develop a linear trend line.
     3. A least squares line is described in terms of its slope and y-intercept with the following equation:
$$\hat{Y} = a + bx$$
Where:
    $\hat{Y}$ = computed value of the variable to be predicted (dependent variable)
    a = y-axis intercept
    b = slope of the regression line
    x = the independent variable (time)

4. The following figure shows the least squares method for finding the best-fitting straight line.

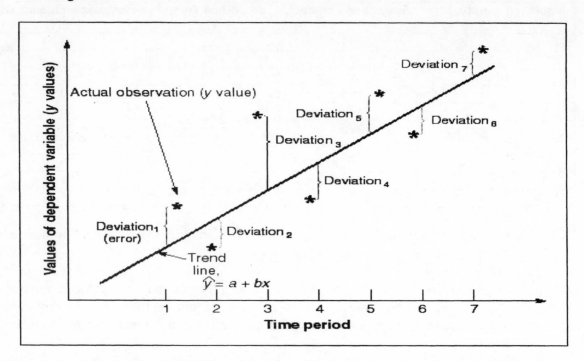

5. To find the values of *a* and *b* for any regressions line, the following equations are used:

a. Slope *b*:

$$b = \frac{\sum xy - n\overline{x}\,\overline{y}}{\sum x^2 - n\overline{x}^2}$$

Where:

b	=	slope of the regression line
x	=	known values for the independent variable
y	=	known values for the dependent variable
$\overline{x}$	=	average of the value of the x's
$\overline{y}$	=	average of the value of the y's
n	=	number of data points or observations

b. Y-intercept:

$$a = \overline{y} - b\overline{x}$$

The demand for electrical power at N.Y. Edison over the period 1997 to 2003 is shown below, in megawatts. Let's forecast 2004 demand by fitting a straight-line trend to these data.

Year	Electrical Power Demand	Year	Electrical Power Demand
1997	74	2001	105
1998	79	2002	142
1999	80	2003	122
2000	90		

Solution:

With a series of data over time, we can minimize the computations by transforming the values of x (time) to simpler numbers. Thus, in this case, we can designate 1997 as year 1, 1998 as year 2, and so on.

Year	Time Period (x)	Electrical Power Demand (y)	x^2	xy
1997	1	74	1	74
1998	2	79	4	158
1999	3	80	9	240
2000	4	90	16	360
2001	5	105	25	525
2002	6	142	36	852
2003	7	122	49	854
	$\sum x = 28$	$\sum y = 692$	$\sum x^2 = 140$	$\sum xy = 3063$

$$\bar{x} = 28/7 = 4 \qquad \bar{y} = 692/7 = 98.86$$

$$b = \frac{3063 - (7)(4)(98.86)}{140 - (7)(4^2)} = \frac{295}{28} = 10.54$$

$$a = 98.86 - 10.54(4) = 56.70$$

Thus, the least squares trend equation is $\hat{Y} = a + bx = 56.70 + 10.54x$. To project demand in 2004, we first denote the year 2004 in our new coding system as x = 8:

Demand in 2004 $= 56.70 + 10.54(8) = 141.02$ or 141 megawatts

We can estimate demand for 2005 by inserting x = 9 in the same equation:

Demand in 2005 $= 56.70 + 10.54(9) = 151.56$ or 152 megawatts

6. Three requirements must be met in order to use the least squares method.
   a. Because least squares data assume a linear relationship, the data must always be plotted.
   b. The time periods far beyond our given database are not predicted; the world is too uncertain.
   c. Deviations around the least squares line are assumed to be random.

K. Seasonal Variations in Data
   1. Seasonal Variations are regular upward or downward movements in a time series that relate to recurring events.
   2. Seasonality may be applied to hourly, daily, weekly, or other recurring patterns.
   3. Being able to understand seasonal variations is important for capacity planning in organizations that handle peak loads.
   4. Seasonality is expressed in terms of the amount that actual values differ from average values in the time series.
   5. A Seasonal Index can be developed by several methods. In a Multiplicative Seasonal Model, seasonal factors are multiplied by an estimate of average demand to produce a seasonal forecast.
   6. The following steps must be followed for a company that has "seasons" of 1 month.
      a. Find the average historical demand of each season by summing the demand for that month in each year and dividing by the number of years of data available.
      b. Compute the average demand over all months by dividing the total average annual demand by the number of seasons.
      c. Compute a seasonal index for each season by dividing that month's actual historical demand by the average demand over all months.
      d. Estimate next year's total annual demand.
      e. Divide this estimate of total annual demand by the number of seasons, then multiply it by the seasonal index for that month. This provides the seasonal forecast.

Example: Seasonal Variations

Monthly demand for IBM laptop computers at a Des Moines distributor for 2000 to 2002 is shown in the following table:

Month	Demand 2000	Demand 2001	Demand 2002	Avg. 2000-2002 Demand	Avg. Monthly Demand	Seasonal Index
Jan.	80	85	105	90	94	.957 (=90/94)
Feb.	70	85	85	80	94	.851 (=80/94)
Mar.	80	93	82	85	94	.904 (=85/94)
Apr.	90	95	115	100	94	1.064 (=100/94)
May	113	125	131	123	94	1.309 (=123/94)
June	110	115	120	115	94	1.223 (=115/94)
July	100	102	113	105	94	1.117 (=105/94)
Aug.	88	102	110	100	94	1.064 (=100/94)
Sept.	85	90	95	90	94	.957 (=90/94)
Oct.	77	78	85	80	94	.851 (=80/94)
Nov.	75	82	83	80	94	.851 (=80/94)
Dec.	82	78	80	80	94	.851 (=80/94)
Total Avg. Annual Demand =				1,128		

Solution:

Avg. Monthly Demand (above) = 1,128 / 12 months = 94

Seasonal Index (S.I.) = Avg. 2000-2002 monthly demand / Avg. monthly demand

S.I. for Jan. = 90 / 94 = .957

If we expected the 2003 annual for computers to be 1,200 units, we would use these seasonal indices to forecast the monthly demand as follows:

Month	Demand	Month	Demand
Jan.	(1200 / 12) x .957 = 96	July	(1200 / 12) x 1.117 = 112
Feb.	(1200 / 12) x .851 = 85	Aug.	(1200 / 12) x 1.064 = 106
Mar.	(1200 / 12) x .904 = 90	Sept.	(1200 / 12) x .957 = 96
Apr.	(1200 / 12) x 1.064 = 106	Oct.	(1200 / 12) x .851 = 85
May	(1200 / 12) x 1.309 = 131	Nov.	(1200 / 12) x .851 = 85
June	(1200 / 12) x 1.223 = 122	Dec.	(1200 / 12) x .851 = 85

Example: Use of Seasonal Index

A San Diego hospital used 66 months of adult inpatient hospital days to reach the following equation: $\hat{Y} = 8090 + 21.5x$.

Solution:

Based on this model, which reflects only trend data, the hospital forecasts patient days for the next month (period 67) to be

Patient days = 8090 + (21.5)(67) = 9530 (trend only)

The table below provides seasonal indices based on the same 66 months. Such seasonal data, by the way, were found to be typical of hospitals nationwide.

SEASONALITY INDICES FOR ADULT INPATIENT DAYS AT SAN DIEGO HOSPITAL			
Month	Seasonal Index	Month	Seasonal Index
Jan.	1.04	July	1.03
Feb.	0.97	Aug.	1.04
Mar.	1.02	Sept.	0.97
Apr.	1.01	Oct.	1.00
May	0.99	Nov.	0.96
June	0.99	Dec.	0.98

However, neither the trend data nor the seasonal data alone provide a reasonable forecast for the hospital. Only when the hospital multiplied the trend-adjusted data times the appropriate seasonal index did it obtain good forecasts. Thus, for period 67 (January):

Patient Days = (trend adjusted forecast) (monthly seasonal index)
              = (9530) (1.04) = 9911

The patient days for each month are:

Period	67	68	69	70	71	72	73	74	75	76	77	78
Month	Jan.	Feb.	Mar.	Apr.	May	June	July	Aug.	Sept.	Oct.	Nov.	Dec.
Forecast w/ Trend & Seasonal	9911	9265	9764	9691	9520	9542	9949	10068	9411	9724	9355	9572

By combining trend and seasonal data, the hospital was better able to forecast inpatient days and the related staffing and budgeting vital to effective operations.

Example

Management at Davis's Department Store has used time-series regression to forecast retail sales for the next 4 quarters. Sales estimates are $100,000, $120,000, and $160,000 for the respective quarters. Seasonal indices for the 4 quarters have been found to be 1.30, .90, .70, and 1.15, respectively.

Solution:
To compute the seasonalized or adjusted sales forecast, we just multiply each seasonal index by the appropriate trend forecast:

$$\hat{Y}_{seasonal} = Index \ x \ \hat{Y}_{trend\ forecast}$$

Thus for:

Quarter I:	$\hat{Y}_1 = (1.30)(\$100,000)$	$= \$130,000$
Quarter II:	$\hat{Y}_2 = (.90)(\$120,000)$	$= \$108,000$
Quarter III:	$\hat{Y}_3 = (.70)(\$140,000)$	$= \$98,000$
Quarter IV:	$\hat{Y}_4 = (1.15)(\$160,000)$	$= \$184,000$

   L. Cyclical Variations in Data
      1. Cycles are patterns in the data that occur every several years – not weeks, months, or quarters.
      2. Finding a leading variable with which the data series seems to correlate is the best way to predict business cycles.

Lecture Key: In business, it is important to forecast demand properly. Forecasting may be done quantitatively or qualitatively, each having different formulas and techniques. Qualitative methods use factors such as opinion, value, and experience. The quantitative forecasting method uses mathematical models that rely on historical data and/or causal variables, and is separated into two categories of models: time-series and associative.

VII. Associative Forecasting Methods: Regression and Correlation Analysis

   A. Associative forecasting considers several variables that are related to the quantity being predicted, unlike time-series forecasting.
      1. A statistical model is generated to forecast the necessary item(s), based on the collected variables.
      2. Associative forecasting is far superior to time-series forecasts, which solely analyze historic values for the forecasted variables.

B. The most common quantitative associative forecasting model is Linear Regression Analysis – a straight-line mathematical model to describe the functional relationships between independent and dependent variables.

C. Using Regression Analysis to Forecast

1. The same equation used in the least squares method of trend projection can be used to perform a linear-regression analysis.

2. Again, the equation is as follows: $\hat{Y} = a + bx$, where $\hat{Y}$ = computed value of the dependent variable, a = y-axis intercept, b = slope of the regression line, and x = the independent variable.

3. The following example shows how to compute linear regression using this equation.

Example

Nodel Construction Company renovates old homes in West Bloomfield, Michigan. Over time, the company has found that its dollar volume of renovation work is dependent on the West Bloomfield area payroll. The following table lists Nodel's revenues and the amount of money earned by wage earners in West Bloomfield during the past 6 years.

Nodel's Sales ($000,000), y	Local Payroll ($000,000,000), x	Nodel's Sales ($000,000), y	Local Payroll ($000,000,000), x
2.0	1	2.0	2
3.0	3	2.0	1
2.5	4	3.5	7

Nodel's management wants to establish a mathematical relationship to help predict sales. First, it needs to determine whether there is a straight-line (linear) relationship between area payroll and sales, so it plots the known data on a scatter diagram.

It appears from the six data points that there is a slight positive relationship between the independent variable (payroll) and the dependent variable (sales): As payroll increases, Nodel's sales tend to be higher.

Solution:
We can find a mathematical equation by using the least squares regression approach.

Sales, y	Payroll, x	x^2	xy
2.0	1	1	2.0
3.0	3	9	9.0
2.5	4	16	10.0
2.0	2	4	4.0
2.0	1	1	2.0
3.5	7	49	24.5
$\Sigma y = 15.0$	$\Sigma x = 18$	$\Sigma x^2 = 80$	$\Sigma xy = 51.5$

$\bar{x} = 18 / 6 = 3 \qquad \bar{y} = 15 / 6 = 2.5$

$b = \dfrac{51.5 - (6)(3)(2.5)}{80 - (6)(3^2)} = 0.25$

$a = 2.5 - 0.25(3) = 1.75$

Thus, the least squares trend equation is $\hat{Y} = a + bx = 1.75 + .25x$.

If the local chamber of commerce predicts that the West Bloomfield area payroll will be $600 million next year, we can estimate sales for Nodel with the regression equation:

Sales (in hundred thousands) = $1.75 + .25(6) = 3.25$ or $325,000

D. Standard Error of the Estimate
   1. The Standard Error of the Estimate ($S_{y,x}$), also called the Standard Deviation of the Regression, is a measure of the variability around the regression line – its standard deviation. It measures the error from the dependent variable, y, to the regression line, rather than to the mean.
   2. There are 2 formulas that may be used to calculate the standard error of the estimate. Both formulas generate identical answers.

$$S_{y,x} = \sqrt{\frac{\Sigma(y - y_c)^2}{n - 2}} \qquad S_{y,x} = \sqrt{\frac{\Sigma y^2 - a\Sigma y - b\Sigma xy}{n - 2}}$$

Where: y = the y-value of each data point
         y_c = the computed value of the dependent variable, from the regression equation
         n = the number of data points

Example: Standard Error of the Estimate

To compute the standard error of the estimate for Nodel's data in the previous example, the only number we need that is not available to solve for Sxy is y2. Some quick addition reveals y2 = 39.5. Therefore:

Solution:

$S_{y,x}$ = $\sqrt{[(\Sigma y^2 - a\Sigma y - b\Sigma xy) / (n - 2)]}$
    = $\sqrt{[(39.5 - 1.75(15.0) - .25(51.5)) / (6 - 2)]}$
    = .306 (in $ hundred thousands)

The standard error of the estimate is then $30,600 in sales.

E. Correlation Coefficients for Regression Lines
   1. The regression equation is one way of expressing the nature of the relationship between two variables – it shows how one variable relates to the value and changes in another variable.
   2. The Coefficient of Correlation (r) can also be used to evaluate the relationship between two variables.
      a. It is a measure of the strength of the relationship between two variables.
         i. It can be any value between +1 and –1.
         ii. The following figure illustrates what different values of r might look like.

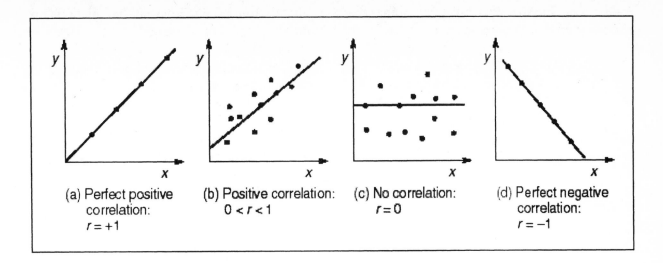

(a) Perfect positive correlation: $r = +1$

(b) Positive correlation: $0 < r < 1$

(c) No correlation: $r = 0$

(d) Perfect negative correlation: $r = -1$

    b. Mathematically, r is expressed as follows:

$$r = \frac{n\Sigma xy - \Sigma x \, \Sigma y}{\sqrt{\left[n\Sigma x^2 - (\Sigma x)^2\right]\left[n\Sigma y^2 - (\Sigma y)^2\right]}}$$

Example: Correlation Coefficients

In the Nodel's example, we looked at the relationship between Nodel Construction Company's renovation sales and payroll in its hometown of West Bloomfield. To compute the coefficient of correlation for the data shown, we need add only one more column of calculations (for y^2) and then apply the equation for r:

Solution:

y	x	x^2	xy	y^2
2.0	1	1	2.0	4.0
3.0	3	9	9.0	9.0
2.5	4	16	10.0	6.25
2.0	2	4	4.0	4.0
2.0	1	1	2.0	4.0
3.5	7	49	24.5	12.25
$\Sigma y = 15.0$	$\Sigma x = 18$	$\Sigma x^2 = 80$	$\Sigma xy = 51.5$	$\Sigma y^2 = 39.5$

$$r = \frac{n\,(\Sigma xy - \Sigma x \, \Sigma y)}{\sqrt{[(\,n\Sigma x^2 - (\Sigma x)^2)]\,[(n\Sigma y^2 - (\Sigma y)^2)]}}$$

$$= \frac{6\,(51.5) - (18)(15.0)}{\sqrt{[(\,6(80) - (18)^2)]\,[(6(39.5) - (15.0)^2)]}}$$

$$= .901$$

This r of .901 appears to be a significant correlation and helps to confirm the closeness of the relationship between the two variables.

3. The Coefficient of Determination (r^2) is another tool used to measure the relationship between two variables.
   a. The coefficient of determination is a measure of the amount of variation in the dependent variable about its mean that is explained by the regression equation.
   b. The value of r^2 will always be a positive number in the range of $0 \leq r^2 \leq 1$.
   c. It is the percentage of variation in the dependent variable (y) that is explained by the regression equation.
F. Multiple Regression Analysis
   1. Multiple Regression is a casual forecasting method with more than one independent variable.
   2. Mathematically, $\hat{Y} = a + b_1x_1 + b_2x_2$, where $\hat{Y}$ is a dependent variable, a is a constant, x_1 and x_2 are values of the two independent variables, and b_1 and b_2 are coefficients for the two independent variables.
   3. Although multiple regression can be quite difficult to calculate, the following example shows how the formula can be interpreted.

Example: Multiple Regression Analysis

The new multiple regression line for Nodel Construction, calculated by computer software, is:
   $\hat{Y} = 1.80 + .30x_1 - 5.0x_2$
We also find that the new coefficient of correlation is .96; implying the inclusion of the variable x2, interest rates, adds even more strength to the linear relationship.

Solution:
We can now estimate Nodel's sales if we substitute values for next year's payroll and interest rate. If West Bloomfield's payroll will be $600 million and the interest rate will be .12 (12%), sales will be forecast as:

Sales ($ hundred thousands) $=$ $1.80 + .30(6) - 5.0(.12) = 3.00$ or $300,000

Lecture Key: *It is important to be able to identify and understand the differences that exist between time-series forecasting and associative forecasting models. Using regression analysis to forecast involves linear-regression and standard error of the estimate. Correlation analysis involves considering the coefficient of correlation and the coefficient of determination. Multiple regression is also a useful forecasting tool when considering more than one independent variable.*

VIII. Monitoring and Controlling Forecasts

A. A forecast must not be forgotten once it is produced.
B. A Tracking Signal is one tool that can be used to monitor forecasts to ensure that they are performing well.
   1. A tracking signal is a measurement of how well the forecast is predicting actual values.
   2. The tracking signal is computed as the running sum of the forecast errors (RSFE) divided by the mean absolute deviation.
   3. Mathematically, the tracking signal is represented as:
      Tracking signal $=$ RSFE / MAD
      $= \sum$ (actual demand in period i
      $-$ forecast demand in period i) / MAD
   Where: MAD $= \sum$ |actual $-$ forecast| / n.

Rick Carlson Bakery's quarterly sales of croissants (in thousands), as well as forecast demand and error computations, are shown below. The objective is to compute the tracking signal and determine whether forecasts are performing adequately.

Quarter	Actual Demand	Forecast Demand	Error	RSFE	Abs. Forecast Error	Cum. Abs. Forecast Error	Cum. MAD	Tracking Signal (RSFE / MAD)
1	90	100	-10	-10	10	10	10.0	-10 / 10 = -1
2	95	100	-5	-15	5	15	7.5	-15 / 7.5 = -2
3	115	100	+15	0	15	30	10.0	0 / 10 = 0
4	100	110	-10	-10	10	40	10.0	-10 / 10 = -1
5	125	110	+15	+5	15	55	11.0	+5 / 11 = +.5
6	140	110	+30	+35	30	85	14.2	+35 / 14.2 = +2.5

At the end of quarter 6, MAD = $\sum$ |forecast errors| / n = 85 / 6 = 14.2 &
Tracking signal = RSFE / MAD = 35 / 14.2 = 2.5 MADs

This tracking signal is within acceptable limits. We see that it drifted from –2.0 MADs to +2.5 MADs.

4. When demand is greater than the forecast, a positive tracking signal results. A negative tracking signal means that demand is less than forecast.
5. A tracking signal is considered to be "good" if it has a low RSFE.
6. Bias occurs when a forecast is consistently higher or lower than actual values of a time series.
7. If a tracking signal exceeds a predetermined upper or lower control limit, there is a problem with the forecasting system, and management should take action. The following figure illustrates this concept graphically.

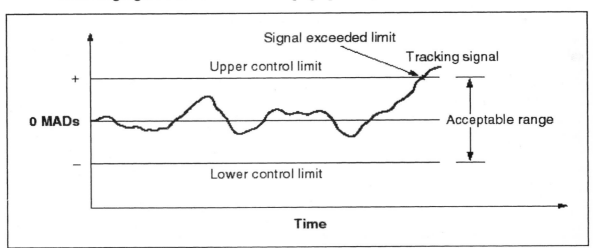

C. Adaptive Smoothing
1. Adaptive Forecasting involves computer monitoring of tracking signals and self-adjustment if a signal passes a preset limit.
2. This process is known as adaptive smoothing – an approach to exponential smoothing in which the smoothing constant is automatically changed to keep errors to a minimum.

D. Focus Forecasting
  1. Focus forecasting utilizes a variety of computer models and selects the best one for a particular application.
  2. It is based on two underlying principles.
     a. Sophisticated forecasting models are not always better than simple ones.
     b. There is no single technique that should be used for all products or services.

Lecture Key: Forecasts must always be monitored after they are produced to ensure efficient business operations. There are many available tools that can be used to monitor many types of forecasts, including tracking signals, adaptive smoothing, and focus forecasting.

IX. Forecasting in the Service Sector

A. Service sector forecasting often presents unique, unusual challenges.
B. Specialty Retail Shops
  1. Many specialty retail firms may often encounter erratic demand patterns.
  2. Therefore, many service firms placed in this situation maintain records of sales, noting the day of the week, along with unusual events, so that patterns and correlations that influence demand can be developed.
C. Fast-Food Restaurants
  1. Most fast-food restaurants monitor variations in demand that influence sales extremely closely.
  2. As a result, they require detailed demand forecasts.

Lecture Key: Oftentimes, service sector forecasting can be quite a unique and even challenging activity. Forecasting for specialty retail shops and fast-food restaurants requires additional work and resources.

Averaging Techniques: Simple Moving Average and Weighted Moving Average

S1.   Quarterly demand for handheld video games at Save-a-Lot closeout store for the past 2 years has been:

Year	Quarter 1	Quarter 2	Quarter 3	Quarter 4
1	611	604	641	622
2	644	572	626	597

a. Develop a 4-quarter moving average for as many periods as possible.
b. Develop a 6-quarter moving average for as many periods as possible.
c. Calculate the weighted moving average for periods 7, 8, and 9 using the following weights for the previous four periods (.10, .20, .30, & .40 respectively).

Solution:

a. MA_4 (Period 5) = (611 + 604 + 641 + 622) / 4 = 619.5
MA_4 (Period 6) = (604 + 641 + 622 + 644) / 4 = 627.75
MA_4 (Period 7) = (641 + 622 + 644 + 572) / 4 = 619.75
MA_4 (Period 8) = (622 + 644 + 572 + 626) / 4 = 616
MA_4 (Period 9) = (644 + 572 + 626 + 597) / 4 = 609.75

b. MA_6 (Period 7) = (611 + 604 + 641 + 622 + 644 + 572) / 6 = 615.67
MA_6 (Period 8) = (604 + 641 + 622 + 644 + 572 + 626) / 6 = 618.17
MA_6 (Period 9) = (641 + 622 + 644 + 572 + 626 + 597) / 6 = 617

c. W MA_4 (Period 7) = (.1 * 641) + (.2 * 622) + (.3 *644) + (.4 * 572) = 610.5
W MA_4 (Period 8) = (.1 * 622) + (.2 * 644) + (.3 *572) + (.4 * 626) = 613
W MA_4 (Period 9) = (.1 * 644) + (.2 * 572) + (.3 *626) + (.4 * 597) = 605.4

S2. Quarterly demand for computer tables at OfficeMart for the past four years has been:

Year	Quarter 1	2	3	4
1	453	345	434	350
2	460	330	390	340
3	500	320	40	390
4	504	330	405	400

a. Develop a 4-quarter moving average for as many periods as possible.
b. Develop an 8-quarter moving average for as many periods as possible.

Solution:

a. MA_4 (period 5) = (453 + 345 + 434 + 350)/4 = 395.5
MA_5 (period 6) = (345 + 434 + 350 + 460)/4 = 397.25
MA_6 (period 7) = (434 + 350 + 460 + 330)/4 = 393.5
MA_7 (period 8) = (350 + 460 + 330 + 390)/4 = 382.5
MA_8 (period 9) = (460 + 330 + 390 + 340)/4 = 380
MA_9 (period 10) = (330 + 390 + 340 + 500)/4 = 390
MA_{10} (period 11) = (390 + 340 + 500 + 320)/4 = 387.5
MA_{11} (period 12) = (340 + 500 + 320 + 403)/4 = 390.75
MA_{12} (period 13) = (500 + 320 + 403 + 390)/4 = 403.25
MA_{13} (period 14) = (320 + 403 + 390 + 504)/4 = 404.25
MA_{14} (period 15) = (403 + 390 + 504 + 330)/4 = 406.75
MA_{15} (period 16) = (390 + 504 + 330 + 405)/4 = 407.25
MA_{16} (period 17) = (504 + 330 + 405 + 400)/4 = 409.75

b. MA8 (period 9) = (453 + 345 + 434 + 350 + 460 + 330 + 390 + 340)/8 = 387.75
   MA9 (period 10) = (345 + 434 + 350 + 460 + 330 + 390 + 340 + 500)/8 = 393.63
   MA10 (period 11) = (434 + 350 + 460 + 330 + 390 + 340 + 500 + 320)/8 = 390.5
   MA11 (period 12) = (350 + 460 + 330 + 390 + 340 + 500 + 320 + 403)/8 = 386.63
   MA12 (period 13) = (460 + 330 + 390 + 340 + 500 + 320 + 403 + 390)/8 = 391.63
   MA13 (period 14) = (330 + 390 + 340 + 500 + 320 + 403 + 390 + 504)/8 = 397.13
   MA14 (period 15) = (390 + 340 + 500 + 320 + 403 + 390 + 504 + 330)/8 = 397.13
   MA15 (period 16) = (340 + 500 + 320 + 403 + 390 + 504 + 330 + 405)/8 = 399
   MA16 (period 17) = (500 + 320 + 403 + 390 + 504 + 330 + 405 + 400)/8 = 406.5

S3.   The manager of the Rose Shop needs to be able to forecast accurately the demand for roses. If the manager doesn't order enough dozens from her supplier, customers will go elsewhere. The manager has collected the following data for the past 9 months.

Month	Demand for Roses (Dozens)
Jan.	40
Feb.	135
March.	50
April	70
May	45
June	90
July	75
Aug.	60
Sept.	20

a. Compute a 3-month simple moving average forecast of demand for April through September.
b. Compute a 3-month weighted moving average forecast for months April through September.

Assign weights of .15, .40, and .45 to the previous months in sequence.

Solution:

Month	Demand for Roses (Dozens)	MA_3	WMA_3
Jan.	40		
Feb.	135		
March	50		
April	70	75	82.5
May	45	85	71.75
June	90	55	55.75
July	75	68.3	69
Aug.	60	70	76.5
		75	70.5

1.   Quarterly demand for portable stereos at a discount electronics store for the past four years has been:

	Quarter			
Year	1	2	3	4
1	500	370	406	444
2	374	304	458	378
3	402	438	330	480
4	376	344	438	372

a. Develop a 4-quarter moving average for as many periods as possible.
b. Develop an 8-quarter moving average for as many periods as possible.
c. Compare the two sets of forecasts with one another and with the actual time series.

2. The Lawn Trimmer Company distributes lawn furniture to various types of shops. The company must base its quarterly distribution schedule on a forecast of how many sets on lawn furniture will be demanded from it. The company has gathered the following data for the past three years from its sales records.

Year	Quarter	# of Sets of Furniture
1	1	100
	2	250
	3	490
	4	220
2	5	140
	6	290
	7	555
	8	150
3	9	165
	10	340
	11	660
	12	200

a. Compute a 3-quarter moving average forecast for quarters 4 through 13 and compute the forecast error for each quarter.
b. Compute a 5-quarter moving average forecast for quarters 6 through 13 and compute the forecast error for each quarter.
c. Compute a weighted 3-quarter moving average forecast using weights of 0.50, 0.33, and 0.17 for the most recent, next recent, and most distant data, respectively, and compute the forecast error for each quarter.
d. Compare the forecast developed in parts (a), (b), and (c) using cumulative error. Which forecast appears to be most accurate? Do any exhibit any bias?

3. The Undergrad program at Bayou University operates on a quarter system. While the number of students enrolled is fairly stable on a yearly basis, there are quarterly seasonal effects, with enrollment lower in the summer due to vacations. Quarterly enrollment for the past three years has been:

	Quarter			
Year	1	2	3	4
1	9319	8289	9295	6190
2	9321	8285	9303	6196
3	9022	8291	9302	6193

a. Estimate the quarterly seasonality using seasonal index.
b. Use a simple moving average to determine the yearly forecast for year 4.
c. Use the indexes found in part a to adjust the forecast for each quarter of year 4.

4. The Play Ball Corp, manufacturer of baseball equipment, wants to accurately forecast for baseball gloves. Because competition is fierce and the demand period limited, it is difficult to service customers and be competitive if the gloves are not ordered a month ahead. From sales records, the dealer has accumulated the following data for the past year.

Month	Glove Sales
January	8000
February	9500
March	10500
April	18000
May	17000
June	12000
July	10000
August	6500
September	2000
October	1000
November	1000
December	4000

a. Compute a 3-month moving average forecast of demand for April through January (of the next year).
b. Compute a 5-month moving average forecast for June through January.
c. Compare the two forecasts computed in parts (a) and (b) using MAD. Which one should the Play Ball Corp. use for January of the next year?

5.   The manager of the Fake Flowers outlet needs to be able to forecast accurately the demand for Silk Flowers. If the manager does not order enough cartoons from the plant, customers will buy their flowers from one of Fake Flowers' many competitors. The manager has collected the following demand data for the past eight months.

Month	Demand for Silk Flowers (Crates)
January	50
February	120
March	75
April	90
May	50
June	25
July	20
August	10

a. Compute a 3-month moving average forecast of demand for April through September.
b. Compute a weighted 3-month moving average forecast for months April through September. Assign weights of 0.15, 0.40, and 0.45 to the months in sequence.
c. Compare the two forecasts computed in parts (a) and (b) using MAD. Which one should the dealer use for January of the next year?

6.   The Lawn Trimmer Company distributes lawn furniture to various types of shops. The company must base its quarterly distribution schedule on a forecast of how many sets on lawn furniture will be demanded from it. The company has gathered the following data for the past three years from its sales records.

Year	Quarter	# of Sets of Furniture
1	1	100
	2	250
	3	490
	4	220
2	5	140
	6	290
	7	555
	8	150
3	9	165
	10	340
	11	660
	12	200

a. Compute a 3-quarter moving average forecast for quarters 4 through 13 and compute the forecast error for each quarter.
b. Compute a 5-quarter moving average forecast for quarters 6 through 13 and compute the forecast error for each quarter.
c. Compute a weighted 3-quarter moving average forecast using weights of 0.50, 0.33, and 0.17 for the most recent, next recent, and most distant data, respectively, and compute the forecast error for each quarter.
d. Compare the forecast developed in parts (a), (b), and (c) using cumulative error. Which forecast appears to be most accurate? Do any exhibit any bias?

Exponential Smoothing

S1. Quarterly demand for handheld video games at Save-a-Lot closeout store for the past 2 years has been:

Year	Quarter 1	Quarter 2	Quarter 3	Quarter 4
1	611	604	641	622
2	644	572	626	597

    a. Develop an exponential smoothing forecast for as many periods as possible with $\alpha = 0.2$ and $\alpha = 0.4$.

    b. Compare the two sets of forecasts wit one another and with the actual time series forecast in the previous problem.

Solution:

a. $\alpha = 0.2$ Period 6 F_{5+1} $= 0.2\,(619.5) + [(1 - 0.2) * 619.5] = 619.5$

              Period 7 F_{6+1} $= 0.2\,(627.75) + [(1 - 0.2) * 619.5] = 621.15$

              Period 8 F_{7+1} $= 0.2\,(619.75) + [(1 - 0.2) * 621.15] = 620.87$

              Period 9 F_{8+1} $= 0.2\,(616) + [(1 - 0.2) * 620.87] = 619.9$

              Period 10 F_{9+1} $= 0.2\,(609.75) + [(1 - 0.2) * 619.9] = 617.87$

    $\alpha = 0.4$ Period 8 F_{7+1} $= 0.4\,(615.67) + [(1 - 0.4) * 615.67] = 615.67$

              Period 9 F_{8+1} $= 0.4\,(618.17) + [(1 - 0.4) * 615.67] = 616.67$

              Period 10 F_{9+1} $= 0.4\,(617) + [(1 - 0.4) * 616.67] = 616.8$

b. The exponential smoothing is the best forecaster of all the techniques.

S2. Quarterly demand for computer tables at OfficeMart for the past four years has been:

Year	\multicolumn{4}{c}{Quarter}

Year	1	2	3	4
1	453	345	434	350
2	460	330	390	340
3	500	320	40	390
4	504	330	405	400

Develop an exponential smoothing forecast for as many periods as possible with $\alpha = 0.1$.

Solution:

$P6 = F6 = .1(395.5) + [1 - .1](395.5) = 395.5$

$P7 = F7 = .1(397.25) + [1 - .1](395.5) = 395.68$

$P8 = F8 = .1(393.5) + [1 - .1](395.68) = 395.46$

$P9 = F9 = .1(382.5) + [1 - .1](395.46) = 394.16$

$P10 = F10 = .1(380) + [1 - .1](394.16) = 392.74$

$P11 = F11 = .1(390) + [1 - .1](392.74) = 392.47$

$P12 = F12 = .1(387.5) + [1 - .1](392.47) = 391.97$

$P13 = F13 = .1(390.75) + [1 - .1](391.97) = 391.85$

$P14 = F14 = .1(403.25) + [1 - .1](391.85) = 393$

$P15 = F15 = .1(404.25) + [1 - .1](393) = 394.13$

$P16 = F16 = .1(406.75) + [1 - .1](394.13) = 395.4$

$P17 = F17 = .1(407.25) + [1 - .1](395.4) = 396.59$

$P18 = F18 = .1(409.75) + [1 - .1](396.59) = 397.91$

S3.   The owner of Addis Café is interested in developing a forecast model for the number of steaks to be sold each night at dinner. She has collected the following data from the registers:

Week	Steaks	Week	Steaks
1	150	6	148
2	132	7	155
3	164	8	137
4	146	9	189
5	99	10	160

Compute exponential smoothing forecasts with $\alpha = 0.2$.

Solution:

Period 2 $= F_{1+1} = .2\,(150) + [1-.2]\,(150)$ $= 150$
Period 3 $= F_{2+1} = .2\,(132) + [1-.2]\,(150)$ $= 146.4$
Period 4 $= F_{3+1} = .2\,(164) + [1-.2]\,(146.4)$ $= 149.92$
Period 5 $= F_{4+1} = .2\,(146) + [1-.2]\,(149.92)$ $= 149.14$
Period 6 $= F_{5+1} = .2\,(99) + [1-.2]\,(149.14)$ $= 139.11$
Period 7 $= F_{6+1} = .2\,(148) + [1-.2]\,(139.11)$ $= 140.89$
Period 8 $= F_{7+1} = .2\,(155) + [1-.2]\,(140.49)$ $= 143.71$
Period 9 $= F_{8+1} = .2\,(137) + [1-.2]\,(143.71)$ $= 142.37$
Period 10 $= F_{9+1} = .2\,(189) + [1-.2]\,(142.37)$ $= 151.70$

S4.   The Quarterly demand for black ink pens from a local office supply store for the past three years are as follows:

Year	Quarter 1	Quarter 2	Quarter 3	Quarter 4
1	15	29	20	18
2	20	25	19	30
3	25	16	18	22

a. Develop a 3-quarter and 5-quarter simple moving average for as many periods as possible.
b. Develop an exponential smoothing forecast for as many periods as possible with $\alpha = .3$ and $\alpha = .5$.
c. Compare all of the forecasts using MAD.

Solution:

a. Simple Moving Average

Step 1:   Using the previous 3 demand periods (year 1: quarters 1, 2, and 3), calculate the average by summing the demand, then divide by the number of periods beginning in period 4.

$MA_3 = (15 + 29 + 20) / 3 = 21.33$

Year	Quarter	Demand	MA$_3$	Error	Absolute Error
1	1	15			
	2	29			
	3	20			
	4	18	21.33	-3.33	3.33
2	1	20	22.33	-2.33	2.33
	2	25	19.33	5.67	5.67
	3	19	21.00	-2.00	2.00
	4	30	21.33	8.67	8.67
3	1	25	24.67	0.33	0.33
	2	16	24.67	-8.67	8.67
	3	18	23.67	-5.67	5.67
	4	22	19.67	2.33	2.33
				$\sum =$	39.00

Step 2:   Calculate the error and absolute error for each forecasted period using:
Error $=$ Demand $-$ Forecast $= 18 - 21.33 = -3.33$ or (for period 4)   Absolute Error $= 3.33$

Step 3:   Calculate the MAD for the forecast periods:
MAD $= \sum$ Absolute Errors / # of periods $= 39.00 / 9 = 4.33$

74

Simple Moving Average for 5 periods:

Year	Quarter	Demand	MA$_5$	Error	Absolute Error
1	1	15			
	2	29			
	3	20			
	4	18			
2	1	20			
	2	25	20.4	4.60	4.60
	3	19	22.4	-3.40	3.40
	4	30	20.4	9.60	9.60
3	1	25	22.4	2.60	2.60
	2	16	23.8	-7.80	7.80
	3	18	23	-5.00	5.00
	4	22	21.6	0.40	0.40
				Σ =	33.40

MAD = 33.40 / 7 = 4.77

b. Exponential Smoothing

Exponential Smoothing (α=0.3):

Step 1: Using the previous demand period and its forecast (year 1: demand for quarter 1 and quarter 1 forecast), calculate the forecast by multiplying the demand (15) by the smoothing constant (α = 0.3) then multiplying the forecast (15) by 1 minus the smoothing constant (1 − 0.3 = 0.7). Add the products together to get the forecast beginning in period 2.

Period 2 = F_{1+1} = .3 (15) + [1-.3] (15) = 15
Period 3 = F_{2+1} = .3 (29) + [1-.3] (15) = 19.2
Period 4 = F_{3+1} = .3 (20) + [1-.3] (19.2) = 19.44

Year	Quarter	Demand	α=0.3	Error	Absolute Error
1	1	15	15		
	2	29	15	14.00	14.00
	3	20	19.2	0.80	0.80
	4	18	19.44	-1.44	1.44
2	1	20	19.008	0.99	0.99
	2	25	19.3056	5.69	5.69
	3	19	21.01392	-2.01	2.01
	4	30	20.409744	9.59	9.59
3	1	25	23.2868208	1.71	1.71
	2	16	23.8007746	-7.80	7.80
	3	18	21.4605422	-3.46	3.46
	4	22	20.4223795	1.58	1.58
				Σ =	49.08

Step 2: Calculate the error and absolute error for each forecasted period using:
Error = Demand − Forecast = 29 − 15 = 14.00 (for period 2)   Absolute Error = 14

Step 3: Calculate the MAD for the forecast periods:
MAD = Σ Absolute Errors / # of periods = 49.08 /11 = 4.46

Exponential Smoothing (α=0.5):

Year	Quarter	Demand	α=0.5	Error	Absolute Error
1	1	15	15		
	2	29	15	14.00	14.00
	3	20	22	-2.00	2.00
	4	18	21	-3.00	3.00
2	1	20	19.5	0.50	0.50
	2	25	19.75	5.25	5.25
	3	19	22.375	-3.38	3.38
	4	30	20.6875	9.31	9.31
3	1	25	25.34375	-0.34	0.34
	2	16	25.171875	-9.17	9.17
	3	18	20.5859375	-2.59	2.59
	4	22	19.2929688	2.71	2.71
				Σ =	52.25

MAD = 52.25 /11 = 4.75

c. Compare the MAD for all the forecasts. The forecast with the lowest MAD would be the best.

Simple Moving Average MAD: 4.33 (3 periods) and 4.77 (5 periods)
Exponential Smoothing MAD: 4.46 (α=0.3) and 4.75 (α=0.5)

Using a simple moving average of 3 periods would be the best.

1. Using the data from problem 1 in the averaging section:
    a. Develop an exponential smoothing forecast for as many periods as possible with $\alpha = 0.2$.
    b. Develop an exponential smoothing forecast for as many periods as possible with $\alpha = 0.4$.
    c. Compare the two sets of forecasts with one another and with the actual time series forecast in the previous problem.

2. The cafeteria supervisor at College hospital is interested in developing a forecast model for the number of meals to be prepared each day at lunch. She has collected the following data from the cafeteria's register:

Week	Meals	Week	Meals	Week	Meals
1	611	6	641	11	626
2	640	7	614	12	597
3	628	8	608	13	622
4	616	9	607	14	645
5	604	10	572	15	619

Compute forecasts for all possible periods using moving averages with three and six weeks and exponential smoothing forecast with $\alpha = 0.3$ and $\alpha = 0.5$.

3. Donut Express, a drive thru donut shop, is open seven days a week. Other than fairly regular fluctuations on a day-of-the-week basis, demand for donuts has remained basically steady. Daily demand over the past four weeks has been:

Day

Week	Mon.	Tues.	Wed.	Thu.	Fri.	Sat	Sun
1	500	350	555	756	868	1212	1036
2	450	320	500	704	1013	1226	999
3	420	310	569	771	761	1200	1048
4	480	309	521	729	826	1327	1028

a. Estimate daily seasonal indexes for donuts demand at Donut Express.
b. Calculate the forecast using exponential smoothing with $\alpha = 0.25$ for year 5.
c. Use the daily seasonal indexes to forecast demand for each day in the week in year 5.

4. The administration at Bayou University wants to forecast the number of students who will enroll at the university next year in order to determine the university budget before the state legislature meets in the spring. The chair has accumulated the following enrollment data for the past eight years.

Year	Students
1	24000
2	25450
3	26350
4	27420
5	29500
6	30575
7	34490
8	34650

a. Compute a 3-semester moving average forecast for semesters 4 through 9.
b. Compute the exponential smoothed forecast ($\alpha = 0.20$) for the enrollment data.
c. Compare the two forecasts using MAD and indicate the most accurate.

5. The manager of the EnviroChem Gas Station wants to forecast the demand for unleaded gasoline next month so that the proper number of gallons can be ordered from headquarters. The manager has accumulated the following data on demand for unleaded gasoline from sales during the past fourteen months.

	Month	Gasoline Demanded (gal)
Year 1 –	October	800
	November	725
	December	630
	January	500
	February	645
	March	690
	April	730
	May	810
	June	1200
	July	1180
	August	1020
	September	940
Year 2 –	October	815
	November	750
	December	650
	January	480

Compute an exponentially smoothed forecast using an $\alpha = 0.3$.

6.   Due the unstable political environments, gas prices have also been very unstable. The state economist has decided to analyze the average weekly price for the past four months.

Month	Week	Price per Gal.
1	1	0.99
	2	1.02
	3	1.08
	4	1.10
2	5	1.12
	6	1.15
	7	1.19
	8	1.18
3	9	1.21
	10	1.25
	11	1.32
	12	1.38
4	13	1.45
	14	1.48
	15	1.48
	16	1.50

Compute the exponentially smoothed forecast with $\alpha = 0.40$, and the linear trend line forecast. Compare the accuracy of the two forecasts using cumulative error and MAD, and indicate which forecast appears to be most accurate.

7.   The Restaurant on the River is minutes from the local casino. The casino is an obvious adult hot spot for gambling and hosts a variety of concerts, shows, and parties throughout the year. The restaurant has experienced the following capacity rates at dinner for the nine years since gambling was legalized.

Year	Occupancy Rate (%)
1989	75
1990	78
1991	82
1992	84
1993	86
1994	85
1995	90
1996	92
1997	94

Compute an exponential smoothing forecast with $\alpha = 0.2$, and a linear trend line forecast. Compare the two forecasts using MAD and average error, and indicate which forecast seems to be most accurate.

8. Strawberries Everywhere makes strawberry pies. It has a production plant in Ponchatoula, La. The manager wants to forecast for the pies, so that they can properly man their plant. They have accumulated the following sales records for their pies for the past 16 months:

Month	Pie Sales (10s)
1	35
2	34
3	41
4	42
5	36
6	41
7	45
8	40
9	42
10	47
11	50
12	48
13	50
14	54
15	58
16	56

Develop an adjusted exponential smoothing model with $\alpha = 0.55$ and $\beta = 0.45$ to forecast demand, and assess its accuracy using cumulative error (E) and average error. Does there appear to be any bias in the forecast?

Linear Trend Line:

S1. Fun in Sun, located in Smalltown, Michigan, is an outdoor furniture and playground center. It has experienced a fairly steady demand growth for most of its product lines for the past few years. However, since using outdoor furniture is a mostly seasonal activity, there has been a strong quarterly seasonality in sales in their outdoor patio furniture line. (a) Use simple linear regression to estimate linear trend, (b) calculate quarterly seasonal adjustment of the trend line, and (c) forecast patio furniture demand for the four quarters of year 5. Quarterly demand for the patio furniture for the past 4 years has been:

Year (T)	Quarter 1	Quarter 2	Quarter 3	Quarter 4
1	321	899	1088	339
2	431	842	1151	399
3	420	825	1002	332
4	376	705	1010	331
10	1548	3271	4251	1401

Solution:

a.

Year (X)	Quarter 1	Quarter 2	Quarter 3	Quarter 4	(Y)	XY	X^2
1	321	899	1088	339	2647	2647	1
2	431	842	1151	399	2823	5646	4
3	420	825	1002	332	2579	7737	9
4	376	705	1010	331	2422	9688	16
10	1548	3271	4251	1401	10471	25718	30

$$B = \frac{\sum XY - N\bar{X}\bar{Y}}{\sum X^2 - N\bar{X}^2} = \frac{25718 - (4)(2.5)(2617.75)}{30 - 4(2.5)^2} = -91.9$$

$$A = \bar{Y} - B\sum \bar{X} = 2617.75 - (-91.9)(2.5) = 2847.5$$

Linear trend line equation: $Y = 2847.5 - 91.9 x$

b. Qtr. 1 $\rightarrow S_t$ = 1548 / 10471 = .148
Qtr. 2 $\rightarrow S_t$ = 3271 / 10471 = .312
Qtr. 3 $\rightarrow S_t$ = 4251 / 10471 = .406
Qtr. 3 $\rightarrow S_t$ = 1401 / 10471 = .134
c. Y_5 = 2847.5 + (-91.9 * 5) = 2388
Qtr. 1 = .148 * 2388 = 353.42
Qtr. 2 = .312 * 2388 = 745.06
Qtr. 3 = .406 * 2388 = 969.53
Qtr. 4 = .134 * 2388 = 319.99

S2.   Being located near the Intercostal Canal, Jet Skies & More has recently experienced a steady growth in demand for some of its product lines. However, since being on the water is definitely a seasonal activity, there has also been strong quarterly seasonality in sales in their Jet Ski lines. Quarterly demand for Jet Skis for the past three years has been:

Year (X)	Quarter 1	Quarter 2	Quarter 3	Quarter 4
1	232	600	456	272
2	200	625	405	238
3	215	681	492	205
6	647	1906	1353	715

a. Use simple linear regression to estimate linear trend.
b. Estimate the quarterly seasonality using a seasonal index.
c. Calculate the quarterly seasonal adjustment of a trend line for year 5.

Solution:

Year (X)	Quarter 1	Quarter 2	Quarter 3	Quarter 4	(Y)	XY	X^2
1	232	600	456	272	1560	1560	1
2	200	625	405	238	1468	2936	4
3	215	681	492	205	1593	4779	9
6	647	1906	1353	715	4621	9275	14

$$B = \frac{\sum XY - N \bar{X} \bar{Y}}{\sum X^2 - N \bar{X}^2} = \frac{9275 - (3)(2)(1540.33)}{14 - 3(2)^2} = 16.51$$

$$A = \bar{Y} - B \sum \bar{X} = 1540.33 - (16.51)(2) = 1507.31$$

Linear trend line equation: Y = 1507.31 + 16.51 x

b. Quarter 1: S_t = 647 / 4621 = .14
   Quarter 2: S_t = 1906 / 4621 = .412
   Quarter 3: S_t = 1353 / 4621 = .292
   Quarter 4: S_t = 715 / 4621 = .155
c. Y_5 = 1507.31 + (16.51* 5) = 1589.86   Qtr. 1 = .14 * 1589.86 = 222.58
                                              Qtr. 2 = .412 * 1589.86 = 655
                                              Qtr. 3 = .292 * 1589.86 = 464.24
                                              Qtr. 4 = .155 * 1589.86 = 246.43

1. The monthly demands for children's books at Children Are Miracles last year were:

Month	Demand	Month	Demand	Month	Demand
Jan.	145	May	286	Sep.	404
Feb.	182	June	273	Oct.	452
Mar.	202	July	328	Nov.	413
Apr.	236	Aug.	375	Dec.	489

   a. Use simple linear regression to fit a linear trend line to the data.
   b. Use the model developed in part (a) to forecast the demand for the magazine in January, June, and December of the current year.

2. As the demand for digital Internet connections increases due to reductions in cost, improvements in quality, and increased availability, the demand for dial-up services has been decreasing. The demand for dial-up services from one local provider for the past 10 months has been:

Month	1	2	3	4	5	6	7	8	9	10
Demand	255	215	190	200	170	150	150	160	140	135

   a. Use simple linear regression to fit a linear trend line to the data.
   b. Use the model developed in part (a) to forecast the demand for dial-up services for each of the next six months.

3. Being located in a rapidly growing area, Hunt's Sun & Fun, a pool supply center, has experienced fairly steady demand growth for most of its product lines over the past few years. However, since swimming is definitely a seasonal activity, there has also been pretty strong quarterly seasonality in sales in their family pool lines. Quarterly demand for chemicals for the past four years has been:

	Quarter			
Year	1	2	3	4
1	339	1088	899	321
2	399	1151	842	431
3	332	1002	825	420
4	331	1010	705	376

   a. Use simple linear regression to estimate linear trend.
   b. Calculate the quarterly seasonal adjustment of a trend line.
   c. Forecast chemical demand for the four quarters of year 5.

4. The department of transportation is analyzing the need for a new light at two local intersections. They select five different time periods per day from 8 weeks to determine the average frequency of cars. The department considers any intersection with an average frequency of 45 cars per hour per day (or better) busy enough for a light. The frequency is listed as follows.

Intersection 1   **Weekly Average**

Time Period	1	2	3	4	5	6	7	8
6am – 9am	62	49	53	35	43	48	56	43
9am – 1pm	73	55	81	77	60	66	85	70
1pm – 4pm	42	38	45	50	29	37	35	44
4pm – 8am	35	40	36	39	26	25	36	31

Intersection 2   **Weekly Average**

Time Period	1	2	3	4	5	6	7	8
6am – 9am	22	20	24	30	33	36	40	45
9am – 1pm	32	30	33	32	45	48	45	52
1pm – 4pm	18	15	18	38	40	38	40	42
4pm – 8am	35	28	32	40	42	42	45	45

a. Develop a seasonally adjusted forecasting model for the traffic frequency and forecast demand for each of the time periods for a single upcoming week using a simple moving average for day 9. Adjust the daily forecast for the various time periods.

b. Develop a trend line using the weekly average (not time period averages). Which light(s) currently need a light? Do you see any trend involved? Do you think any lights will be needed in the future? When?

5.   The Snow Ski tour guide company is a recreational tour guide company that takes groups cross-country skiing across the Rocky Mountains. Demand for its services is very seasonal, peaking during the holiday season and during the spring. It has accumulated the following data for tours per "season" (quarter) during the past five years.

Orders (1,000s)

Quarter	1993	1994	1995	1996	1997
1	10	12	18	24	25
2	20	21	24	28	30
3	21	20	25	29	32
4	31	38	42	48	50

a. Develop a model to forecast demand for each Quarter in 1998 using linear trend line.

b. Develop a seasonally adjusted forecast model for these order data by using the linear trend line and determining any seasonal adjustments.

c. Which model is most accurate?

d. If each guide can make at most 2 guides per day, how many guides are needed during 1998 based on the annual demand for tours? Calculate the maximum guides needed for any quarter in 1998.

6.   Using the demand in Problem 8 in the exponential smoothing section, develop a seasonally adjusted forecast of the next year's (year 5) quarters. To begin, you will have to break the 16 months of demand into quarters. Which forecast model do you think is better? Why?

5

Design of Goods and Services

I. Goods and Services Selection

A. Product Strategy Options Support Competitive Advantage
   1. Product selection is choosing the good or service to provide customers or clients.
   2. Product decisions are fundamental to an organization's strategy and have major implications throughout the operations function.

B. Product Life Cycles
   1. A successfully chosen product moves through the four phases of the product life cycle: introductory phase, growth phase, maturity phase, and decline phase, as shown in the figure below.
   2. Regardless of the length of the cycle, the task for the operations manager is the same: to design a system that helps introduce new products successfully.
   3. If the operations function cannot be produced effectively at this stage, the firm may be stuck with products that cannot be produced efficiently and perhaps not at all.

Product Life Cycle, Sales, Cost, and Profit

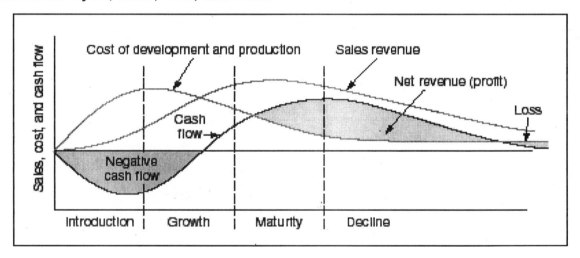

C. Product-by-Value Analysis
   1. Lists products in descending order of their individual dollar contribution to the organization.
   2. It also lists the total annual dollar contribution of the product.
   3. A product-by-value report allows management to evaluate possible strategies for each product.
   4. The report may also tell management which product offerings should be eliminated and which fail to justify further investment in research and development or capital equipment.

Lecture Key: When selecting a product to promote, you must be able to differentiate your product from other products. You have to be conscious of changes in the society in which you market your product. The product will go through a series of stages; going from negative cash flow, to making a profit, to the decline in demand, thus, creating new demand for a new product. Management determines which products will be successful or fail by creating a product-by-value analysis to show how much individual dollar contribution to the firm is made and how much the total annual dollar contribution of the product will be.

II. **Generating New Products**

    A. New Product Opportunities

        1. Brainstorming

            a. Used among a diverse group of people that share, without criticism, ideas on a particular topic.

            b. The goal is to generate an open discussion that will yield creative ideas about possible products and product improvements.

            c. Six specific opportunities which are rewarding to focus on:

                1. Understanding the customer

                2. Economic change

                3. Sociological and demographic change

                4. Technological change

                5. Political /legal change

                6. Changes in market practice, professional standards, suppliers, and distributors

        2. Operations managers must be aware of these factors and be able to anticipate changes in product opportunities, the products themselves, product volume, and product mix.

    B. Importance of New Products

        1. Importance of new products cannot be overestimated.

        2. Leading companies generate a substantial portion of their sales from products less than 5 years old, as seen here:

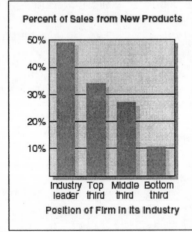

FIGURE 5.2 ■

Percent of Sales from Products Introduced in the Last 5 Years

The higher the percent of sales from products introduced in the last 5 years, the more likely the firm is to be a leader.

        3. Operations managers and their organizations must be able to accept risk and tolerate failure and must be able to accommodate a high volume of new product ideas while maintaining the activities to which they are already committed.

Lecture Key: Generating new product ideas alone will not be enough to come up with a successful product. Firms must focus on understanding the customer, economic changes, sociological and demographic changes, technological changes, political/legal changes, and other changes related to business, such as, market practice, suppliers, and distributors. Not making yourself aware of these changes may lead to failure because it may not be something the people, economy, or business world can handle or want at that time.

III. Product Development

A. Product Development System
1. May well determine not only product success but also a firm's future.
2. Stages of the product development system are shown below.
3. Product options go through a series of steps, each having its own screening and evaluation criteria and providing feedback to prior steps.

Product Development Stages

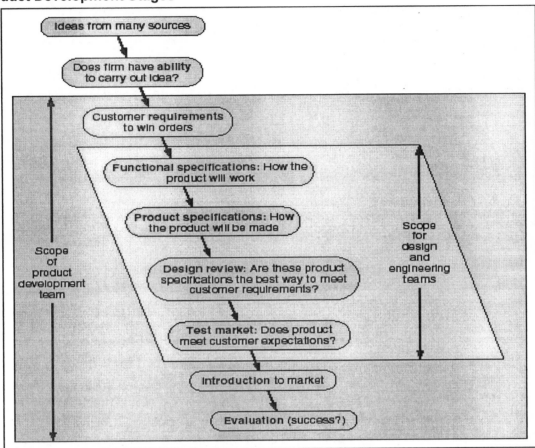

IV. Quality Function Deployment (QFD)

1. Refers to both determining what will satisfy the customer and translating those customer desires into the target design.
2. Used early in the design process to help determine what will satisfy the customer and where to deploy quality efforts.
3. One of the tools of QFD is the house of quality, which is a graphic technique for defining the relationship between customer desires and product/service; to build the house of quality, we perform six basic steps. (Steps are shown in Example 1 on pg. 162 of the text.)

First, through extensive market research, Great Cameras, Inc., determined what the customer *wants*. Those *wants* are shown on the left of the house of quality and are: lightweight, easy to use, reliable, easy to hold steady, and no double exposures. Second, the product development team determined *how* the organization is going to translate those customer *wants* into product design and process attribute targets. These *hows* are entered across the top portion of the house of quality. These characteristics are low electricity requirements, aluminum components, auto focus, auto exposure, auto film advance, and ergonomic design.

Third, the product team evaluated each of the customer *wants* against the *hows*. In the relationship matrix of the house, the team evaluated how well its design will meet customer needs. Fourth, in the "roof" of the house, the product development team developed the relationship between the attributes.

Fifth, the team developed importance ratings for its design attributes on the bottom row of the table. This was done by assigning values (5 for high, 3 for medium, and 1 for low) to each entry in the relationship matrix, and then multiplying each of these values by the customer's importance rating. These values in the "Our importance ratings" row provide a ranking of how to proceed with product and process design, with the highest values being the most critical to a successful product.

Sixth, the house of quality is also used for the evaluation of competitors. How well do *competitors* meet customer demand? The two columns on the right indicate how market research thinks competitors satisfy customer wants (Good, Fair, or Poor). So company A does a good job on "lightweight," "easy to use," and "easy to hold steady," a fair job on "reliability," and a poor job on "no double exposures." Company B does a good job with "reliability" but poor on other attributes. Products from other firms and even the proposed product can be added next to company B.

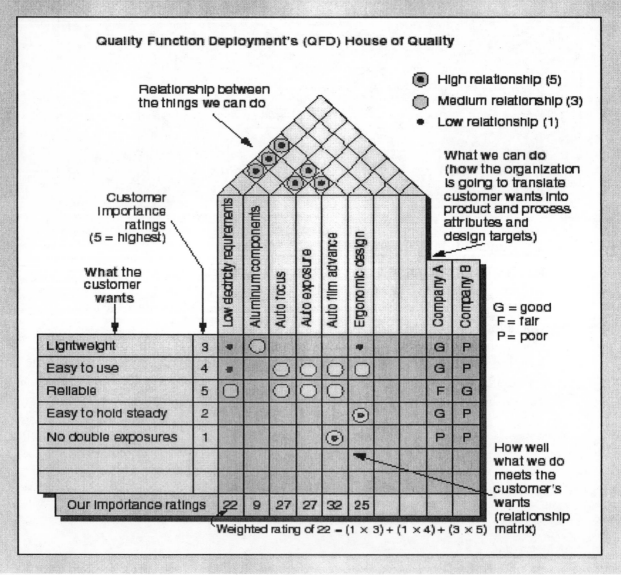

4. Another use of QFD is to show how the quality effort will be deployed as shown in a house of quality sequence.
    a. An effective way of identifying, communicating, and allocating resources throughout the system.
    b. The series of houses also helps operations managers determine where to deploy quality resources; that way we meet customer requirements, produce quality products, and win orders.
C. Organizing for Product Development – Product Development Teams
    1. Charged with the responsibility of moving from market requirements for a product to achieving a product success (Figure 5.3 on pg. 161 of the text).
    2. The objective of a team is to make the good or service a success, including marketability, manufacturability, and serviceability.
    3. Use of such teams is also called concurrent engineering and implies a team representing all affected areas (known as a cross-functional team).
    4. The team approach is the dominant structure for product development by leading organizations in the U.S.

Lecture Key: A product may look like a good choice, but without careful screening and evaluating every angle of the product, you could end up with a product that will fail. Also, you must pay attention to customers' wants and needs or else your product may fail once on the market. To look at how well a product will perform, product development teams are put together to research, design, and manufacture the product. Since product design affects all aspects of operating expense, manufacturability and value engineering activities do a thorough evaluation of the design and specifications to assess if there can be any improvements to the product.

V.   Issues for Product Design

A. Robust design means that the product is designed so that small variations in production or assembly do not adversely affect the product.
B. Modular designs are products that are designed in easily segmented components.
C. Computer-Aided Design is the use of computers to interactively design products and prepare engineering documentation.
D. Computer-Aided Manufacturing refers to the use of specialized computer programs to direct and control manufacturing equipment.
E. Virtual Reality Technology is a visual form of communication in which images substitute for the real thing, but still allow the user to respond interactively.
F. Value analysis seeks improvements that lead to either a better product or a product made more economically.
G. To aid in creating environmentally friendly designs, the use of Environmental Teams is helpful. The concept of green manufacturing is making environmentally sound products through efficient processes.

Lecture Key: The design of products can affect production costs, which can affect your total profits. These product design tools aid in different ways. The first helps in manufacturing a lot of one product to be used in many different other products. The second is helpful for production and sales because you are creating one product that is not specially made, but customers can mix and match to make it customized to their needs. The third aids in analyzing the design and avoiding mistakes. The fourth helps in the production line when manpower is not accurate enough. The fifth is used as a "what if" situation to aid in the design of the product. The sixth is similar to value engineering, yet it is used during the production process. And the last design tool is important for the environment, but it can also affect sales based on public opinion.

VI.   Time-Based Competition

A. As product life cycles shorten, the need for faster product development increases. The concept of time-based competition is that the quick will gain the competitive advantage.

B. Because time-based competition is so important, instead of developing new products from scratch, a number of other strategies can be used. Enhancements and migrations use the organization's existing product strengths for innovation and therefore are typically faster, while at the same time being less risky than developing entirely new products.

C. The external strategies for product development include:
1. Purchasing technology by acquiring a firm.
2. Joint ventures are combined ownership, usually between just two firms, to form a new entity.
3. Alliances are cooperative agreements that allow firms to remain independent, but use complementing strengths to pursue strategies consistent with their individual missions.

Lecture Key: *Time-based competition not only refers to faster production times but also the time it takes to get that product to market. These strategies can sometimes reduce the risk that goes with product development, but at the same time they enhance your human and capital resources available.*

VII.   Defining the Product

A. Once new goods or services are selected for introduction, they must be defined in terms of their functions.

B. Engineering drawings show the dimensions, tolerances, materials, and finishes of a component.

C. Bill of material lists the components, their description, and the quantity of each required to make one unit of a product.

D. Make-or-buy decisions distinguish between what the firm wants to produce and what it wants to purchase.

E. Group technology requires that components be identified by a coding scheme that specifies the type of processing and the parameters of the processing.

Lecture Key: *A good must be determined on the basis of what it is to do. You must then decide how you will achieve these functions. You must have documents to define your products, which include specifications and standards. Sometimes items are defined by drawings along with the bill of material. Products may also be defined by formulas and portion-control documents, depending on the product and what it contains. Some firms also have to decide if they will produce everything that goes into their product or purchase some of its components. Also, different parts must be grouped together, along with their parameters, to determine if an existing part would suffice.*

VIII. Documents for Production

A. Once a product is selected and designed, its production is assisted by a variety of documents.
B. An assembly drawing simply shows an exploded view of the product.
C. The assembly chart shows in schematic form how a product is assembled.
D. The route sheet lists the operations necessary to produce the component.
E. The work order is an instruction to make a given quantity of a particular item, usually to a given schedule.
F. Engineering change notices change some aspect of the product's definition or documentation, such as an engineering drawing or a bill of material.
G. Configuration management is the system by which a product's planned and changing configurations are accurately identified and for which control and accountability of change are maintained.

Lecture Key: Different documents must be used to produce the product. Some which show it in a three-dimensional way, others that show exactly how it is to be put together. Others list the operations needed to produce it and what material is needed and some that list given quantities so that every item is uniform in production.

IX. Service Design

A. Service industries include banking, finance, insurance, transportation, and communications.
B. Like goods, a large part of the cost and quality of a service is defined at the design stage.
   1. One technique is to design the product so that customization is delayed as late in the process as possible.
   2. The second approach is to modularize the product so that customization takes the form of changing modules.
   3. A third approach to the design of services is to divide the service into small parts and identify those parts that lend themselves to automation or reduced customer interaction.
C. The moment-of-truth is the moment that exemplifies, enhances, or detracts from the customer's expectations.
D. Documents for Services will often take the form of explicit job instructions that specify what is to happen at the moment-of-truth. Because of the high customer interaction of most services, the documents for moving the product to production are different from those used in goods-producing operations.

Customers who use drive-up teller stations rather than walk-in lobbies require different customer relations techniques. The distance and machinery between you and the customer raises communication barriers. Communication tips to improve customer relations at a drive-up window are:

- Be especially discreet when talking to the customer through the microphone.
- Provide written instructions for customers who must fill out forms you provide.
- Mark lines to be completed or attach a note with instructions.
- Always say "please" and "thank you" when speaking through the microphone.
- Establish eye contact with the customer if the distance allows it.
- If a transaction requires that the customer park the car and come into the lobby, apologize for the inconvenience.

Source: Adapted with permission from Teller Operations (Chicago, IL: The Institute of Financial Education, 1999): page 32.

Lecture Key: Service design is much different from product design. It is not a tangible good, so customer interaction is needed to achieve successful productivity improvements. You want customer satisfaction to be known in the design process so that costs concerning improvements may not be incurred. You want to design to meet or exceed customer expectations.

X. **Application of Decision Trees to Product Design**

A. Decision trees can be used for new product decisions as well as for a wide variety of other management problems.
B. To form a decision tree, we use the following procedure:
  1. Be sure that all possible alternatives and states of nature are included in the tree; this includes an alternative of "doing nothing."
  2. Payoffs are entered at the end of the appropriate branch. This is the place to develop the payoff of achieving this branch.
  3. The objective is to determine the expected value of each course of action. We accomplish this by starting at the end of the tree and working toward the beginning of the tree, calculating values at each step and "pruning" alternatives that are not as good as others from the same node.

Example: Decision Trees

Silicon, Inc., a semiconductor manufacturer, is investing the possibility of producing and marketing a microprocessor. Undertaking this project will require either purchasing a sophisticated CAD system or hiring and training several additional engineers. The market for the product could be either favorable or unfavorable. Silicon, Inc., of course, has the option of not developing the new product at all.

With favorable acceptance by the market, sales would be 25,000 processors selling for $100 each. With unfavorable acceptance, sales would be only 8,000 processors selling for $100 each. The cost of CAD equipment is $500,000, but that of hiring and training three new engineers is only $375,000. However, manufacturing costs should drop from $50 each when manufacturing without CAD to $40 each when manufacturing with CAD.

The probability of favorable acceptance of the new microprocessor is .40; the probability of unfavorable acceptance is .60.

Solution:

Step 1: Illustrate the decision possibilities with a decision tree.

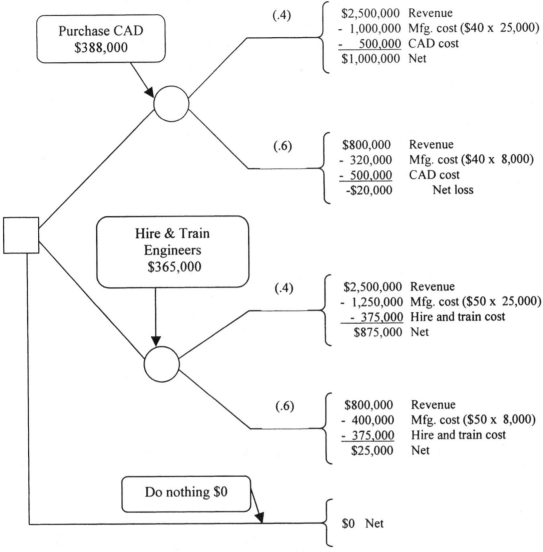

Step 2: Calculate the Expected Monetary Value (EMVs).

The EMVs have been circled at each step of the decision tree above. For the top branch:

EMV (purchase CAD system)   =   (.4)($1,000,000) + (.6)(−$20,000)
        = $388,000

This figure represents the results that will occur if Silicon, Inc., purchases CAD. The expected value of hiring and training engineers is the second series of branches:

EMV (hire/train engineers)   =   (.4)($875,000) + (.6)($25,000)
        = $365,000

The EMV of doing nothing is $0.

Because the top branch has the highest expected monetary value (an EMV of $388,000 vs. $0), it represents the best decision. Management should purchase the CAD system.

Lecture Key: *A decision tree is used almost in the same manner as you would use thought bubbles when writing a paper. You must consider every possible option/outcome and gather your thoughts.*

XI. Transition to Production

A. One of the arts of modern management is knowing when to move a product from development to production; this move is known as transition to production.
B. Management must make a decision—more development or production.
C. Once this decision is made, there is usually a period of trial production to ensure that the design is indeed producible.
D. Some companies appoint a project manager, while others use product development teams to ensure that the transition from development to production is successful. Another approach is integration of the product development and manufacturing organizations.
E. Assembly drawings, assembly charts, route sheets, and work orders are often used to assist in the actual production of the product.

Lecture Key: *A product will eventually go to production. Design is the first step, but some people that are part of the production process see production as the first step. If a product does not make it to market in time it can be costly. So you must make the decision to keep the product for more development or production. The operations manager's job is to make the transition from research and design to production as smooth as possible.*

Decision Trees

S1.   Kurt Wayne is interested in interviewing applicants for an open position in his company. From past experience, Kurt has determined that 90% of applicants are considered qualified (or good) and 10% are not qualified (or bad). He has also determined that if the applicant is qualified, he has a 90% chance of being successful. If the applicant is not qualified, then the applicant has only a 20% chance of being successful. What is the probability that a person will be successful if they are really not qualified? What is the probability that a person will not be successful if they are really qualified? What is the probability that the applicant will not be successful?

Solution:

Step 1:   The decision tree is below. It represents the series of sequential decision-making.

Step 2:   Calculate the expected values for each branch of the tree.

Branch 1: Probability (Qualified applicant) x Probability (successful given qualified)
EV = 0.90 x 0.90 or 0.81

Branch 2: Probability (Qualified applicant) x Probability (not successful given qualified)
EV = 0.90 x 0.10 or 0.09

Branch 3: Probability (Not Qualified applicant)
x Probability (successful given not qualified)
EV = 0.10 x 0.20 or 0.02

Branch 4: Probability (Not Qualified applicant)
x Probability (successful given not qualified)
EV = 0.10 x 0.80 or 0.08

Step 3:   Analysis:
What is the probability that a person will be successful if they are really not qualified?

Follow the branch for not qualified and successful (branch #3). The expected value is 0.02 or 2% will not be qualified and be successful anyway.

What is the probability that a person will not be successful if they are really qualified?

Follow the branch for qualified and not successful (branch #2). The expected value is 0.09 or 9% will be qualified and not successful.

What is the probability that the applicant will not be successful?

For this one, you have two branches to consider, qualified and not successful (branch #2) and not qualified and not successful (branch #4). Follow the branches for both and calculate the expected value as 0.09 or 9% (for branch #2) and 0.08 or 8% (for branch #4). To calculate the probability that the applicant will not be successful, add the individual probabilities for each branch together to get 17%.

P(not successful) = 9% + 8% = 17%

Decision Tree:

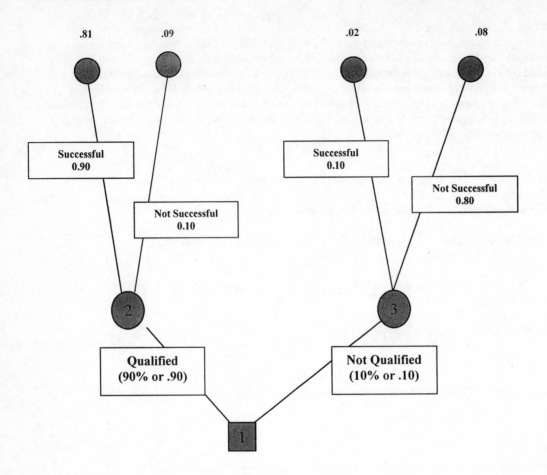

S2.   ComTech is bidding for a new state contract. The manager expects that his company has a 40% chance of getting the contract. The bidding process costs $50,000 (a cost that will be lost either way). If ComTech gets the contract, then they have two options (use current equipment and labor or buy new equipment). If they use current resources, then the cost is $40,000 (fixed) plus $20 per unit (variable). The new equipment and labor will cost $260,000 (fixed) plus $10 per unit (variable). The manager does have another concern if they use the current resources, and that is what to do if demand changes. If other demand is light (only 10% of the time), the cost is $0 since it can be absorbed. If other demand is normal (only 70% of the time), the cost is $100,000. If other demand is heavy (only 20% of the time), the cost is $200,000. Should the manager go after the state bid?

Solution:

Step 1:   Draw the decision tree. The table below represents the series of sequential decision-making.

Step 2:   Calculate the expected values of the end nodes (6, 7, and 8). The analysis begins by calculating the expected values of nodes 6 and 7 (work backwards through the decision tree).

EV (node 6) = 0.20 ($200,000) = $40,000
EV (node 7) = 0.70 ($100,000) = $70,000
EV (node 8) = 0.10 ($0) = $0

Step 3:   Calculate the expected values for node 4 and node 5.
EV (node 4) = (Cost of production using the old resources)
                             + [EV (node 6) + EV (node 7) + EV (node 8)]
              = (40,000 + 20x) + [40,000 + 70,000 + 0]
              = (40,000 + 20(10,000 units of production)) + [40,000 + 70,000 + 0]
              = −$350,000
EV (node 5) = 260,000 +10x = 260,000 + 10(10,000 units of production)
              = −$360,000

Step 4:   Make decision for the value for node 2.
EV (node 4) = −$350,000
EV (node 5) = −$360,000
Since these are costs, you would want to choose node 4.
                (Use current resources at cost of $350,000)

Step 5:   Calculate the expected cost of node 1 given the two states of nature.
                (get contract 40% of time and don't get contract 60% of the time)

Revenue from contract production = Revenue in $ x units of production
                                  = $50 x 10,000 units
                                  = $500,000
Cost of getting contract = Cost of bidding + Cost of production
                          = $50,000 + 350,000
                          = $400,000
EV (node 2) = Probability on getting contract
                        x (Revenue from contract − Cost of getting contract)
              = .40 x ($500,000 − $400,000)
              = $40,000 in profit
EV (node 3) = Probability of not getting a contract x cost of bidding
              = 0.60 x −$50,000
              = −$30,000 in loss
EV (node 1) = EV (node 2) + EV (node 3)
              = $40,000 – 30,000 = $10,000

Step 6:   Analysis: Based on this decision tree, the manager expects to make $10,000 in profit. The recommendation would be to bid for the contract and produce using the current resources if the contract is received.

Decision Tree:

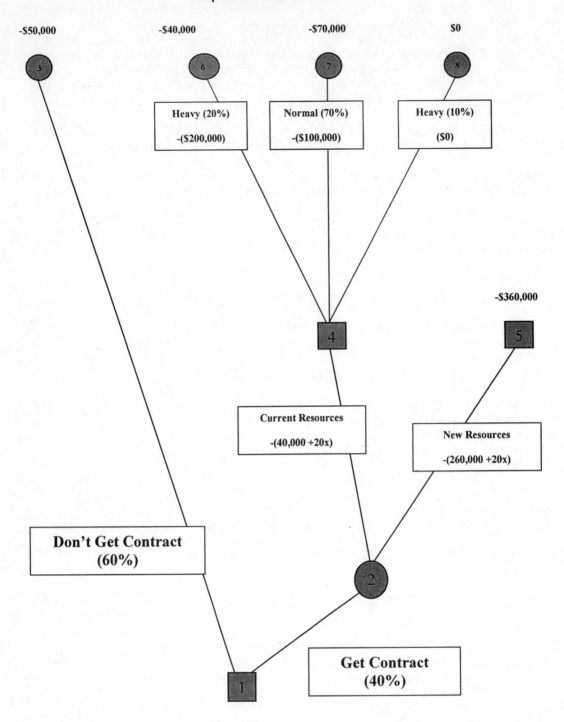

Expected Values

-$50,000   -$40,000   -$70,000 $0

③   ⑥   ⑦   ⑧

Heavy (20%)   Normal (70%)   Heavy (10%)

-($200,000)   -($100,000)   ($0)

4

-$360,000

5

Current Resources

-(40,000 +20x)

New Resources

-(260,000 +20x)

Don't Get Contract
(60%)

2

Get Contract
(40%)

1

1. Lower State University is being sued for damages as a result of injuries incurred during the university's 75th Anniversary celebration. The lawyers suggest taking a low/medium/high offer approach for settling the suits out of court. The city will initially offer $100,000, an amount that the lawyers feel has a 20% chance of being accepted. Alternatively, the city could offer $150,000, which the lawyers feel would have a 50-50 chance of being accepted, or they could offer $200,000, which would definitely be accepted.

   If the initial offer is not accepted, the city would make a second, higher offer of $175,000, which the lawyers feel would have a 50-50 chance of acceptance. If this were rejected, the city would have to offer $225,000 to guarantee acceptance. If the plaintiffs accepted neither offer, the lawyers felt that an offer of $250,000 would definitely be accepted.

   a. Draw a decision tree for this problem.
   b. What strategy should the city follow to minimize the expected cost of settlement? That is, what should be the first offer, the second offer?
   c. If the probability of acceptance of the first offer changes to 30%, does this change the city's strategy?
   d. Determine the minimum probability of acceptance of an initial offer of $100,000 that would make the strategy starting with that amount optimal.

2. Kurt Wayne is the president of Factory Sheet Metal Company. Kurt is considering whether or not to build a manufacturing plant in New Orleans to supply the local petroleum plants. His decision is laid out in the following table:

Alternatives	Positive Market	Negative Market
Large Plant	$200,000	-$150,000
Small Plant	$40,000	-$5,000
Do Nothing	$0	$0
Market Probabilities	0.35	0.65

   a. Construct a decision tree.
   b. Determine the best strategy, using expected monetary value (EMV).
   c. What is the expected value of perfect information (EVPI)?

3. Lawn Trimmer Tractors buys batteries from two suppliers. The quality of the batteries from the suppliers is indicated below:

Percent Defective	Probability for Supplier #1	Probability for Supplier #2
1	.70	.30
3	.20	.40
5	.10	.30

   This means that the probability of getting a batch of batteries that are 1% defective from Supplier #1 is .70. This means that every time Lawn Trimmer makes an order of 1,000 batteries, then 10 will be defective. A defective battery can be repaired for $1.50. Although the quality of Supplier #2 is lower, it will sell an order of 1,000 for $37 less than Supplier #1.

   a. Develop a decision tree.
   b. Which supplier should Lawn Trimmer use?

4. Bonnie Hunt, manager of the Lake Arena that will be home to the new professional basketball team, wants to make plans for the gift shop needs for next season. She has developed a table of conditional values for the various alternatives (inventory for memorabilia) and states of nature (size of crowd).

Alternatives	STATES OF NATURE (size of crowd)		
	Large	Average	Small
Large force	$20,000	$10,000	$2,000
Average force	$15,000	$12,000	$6,000
Small force	$9,000	$6,000	$5,000

If the probabilities associated with the states of nature are 0.40 for a large crowd, 0.40 for an average crowd, and 0.20 for a small crowd, determine:

a. The alternative that provides the greatest expected monetary value (EMV).
b. The expected value of the perfect information (EVPI).

5. Shelia Rock is the Technology Manager for a local university. She is trying to determine whether to build a large annex on the Business Center. She has to determine if a large, small, or no annex is needed to meet the needs of the students and faculty. If the size of the university continues to grow, a large wing could return $500,000 in grant money and user fees each year. If the small annex were built, it would return $100,000 to the university each year if the population continues to grow. If the size of the university remains the same, the university would encounter a loss of $85,000 if the large annex were built. Furthermore, a loss of $45,000 would be realized if the small annex was constructed and the size remains the same. Unfortunately, Shelia does not have any information about the future size of the university.

a. Construct a decision tree.
b. Construct a decision table.
c. Using an equal likelihood criteria, determine the best alternative.
d. If the probabilities changed to: Growth = 0.60 and Remaining the Same = 0.40, what decision should Shelia make?

6

Managing Quality

I. **Quality and Strategy**

  A. Quality is a wonderful tonic for improving operations.
    1. Helps build successful strategies of differentiation, low cost, and response.
    2. Quality may be the critical success factor.
  B. Improvements in quality help firms increase sales and reduce costs, both of which can increase profitability.
    1. Increases in sales often occur as firms speed response, lower selling prices as a result of economies of scale, and improve their reputation for quality products.
    2. Improved quality allows costs to drop as firms increase productivity and lower rework, scrap, and warranty costs.

WAYS QUALITY IMPROVES PROFITABILITY

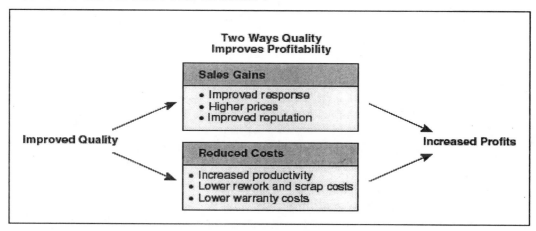

  C. Quality and productivity are positively related. Companies with the highest quality were five times as productive as companies with the poorest quality.
  D. Quality, or the lack of quality, impacts the entire organization from supplier to customer and from product design to maintenance.
    1. Building an organization that can achieve quality also affects the entire organization—and it is a demanding task.
    2. Flow of activities for an organization to use to achieve total quality management (TQM).
      i. Begins with an organizational environment that fosters quality, followed by an understanding of the principles of quality, and then an effort to engage employees in the necessary activities to implement quality.
      ii. When done well, the organization typically satisfies its customers and obtains a competitive advantage.
      iii. The ultimate goal is to win customers.

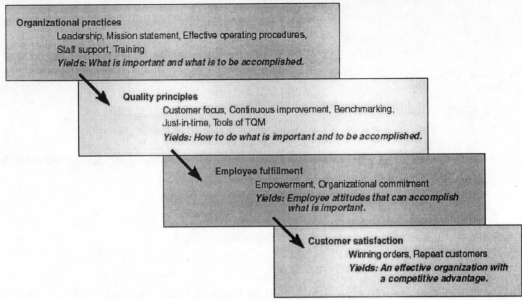

Organizational practices
Leadership, Mission statement, Effective operating procedures,
Staff support, Training
Yields: What is important and what is to be accomplished.

Quality principles
Customer focus, Continuous improvement, Benchmarking,
Just-in-time, Tools of TQM
Yields: How to do what is important and to be accomplished.

Employee fulfillment
Empowerment, Organizational commitment
*Yields: Employee attitudes that can accomplish
what is important.*

Customer satisfaction
Winning orders, Repeat customers
*Yields: An effective organization with
a competitive advantage.*

FIGURE 6.2 ■ The Flow of Activities that Are Necessary to Achieve Total Quality Management

Lecture Key: As you can see, quality is the critical success factor for managing a firm. This impacts the organization from supplier to customer, and from product design to maintenance. Although demanding, when quality is achieved, the organization usually satisfies its customers and obtains a competitive advantage, which is the ultimate goal.

II.   Defining Quality

A. Total Quality Management systems are driven by identifying and satisfying customer needs.
  1. Quality is the ability of a product or service to meet customer needs. It is also defined as, "The totality of features and characteristics of a product or service that bears on its ability to satisfy stated or implied needs."
  2. Other definitions:
      a. User-based: lies in the eyes of the beholder; marketing and customer based.
      b. Manufacturing-based: making it right the first time; production managers.
      c. Product-based: views quality as a precise and measurable variable.
  3. Characteristics that connote quality must first be identified through research; then the manufacturing process is organized to ensure that products are made precisely to specifications. A process that ignores any one of these steps will not result in a quality product.
B. Implications of Quality/ Why Quality is Important
  1. Company Reputation
      a. Perceptions about the firm's new products.
      b. Employment practices.
      c. Supplier relations.
      d. Self-promotion is not a substitute for quality products.
  2. Product Liability
      a. Courts hold organizations that design, produce, or distribute faulty products or services liable for damages or injuries resulting from their use.
      b. Consumer Product Safety Acts set and enforce product standards by banning products that do not reach those standards.
      c. Huge legal expenses, large settlements or losses, and terrible publicity.

100

3. Global Implications
   a. Quality is an international, as well as OM, concern.
   b. To compete effectively in the global economy, products must meet global quality, design, and price expectations.
   c. Inferior products harm a firm's profitability and a nation's balance of payments.
C. Malcolm Baldridge National Quality Award
   1. Award for quality achievement.
   2. Named for former Secretary of Commerce Malcolm Baldridge.
   3. Firm winners include: Motorola, Milliken, Xerox, Federal Express.
D. Cost of Quality (COQ)
   1. The cost of doing things wrong, that is, the price of nonconformance.
   2. Four major categories of costs:
      a. Prevention costs—associated with the potential for defective parts or services; Examples: training, quality improvement programs.
      b. Appraisal costs—related to evaluating products, processes, parts, and services; testing, labs, inspectors.
      c. Internal failure—costs that result from production of defective parts or services before delivery to customers; rework, scrap, downtime.
      d. External costs—occur after delivery of defective parts or services; rework, returned goods, liabilities, lost goodwill, costs to society.
   3. First three costs can be reasonably estimated, but external costs are very hard to quantify.
   4. Cost of poor quality is consistently underestimated.
   5. Philip Crosby stated that quality is free. "It is not a gift, but it is free. What costs money are the unquality things—all the actions that involve not doing it right the first time."

Lecture Key: *Quality can lie in the eyes of the customer, marketing people, or production managers. Although this is the case, operations managers must define what the beholder, or customer, expects. Quality is important for the company's reputation, product liability, and its global implications. There are also costs associated with obtaining quality, with greater costs coming with poor quality.*

III.   International Quality Standards

A. ISO 9000
   1. A set of quality standards developed by the International Standards Organization.
   2. 91 member nations (including the U.S.) published a series of quality assurance standards.
   3. Focus of the standards is to establish quality management procedures, through leadership, detailed documentation, work instructions, and record keeping.
   4. Procedures say nothing about the actual quality of the product—they deal entirely with standards to be followed.
   5. Organizations go through a 9-to-18-month process that involves documenting quality procedures, an on-site assessment, and an ongoing series of audits of their products or services.

B. ISO 14000
    1. An environment management standard established by the International Standards Organization (ISO).
    2. Contains five core elements:
       a. Environmental management
       b. Auditing
       c. Performance evaluation
       d. Labeling
       e. Life-Cycle assessment
    3. Several Advantages
       a. Positive public image and reduces exposure to liability.
       b. Good systematic approach to pollution prevention through the minimization of ecological impact of products and activities.
       c. Compliance with regulatory requirements and opportunities for competitive advantage.
       d. Reduction in need for multiple audits.
    4. Accepted worldwide

Lecture Key: *It is important that the U.S. pushed for this series of quality assurance standards. This is important for corporations doing business globally. ISO 14000 is an environmental management standard established by the International Standards Organization. This standard is being accepted worldwide.*

IV.   **Total Quality Management**

  A. Management of an entire organization so that it excels in all aspects of products and services that are important to the customer.
    1. Quality emphasis that encompasses the entire organization, from supplier to customer.
    2. Commitment by management to have a continuing company-wide drive toward excellence in all aspects of products and services that are important to the customer.
    3. Quality expert W. Edwards Deming used 14 points to indicate how he implemented TQM. The list below is Deming's 14 Points for Implementing Quality Improvement.

Deming's 14 Points:
1. Create consistency of purpose.
2. Lead to promote change.
3. Build quality into the product; stop depending on inspections to catch problems.
4. Build long-term relationships based on performance, instead of awarding business on the basis of price.
5. Continuously improve product, quality, and service.
6. Start training.
7. Emphasize leadership.
8. Drive out fear.
9. Break down barriers between departments.
10. Stop haranguing workers.
11. Support, help, and improve.
12. Remove barriers to pride in work.
13. Institute a vigorous program of education and self-improvement.
14. Put everybody in the company to work on the transformation.

---

4. We develop these into six concepts for an effective TQM program:
   a. Continuous improvement
   b. Employee empowerment
   c. Benchmarking
   d. Just-in-time
   e. Taguchi concepts
   f. Knowledge of TQM tools

B. Continuous Improvement – Never-ending process of continuous improvement that covers people, equipment, suppliers, materials, and procedures.
   1. Basis of philosophy is that every aspect of an operation can be improved.
   2. End goal is perfection, which is never achieved but always taught.

C. Plan-Do-Check-Act (PDCA) – a continuous improvement model of plan, do, check, act.
   1. Walter Shewhart, developed the PDCA circular model as his version of continuous improvement.
   2. W. Edward Deming later took Shewhart's concept to Japan.

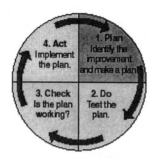

3. Six Sigma:
   a. Kaizan – Japanese word for the ongoing processes of incremental improvement.
   b. In the U.S., TQM and zero defects are also used to describe continuous improvement efforts.
   c. Six Sigma – a quality program that yields 99.9997% accurate products or services.
   d. Whether it's PDCA, kaizan, a zero defects, or six sigma, the operations manager is a key player in building a work culture that endorses continuous improvement.

D. Employee Empowerment
   1. Employee Empowerment – enlarging employee jobs so that the added responsibility and authority is moved to the lowest level possible in the organization.
   2. 85% of quality problems have to do with materials and processes, not with employee performance.
   3. Techniques for building employee empowerment:
      a. Building communication networks that include employees.
      b. Developing open, supportive supervisors.
      c. Moving responsibility from both managers and staff to production employees.
      d. Building high-morale organizations.
      e. Creating such formal organization training structures as teams and quality circles.
   4. Quality circle – a group of employees meeting regularly with a facilitator to solve work related problems in their work area. Members receive training in group planning, problem solving, and statistical quality control.

E. Benchmarking
    1. Selecting a demonstrated standard of performance that represents the very best performance for a process or activity.
    2. Steps for developing benchmarks:
        a. Determine what to benchmark.
        b. Form a benchmark team.
        c. Identify benchmarking partners.
        d. Collect and analyze benchmarking information.
        e. Take action to meet or exceed the benchmark.
    3. Benchmarks often take the form of "best practices" found in other firms.
    4. Best practices for resolving customer complaints:
        a. Make it easy for clients to complain: It is free market research.
        b. Respond quickly to complaints: It adds customers and loyalty.
        c. Resolve complaints on the first contact: It reduces cost.
        d. Use computers to manage complaints: Discover trends, share them, and align your services.
        e. Recruit the best for customer service jobs: It should be part of formal training and career advancement.
F. Just-in-Time (JIT)
    1. Just-in-time (JIT) is one of continuing improvement and enforced problem solving
    2. Designed to produce or deliver goods just as they are needed
    3. JIT is related to quality in (3) ways:
        a. JIT cuts the cost of quality –
            This occurs because scrap, rework, inventory investment, and damage costs are directly related to inventory on hand, there is less inventory on hand with JIT, costs are lower, inventory hides bad quality, whereas JIT immediately exposes bad quality.
        b. JIT improves quality –
            JIT shrinks lead time, it keeps evidence of errors fresh and limits the number of potential sources of error; JIT creates, in effect, an early warning system for quality problems, both within the firm and with vendors.
        c. Better quality means less inventory and a better, easier-to-employ JIT system –
            The purpose of keeping inventory is to protect against poor production performance resulting from unreliable quality; JIT allows firms to reduce all the costs associated with inventory.
G. Taguchi Concepts
    1. Most quality problems are the result of poor product and process design.
    2. Genichi Taguchi has provided us with three concepts aimed at improving both product and process quality, which are:
        a. Quality robust – Products that are consistently built to meet customer needs in spite of adverse conditions in the production process.

b. Quality loss function (QLF) – A mathematical function that identifies all costs connected with poor quality and shows how these costs increase as product quality moves from what the customer wants. QLF takes the general form of a simple quadratic formula:

$$L = D^2C$$

Where: L = loss to society
D^2 = square of the distance from the target value
C = cost of the deviation at the specification limit

i. All the losses to society due to poor performance are included in the loss function.
ii. The smaller the loss, the more desirable the product.
iii. The farther the product is from the target value, the more severe the loss.

c. Target-oriented quality – A philosophy of continuous improvement to bring the product exactly on target.

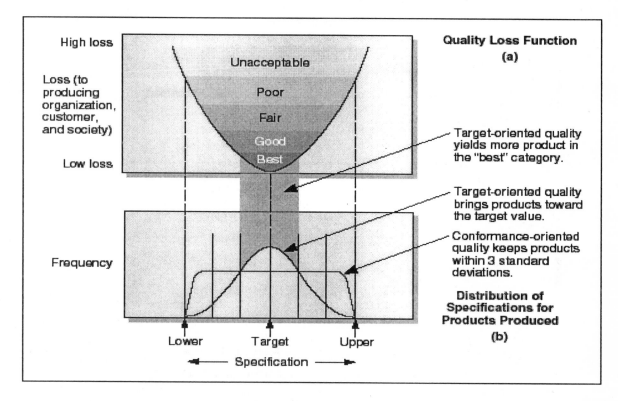

Lecture Key: Taguchi aims for the target because products produced near the upper and lower acceptable specifications result in higher quality loss function.

H. Knowledge of TQM Tools – To empower employees and implement TQM as a continuing effort, everyone in the organization must be trained in the techniques of TQM.

Lecture Key: Because quality is so important, the TQM approach is essential. Just as important as quality is requiring a never-ending process of a continuous improvement model such as plan, do, check, act or the PDCA Cycle. Techniques include building employee empowerment and developing benchmarks. The just-in-time philosophy and Taguchi concepts are aimed at improving delivery, and product and process quality. Most importantly, for the concept of TQM to work, you have to train your employees with the knowledge of this approach and continuous effort.

V.   Tools of TQM

A. Check Sheets
1. Any kind of a form that is designed for recording data is done so the patterns are easily seen while the data are being taken.
2. Help analysts find the facts or patterns that may aid subsequent analysis.
3. A drawing that shows a tally of the areas where defects are occurring or a check sheet showing the type of customer complaints.

Example

(a) *Check Sheet:* An organized method of recording data.

Defect	Hour							
	1	2	3	4	5	6	7	8
A	III	I		I	I	I	III	I
B	II	I	I	I			II	III
C	I	II					II	IIII

B. Scatter Diagrams
1. Show the relationship between two measurements.
2. The positive relationship between length of a service call and the number of trips the repairperson makes back to the truck for parts.

Example

(b) *Scatter Diagram:* A graph of the value of one variable vs. another variable.

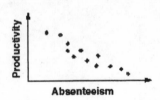

C. Cause-and-Effect Diagrams
1. A schematic technique used to discover possible locations of quality problems.
2. Also known as an Ishikawa diagram or a fish-bone chart.
3. Highlights possible quality problems and inspection points.
4. Cause and Effect Diagram for problems with airline customer service. Each "bone" represents a possible source of error (Figure on next page and pg. 199 of text).
5. The operations manager starts with four "causes" known as the four M's: Material, Machinery/Equipment, Manpower, and Methods.
6. Individual causes associated with each category are tied in as separate bones along that branch.
7. I.E. in figure on next page, the machinery branch has problems caused by deicing equipment, mechanical delays, and broken carousels.

Example

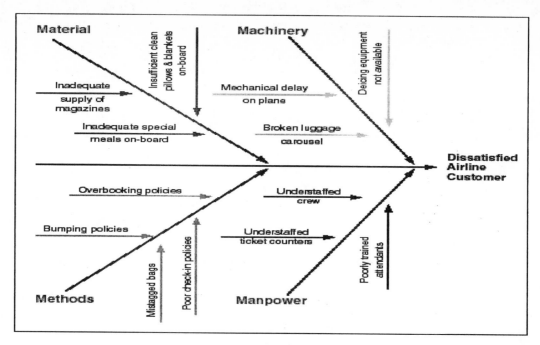

(c) *Cause and Effect Diagram:* A tool that identifies process elements (causes) that might effect an outcome.

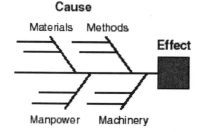

D. Pareto Charts
1. A method of organizing errors, problems, or defects graphically to help focus on problem-solving efforts.
2. Popularized by Joseph M. Juran when he suggested that 80% of a firm's problems are a result of only 20% of the problems.
3. Indicates which problems may yield the greatest payoff.

Example: Pareto Charts

The Hard Rock Hotel in Bali has just collected the data from 75 complaint calls to the general manager during the month of October. The manager decides to prepare a Pareto analysis of the complaints. The data provided are room service, 54; check-in delays, 12; hours the pool is open, 4; minibar prices, 3; and miscellaneous, 2.

Solution:
The Pareto chart shown indicates that 72% of the calls were the result of one cause, room service. The majority of complaints will be eliminated when this one cause is corrected.

    E. Flow Charts
        1. Block diagrams that graphically describe a process or system.
        2. Used to make sense of a process or explain a process.

Example: Flow Charts

The WJC Chicken Processing Plant in Little Rock, Arkansas, would like its new employees to understand more about the packing and shipping process. They have prepared the following chart to aid the new-employee training program.

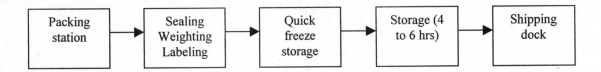

    F. Histograms
        1. Show the range of values of a measurement and the frequency with which each value occurs.
        2. Show the most frequently occurring readings as well as the variations in the measurements.

Example

Tools for Identifying Problems
(f) *Histogram:* A distribution showing the frequency of occurrences of a variable.

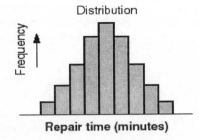

G. Statistical Process Control (SPC)
   1. A process used to monitor standards, make measurements and take corrective action as a product or service is being produced.
   2. Samples of process outputs are examined.
   3. If they are within acceptable limits, the process continues.
   4. If they fall outside certain specific ranges, the process is stopped. The assignable cause is located and removed.
   5. Control charts: graphic presentation of data over time that shows upper and lower limits for the process we want to control.
   6. Constructed in such a way that new data can be quickly compared to past performance data.
   7. Take samples of the process output and plot the averages of these samples on a chart that has the limits on it.

Example

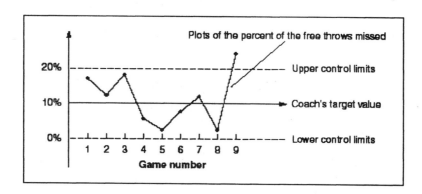

Plots of the percent of the free throws missed

Lecture Key: *The seven tools of TQM are helpful in monitoring processes. The tools used to generate ideas include check sheets, scatter diagrams, and cause and effect diagrams. The tools used to organize data include Pareto charts and flow charts. The tools for identifying problems are histograms and statistical process control charts.*

VI.   The Role of Inspection

A. To make sure a system is producing at the expected quantity level, control of the process is needed.
B. The best processes have little variation from the standard expected.
C. The operations manager's task is to build such systems and to verify, often by inspection, that they are performing to standard.
D. Inspection: a means of ensuring that an operation is producing at the quality level expected.
E. Can involve measurement, tasting, touching, weighing, or testing of the product.
F. Goal is to detect a bad process immediately.
G. Finds deficiencies and defects, does not correct them.
H. Generally expensive.
I. When and Where to Inspect – Two basic issues relating to inspection:
   1. Depends on the type of process and the value added at each stage.
   2. Can take place at any of the following points:
      a. At your supplier's plant while the supplier is producing.
      b. At your facility upon receipt of goods from your supplier.

    c. Before costly or irreversible processes.
    d. During the step-by-step production process.
    e. When production or service is complete.
    f. Before delivery from your facility.
    g. At the point of customer contact.
   3. There is variability in the inspection process.
   4. Good processes and employee empowerment are a better solution than trying to find defects by inspection.
J. Source Inspection
   1. Controlling or monitoring at the point of production or purchase – at the source.
   2. Consistent with the concept of employee empowerment, where individual employees self-check their own work. May be assisted by the use of checklists and controls such as a fail-safe device called a poka-yoke.
      a. Poka-yoke: literally translated, "foolproof." It has come to mean a device or technique that ensures the production of a good unit every time.
      b. Avoid errors and provide quick feedback of problems.
      c. Example: Diesel or leaded gas pump nozzle that will not fit into the "unleaded" gas tank opening on your car.
K. Service Industry Inspection – inspection points can be assigned at a wide range of locations.

ORGANIZATION	WHAT IS INSPECTED	STANDARD
Jones Law Offices	Receptionist performance Billing Attorney	Phone answered by the second ring. Accurate, timely, and correct format. Promptness in returning calls.
Hard Rock Hotel	Reception desk Doorman Room Minibar	Use customer's name. Greet guest in less than 30 seconds. All lights working, spotless bathroom. Restocked and charges accurately posted to bill.
Bayfield Community Hospital	Billing Pharmacy Lab Nurses Admissions	Accurate, timely, and correct format. Prescription accuracy, inventory accuracy. Audit for lab-test accuracy. Charts immediately updated. Data entered correctly and completely.
Hard Rock Cafe	Busboy Busboy Waiter	Serves water and bread within 1 minute. Clears all entree items and crumbs prior to dessert. Knows and suggests specials, desserts.
Nordstrom's Department Store	Display areas Stockrooms Salesclerks	Attractive, well organized, stocked, good lighting. Rotation of goods, organized, clean. Neat, courteous, very knowledgeable.

L. Inspection of Attributes versus Variables
   1. Attribute inspection: classifies items as being either good or defective.
      a. Does not address the degree of failure.
      b. Example: the light bulb burns or it does not.
   2. Variable inspection: measures such dimensions as weight, speed, height, or strength to see if an item falls within an acceptable range.
      a. Example: If a piece of electrical wire is supposed to be 0.01 inch in diameter, a micrometer can be used to see if the product is close enough to pass inspection.

VII. TQM in Services

A. The personal component of services is more difficult to measure than the quality of the tangible component.

B. What make the selection of services different from that of products?
1. The intangible differences between products.
2. The intangible expectations customers have of those products.

C. The operations manager plays a significant role in addressing several major aspects of service quality.
1. The tangible component of many services is important. How well the service is designed and produced does make a difference.
2. Another aspect of service and service quality is the process. 9 of the 10 determinates of service quality are related to the service process.
3. The operations manager should realize that the customer's expectations are the standard against which the service is judged. Service quality is judged on the basis of whether it meets expectations.
4. The manager must expect exceptions.
   a. There are "exceptions" or "problems" initiated by the customer or by less than optimal operating conditions (for example, the computer "crashed").
   b. This implies that the quality control system must recognize and have a set of alternative plans for less than optimal operating conditions.

Determinants of Service Quality

- Reliability involves consistency of performance and dependability. It means that the firm performs the service right the first time and that the firm honors its promises.

- Responsiveness concerns the willingness or readiness of employees to provide service. It involves timeliness of service.

- Competence means possession of the required skills and knowledge to perform the service.

- Access involves approachability and ease of contact.

- Courtesy involves politeness, respect, consideration, and friendliness of contact personnel (including receptionists, telephone operators, etc.).

- Communication means keeping customers informed in language they can understand and listening to them.

- It may mean that the company has to adjust its language for different consumers – increasing the level of sophistication with a well-educated customer and speaking simply and plainly with a novice.

- Credibility involves trustworthiness, believability, and honesty. It involves having the customer's best interests at heart.

- Security is the freedom from danger, risk, or doubt.

- Understanding/knowing the customer involves making the effort to understand the customer's needs.

- Tangibles include the physical evidence of the service.

Lecture Key: It is much more difficult to measure the quality of a service organization as compared to a manufacturer of products. The operations manager plays a significant role in addressing several major aspects of service quality. Designing the product, managing the service process, matching customer expectations to the product, and preparing for the exceptions are keys to quality services.

Supplement 6
Statistical Process Control

I.   **Statistical Process Control (SPC)**

   A. A statistical technique that is widely used to ensure that processes meet standards.

      1. Uses control charts as a tool for measuring the performance of a process.

      2. A process is operating "in statistical control" when the only source of variation is common (natural) causes.

         a. Natural variations affect most production processes and are to be expected.

         b. These causes are considered random or chance variation.

      3. SPC and control charts look to detect and eliminate special (assignable) causes of variation, so that the process can be brought into statistical control.

         a. Assignable variation is a variation that can be traced to a specific reason.

         b. Examples include machine wear, misadjusted equipment, fatigue or untrained workers, or new batches of raw material.

      4. Objective of the process control system is to provide a statistical signal when assignable causes of variation are present.

      5. Samples –

         a. SPC uses averages of small samples (often of 4 to 8 items) to determine control.

         b. Individual pieces tend to be erratic in variation and make identifying visible trends difficult.

      6. Control Charts – the purpose is to help distinguish between natural variations and variations from assignable causes.

   B. Control Charts for Variables

      1. Variables – characteristics that have continuous dimensions, or infinite number of possibilities. Examples include weight, speed, length, or strength.

      2. Two types of variable charts are used:

         a. x-chart – used to measure changes in the central tendency (the mean) of a process.

         b. R-chart – used to measure changes in the dispersion of a process.

      3. The two charts are used together to monitor the control of variable for a process.

      4. The Central Limit Theorem – foundation of the x-chart. The distribution of samples will follow a normal curve. However, it should be noted that samples will have less variability than the process distribution.

         a. 95.45% of the time, the sample averages will fall within $\pm 2\sigma_{\bar{x}}$ if the process has only natural variations.

         b. 99.73% of the time, the sample averages will fall within $\pm 3\sigma_{\bar{x}}$ if the process has only natural variations.

         c. If a point on the control chart falls outside of the $\pm 3\sigma_{\bar{x}}$ control limits, then we are 99.73% sure the process has changed.

C. Setting Mean Chart Limits (x-charts)
1. If we know from past data, the standard deviation of the process population, σ, we can set upper and lower control limits by these formulas:

$$UCL_{\text{x-bar}} = \text{x-bar} + (z * \sigma_{\bar{x}})$$
$$LCL_{\text{x-bar}} = \text{x-bar} - (z * \sigma_{\bar{x}})$$

Where:
- x-bar = mean of the sample means or a target value
- z = # of normal std. dev. (2 for 95.45% confidence)
- $\sigma_{\bar{x}}$ = std. dev. of the sample means = $\sigma / \sqrt{n}$
- σ = population (process) std. dev.
- n = sample size

Example: X-Chart with Sample Data

The weights of boxes of Oat Flakes within a large production lot are sampled each hour. To set control limits that include 99.73% of the sample means, samples of nine boxes are randomly selected and weighted. Here are the nine boxes chosen for Hour 1:

Samples:								
17 oz.	13 oz.	16 oz.	18 oz.	17 oz.	16 oz.	15 oz.	17 oz.	16 oz.

Solution:

The average weight in the first sample $= \dfrac{17 + 13 + 16 + 18 + 17 + 16 + 15 + 17 + 16}{9}$

x-bar $= 16.1$ oz.

Also, the population standard deviation (σ) is known to be 1 ounce. We do not show each of the boxes sampled in Hours 2 through 12, but here are the rest of the results:

Hour	Weight of Sample (Avg. of 9 boxes)	Hour	Weight of Sample (Avg. of 9 boxes)	Hour	Weight of Sample (Avg. of 9 boxes)
1	16.1	5	16.5	9	16.3
2	16.8	6	16.4	10	14.8
3	15.5	7	15.2	11	14.2
4	16.5	8	16.4	12	17.3

The average mean of the 12 samples is calculated to be exactly 16 ounces. We therefore have x-bar = 16 ounces, σ = 1 ounce, n = 9, and z = 3. The control limits are:

$$UCL_{\text{x-bar}} = \text{x- double bar} + (z * \sigma_{\bar{x}}) = 16 + 3(1 / \sqrt{9}) = 17 \text{ ounces}$$
$$LCL_{\text{x-bar}} = \text{x- double bar} - (z * \sigma_{\bar{x}}) = 16 - 3(1 / \sqrt{9}) = 15 \text{ ounces}$$

The 12 samples are then plotted on the control chart shown below. Because the means of recent sample averages fall outside the upper and lower control limits of 17 and 15, we can conclude that the process is becoming erratic and not in control.

2. If we don't know process standard deviation (either not available or difficult to compute), we use the range of the process to calculate the control limits using the following formulas:

$$UCL_{x\text{-}bar} = x\text{-}bar + (A_2 * \bar{R})$$
$$LCL_{x\text{-}bar} = x\text{-}bar - (A_2 * \bar{R})$$

Where: $\bar{R}$ = average range of the samples
A_2 = constant value found in Table S6.1 on pg. 219 of text
x-bar = mean of the sample means

Example: X-Chart with Process Data

Super Cola bottles soft drinks labeled "net weight 16 ounces." An overall process average of 16.01 ounces has been found by taking several batches of samples, in which each sample contained 5 bottles. The average range of the process is .25 ounces. Determine the upper and lower control limits for averages in the process.

Solution:
Looking in Table S6.1 on pg. 219 of the text for a sample size of 5 in the mean factor A_2 column, we find the number .577. Thus, the upper and lower control chart limits are:

$$UCL_{x\text{-}bar} = x\text{-}bar + (A_2\,\bar{R}) = 16.01 + (.577)(.25) = 16.154 \text{ ounces}$$
$$LCL_{x\text{-}bar} = x\text{-}bar - (A_2\,\bar{R}) = 16.01 - (.577)(.25) = 15.866 \text{ ounces}$$

D. Setting Range Chart Limits (R-charts)
1. Operations managers are interested in the process dispersion, or range.
2. The process average may be in control, but the dispersion of the process may not be.
3. Operations managers use R-charts to monitor the process variability. The R-chart is computed using the following formulas:

$$UCL_{\bar{R}} = D_4 * \bar{R}$$
$$LCL_{\bar{R}} = D_3 * \bar{R}$$

Where: D_4 = constant value found in Table S6.1 on pg. 219 of the text
D_3 = constant value found in Table S6.1 on pg. 219 of the text

Example: R-Chart

The average range of a process for loading trucks is 5.3 pounds. If the sample size is 5, determine the upper and lower control chart limits.

Solution:
Looking in Table S6.1 on pg. 219 of the text for a sample size of 5, we find that $D_4 = 2.115$ and $D_3 = 0$. The range control chart limits are:

$$UCL_{\bar{R}} = D_4 * \bar{R} = 2.115 * 5.3 \text{ pounds} = 11.2 \text{ pounds}$$
$$LCL_{\bar{R}} = D_3 * \bar{R} = 0 * 5.3 \text{ pounds} = 0 \text{ pounds}$$

E. Using Mean and Range Charts
   1. The x-chart is sensitive to shifts in the process mean, and R-charts are sensitive to shifts in the process standard deviation.
   2. Using them together allows for tracking changes in the process distribution.
   3. Steps to follow when using control charts:
      a. Collect 20 to 25 samples of n = 4 or n = 5, each from a stable process, and compute the mean and range of each.
      b. Compute the overall means (x-bar and R), set appropriate control limits, usually at the 99.73% level, and calculate the preliminary upper and lower control limits. If the process is not currently stable, use the desired mean, μ, instead of x-bar to calculate limits.
      c. Graph the sample means and ranges on their respective control charts and determine whether they fall outside the acceptable limits.
      d. Investigate points or patterns that indicate the process is out of control. Try to assign causes for the variation and then resume the process.
      e. Collect additional samples and, if necessary, revalidate the control limits using the new data.
F. Control Charts for Attributes
   1. Attributes – characteristics of a product that are typically classified as defective or nondefective.
   2. P-charts –
      a. Chief way to control attributes.
      b. Monitor the proportion or percentage of defects in a lot.
      c. Follow the binomial distribution.
      d. Use the following formulas:

$$UCL_{\bar{p}} = \bar{p} + (z * \sigma_{\bar{p}})$$

$$LCL_{\bar{p}} = \bar{p} - (z * \sigma_{\bar{p}})$$

$$\text{Where:} \quad \bar{p} = \text{mean fraction defective in the sample}$$

$$z = \text{\# of normal std. dev. (2 for 95.45\% confidence)}$$

$$\sigma_{\bar{p}} = \text{std. dev. of the sampling distribution}$$

$$= \sqrt{\bar{p}(1-\bar{p})/n}$$

Example: P-Chart

Data-entry clerks at ARCO key in thousands of insurance records each day. Samples of the work of 20 clerks are shown in the table. One hundred records entered by each clerk were carefully examined and the number of errors counted. The fraction defective in each sample was then computed.

Set the control limits to include 99.73% of the random variation in the entry process when it is in control.

Sample Number	Number of Errors	Fraction Defective	Sample Number	Number of Errors	Fraction Defective
1	6	.06	11	6	.06
2	5	.05	12	1	.01
3	0	.00	13	8	.08
4	1	.01	14	7	.07
5	4	.04	15	5	.05
6	2	.02	16	4	.04
7	5	.05	17	11	.11
8	3	.03	18	3	.03
9	3	.03	19	0	.00
10	2	.02	20	4	.05

Solution:

$$\bar{p} = \text{total \# of errors} / \text{total \# of records examined}$$
$$= 80 / (100)(20)$$
$$= .04$$

$$\sigma_{\bar{p}} = \sqrt{.04(1 - .04)/100}$$
$$= .02 \text{ (rounded up from 0.196)}$$

$$\text{UCL}_{\bar{p}} = \bar{p} + (z * \sigma_{\bar{p}}) = .04 + 3(.02) = .10$$
$$\text{LCL}_{\bar{p}} = \bar{p} - (z * \sigma_{\bar{p}}) = .04 - 3(.02) = 0$$

If we plot the control limits and the sample fraction defectives below, we find that only one data-entry clerk (#17) is out of control. The firm may wish to examine that individual's work a bit more closely to see if a serious problem exists.

3. c-charts –
   a. Used to control the number of defects per unit of output.
   b. Control charts for defects are helpful for monitoring processes in which a large number of potential errors can occur, but the actual number that do occur is relatively small.
   c. Based on the Poisson probability distribution.
   d. Calculate using the following formulas:
      $$\text{Control limits} = \bar{c} + 3\sqrt{\bar{c}}$$
      Where: $\bar{c}$ = mean number of defects per unit

116

Example: C-Chart

Red Top Cab Company receives several complaints per day about the behavior of its drivers. Over a 9-day period (where days are the units of measure), the owner received the following numbers of calls from irate passengers: 3, 0, 8, 9, 6, 7, 4, 9, and 8, for a total of 54 complaints.

Solution:

$$\bar{c} = 54 \text{ defects} / 9 \text{ samples} = 6 \text{ complaints per day}$$

Thus,

$$UCL_{\bar{c}} = \bar{c} + 3\sqrt{\bar{c}} = 6 + 3\sqrt{6} = 13.35 \text{ defects}$$
$$LCL_{\bar{c}} = \bar{c} + 3\sqrt{\bar{c}} = 6 - 3\sqrt{6} = 0 \text{ defects (cannot be negative)}$$

    G. Managerial Issues and Control Charts
       1. Managers must select the points in the process that need SPC.
       2. Managers need to decide between variable charts (i.e., x-bar and R) and attribute charts (i.e., p and c).
       3. The company must set clear and specific SPC policies for employees to follow.

II.   Process Capability

    A. The natural variation of the process must be small (narrow) enough to produce products that meet the standards (quality) required.
    B. A process that is in statistical control may not yield goods and services that meet their design specifications (tolerances).
    C. Process Capability – the ability of a process to meet design specifications, which are set by engineering design or customer requirements.
    D. Two measures of process capability:
       1. Process Capability Ratio (C_p)
          a. A process is capable as its values fall within upper and lower specifications.
          b. A capable process tolerance, which is the difference between the upper and lower specifications, must be greater than or equal to 6.
          c. Compute using the following formula:
            Capability ratio (C_p):

$$C_p = \frac{\text{upper specification} - \text{lower specification limit}}{6\sigma}$$

            i. If $C_p < 1.0$, process range is greater than tolerance range, and process is not capable of producing with specifications.
            ii. If $C_p = 1.0$, the tolerance range and process range are the same.
            iii. If $C_p > 1.0$, the tolerance range is greater than process range.
            iv. Companies want C_p of 1.0 or better to meet specifications.
          d. With a C_p of 1.0, 2, 7 parts in 1,000 can be expected to be "out of spec."

In a GE insurance claims process, $\overline{x}$ = 210.0 minutes, and σ = .516 minutes. The design specification to meet customer expectations is 210 ± 3 minutes. So the upper specification is 213 minutes and the lower specification is 207 minutes.

Solution:

$$C_p = \frac{\text{upper specification} - \text{lower specification limit}}{6\sigma}$$

$$C_p = \frac{213 - 207}{6(0.516)} = 1.938$$

Since a ratio of 1.00 means that 99.73% of a process' outputs are within specifications, the ratio suggests a very capable process, with nonconformance of less than 4 claims per million.

2. Process Capability Index (C$_{pk}$)
    a. Measures the difference between the desired and actual dimensions of goods or services produced.
    b. Shows whether process mean has shifted away from the design target and the direction of shift.
    c. Computed using the following formula:

$$C_{pk} = \text{minimum of} \left[\frac{\text{upper specification} - \overline{x}}{3\sigma}, \frac{\overline{x} - \text{lower specification}}{3\sigma} \right]$$

    i. If C$_{pk}$ > 1.0, process is capable of meeting design specifications.
    ii. If C$_{pk}$ < 1.0, process mean has moved closer to one of the upper or lower design specifications. This will result in defects.
    iii. When C$_{pk}$ = C$_p$, process mean is centered on the design (nominal) target.

Example: Computing C$_{pk}$

You are the process improvement manager and have developed a new machine to cut insoles for the company's top-of-the-line running shoes. You are excited because the company's goal is no more than 3.4 defects per million and this machine may be the innovation you need. The insoles cannot be more than ±.001 of an inch from the required thickness of .250". You want to know if you should replace the existing machine, which has a C$_{pk}$ of 1.0. You decide to determine the C$_{pk}$ for the new machine and make a decision on that basis.

Upper Specification Limit	=	.251 inches
Lower Specification Limit	=	.249 inches
Mean of the new process $\overline{x}$	=	.250 inches
Estimated standard deviation of the new process	= σ =	.0005 inches

Solution:

$$C_{pk} = \text{minimum of} \left[\frac{\text{upper specification} - \bar{x}}{3\sigma}, \frac{\bar{x} - \text{lower specification}}{3\sigma} \right]$$

$$C_{pk} = \text{minimum of} \left[\frac{.251 - .250}{3(.0005)}, \frac{.250 - .249}{3(.0005)} \right]$$

Both calculations result in: $.001 / .0015 = 0.67$

Because the new machine has a C_{pk} of only 0.67, the new machine should not replace the existing machine.

III. Acceptance Sampling

A. A form of testing that involves taking random samples of "lots," or batches, of finished products and measuring them against predetermined standards.
B. Sampling is more economical than 100% inspection.
C. Sample quality is used to judge the quality of all items in the lot.
D. Operating Characteristic Curve
   1. Describes how well an acceptance plan discriminates between good and bad lots.
   2. Represents a specific plan defining n, sample size, and c, acceptance level.
   3. Two risks associated with a sampling plan:
      a. Producer's risk
         i. Defined as rejecting a good lot by mistake.
         ii. Also known as alpha (α).
         iii. Also referred to as a Type I error.
      b. Consumer's risk
         i. Defined as accepting a bad lot by mistake.
         ii. Also known as beta (β).
         iii. Also referred to as a Type II error.
         iv. Risk assumed by the manufacturer for the consumer.
   4. Standards for the sampling plan and operation curve.
      a. Acceptance Quality Level (AQL) – poorest level of quality that we are willing to accept. We want this level of quality or better.
      b. Lot Tolerance Percent Defective (LTPD) – the quality level of a lot that we consider bad. We wish to reject this or poorer quality levels.
E. Average Outgoing Quality
   1. When a lot is rejected, the entire lot is inspected and all defective items are replaced.
   2. This replacement technique improves the average outgoing quality in terms of percent defective.

$$AOQ = \frac{(P_d)(P_a)(N - n)}{N}$$

Where: P_d = true percent defective of the lot
           P_a = probability of accepting the lot
           N = number of items in the lot
           n = number of items in the sample

   3. The maximum value of AOQ corresponds to the highest average percent defective or the lowest average quality for the sampling plan, called average outgoing quality limit (AOQL).

X-Bar and R-Charts for Variables

S1.   The Creamery Inc. has a large refrigeration locker in which a constant temperature of approximately 40° F should be maintained with very little variation (target range is 5 degrees). The market manager has decided to construct an R-chart to monitor the temperature inside the locker. The manager had one of the market employees take sample temperature readings randomly five times each day for 15 days in order to gather data for the control chart. Following are the temperature sample observations.

Sample	Temperature (° F)				
1	46.3	40.1	35.2	38.4	44.1
2	41.2	42.2	40.6	38.4	45.3
3	40.1	35.2	33.2	41.5	36.4
4	42.2	40.6	41.8	40.1	40.5
5	35.2	33.2	42.4	42.2	39.5
6	40.6	41.8	44.7	35.2	46.7
7	33.2	42.4	42.7	40.6	44.8
8	41.8	44.7	40.1	33.2	40.7
9	42.4	42.6	42.2	41.8	42.2
10	44.7	40.5	35.2	42.4	35.2
11	42.6	45.3	40.6	44.7	40.6
12	40.5	36.4	33.2	42.6	33.2
13	45.3	40.5	41.8	40.5	41.8
14	36.4	39.5	42.4	45.3	42.4
15	40.5	42.8	44.7	36.4	44.7

a. Construct an R-chart based on these data using $\pm 3\sigma$ (99.9%) control limits, and plot the 15 sample range values.

   Step 1: Identify as an R-chart

   Step 2: Identify N (n = 5; D4 = 2.11; D3 = 0)

   Step 3: Calculate control limits – LCL = 0 * 5 = 0
              UCL = 2.11 * 5 = 10.55

b. Does it appear that the temperature is in control according to the criteria established by management?

   Step 4: Not all data points fall between control limits, so the process is out of control.

c. Construct an x-chart in conjunction with the above R-chart, plot the sample observations, and, using both the x-chart and R-chart, comment on the process control.

   Step 1: Identify as an x-chart (n = 5; A2 = .58)

   Step 2: Calculate control limits – CL = $40 \pm (.58 * 5)$ = 42.9 ~ 37.1

   Step 3: All the sample points fall between control limits, so the process is in control.

S2.   The Spantech Company manufactures expensive, polo-style men's and women's short-sleeve knit shirts at its plant in Mexico. The first step in the production process requires that material be cut into large patterned squares by operators, which are then sewn together at another stage of the process. If the squares are not of a correct length, the final shirt will be either too large or too small. In order to monitor the cutting process, management takes a sample of five squares of cloth every other hour and measures the length. The length of a cloth should be 36.5 inches, and historically, the company has found the length to vary across an acceptable average range of 2 inches and standard deviation of 1.92.

a. Construct an R-chart for the cutting process using $\pm 3\sigma$ (99.9%) control limits.

Step 1: Identify as an R-chart

Step 2: Identify N (n = 5; D4 = 2.11; D3 = 0)

Step 3: Calculate control limits – LCL $= 0 * 2 = 0$
$$UCL = 2.11 * 2 = 4.22$$

b. The company has taken ten additional samples with the following results.

Sample	Measurements (in.)				
1	37.3	36.5	37.1	38.2	36.1
2	33.4	35.8	34.8	37.9	36.2
3	32.1	34.8	36.4	39.1	35.3
4	36.1	37.2	36.8	36.7	34.2
5	35.1	38.6	35.9	37.2	33.6
6	33.4	34.5	37.0	36.7	32.4
7	38.1	39.2	36.8	35.3	32.7
8	35.4	36.2	36.7	36.3	34.3
9	37.1	39.4	35.9	38.1	36.2
10	32.1	34.0	36.8	35.6	36.1

Plot the new sample data on the control chart constructed in part (a) and comment on the process variability.

Step 4: Not all data points fall between control limits, so the process is out of control.

Now, construct an x-chart at a 95% confidence level in conjunction with the above R-chart, plot the sample observations provided in part (b), and, using both the x-chart and R-chart, comment on the process control.

Step 1: Identify as an x-chart

Step 2: Calculate control limits – CL $= 36.5 \pm (1.96 * (1.92/\sqrt{5})) = 38.183 \sim 34.82$

Step 3: Not all data points fall between control limits, so the process is out of control.

1.   The Little Slugger Company manufactures wooden and aluminum baseball bats along with other equipment at its plant in New England. Wooden bats produced for the mass market are turned on a lathe, where a piece of wood is shaped into a bat with a handle and barrel. The bat is cut to its specified length and then finished in subsequent processes. Once bats are cut to length, it is difficult to rework them into a different style, so it is important to catch defects before this step. As such, bats are inspected at this stage of the process. A specific style of wooden bat has a mean barrel circumference of 9 inches at its thickest point with a standard deviation of 0.1 inches. (The process variability is assumed to be normally distributed.)

a. Construct a mean control chart for this process for $\pm 3\sigma$ (99.7%) limits and a sample size of 10 bats.
b. Three samples are taken, and they have average bat diameters of 9.08 inches, 9.02 inches, and 9.04 inches. Is the process in control?
c. What effect will increasing the sample size to 20 bats have on the control charts? Will the conclusions reached in part (b) change for this sample size?

d. Construct a control chart for this process variation if the average range is .64 and the sample size remains constant at 10 bats. Determine if the process is in control if the ranges for the three samples above are .69, .57, and .71.

e. Construct a mean control chart for this process at confidence levels of 85, 90, and 95. Which do you think is the best alternative along with the $\pm 3\sigma$ limits for this process? What things do you need to consider? If I mentioned that the rules specified by the league are very strict (9.25 inches), does that have an impact on your first decision?

2. The Little Slugger Company manufactures basketball goals along with other equipment at its plant in Florida. Goals produced for the mass market are cut with a programmable laser cutter. The poles are cut to a specified length and then finished in subsequent processes. Once goals are cut to length, it is difficult to rework them into a different model goal, so it is important to catch defects before this step. As such, goals are inspected at this stage of the process. A specific model of basketball goals has a mean barrel length of 8.75 feet with a standard deviation of 0.14 feet. (The process variability is assumed to be normally distributed.)

a. Construct a mean control chart for this process for $\pm 3\sigma$ (99.7%) limits and a sample size of 10 goals.
b. Three samples are taken, and they have average bat diameters of 8.78 feet, 9.02 feet, and 8.94 feet. Is the process in control?
c. What effect will increasing the sample size to 20 bats have on the control charts? Will the conclusions reached in part (b) change for this sample size?
d. Construct a control chart for this process variation if the average range is .84 and the sample size remains constant at 10 poles. Determine if the process is in control if the ranges for the three samples above are .69, 1.27, and .71.
e. Construct a mean control chart for this process at confidence levels of 85, 90, and 95. Which do you think is the best alternative along with the $\pm 3\sigma$ limits for this process? What things do you need to consider?

3. An automated filling machine at Celebration Cereal Company fills boxes with healthy dry cereal. The labeled weight of the boxes is 10 ounces. The company wants to construct an R-chart to monitor the filling process and make sure the box weights are in control. The quality control department for the company sampled five boxes every two hours for twelve consecutive working days. The sample observations are as follows.

Sample	Box Weights (oz)				
1	9.06	9.13	8.97	8.85	8.46
2	8.52	8.61	9.09	9.21	8.95
3	9.35	8.95	9.20	9.03	8.42
4	9.17	9.21	9.05	9.01	9.53
5	9.21	8.87	8.71	9.05	9.35
6	8.74	8.35	8.50	9.06	8.89
7	9.00	9.21	9.05	9.23	8.78
8	9.15	9.20	9.23	9.15	9.06
9	8.98	8.90	8.81	9.05	9.13
10	9.03	9.10	9.26	9.46	8.47
11	9.53	9.02	9.11	8.88	8.92
12	8.95	9.10	9.00	9.06	8.95

Construct an R-chart from these data with $\pm 3\sigma$ (99.7%) control limits, and plot the sample range values.

a. What does the R-chart suggest about the process variability?
b. Construct an x-chart in conjunction with the above R-chart, plot the sample observations, and, using both the x-chart and R-chart, comment on the process control.

4. Big D's Grill has added a drive-through window and is concerned with complaints from customers about its drive-through window operation. Customers complain that it sometimes takes too long to be served and since there are often cars in front and back of a customer, they cannot leave if the service is taking a long time. To correct this problem the bank installed an intercom system so the drive-through window teller can call for assistance if the line backs up or a customer has an unusually long order. John's objective is an average customer's waiting and service time of approximately three minutes. The restaurant's operations manager wants to monitor the new drive-through window system with SPC. The manager has timed five customers' waiting and service times at random for eight days as follows.

Sample	Observation Times (min)				
	1	2	3	4	5
1	3.05	6.27	1.35	2.56	1.05
2	7.21	1.50	2.66	3.45	3.78
3	3.12	5.11	1.37	5.2	2.65
4	2.96	3.81	4.15	5.01	2.15
5	3.25	3.11	1.63	1.29	3.74
6	2.47	2.98	2.15	1.88	4.95
7	6.05	2.03	3.17	3.18	2.34
8	1.87	2.65	1.98	2.74	3.63

Construct the appropriate charts to determine given *ALL* the information provided.

a. Construct the control charts using the manager's raw data from the sampling.
b. The manager wants to be confident that the central tendency of his restaurant is meeting a quality level of 90% of other restaurants in the chain and the variability is meeting a quality level of 99.7%. Based on the fact that the restaurants have an expected wait and service times are 4.5 minutes, a range or .2 minutes, and standard deviation of .95 minutes. (All of this information is *sample information* obtained from headquarters.) You will need to construct a control chart for the chain, and then plot your sampling information against their control limits.
c. Do you think that your process is in control based on your study? Will you be able to meet the same quality levels as the neighboring bank?

5. Bayou Bonanza is a mail-order catalog operation for fishing and camping equipment. The company has never worried about recording quality, but under recent pressures from national competitors, the company realized that they have to start recording their quality measurements. The company has several models of reels for fishing poles that have varying tensions based on tension. The model that they will inspect and are most concerned with is their economy freshwater model, so they want to do a quality study. The company has set a target tension of 50 lbs, standard deviation of 0.75 lbs, and range of 0.5 lbs. They have inspected the next 20 production runs for average tensions and variability measurements. Each run consists of 100 reels, of which 5 will be inspected. The following represent the average tension and range levels for each inspection.

Sample	Average	Range	Sample	Average	Range
1	51.2	.18	11	49.8	.54
2	49.9	.26	12	48.7	.37
3	50.7	.43	13	51.2	.26
4	52.4	.27	14	50.1	.29
5	50.7	.14	15	50.5	.37
6	49.8	.36	16	49.9	.65
7	51.4	.42	17	52.1	.54
8	50.2	.28	18	50.4	.31
9	50.6	.61	19	50.2	.28
10	51.3	.37	20	50.8	.25

a. Construct the appropriate control chart for central tendency using a 95% confidence interval for this data.
b. Construct the chart for variability using a ± 3σ (99.7%).
c. Do you think that the company should be worried about these results?

6.   Dixieland Delights would like each cake to average approximately eighty full chips per cake. Too few or too many chips can change the desired taste. Ten samples of five pies each during a week have been taken and the chips counted. The sample observations are as follows. The company only counts full and half chips, but the target is 80 total.

Sample	Chip Per Cake				
1	78	74.5	90	80	82.5
2	79.5	79	85	81	100
3	59.5	85	78.5	76.5	81
4	80.5	95	79	91	79
5	89	87	79.5	100	88
6	79.5	86	95	84	84
7	91	88	100	88	78
8	78	76	81.5	84	85
9	95	100	84.5	92	87
10	81.5	91	90.5	100	86

Construct an x-chart at a 99% confidence level in conjunction with an R-chart using a 3σ limits or 99.7% confidence level for this data and comment on the pie production process.

7.   An important aspect of customer service and satisfaction at the Lake Arena is the maintenance of the facilities of the complex including parking lots, courts, bleachers, concession stands, and bathrooms. Customers expect the facilities to be kept up since they are charged taxes and user fees. They expect no potholes in the parking lots, boards to be replaced, rest rooms to be clean; odorless; well-stocked with soap, paper towels, and toilet paper, and to have a comfortable temperature. In order to maintain quality, park quality control inspectors randomly inspect all facilities daily (during the day and evening) and record the number of defects (incidences of poor maintenance). For the next year, the park will perform a study to see what their average numbers of defects are. The goal of park management is approximately 15 defects per inspection period. Each month has five individual inspections to determine the quality level of the month. Following is a summary of the observations taken by these inspectors for 12 consecutive inspection periods.

Sample	Inspection Time (days)					Sample	Inspection Time (days)				
1	2	3	3	4	3	7	2	3	3	1	2
2	5	3	6	2	1	8	1	1	3	2	1
3	4	3	3	2	2	9	6	3	3	3	3
4	6	1	5	3	3	10	6	7	5	6	5
5	2	4	1	4	4	11	6	1	1	2	3
6	5	1	3	3	3	12	5	5	3	3	1

Construct an x-chart at a 99.7% confidence level in conjunction with an R-chart (99.7%) based upon the sample data. Comment on the process in terms of the company's objective.

8.   The Department of Highway Systems wants to monitor the quality of the highway signs that it contracts for the Federal Highway system. The department has three different signs produced based on specified sizes. Since this is a federal contract, quality records have to be maintained to ensure that the contract is renewed. The manager orders the hardware and poles from another supplier, so the size of each sign has to be precise for assembly to go smoothly. The company will sample 10 items from each model to determine if the sizes are being cut properly. The first model (FW#10) has to be at least 575 square inches. The second model (FW#20) has to be 1300 square inches. The third model (FW#30) has to be 5100 square inches. The company's manager is budgeting for next year and is trying to determine if they will get the contracts for all three signs based on their quality test results. The results of 30 samples have been recorded as follows.

Sample(FW10)	Sq. Inches	Sample(FW20)	Sq. Inches	Sample(FW30)	Sq. Inches
1	590	1	1310	1	5120
2	580	2	1305	2	5116
3	576	3	1309	3	5105
4	581	4	1311	4	5099
5	570	5	1316	5	5111
6	579	6	1301	6	5114
7	580	7	1300	7	5107
8	590	8	1302	8	5105
9	592	9	1299	9	5101
10	580	10	1312	10	5110

a. Construct a chart to monitor the average size of the signs to determine if the cutting process is operating correctly. Use a 99.7% quality level if the sample range is used to estimate process variability.
b. Do you think that the company is in danger of losing any of the sign contracts?
c. The company had determined that they want the FW#10 model to have control limits set at 573 and 577. What would the confidence level be if the average is 575 and the standard deviation is 2.84 for the process?
d. What would the average size for the process have to be if the lower control limit is set at 575, the standard deviation is constant at 2.90, and the company is using a 99.7% confidence level? If the maximum size were set at 585 sq. inches, would the upper control limit associated with this information be appropriate to keep the process in control?

Attribute Charts

C-Charts:

S1. Big D's Grill is a chain that uses planted customers to determine the quality of its restaurants and assess the quality of the service by filling out a questionnaire. The company evaluates restaurants in three categories: products (the food), environment (the atmosphere), and service (promptness, order accuracy, courtesy, friendliness, etc.). These "customers" consider not only their order experiences but also observations throughout the restaurant. Following are the results of an evaluator's 20 visits to one particular restaurant during a month showing the number of "defects" noted in the service category.

Sample	# of Defects	Sample	# of Defects
1	4	11	9
2	6	12	4
3	10	13	3
4	3	14	4
5	6	15	13
6	7	16	9
7	8	17	10
8	5	18	11
9	2	19	15
10	5	20	12

a. Construct a control chart for this restaurant using $\pm 3\sigma$ limits or 99.7% confidence level to monitor quality service and indicate if the process is in control.

Step 1: Identify the control chart as a c-chart

Step 2: Calculate the c value – $c = 146/20 = 7.3$

Step 3: Calculate the control limits – $CL = 7.3 \pm (3 * \sqrt{7.3}) = 15.40 \sim 0$

Step 4: Process is in control when looking at the samples

b. Construct a control chart for this restaurant using a 95% confidence level to monitor quality service and indicate if the process is in control.

Step 1: Identify the control chart as a c-chart

Step 2: Calculate the c value – c = 146/20 = 7.3

Step 3: Calculate the control limits – CL = 7.3 ± (1.96 * $\sqrt{7.3}$) = 12.60 ~ 2.0

Step 4: Process is out of control since some of the samples have more than 12.6 defects

c. Construct a control chart for this restaurant using a 75% confidence level to monitor quality service and indicate if the process is in control.

Step 1: Identify the control chart as a c-chart

Step 2: Calculate the c value – c = 146/20 = 7.3

Step 3: Calculate the control limits – CL = 7.3 ± (1.15 * $\sqrt{7.3}$) = 10.41 ~ 4.19

Step 4: Process is out of control since some of the samples have more than 10.41 defects

S2.   Dixieland Delights makes a variety of pastries, but their specialty is chocolate chip cakes. The company would like each cake to average approximately eighty full chips per cake. Too few or too many chips can change the desired taste. Thirty samples (1 cake = 1 sample) have been taken and the total defects on a cake are counted. The sample observations are as follows. Any bad chips, uneven cooking, cracks, or burnt spots are considered defective. The company is interested in determining if they are averaging less than 3 defectives per cakes from the process.

Sample	# of defects	Sample	#of defects	Sample	#of defects
1	0	11	8	21	1
2	1	12	4	22	6
3	2	13	0	23	2
4	5	14	0	24	2
5	1	15	1	25	3
6	3	16	2	26	1
7	1	17	0	27	0
8	1	18	5	28	5
9	0	19	3	29	0
10	2	20	1	30	1

Construct a control chart at a 90% confidence level using the sample data. Determine if the process will be able to meet the target number of defectives per cake based on these control limits. Is this confidence level high enough to ensure an average number of defects of 3? If the next sample contains the following defects, is the process in control (6, 3, 1, 5, and 8)?

Step 1: Identify the control chart as a c-chart

Step 2: Calculate the c value – c = 61/30 = 2.03

Step 3: Calculate the control limits – CL = 3 ± (1.65 * $\sqrt{2.03}$) = 5.35 ~ 0

Step 4: Process is out of control since some of the samples have more than 5.35 defects

P-Charts:

S3.   Big D's Grill has added a drive-through window and is concerned with complaints from customers about its drive-through window operation. Customers complain that it sometimes takes too long to be served and since there are often cars in front and back of a customer, they cannot leave if the service is taking a long time. To correct this problem, the restaurant installed an intercom system so the drive-through window teller can call for assistance if the line backs up or a customer has an unusually long order. John's objective is an average customer's waiting and service time of approximately three minutes. The restaurant's operations manager wants to monitor the new drive-through window system with SPC. The manager has timed five customers' waiting and service times at random for eight days as follows. Any service that takes longer than 3 minutes is considered a defect. Using the data that the manager gathered, determine the proportion of services that the restaurant considers defective.

Observation Times (min)

Sample	1	2	3	4	5
1	3.05	6.27	1.35	2.56	1.05
2	7.21	1.50	2.66	3.45	3.78
3	3.12	5.11	1.37	5.2	2.65
4	2.96	3.81	4.15	5.01	2.15
5	3.25	3.11	1.63	1.29	3.74
6	2.47	2.98	2.15	1.88	4.95
7	6.05	2.03	3.17	3.18	2.34
8	1.87	2.65	1.98	2.74	3.63

Construct the control charts using the manager's raw data from the sampling (you will have to convert the data). The manager wants to be confident that the proportion of services is meeting a quality level of 90% of your target service time. Do you think that your process is in control based on your study? Will you be able to meet your quality levels?

Step 1: Identify the control chart as a p-chart

Step 2: Calculate the p value – p = 19/40 = .475

Step 3: Calculate the control limits – CL = .475 ± (1.65 * $\sqrt{[.475(1-.475)/5]}$) = .843 ~ .106

Step 4: Process is in control since no sample of observations is out of control

S4.   Bayou Bonanza is a mail-order catalog operation for fishing and camping equipment. Whenever a customer returns an item for a refund, credit, or exchange, he or she is asked to complete a return form. For each item returned, the customer is asked to insert a code indicating the reason for the return. The company does not consider the returns related to style, size, or "feel" of the material to be a defect. However, it does consider the returns because the item "was not as described in the catalog," "didn't look like what was in the catalog," or "the color was different than shown in the catalog," to be defects in the catalog. The company has randomly checked 100 customers' return forms for 20 days and collected the following data for catalog defects.

Sample	# of Catalog Defects	Sample	# of Catalog Defects
1	18	11	54
2	26	12	37
3	43	13	26
4	27	14	29
5	14	15	37
6	36	16	65
7	42	17	54
8	28	18	31
9	61	19	28
10	37	20	25

Construct the appropriate control chart using a 95% confidence interval for this data.

Step 1: Identify the control chart as a p-chart

Step 2: Calculate the p value – p = 718/2000 = .359

Step 3: Calculate the control limits – CL = .359 ± (1.96 * $\sqrt{[.359(1-.359)/100]}$) = .453 ~ .265

Step 4: Process is out of control since 4 of the samples are out of control

1. Dixieland Delights makes a variety of pastries, but their specialty is chocolate chip cakes. The company would like each cake to average approximately eighty full chips per cake. Too few or too many chips can change the desired taste. Ten samples of five cakes each during a week have been taken and the chips counted. The sample observations are as follows. The company only counts full and half chips, but the target is 80 total. Any cake that has less than 75 total full chips is considered defective. The company is interested in determining if they are averaging less than 2% defective chips from the process. You will have to convert the sample data to defective chips.

Sample	Chips Per Cake				
1	78	74.5	90	80	82.5
2	79.5	79	85	81	100
3	59.5	85	78.5	76.5	81
4	80.5	95	79	91	79
5	89	87	79.5	100	88
6	79.5	86	95	84	84
7	91	88	100	88	78
8	78	76	81.5	84	85
9	95	100	84.5	92	87
10	81.5	91	90.5	100	86

Construct a control chart at a 99% confidence level to determine if the proportion of defective cakes is acceptable for this data and comment on the production process. Why do you choose a 99% confidence level if you are targeting 98% quality levels?

UCL = .18 LCL = 0   All samples are within control limits. Process in control.

2. Forty customers who check out of the Pitre Street Market each week are asked to complete a questionnaire about the general quality of the produce. Since customers are very picky when it comes to produce, they typically are very critical of the quality. The number of customers who indicated dissatisfaction of any kind with the produce for each 40-customer sample for a 16-week period is as follows.

Sample	# of Dissatisfied Cust.	Sample	# of Dissatisfied Cust.
1	6	9	6
2	3	10	6
3	10	11	5
4	7	12	3
5	2	13	2
6	9	14	8
7	11	15	12
8	7	16	8

Construct a control chart to monitor customer satisfaction at the hospital using an 85% confidence level.

UCL = .2483   LCL = 0.0796   All samples are not within control limits. Process out of control.

3. Bayou Bonanza sells specialty outdoor equipment through its catalog. A quality problem that generates customer complaints occurs when a warehouse employee fills an order with the wrong items. The company has decided to implement a process control plan by inspecting the ordered items after they have been obtained from the warehouse and before they have been packaged. The company has taken 30 samples (during a 30-day period), each for 100 orders, and recorded the number of "defective" orders in each sample, as follows.

Sample	Number of Defectives	Sample	Number of Defectives
1	12	16	6
2	14	17	3
3	10	18	7
4	16	19	10
5	18	20	14
6	19	21	18
7	14	22	22
8	20	23	26
9	18	24	20
10	17	25	24
11	9	26	18
12	11	27	19
13	14	28	20
14	12	29	17
15	7	30	18

Construct a p-chart for the company that describes 99.7 percent ($\pm 3\sigma$) of the random variation in the process, and indicate if the process seems to be out of control at any time.

UCL = .258   LCL = 0.044   All samples are not within control limits. Process out of control.

4. An important aspect of customer service and satisfaction at the Lake Arena, home of the new professional basketball team, is the maintenance of the facilities of the complex including parking lots, courts, bleachers, concession stands, and bathrooms. Customers expect the facilities to be kept up since they are charged taxes and user fees. They expect no potholes in the parking lots, boards to be replaced, rest rooms to be clean; odorless; well-stocked with soap, paper towels, and toilet paper, and to have a comfortable temperature. In order to maintain quality, park quality control inspectors randomly inspect all facilities daily (during the day and evening) and record the number of defects (incidences of poor maintenance). The goal of park management is to have poor quality for its customers no more than 95% of the time. The complex considers more than four defects per inspection to be "Poor Quality." The company has randomly selected five of its daily inspections per month to determine if they are meeting their desired quality level. The following is a summary of the randomly selected inspections that will be used to determine compliance.

Month	Defects Per Inspection				
1	2	3	3	4	3
2	5	3	6	2	1
3	4	3	3	2	2
4	6	1	5	3	3
5	2	4	1	4	4
6	5	1	3	3	3
7	2	3	3	2	1
8	1	1	3	1	2
9	6	3	3	3	3
10	6	7	5	5	6
11	6	1	1	3	2
12	5	5	3	1	3

Construct a p-chart at a 95% confidence level based upon the sample data. Comment on the process in terms of the complex's objective.

p = .05   UCL = .24   LCL = 0

All samples are not within control limits. Process out of control.

5.   An important aspect of customer service and satisfaction at the Lake Arena is the maintenance of the facilities of the complex including parking lots, courts, bleachers, concession stands, and bathrooms. Recently, the complex has been contacted about the conditions of the courts and the hazards for children using the courts. The complex considers more than three hazards per inspection to be "Poor Quality." The complex will check all courts for holes, uneven spots, condensation from the hockey ice, standing water, garbage, and sharp objects near the courts. The complex plans daily maintenance and inspections. The complex has randomly selected five days per month to determine if they are meeting their desired quality level. The complex has set the limit at 3 hazards, and anything over that will require the courts to be shut down. This could be detrimental to the usage and survival of the arena during the off-season. The following is a summary of the randomly selected inspections that will be used to determine compliance. Each sample represents a unit of quality.

Month	Defects Per Inspection (Samples)				
1	2	3	3	4	3
2	5	3	6	2	1
3	4	3	3	2	2
4	6	1	5	3	3
5	2	4	1	4	4
6	5	1	3	3	3
7	2	3	3	2	1
8	1	1	3	1	2
9	6	3	3	3	3
10	6	7	5	5	6
11	6	1	1	3	2
12	5	5	3	1	3

Construct a c-chart at a 95% confidence level based upon the sample data. Comment on the maintenance process in terms of the arena's objective.

Since any sample with an average number of defects greater than 3 causes the arena to immediately be shut down, the upper control limit is going to be set at 3.0. This gives the average number of defects per sample equal to 1 defect if the confidence level is set at 95%.

$$UCL = c + (1.96 \times \sqrt{})$$

6.   Department of Federal Highway Development wants to monitor the quality of the highway signs that it contracts for the Federal Highway System. Each day the company quality control manager takes a sample of 50 signs, tests them for flaking, discoloration, etc., and determines the number of defective signs. The results of 20 samples have been recorded as follows.

Sample	# of Defectives	Sample	# of Defectives
1	5	11	3
2	12	12	4
3	7	13	1
4	1	14	0
5	1	15	0
6	2	16	5
7	8	17	2
8	4	18	1
9	6	19	3
10	5	20	2

Construct a chart to monitor the proportion of defects in these samples at a 95% quality level.

Computing C_p (Process Capability Ratio):

S1.   YumYum Bakery produces and packages chocolate candies in box containers. The net weight of the chocolate in the container is designed to be 30 grams, with a tolerance of ±2 grams. The packaging process results in bags with an average net weight of 29.15 grams and a standard deviation of 0.50 grams. The company wants to determine if the process is capable of meeting design specifications.

Solution:

Step 1:   Identify or calculate the following information:
Upper Specification Limit = average + tolerance level = 30 grams + 2 grams = 32 grams
Lower Specification Limit = average – tolerance level = 30 grams – 2 grams = 28 grams
Standard Deviation (σ) = 0.25

Step 2:   Calculate the process capability ratio (C_p) using the following formula.
$$C_p = \frac{\text{upper specification} - \text{lower specification limit}}{6\sigma}$$
$$C_p = \frac{32 - 28}{6(0.25)} = 2.66$$

Step 3:   Analysis: Thus, according to this process capability ratio of 2.66, the process is capable of being within design specifications since the process capability ratio is greater than 1.0.

S2.   YumYum Bakery wants to respond to market demand to reduce the size of their portions and reduce the calories of their product. Now, they will produce and package chocolate candies in box containers with a net weight of the chocolate per container reduced to 20 grams, with a tolerance of ±1 gram. The packaging process results in boxes with an average net weight of 19.15 grams and a standard deviation of 0.75 grams. The company wants to determine if the process is capable of meeting design specifications.

Solution:

Step 1:   Identify or calculate the following information:
Upper Specification Limit = average + tolerance level = 20 grams + 1 grams = 21 grams
Lower Specification Limit = average – tolerance level = 20 grams – 1 grams = 19 grams
Standard Deviation (σ) = 0.75

Step 2:   Calculate the process capability ratio (C_p) using the following formula.
$$C_p = \frac{\text{upper specification} - \text{lower specification limit}}{6\sigma}$$
$$C_p = \frac{21 - 19}{6(0.75)} = 0.44$$

Step 3:   Analysis: Thus, according to this process capability ratio of 0.44, the process is not capable of being within design specifications since the process capability ratio is less than 1.0.

Since the process capabilities were not sufficient, management imposed a strict quality program that has helped with the process. Has the process shifted and changed this process drastically? The process is now producing boxes with a mean of 19.80 and a standard deviation that has been reduced to 0.20 grams.

Step 4:   Calculate the process capability ratio (C_p) using the following formula at the new mean.
$$C_p = \frac{\text{upper specification} - \text{lower specification limit}}{6\sigma}$$
$$C_p = \frac{21 - 19}{6(0.20)} = 1.66$$

Step 5:   Calculate the capability index (C_{pk}) using:
$$C_{pk} = \text{minimum} \left[\frac{\bar{x} - \text{lower specification}}{3\sigma}, \frac{\text{upper specification} - \bar{x}}{3\sigma} \right]$$
$$C_{pk} = \text{minimum} \left[\frac{19.80 - 19.00}{3(0.20)}, \frac{21.0 - 19.80}{3(0.20)} \right]$$

C_{pk} = minimum [1.33, 2.0] = 1.33 is the minimum

Step 6:   Analysis: Although the C_p of 1.66 computed earlier indicated that the process is capable of being within design specifications, the C_{pk} value of 1.33 indicates the process mean is back on center. It has shifted toward the lower specification limit, but not enough to stop the process; that means quality packages of chips will be produced on average.

1.   Using the data and target levels in problem 4 in the variable section, determine the process capability ratio and index, and comment on the capability of the process to meet Big D's requirements.

2.   Using the data and target levels in problem 5 in the variable section, determine the process capability ratio and index, and comment on the capability of the process to meet Bayou Bonanza's requirements.

3.   Using the data and target levels in problem 6 in the variable section, determine the process capability ratio and index, and comment on the capability of the process to meet Dixieland Delight's requirements.

Acceptance Sampling

Use computer software to help develop these sampling plans.

1.   The Great Lakes Company, a grocery store chain, purchases apples from a produce distributor in Virginia. The grocery company has an agreement with the distributor that it desires shipments of 10,000 apples with no more than 2 percent defective (i.e., severely blemished apples), although it will accept shipments with up to a maximum of 8 percent defective. The probability of rejecting a good lot is set at 0.05, whereas the probability of accepting a bad-quality lot is 0.10.

   a. Determine a sampling plan that will approximately achieve these quality performance criteria, and the operating curve.
   b. Determine the average outgoing quality limit for this plan.

2.   The Academic House Publishing Company sends out the textbooks it publishes to an independent bookbinder. When the bound books come back, they are inspected for defective bindings (e.g., warped boards, ripples, cuts, poor adhesion). The publishing company has an acceptable quality level of 4 percent defective but will tolerate lots of up to 10 percent defective. What (approximate) sample size and acceptance level would result in a probability of 0.05 that a good lot will be rejected and a probability of 0.10 that a bad lot will be accepted?

3.   The Metro Packaging Company in Richmond produces clear plastic bottles for the Kooler Cola Company, a soft-drink manufacturer. Metro inspects each lot of 5000 bottles before they are shipped to the Kooler Company. The soft-drink company has specified an acceptable quality level of 0.06 and a lot tolerance percent defective of 0.12. Metro currently has a sampling plan with $n = 150$ and $c \leq 4$. The two companies have recently agreed that the sampling plan should have a producer's risk of 0.05 and a consumer's risk of 0.10. Will the current sampling plan used by Metro achieve these levels of α and β?

4.   The Discount Warehouse purchases produce from a produce distributor upstate. The Warehouse has an agreement with the distributor that it desires shipments of 20,000 lbs of produce weekly with no more than 2 percent defective, although it will accept shipments with up to a maximum of 6 percent defective. The probability of rejecting a good lot is set at 0.05, whereas the probability of accepting a bad-quality lot is 0.10.

   a. Determine a sampling plan that will approximately achieve these quality performance criteria, and the operating curve.
   b. Determine the average outgoing quality limit for this plan.

5.   KidCo is introducing a new line of rag toys for infants to play with while they are teething. It contracts out the stitching to an independent tailor company. When the toys come back, they are inspected for defectives and safety hazards. KidCo has an acceptable quality level of 2 percent defective but will tolerate lots of up to 12 percent defective. What (approximate) sample size and acceptance level would result in a probability of 0.02 that a good lot will be rejected and a probability of 0.08 that a bad lot will be accepted?

132

6.   LabelIt produces advertising labels for Butcher Mart. LabelIt inspects each lot of 20,000 labels before they are shipped to Butcher Mart. It is important for Butcher Mart since they must comply with the FDA policies or risk being shut down. Butcher Mart has specified an acceptable quality level of 0.04 and a lot tolerance percent defective of 0.10. LabelIt currently has a sampling plan with $n = 100$ and $c \leq 1$. The two companies have recently agreed that the sampling plan should have a producer's risk of 0.01 and a consumer's risk of 0.08. Will the current sampling plan used by LabelIt achieve these levels of α and β?

7.   Jason Lewis assembles computers and sells them to resale shops. He purchases keyboards for the PCs from a manufacturer in India. The keyboards are shipped in lots of 1200 units, and when they arrive, Jason takes samples to inspect. Jason's contract with the overseas manufacturer specifies that the quality level that they will accept is 5 percent defective. Jason wants to avoid sending a shipment back because the distance involved would delay and disrupt the assembly process; thus, they want only a 2 percent probability of sending a good lot back. The worst level of quality the Fast Break Company will accept is 10 percent defective items. Using POM/QM for Windows, develop a sampling plan that will achieve these quality-performance criteria.

8.   The DL Hunt Department store has arranged to purchase specially designed sweatshirts with the State University Mascot from a clothing manufacturer in South Carolina. When the sweatshirts arrive in lots of 1000 units, they are inspected. The store's management and manufacturer have agreed on quality criteria of AQL = 2 percent defective and LTPD = 8 percent defective. Because sending poor-quality shipments back to South Carolina would disrupt sales at the stores, management has specified a low producer's risk of 0.01 and will accept a relatively high consumer's risk of 0.10. Using POM/QM for Windows, develop a sampling plan that will achieve these quality-performance criteria, and determine average outgoing quality.

7
Process Strategy

I.　**Process Strategy**

　A. An organization's approach to transform resources into goods and services.

　B. Choosing which process strategy to employ is one of the ten strategy decisions that operations managers must face.

　C. The objective of process strategy is to find the best ways to produce goods and services, while meeting customer demands and proper product specifications within costs and other constraints.

　D. Four approaches have developed over time and now present operations managers with the ability to fit their company's mission with its process strategy.

II.　**Four Process Strategies**

　A. Process Focused
　　1. Production facility organized around processes.
　　2. Produce low volume but high variety of products.
　　3. High degree of flexibility.
　　4. High variable costs.
　　5. Low utilization of facilities.
　　6. Also called: Intermittent Processes.

Example: Process Focus

If you've had a pizza delivered to your home recently, there is a good chance that Standard Register printed the order and delivery tag on the box. You probably came in contact with one of Standard's forms this week without knowing it. Thousands of different products are made by the firm, a typical one being a multisheet (3- or 4- layer) business form. Forms used for student college applications, hospital patient admissions, bank drafts, store orders, and job applications are examples. The company has 11 U.S. plants in its Forms Division.

A flow diagram of the entire production process, form order submission to shipment, at Standard's Kirksville, Missouri, plant is illustrated on the next page. This job shop groups people and machines that perform specific activities, such as printing, cutting, or binding, into departments. Entire orders are processed in batches, moving from department to department, rather than in a continuous flow or one at a time.

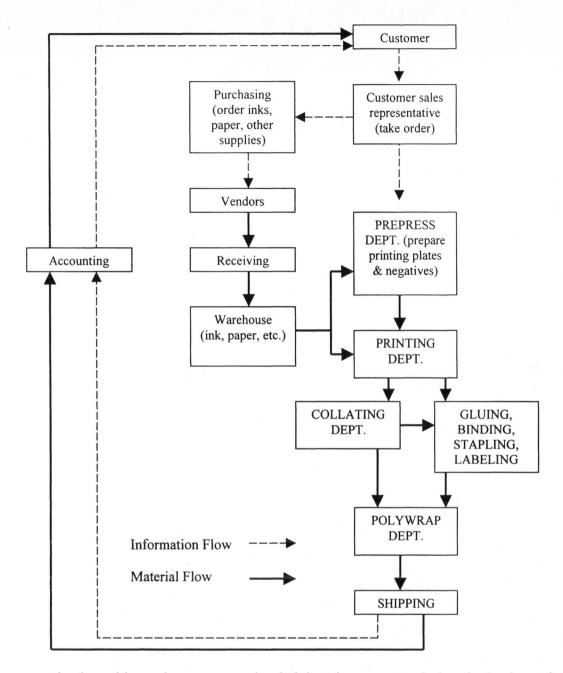

The process begins with a sales representative helping the customer design the business form. Once the form is established, the order is transmitted electronically to the Sales Support Department at the manufacturing plant. An order coordinator determines what materials will be needed in production (ink, paper, labels, etc.), computes the production time needed, and schedules the job on a particular machine.

The Prepress Department uses computer-aided design (CAD) to convert the product design into printing plates for the presses and then "burns" the image of the form onto an aluminum printing plate. Machine operators in the Printing Department install the plates and inks on their presses and print the forms. After leaving the presses, most products are collated on a machine that places up to 14 copies together, possibly with carbon paper between them. Some products undergo additional processing (for example, gluing, binding, stapling, or labeling). When the forms are completed, most are wrapped in polyethylene before being placed in cartons for shipping. The order is shipped, a "job ticket" is sent to Accounting, and an invoice goes to the customer.

B. Repetitive Focused
   1. Product-oriented production process.
   2. Use modules (parts or component parts of previously prepared items).
   3. Classic assembly line layout.
   4. Produce quasi-custom products.
   5. Incorporates advantages of both process and product focused.
      a. Economic advantages of product focused.
      b. Custom advantages of process focused.

Example: Repetitive Focus

Harley-Davidson assembles modules. Most repetitive manufacturers produce on a form of assembly line where the end product can take a variety of shapes depending on the mix of modules. This is the case at Harley, where the modules are motorcycle components and options.

Harley engines are produced in Milwaukee and shipped on a just-in-time basis to the company's York, Pennsylvania, plant. At York, Harley groups parts that require similar processes together into families (see figure below). The result is work cells. Work cells feed the assembly line.

Harley-Davidson assembles 2 engine types in 3 displacement sizes for 20 street bike models, which are available in 13 colors and 2 wheel options, adding up to 95 total combinations. Harley also produces 4 police and 2 Shriner motorcycles, and offers many custom paint options. This strategy requires that no fewer than 20,000 different pieces be assembled into modules and then into motorcycles.

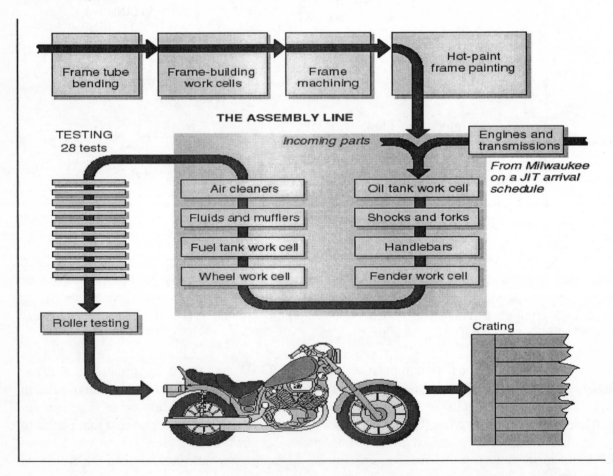

C. Product Focused (also called Continuous Processes)
  1. Production facilities organized around the products.
  2. Produce high volume but low variety of products.
  3. Require standardization and effective quality controls.
  4. Has ability to set and maintain quality standards.
  5. High fixed costs; low variable costs.
  6. High facility utilization.
D. Mass Customization Focus
  1. Focused around economically producing what the customer wants, when the customer wants it.
  2. Rapid, low-cost production of goods and services.
  3. High variety of products at the cost of standardized high-volume.
  4. Examples: Dell Computers and General Motors.
  5. High reliance on modular design. OM managers use imaginative, modularization, powerful scheduling, and rapid throughput to achieve.
E. Comparison of Process Choices
  1. Strategic advantages to each process.
  2. Match company's volume, cost, and utilization standards to process.

Comparison of the Characteristics of Four Types of Processes			
Process Focus	**Repetitive Focus**	**Product Focus**	**Mass Customization**
1. Small quantity and large variety of products are produced.	Long runs, usually a standardized product with options, are produced from modules.	Large quantity and small variety of products are produced.	Large quantities of large variety of products are produced.
2. Equipment used is general purpose.	Special equipment aids in use of an assembly.	Equipment used is special purpose.	Rapid changeover on flexible equipment.
3. Operators are broadly skilled.	Employees are modestly trained.	Operators are less broadly skilled.	Flexible operators are trained for the necessary customization.
4. There are many job instructions because each job changes.	Repetitive operations reduce training and changes in job instructions.	Work orders and job instructions are few because they are standardized.	Custom orders require many job instructions.
5. Raw material inventories are high relative to the value of the product.	Just-in-time procurement techniques are used.	Raw material inventories are low relative to the value of the product.	Raw material inventories are low relative to the value of the product.
6. Work-in-process is high compared to output.	Just-in-time inventory techniques are used.	Work-in-process inventory is low compared to output.	Work-in-process inventory is driven down by JIT, kanban, lean production.
7. Units move slowly through the plant.	Movement is measured in hours and days.	Swift movement of units through the facility is typical.	Goods move swiftly through the facility.
8. Finished goods are usually made to order and not stored.	Finished goods are made to frequent forecasts.	Finished goods are usually made to a forecast and stored.	Finished goods are often made to order.
9. Scheduling orders is complex and concerned with the trade-off between inventory availability, capacity, and customer service.	Scheduling is based on building various models from a variety of modules to forecasts.	Scheduling is relatively simple and concerned with establishing a rate of output sufficient to meet sales forecasts.	Sophisticated scheduling is required to accommodate custom orders.
10. Fixed costs tend to be low and variable costs high.	Fixed costs are dependent on flexibility of the facility.	Fixed costs tend to be high and variable costs low.	Fixed costs tend to be high, but variable costs must be low.
11. Costing, often done by the job, is estimated prior to doing the job, but known only after the job.	Costs are usually known because of extensive prior experience.	Because fixed costs are high, costs are highly dependent on utilization of capacity.	High fixed costs and dynamic variable costs make costing a challenge.

3. Use Crossover charts to compare processes.
   a. Chart of costs at possible volumes over different processes.
   b. Compares likely fixed costs and variable costs to determine lowest cost at any given volume.

Example

Kleber Enterprises is evaluating three accounting software products (A, B, and C) to support changes in its internal accounting processes. The resulting processes will have cost structures similar to those shown in the figure below. The costs of the software for these processes are:

	Total Fixed Cost	$ Required per Accounting Report
Software A	$200,000	$60
Software B	$300,000	$25
Software C	$400,000	$10

Solution:
Software A yields a process that is most economical up to V_1, but to exactly what number of reports (volume)? To determine the volume at V_1, we set the cost of software A equal to the cost of software B. V_1 is the unknown volume.

$$
\begin{aligned}
200,000 + (60) V_1 &= 300,000 + (25) V_1 \\
35 V_1 &= 100,000 \\
V_1 &= 2,857
\end{aligned}
$$

This means that software A is most economical from 0 reports to 2,857 reports (V_1). Similarly, to determine the crossover point for V_2, we set the cost of software B equal to the cost of software C.

$$
\begin{aligned}
300,000 + (25) V_2 &= 400,000 + (10) V_2 \\
15 V_2 &= 100,000 \\
V_2 &= 6,666
\end{aligned}
$$

This means that software B is most economical if the number of reports is between 2,857 (V_1) and 6,666 (V_2) and that software C is most economical if reports exceed 6,666 (V_2).

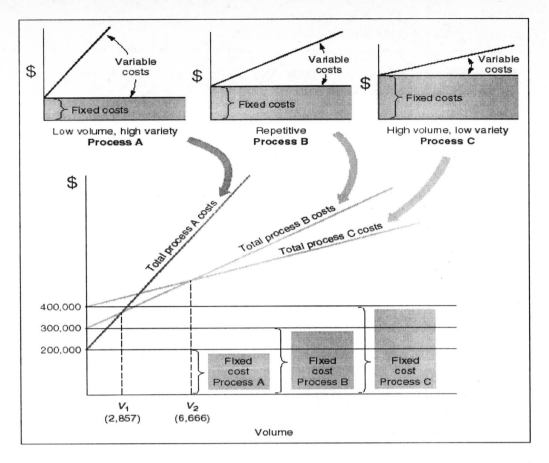

4. Changing processes from one production system to another is difficult and expensive.
   a. Changes may be necessary in:
      i. Purchasing
      ii. Quality Standards
      iii. Equipment
      iv. Layout
      v. Training
   b. Crucial to make correct process decision the first time.

III. **Process Analysis and Design**

   A. Flow Diagrams – Drawings used to analyze movement of people, material, or product.
   B. Time-Function Mapping
      a. A flow diagram with time element on horizontal axis.
      b. Nodes indicate activities; arrows indicate the flow direction.
      c. Helps identify and eliminate waste such as extra steps, duplicates, and delays.

Example: Process Mapping

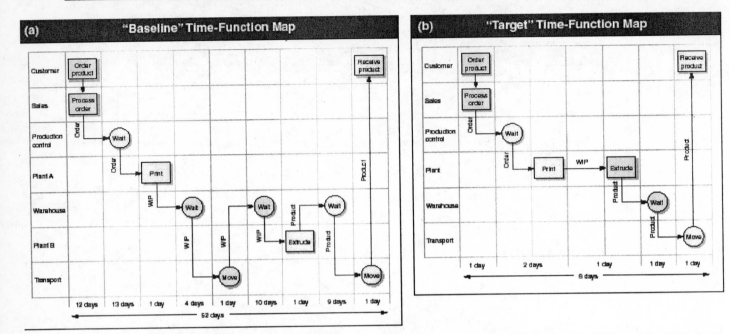

FIGURE 7.7 ■ Time-Function Mapping (Process Mapping) for a Product Requiring Printing and Extruding Operations at American National Can Company

C. Process Charts
  a. Use symbols (time and distance) to analyze the movement of people or material.
  b. Focus on value-added activities.
  c. Do not focus on "waste" activities (actions that do not add value).
    i. Resources lost to a firm or society forever.
    ii. Examples include: storage, delay, transportation, inspection.

Present Method ☒	**PROCESS CHART**		Proposed Method ☐

SUBJECT CHARTED *Hamburger Assembly Process*   DATE *1/1/03*

CHART BY *KH*

CHART NO. *1*

DEPARTMENT _____   SHEET NO. *1* OF *1*

DIST. IN FEET	TIME IN MINS.	CHART SYMBOLS	PROCESS DESCRIPTION
	—	○ ⇨ ☐ D ▽	Meat Patty In Storage
1.5	.05	○ ⇨ ☐ D ▽	Transfer to Broiler
	2.50	○ ⇨ ☐ D ▽	Broiler
	.05	○ ⇨ ☐ D ▽	Visual Inspection
1.0	.05	○ ⇨ ☐ D ▽	Transfer to Rack
	.15	○ ⇨ ☐ D ▽	Temporary Storage
.5	.10	○ ⇨ ☐ D ▽	Obtain Buns, Lettuce, etc.
	.20	○ ⇨ ☐ D ▽	Assemble Order
.5	.05	○ ⇨ ☐ D ▽	Place In Finish Rack
		○ ⇨ ☐ D ▽	
3.5	3.15	2 4 1 – 2	TOTALS

Value-added time = Operation time/Total time = (2.50+.20)/3.15 = 85.7%

○ = operation; ⇨ = transportation; ☐ = inspection; D = delay; ▽ = storage.

FIGURE 7.8 ■ Process Chart Showing a Hamburger Assembly Process at a Fast-Food Restaurant

D. Service Blueprinting
   a. Focuses on the customers and the provider's interaction with the customer.
   b. Different levels that have different management issues:
      i. Level one – the customer is in control.
      ii. Level two – the customer interacts with service provider.
      iii. Level three – service is removed from customer's control and interaction.

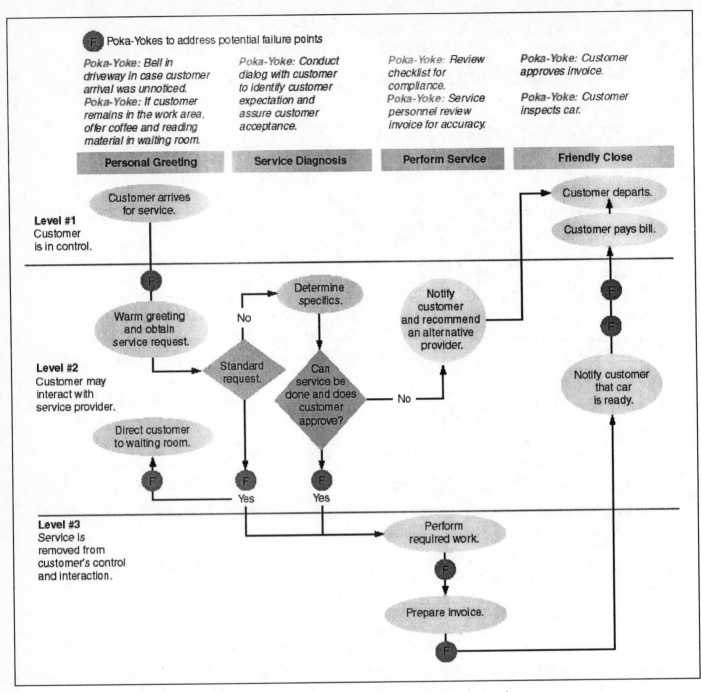

FIGURE 7.9 ■ Service Blueprint for Service at Speedy Lube, Inc.

Lecture Key: Customer service is the most important aspect of the service process design. These four tools help us to see the processes that occur from transforming resources into goods and services. These tools provide an easy way to see the strengths and weaknesses throughout the complexities of the process.

IV. Service Process Design

A. Customer Interaction and Process Design
   1. Service Process Matrix
      a. Upper section, mass service, and professional service focus on human resources.
         i. Managers find ways to address issues to satisfy customers and win orders.
         ii. Done with personalized service, requiring high labor involvement.
      b. Quadrant with low customization.
         i. To standardize or restrict some offerings of the service.
         ii. To automate.
         iii. To remove some services.
      c. Customer service is lower in quadrants with low customization.
      d. Operations with low labor intensity will lend themselves to innovations in process technology and scheduling.
   2. Manager should focus on designing a process that enhances service.

Example: Operation Changes Within the Service Process Matrix

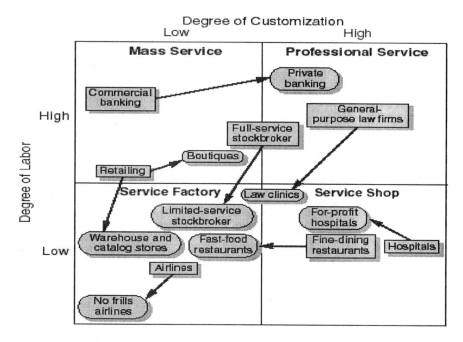

Lecture Key: Interaction with customers often has an adverse effect on process performance, but service providers must regard these likely challenges as opportunities. Managers must design processes to accommodate the special requirements of customers, in order to ensure effectiveness and efficiency. There are many different techniques for improving service productivity. Some common strategies include: separating services from other operations; scheduling personnel to be available to aid customers, employing modules, and customizing products at the time of delivery rather than during production.

B. More Opportunities
    1. Layout Design
        a. Integral part of service process, particularly in retailing, dining, and banking.
        b. Provides product exposure, customer education, product enhancement, security, and personal comfort.
        c. Provides continuing opportunity for winning orders.
    2. Human Resources
        a. Recruiting and training are important for service processes.
        b. Committed workforce that provides flexibility has a great impact on process performance.

V.   Selection of Equipment and Technology

A. Process decisions require subsequent decisions about proper equipment and technology.
B. Proper equipment choices require knowledge of the industry, available processes, and technology.
C. Selection of equipment can provide competitive advantage.
D. Modern technology allows enlargement of the scope of operations processes.
E. Flexibility (the ability to respond with little penalty in time, cost, or customer value) is an important attribute of new equipment.

VI.   Production Technology

A. Machine Technology
    1. Recent improvements in machinery involved in operations (such as cutting, drilling, boring, and milling) have decreased the time, space, and power needed for production.
    2. Computer numerical control (CNC) machinery (with its own computer and memory) increases speed (by reducing changeover time), reduces waste, and enhances flexibility.
B. Automatic Identification System (AIS)
    1. AIS is a system for transforming data into electronic form.
    2. Because most Operations Management data does not begin with bits and bytes, electrons cannot assist in transforming data.
    3. AIS is done via computer, keyboards, bar codes, and radio frequencies. Example: Nurses reducing errors in hospitals by matching bar codes on medication to ID bracelets on patients.
C. Process Control
    1. Use of information technology to monitor and control a physical process.
    2. Process control systems commonly operate using the following steps:
        a. Sensors collect data.
        b. Analog devices read data on some periodic basis.
        c. Measurements are translated into digital signals, which are transmitted to a digital computer.
        d. Computer programs read, file, and analyze data.
        e. Output is displayed.
D. Vision Systems
    1. Vision systems combine video cameras and computer technology in inspection roles.
    2. Are used mostly in food processing and manufacturing organizations.
    3. Vision systems are superior to human inspection, which is tedious and error-prone.
    4. Is widely used when the items being inspected are similar.

E. Robots
   1. A robot is a flexible machine with the ability to hold, move, or grab items.
   2. A robot functions through electronic impulses that activate motors and switches.
   3. It performs tasks that are monotonous or dangerous.
   4. Consistency, accuracy, speed, and power are enhanced by robots.

F. Automated Storage and Retrieval System (ASRS)

   1. ASRS are computer-controlled warehouses that provide automatic placement of parts into and from designated places within the warehouse.
   2. They are commonly used in distribution facilities of retailers.

G. Automated Guided Vehicle (AGV)

   1. AGV is an electronically guided and controlled cart used to move materials.
   2. Used in offices to move mail, and in hospitals and jails.

H. Flexible Manufacturing Systems (FMS)

   1. FMS is a system using an automated work cell controlled by electronic signals from a common centralized computer facility.
   2. Economically produces low volume but high variety.
   3. FMS bridges gap between product-focused and process-focused facilities.
   4. It has the flexibility to provide customized products, improved utilization, reduced costs, and improved throughput in order to improve response.

I. Computer-Integrated Manufacturing (CIM)

   1. CIM is a manufacturing system in which computer aided design, flexible manufacturing system, inventory control, warehousing and shipping are integrated.
   2. Reduces distinction between low-volume/high-variety and high-volume/low-variety.

Lecture Key: *Advances in technology enhance production and productivity. They have a wide range of applications in manufacturing as well as services.*

VII. Technology in Services

A. Examples include:
   1. Electronic diagnostic equipment at auto repair shops, blood and urine testing equipment in hospitals, retinal security scanners at airports, and high-security facilities.
   2. User-friendly computer software that enables customers to design their own window specifications.
B. Operations managers must be able to evaluate the impact of technology on their firm.

Lecture Key: *Just as in manufacturing production facilities, technology has advanced the capabilities of the service industry. Today, operations managers must be able to adapt to changes in technology quickly to maintain their market share. Their responses require special skills when evaluating reliability, investment analysis, human resource requirements, and maintenance.*

VIII.   Process Reengineering

A. Process Reengineering is the fundamental rethinking and redesign of business processes to bring about dramatic improvements in performance.
B. Relies on reevaluating the purpose of the process and questioning both the purpose and underlying assumptions.
C. Focuses on activities that cross functional lines and make dramatic improvements in cost, time, and customer value.

IX.   Environmentally Friendly Processes

A. Process approaches that address social responsibility and environmental concerns.
B. May range from activities that include a focus on issues such as efficient use of resources, reduction of waste by-products, emission controls, and recycling.
C. Some examples of environmentally sensitive and low-cost advantage processes:
   1. Ben and Jerry's use of energy-efficient lighting.
   2. Anheuser-Busch's use of wastewater to generate the gas that powers its St. Louis brewery.

Lecture Key: As consumer awareness and concerns grow and shift, firms must respond to those changes in order to continue winning orders. The rise in consumer concern with regard to the environment has forced many firms to alter their production processes to ensure environmental safety. The challenge for operations managers lies in integrating processes that meet customer expectations in terms of quality and environmental safety along with the company's strategy, cost requirements and product/service specifications.

Supplement 7
Capacity Planning

I. Capacity

A. Refers to the throughput or number of units a facility can hold, receive, store, or produce in any given period of time.

B. Capacity can affect a facility's fixed cost, and its management of demand. Therefore, determining proper capacity is crucial to the success of the company. The following information lays out the groundwork for examining capacity and capacity decisions.

C. Capacity must be measured, evaluated, incorporated into the company's overall strategic plan, and adequately respond to changes in the marketplace.

D. Design and Effective Capacity
   1. Design Capacity
      a. Maximum theoretical output of a system in a given period.
      b. Usually expressed as a rate.
      c. Some firms find that they operate more efficiently at less than design capacity.
   2. Effective Capacity
      a. The capacity a firm expects to achieve given its product mix, methods of scheduling, maintenance, and standards of capacity.
      b. Often lower than design capacity.
   3. Utilization
      a. Measure of performance.
      b. Equal to the percent of design capacity actually achieved.

      Utilization = Actual output / Design capacity
   4. Efficiency
      a. Measure of performance.
      b. Equal to the percent of effective capacity actually achieved.
      c. Improved by correcting quality problems.

      Efficiency = Actual output / Effective capacity

Example: Efficiency & Utilization

Sara James Bakery has a plant for processing breakfast rolls. Last week the facility produced 148,000 rolls. The effective capacity is 175,000 rolls. The production line operates 7 days per week with three 8-hour shifts per day. The line was designed to process a nut-filled, cinnamon-flavored, sugar-coated Deluxe roll at the rate of 1,200 per hour. Determine the design capacity, utilization, and efficiency for this plant when producing the Deluxe roll.

Solution:

Design Capacity = (7 days x 3 shifts x 8 hours) x (1,200 rolls per hour) = 201,600 rolls

Utilization = Actual Output / Design Capacity = 148,000 / 201,600 = 73.4%

Efficiency = Actual Output / Effective Capacity = 148,000 / 175,000 = 84.6%

The manager of Sara James Bakery now needs to increase production of the increasingly popular Deluxe roll. To meet this demand, the operations manager will be adding a second production line. The manager must determine the expected output of this second line for the sales department. Effective capacity on the second line is the same as on the first line, which is 175,000 Deluxe rolls. The first line is operating at an efficiency of 84.6% (from above). But output on the second line will be less than the first line because the crew will be primarily new hires; so the efficiency can be expected to be no more than 75%. What is the expected output?

Solution:
Expected Output = (Effective Capacity)(Efficiency) = (175,000)(.75) = 131,250 rolls
The sales department should be told the expected output is 131,250 Deluxe rolls.

 E. Capacity and Strategy
  1. Capacity decisions must be integrated into the organization's mission and strategy.
  2. The majority of OM decisions are impacted by changes in capacity.
 F. Capacity Considerations
  1. Forecast demand accurately.
   a. Accurate forecasting is extremely important to capacity decisions, therefore managers must determine the product life cycle and its prospects.
   b. Products being added/dropped must be known.
  2. Understand the technology and capacity increments.
   a. Technology decisions may be aided by cost analysis, human resources required, quality, and reliability once volume is determined.
   b. The operations manager is responsible for applying correct capacity increments.
  3. Find the optimum operating level (volume).
  4. Build for change.
   a. Operations managers build flexibility into the facility and equipment.
   b. Decisions about flexibility are made by testing several revenue projections on both the upside and downside of potential risks.
 G. Managing Demand
  1. Demand Exceeds Capacity
   a. The firm may be able to curtail demand by raising prices, scheduling long lead times, and discouraging marginally profitable business.
   b. Long term solution: increase capacity.
  2. Capacity Exceeds Demand
   a. Firm may stimulate demand through price reductions or aggressive marketing.
   b. Firm may accommodate market through product changes.
  3. Adjusting to Seasonal Demand
   a. Possible helpful action: offer products with complementary product designs.
   b. Appropriate complementing of products can lead to more consistency in the utilization of facilities, equipment, and personnel.
  4. Tactics for Matching Capacity to Demand
   i. Making staffing changes.
   ii. Adjusting equipment and processes (may involve purchasing new equipment).
   iii. Improving methods to increase throughput.
   iv. Redesigning the product to facilitate more throughputs.

Lecture Key: Although good forecasting may relieve some external pressures of the market place, operations managers may run into problems caused by poorly matching actual demand and available capacity. It is also important to remember that some external factors cannot be predicted or controlled (i.e., drastic drop in economy onset by the September 11th attacks). The following four points discuss possible approaches to minimizing the gap between actual demand and available capacity.

II.   Capacity Planning

A. Setting future capacity requirements is mostly based on future demand.
B. Determining capacity requires two phases.
   1. Future demand is forecast with traditional models in the first phase.
   2. Forecast is used to determine capacity requirements and the incremental size of each addition to capacity.
C. Capacity additions are usually instantaneous in large units.
D. Demand growth is usually gradual in small units.
E. Four approaches to capacity expansion:
   1. Leading demand with an incremental expansion –
      a. New capacity is acquired which handles demand until and given period.
      b. The process continues indefinitely into the future.
   2. Leading demand with a one-step expansion – large increase in capacity is acquired, which satisfies demand until demand levels out.
   3. Capacity lags demand with incremental expansion – shows a lag of capacity probably due to overtime or outsourcing.
   4. Attempts to have an average capacity with incremental expansion – attempts to build average capacity, sometimes lagging and sometimes leading.
F. The alternative with the lowest total cost is selected.

III.   Break-Even Analysis

A. What is Break-Even Analysis?
   1. Determining the capacity a facility must have to achieve profitability.
   2. Finding the point, in dollars and units, at which cost equals revenues.
B. Fixed Costs
   1. Costs that vary with the volume of units produced.
   2. Examples include: depreciation, taxes, debt, and mortgage payments.
C. Variable Costs
   1. Costs that vary with the volume of units produced.
   2. Major components are labor and materials.
D. Contribution
   1. Difference between selling price and variable costs.
   2. When total contribution exceeds total fixed costs, there will be profit.
E. Revenue Function
   1. Function that increases by the selling price of each unit.
   2. Where the revenue function crosses the total cost line is the break-even point.
F. Assumptions
   1. Cost and revenue are straight lines that are shown to increase linearly, in direct proportion to the volume of units being produced.
   2. Neither fixed cost nor variable cost needs to be a straight line.
   3. Revenue function may change with such factors as volume discounts.

G. Graphic Approach
   1. First step is to define the fixed cost and sum them up.
      a. Drawn as a horizontal line beginning at the dollar amount on the vertical axis.
      b. Does not remain constant over all volume.
   2. Variable cost is estimated by labor, material, and other costs connected with the production.
      a. Shown as increasing cost.
      b. Originates at the intersection of fixed cost on vertical axis and increases with change in volume as we move to the right on the volume axis.
H. Algebraic Approach
   1. Break-even occurs where total revenue equals total cost.
   2. Break-even point in dollars equals the fixed cost divided by the selling price minus the variable cost.
   3. Formulas given allow us to solve for not only break-even point but also profitability.

   BEP_x = Break-even point in units TR = Total revenue = Px
   BEP_s = Break-even point in dollars F = Fixed costs
   P = Price per unit (after all discounts) V = Variable costs / unit
   x = Number of units produced TC = Total costs = $F + Vx$

I. Single-Product Case
   1. Break-even point in dollars and units is determined for one product.
   2. Formulas for algebraic approach are used.

   BEP_x = Total fixed cost / (Price – Variable cost)
   BEP_s = Total fixed cost / (1 – (Variable cost / Selling price))

Example: Single-Product Case

Jimmy Stephens, Inc., has a fixed cost of $10,000 this period. Direct labor is $1.50 per unit, and material is $.75 per unit. The selling price is $4.00 per unit.

Solution:
The break-even point in dollars is computed as follows:
BEP_s = F / 1 – (V / P) = $10,000 / [(1 – (1.50 + .75)) / (4.00)]
= $22,857.14

The break-even point in units is computed as follows:
BEP_s = F / (P – V) = $10,000 / [4.00 – (1.50 + .75)]
= 5,714 units

J. Multiproduct Case
   1. Break-even point in dollars and units is determined for two or more products.
   2. Each product's contribution is weighted by its portion of sales.
   3. Formula:

   BEP_s = F / $\sum[(1 – (V_i / P_i)) \times (W_i)]$

Example: Multiproduct Case

Information for LeBistro, a French-style deli, follows. Fixed costs are $3,500 per month.

Item	Price	Cost	Annual Forecasted Sales Units
Sandwich	$2.95	$1.25	7,000
Soft drink	.80	.30	7,000
Baked potato	1.55	.47	5,000
Tea	.75	.25	5,000
Salad bar	2.85	1.00	3,000

Solution:
With a variety of offerings, we proceed with break-even analysis just as in a single-product case, except that we weight each of the products by its proportion of total sales.

MULTIPRODUCT BREAK-EVEN-DETERMINING CONTRIBUTION							
1	2	3	4	5	6	7	8
Item (i)	Selling Price (P)	Variable Cost (V)	(V / P)	1 – (V / P)	Annual Forecasted Sales $	% of Sales	Weighted Contribution (Col. 5 x Col. 7)
Sandwich	$2.95	$1.25	.42	.58	$20,650	.446	.259
Soft drink	.80	.30	.38	.62	5,600	.121	.075
Baked potato	1.55	.47	.30	.70	7,750	.167	.117
Tea	.75	.25	.33	.67	3,750	.081	.054
Salad bar	2.85	1.00	.35	.65	8,550	.185	.120
					$46,300	1.000	.625

For instance, revenue for sandwiches is $20,650 (2.95 x 7,000), which is 44.6% of the total revenue of $46,300. Therefore, the contribution for sandwiches is "weighted" by .446. The weighted contribution is .446 x .58 = .259. In this manner, its relative contribution is properly reflected.

Using this approach for each product, we find that the total weighted contribution is .625 for each dollar sales, and the break-even point in dollars is $67,200.

$$BEP_s = F / \Sigma[(1 - (V_i / P_i)) \times (W_i)] = \$3,500 \times 12 / .625 = \$67,200$$

The information given in this example implies total daily sales (52 weeks at 6 days each) of

$$\$67,200 / 312 \text{ days} = \$215.30$$

Using the data above, we take the forecast sandwich sales of 44.6% times the daily break-even of $215.38 divided by the selling price of each sandwich ($2.95). Then sandwich sales must be:

$$.446 \times \$215.38 / \$2.95 = \# \text{ of sandwiches} = 32.6 \sim 33 \text{ sandwiches each day.}$$

Lecture Key: *Just as it is important for individuals to budget their income and spending, companies must do the same. One way that companies can set budget standards is by performing break-even analysis. Break-even analysis allows the operations manager to determine how many units of product/service must be sold in order to cover the company's cost. Coupled with adequate forecasting of demand, an operations manager can plot the company's likely revenue, and thus profit.*

IV. Applying Decision Trees to Capacity Decisions

A. Decision trees require specifying alternatives and various states of nature.

B. By assigning probability values to the various states of nature, we can make decisions that maximize the expected value of the alternatives.

Example: Decision Trees

Southern Hospital Supplies, a company that makes hospital gowns, is considering capacity expansion. Its major alternatives are to do nothing, build a small plant, build a medium plant, or build a large plant. The new facility would produce a new type of gown, and currently the potential or marketability for this product is unknown. If a large plant is built and a favorable market exists, a profit of $100,000 could be realized. An unfavorable market would yield a $90,000 loss. However, a medium plant would earn a $60,000 profit with a favorable market. A $10,000 loss would result from an unfavorable market. A small plant, on the other hand, would return $40,000 with favorable market conditions and lose only $5,000 in an unfavorable market. Of course, there is always the option of doing nothing.

Solution:

Step 1: Illustrate the decision possibilities with a decision tree.

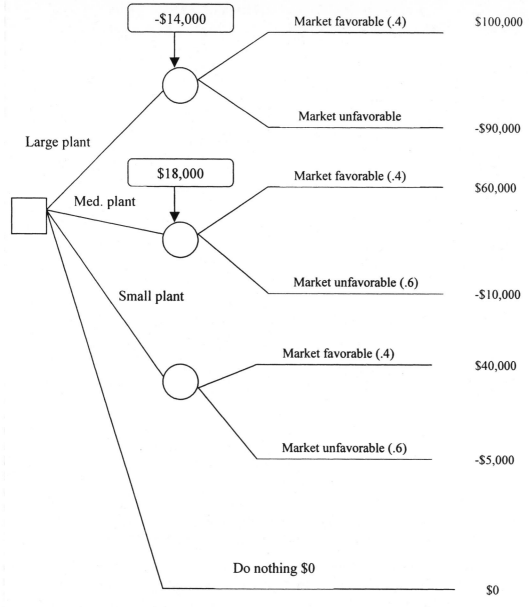

Step 2: Calculate the Expected Monetary Value (EMVs).

Recent market research indicates that there is a .4 probability of a favorable market, which means that there is also a .6 probability of an unfavorable market. With this information, the alternative that will result in the highest expected monetary value (EMV) can be selected:

$$
\begin{aligned}
\text{EMV (large plant)} &= (.4)(\$100{,}000) + (.6)(-\$90{,}000) \\
&= -\$14{,}000 \\
\text{EMV (large plant)} &= (.4)(\$60{,}000) + (.6)(-\$10{,}000) \\
&= \$18{,}000 \\
\text{EMV (small plant)} &= (.4)(\$40{,}000) + (.6)(-\$5{,}000) \\
&= \$13{,}000 \\
\text{EMV (do nothing)} &= \$0
\end{aligned}
$$

Based on EMV criteria, Southern should build a medium plant.

V. Strategy-Driven Investments

A. Investment, Variable Cost, and Cash Flow
   1. Managers must choose from among different financial options.
   2. Capital investment, variable cost, and cash flows should be examined in the decision making process.

B. Net Present Value
   1. Way of determining the discounted value of future income (called present value).
   2. Accounts for the time value of money (premise that cash today is worth more than cash tomorrow).
   3. Present value formulas and tables are used to determine the present value of one future cash amount.
   4. Annuity formulas and tables are used to determine the present value of a uniform series of amounts paid annually.
   5. Formulas:

$$\text{Future Value: } F = P(1 + i)^N$$

Where: F = future value
P = present value
i = interest rate
N = number of years

Present Value for small number of years:

$$P = F / (1 + i)^N$$

$$\text{Present Value: } P = F / (1 + i)^N = FX$$

Where: X = a factor from Table S7.1 defined as $= 1/(1 + i)^N$
F = future value

$$\text{Annuity: } S = RX$$

Where: X = a factor from Table S7.2
S = present value of a series of uniform annual receipts
R = receipts that are received every year for the life of the investment (the annuity)

Example: Investments (Annuity)

River Road Medical Clinic is thinking of investing in a sophisticated new piece of medical equipment. It will generate $7,000 per year in receipts for 5 years. What is the present value of this cash flow? Assume an interest rate of 6%.

Solution:

$$\text{Annuity: } S = RX = \$7,000(4.212) = \$29,484$$

The factor from Table 7.2 (=4.212) was obtained by finding that value when the interest rate is 6% and the number of years is 5. There is another way of looking at this example. If you went to a bank and took a loan for $29,484 today, your payments would be $7,000 per year for 5 years if the bank used an interest rate of 6% compounded yearly. Thus, $29,484 is the present value.

Example: Investments

Quality Plastics, Inc., is considering two different investment alternatives. Investment A has an initial cost of $25,000, and investment B has an initial cost of $26,000. Both investments have a useful life of 4 years. The cash flows for these investments follow. The cost or the interest rate (i) is 8%. (Factors come from Table S7.1 on pg. 287 of the text).

Investment A's Cash Flow	Investment B's Cash Flow	Year	Present Value Factor at 8%
$10,000	$9,000	1	.926
9,000	9,000	2	.857
8,000	9,000	3	.794
7,000	9,000	4	.735

Solution:

To find the present value of the cash flows for each investment, we multiply the present value factor by the cash flow for each investment for each year. The sum of these present value calculations minus the initial investment is the net present value of each investment. The computations appear in the following table:

Year	Investment A's Present Values	Investment B's Present Values
1	$9,260 = (.926)($10,000)	$8,334 = (.926)($9,000)
2	$7,713 = (.857)($9,000)	$7,713 = (.857)($9,000)
3	$6,352 = (.794)($8,000)	$7,146 = (.794)($9,000)
4	$5,145 = (.735)($7,000)	$6,615 = (.735)($9,000)
Totals	$28,470	$29,808
Minus initial investment	-25,000	-26,000
Net present value	$3,470	$3,808

The net present value criterion shows investment B to be more attractive than investment A because it has a higher present value.

Lecture Key: *Because the operations manager may be held responsible for the production/service process' return on investment, it is necessary to conduct investment analysis. We can do that by evaluating the company's capital investment needs, cash flow, and value of future cash receipts. We will examine the Net Present Value method to determine the discounted value of a series of future cash receipts.*

SUPPLEMENT 7 PROBLEMS

Break-Even Point

S1.   The Vicksburg Visitor Center has decided to put together a booklet of attractions for the city. The cost of producing the booklet is $2000, but copies of the booklet are $2.50 a piece. If they will be sold for $5 a piece, how many does the visitor center have to sell to break even? What is the break-even point in dollars?

Solution:

Step 1:   Determine the following information:
Total Fixed Cost (FC) = $2,000   Price = $5.00   Total Variable Cost = $2.50

Step 2:   Calculate the break-even point or volume using: $V = FC/(P - VC)$
V_{BEP} = 2000 / (5 – 2.5) = 800 booklets

Step 3:   Analysis: The Visitor Center needs to sell 800 booklets to break even. The center must now determine what the capacity constraints may be (can they make 800 books?) and what demand levels will be (can they sell 800 books?).

Step 4:   Convert the break-even volume into dollars by multiplying the V_{BEP} by the price at which the books will be sold (BEP$_s$ = V*P).
BEP$_s$ = 800 * 5 = $4000

S2.   Missy is about to produce a new album entitled "Madonna Wannabe." It costs $800 to write and produce the album. The copies are $12 a piece. If the CDs are sold at Music and More for $17 each, how many CDs must be sold to break even? What's the break-even point in dollars?

Solution:

Step 1:   Determine the following information:
Total Fixed Cost (FC) = $800   Price = $17.00   Total Variable Cost = $12

Step 2:   Calculate the break-even point or volume using: $V = FC/(P - VC)$
V_{BEP} = 800 / (17 – 12) = 160 CDs

Step 3:   Analysis: Missy needs to sell 160 CDs to break even. Missy must now determine what capacity constraints may be (can they make 160 books?) and what demand levels will be (can they sell 160 books?).

Step 4:   Convert the break-even volume into dollars by multiplying the V_{BEP} by the price at which the books will be sold (BEP$_s$ = V*P).
BEP$_s$ = 160 * 17 = $2720

1.   River Road Recipes is preparing to produce its first book. The cost of writing and printing the book is $3000, but copies are $12 apiece. If the books will be sold through the local bookstore for $17 each, how many books must be sold to break even? What is the break-even point in dollars?

2.   River Road Recipes is confident that demand for its book will exceed the break-even point computed in Problem 1. So, River Road Recipes is contemplating having its book produced with color photos throughout to depict bayou scenes. The cost to print the book would rise to $15,000. River Road Recipes will be able to do most of the writing, editing, and production work themselves and reduce outsourcing the work to the printer, and productivity cost would fall to $1.50 per book.

   a. What is the break-even point for this new process?
   b. Compare this process to the process proposed in the previous problem. For what volume of demand should River Road Recipes choose to use the color photos?

3.   Roxie, a local artist, is interested in the mass marketing and production of her latest work, French Market. The initial investment required for plant and equipment is estimated at $35,000. Labor and material costs are approximately $15 per print. If the prints can be sold for $75 each, what volume of demand is necessary for the prints to break even?

4.   Roxie is not confident that demand for her print will exceed the break-even point computed in Problem 3. If she chooses a less appealing site for the printing and does more of the framing work herself, her initial investment cost can be reduced to $5,000, but her per-unit cost to manufacture will rise to $25 per print.

        a. What is the break-even point for this new process?
        b. Compare this process to the process proposed in the previous problem. For what volume of demand should Roxie choose this process?

5.   Since Roxie has never used or considered mass printing, she is obviously very concerned about how this will affect demand for her work. Over her career, Roxie has averaged a yearly demand of 20 original paintings and has always commanded a very high price tag with her originals. The average selling price of her works is $2,500 per painting. What do you think is the best alternative of the three displayed here? Why? What is your quantitative logic or reasoning to back your decision?

6.   Allison recently purchased a chain of photo processing centers. Although the business is doing well now, Allison suspects that if she invests in a new processor for printing digital photos, she would attract a new market and increase profits. The new processor costs $25,000 to purchase and install and can process 50 rolls an hour (or 500 per day). Allison estimates that with the new processor, it will cost $1.50 to process each roll. Customers are charged $5.00 per roll.

        a. How many rolls will Allison have to process to break even?
        b. So far, Allison's workload has varied from 50 to 200 rolls. How long would it take to break even on the new equipment at the low demand estimates? At the high demand estimate?
        c. If Allison cuts her price to $4.00 a roll, she expects to be able to stabilize her customer base at 300 rolls per day. How long would it take to break even at the reduced price of $4.00? Should Allison cut her price and buy the new processor?

7.   Allison also has the option to purchase a laser copier that can be used for printing color photos for her chain of photo processing centers, or it could be used to expand the business into the general media-printing sector. Allison suspects that if she invests in the new equipment for printing digital photos and expands the business, she would attract a new market and increase profits substantially. The new printer would double the costs of purchasing and installing the other equipment. Production would increase to 90 jobs an hour (or 900 per day). Allison estimates that with the new printer, it will cost on average $0.50 to process each job. Customers are charged $8.00 per job.

        a. How many rolls will Allison have to process to break even?
        b. So far, Allison's workload has varied from 150 to 500 jobs. How long would it take to break even on the new equipment at the low demand estimates? At the high demand estimate?
        c. Based on the information provided, should Allison buy the new printer?

Decision Tree:

S1.   Kurt Wayne is interested in interviewing applicants for an open position in his company. From past experience, Kurt has determined that 90% of applicants are considered qualified (or good) and 10% are not qualified (or bad). He has also determined that if the applicant is qualified, he has a 90% chance of being successful. If the applicant is not qualified, then the applicant has only a 20% chance of being successful. What is the probability that a person will be successful if they are really not qualified? What is the probability that a person will not be successful if they are really qualified? What is the probability that the applicant will not be successful?

Solution:

Step 1:   The decision tree is below. It represents the series of sequential decision-making.

Step 2:   Calculate the expected values for each branch of the tree.

Branch 1: Probability (Qualified applicant) x Probability (successful given qualified)
EV = 0.90 x 0.90 or 0.81

Branch 2: Probability (Qualified applicant) x Probability (not successful given qualified)
EV = 0.90 x 0.10 or 0.09

Branch 3: Probability (Not Qualified applicant) x Probability (successful given not qualified)
EV = 0.10 x 0.20 or 0.02

Branch 4: Probability (Not Qualified applicant) x Probability (successful given not qualified)
EV = 0.10 x 0.80 or 0.08

Step 3:   Analysis:
What is the probability that a person will be successful if they are really not qualified?

Follow the branch for not qualified and successful (branch #3). The expected value is 0.02 or 2% will not be qualified and be successful anyway.

What is the probability that a person will not be successful if they are really qualified?

Follow the branch for qualified and not successful (branch #2). The expected value is 0.09 or 9% will be qualified and not successful.

What is the probability that the applicant will not be successful?

For this one, you have two branches to consider, qualified and not successful (branch #2) and not qualified and not successful (branch #4). Follow the branch for both and calculate the expected value as 0.09 or 9% (for branch #2) and 0.08 or 8% (for branch #4). To calculate the probability that the applicant will not be successful, add the individual probabilities for each branch together to get 17%.

P(not successful) = 9% + 8% = 17%

Decision Tree:

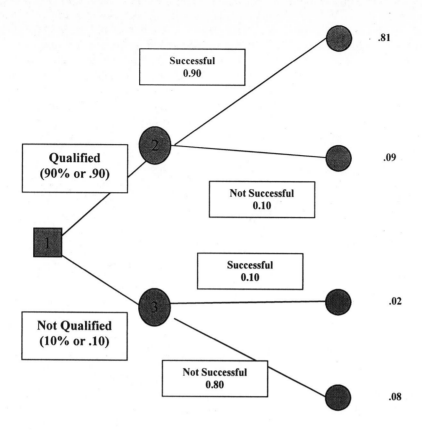

S2.   ComTech is bidding for a new state contract. The manager expects that his company has a 40% chance of getting the contract. The bidding process costs $50,000 (a cost that will be lost either way). If ComTech gets the contract, then they have two options (use current equipment and labor or buy new equipment). If they use current resources, then the cost is $40,000 (fixed) plus $20 per unit (variable). The new equipment and labor will cost $260,000 (fixed) plus $10 per unit (variable). The manager does have another concern if they use the current resources and that is what to do if demand changes. If other demand is light (only 10% of the time), the cost is $0 since it can be absorbed. If other demand is normal (only 70% of the time), the cost is $100,000. If other demand is heavy (only 20% of the time), the cost is $200,000.   Should the manager go after the state bid?

Solution:

Step 1:   Draw the decision tree. The table below represents the series of sequential decision-making.

Step 2:   Calculate the expected values of the end nodes (6, 7, and 8). The analysis begins by calculating the expected values of nodes 6 and 7 (work backwards through the decision tree).

   EV (node 6) = 0.20 ($200,000) = $40,000
   EV (node 7) = 0.70 ($100,000) = $70,000
   EV (node 8) = 0.10 ($0) = $0

Step 3:   Calculate the expected values for node 4 and node 5.

   EV (node 4) = (Cost of production using the old resources)
                   + [EV (node 6) + EV (node 7) + EV (node 8)]
              = (40,000 + 20x) + [40,000 + 70,000 + 0]
              = (40,000 + 20(10,000 units of production)) + [40,000 + 70,000 + 0]
              = –$350,000
   EV (node 5) = 260,000 +10x = 260,000 + 10(10,000 units of production)
              = –$360,000

Step 4:   Make decision for the value for node 2.

   EV (node 4) = –$350,000
   EV (node 5) = –$360,000

   Since these are costs, you would want to choose node 4.
                   (Use current resources at cost of $350,000)

Step 5:   Calculate the expected cost of node 1 given the two states of nature.
                   (get contract 40% of time and don't get contract 60% of the time)

   Revenue from contract production = Revenue in $ x units of production
                   = $50 x 10,000 units
                   = $500,000
   Cost of getting contract = Cost of bidding + Cost of production
                   = $50,000 + 350,000
                   = $400,000
   EV (node 2) = Probability on getting contract
                   x (Revenue from contract – Cost of getting contract)
              = .40 x ($500,000 – $400,000)
              = $40,000 in profit
   EV (node 3) = Probability of not getting a contract x cost of bidding
              = 0.60 x –$50,000
              = –$30,000 in loss
   EV (node 1) = EV (node 2) + EV (node 3)
              = $40,000 – 30,000 = $10,000

Step 6:   Analysis: Based on this decision tree, the manager expects to make $10,000 in profit.   The recommendation would be to bid for the contract and produce using the current resources if the contract is received.

Decision Tree:

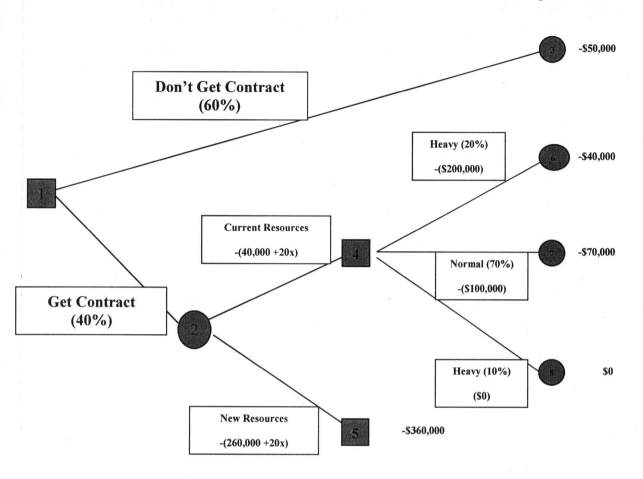

Expected Values

Don't Get Contract (60%) → ③ -$50,000

Get Contract (40%) → ②

Current Resources -(40,000 +20x) → ④

Heavy (20%) -($200,000) → ⑥ -$40,000

Normal (70%) -($100,000) → ⑦ -$70,000

Heavy (10%) ($0) → ⑧ $0

New Resources -(260,000 +20x) → ⑤ -$360,000

1. Lower State University is being sued for damages as a result of injuries incurred during the university's 75th Anniversary celebration. The lawyers suggest taking a low/medium/high offer approach for settling the suits out of court. The city will initially offer $100,000, an amount that the lawyers feel has a 20% chance of being accepted. Alternatively, the city could offer $150,000, which the lawyers feel would have a 50–50 chance of being accepted, or they could offer $200,000, which would definitely be accepted.

   If the initial offer is not accepted, the city would make a second, higher offer of $175,000, which the lawyers feel would have a 50–50 chance of acceptance. If this were rejected, the city would have to offer $225,000 to guarantee acceptance. If the plaintiffs accepted neither offer, the lawyers felt that an offer of $250,000 would definitely be accepted.

   a. Draw a decision tree for this problem.
   b. What strategy should the city follow to minimize expected cost of settlement? That is, what should be the first offer, the second offer?
   c. If the probability of acceptance of the first offer changes to 30%, does this change the city's strategy?
   d. Determine the minimum probability of acceptance of an initial offer of $100,000 that would make the strategy starting with that amount optimal.

2. Kurt Wayne is the president of Factory Sheet Metal Company. Kurt is considering whether or not to build a manufacturing plant in New Orleans to supply the local petroleum plants. His decision is laid out in the following table:

Alternatives	Positive Market	Negative Market
Large Plant	$200,000	-$150,000
Small Plant	$40,000	-$5,000
Do Nothing	$0	$0
Market Probabilities	0.35	0.65

   a. Construct a decision tree.
   b. Determine the best strategy, using expected monetary value (EMV).
   c. What is the expected value of perfect information (EVPI)?

3. Lawn Trimmer Tractors buys batteries from two suppliers. The quality of the batteries from the suppliers is indicated below:

Percent Defective	Probability for Supplier #1	Probability for Supplier #2
1	.70	.30
3	.20	.40
5	.10	.30

   This means that the probability of getting a batch of batteries that are 1% defective from Supplier #1 is .70. This means that every time Lawn Trimmer makes an order of 1,000 batteries, then 10 will be defective. A defective battery can be repaired for $1.50. Although the quality of Supplier #2 is lower, it will sell an order of 1,000 for $37 less than Supplier #1.

   a. Develop a decision tree.
   b. Which supplier should Lawn Trimmer use?

4. Bonnie Hunt, manager of the Lake Arena that will be home to the new professional basketball team, wants to make plans for the gift shop needs for next season. She has developed a table of conditional values for the various alternatives (inventory for memorabilia) and states of nature (size of crowd).

Alternatives	STATES OF NATURE (size of crowd)		
	Large	Average	Small
Large force	$20,000	$10,000	$2,000
Average force	$15,000	$12,000	$6,000
Small force	$9,000	$6,000	$5,000

If the probabilities associated with the states of nature are 0.40 for a large crowd, 0.40 for an average crowd, and 0.20 for a small crowd, determine:

    a. The alternative that provides the greatest expected monetary value (EMV).
    b. The expected value of the perfect information (EVPI).

5.   Shelia Rock is the Technology Manager for a local university. She is trying to determine whether to build a large annex on the Business Center. She has to determine if a large, small, or no annex is needed to meet the needs of the students and faculty. If the size of the university continues to grow, a large wing could return $500,000 in grant money and user fees each year. If the small annex were built, it would return $100,000 to the university each year if the population continues to grow. If the size of the university remains the same, the university would encounter a loss of $85,000 if the large annex were built. Furthermore, a loss of $45,000 would be realized if the small annex was constructed and the size remains the same. Unfortunately, Shelia does not have any information about the future size of the university.

    a. Construct a decision tree.
    b. Construct a decision table.
    c. Using an equal likelihood criteria, determine the best alternative.
    d. If the probabilities changed to: Growth = 0.60 and Remaining the Same = 0.40, what decision should Shelia make?

Investments (Annuity & Net Present Value)

S1.   An investment will produce $1800 three years from now. What is the amount worth today? What is the present value if the interest rate is 9%?

Solution:
Step 1:   Identify the following information:
           $FV = 1800$ $I = 9$ $N = 3$

Step 2:   You can use one of two formulas to complete the problem.
           #1: Using a financial calculator.
$$P = FV / (1 + i)^n = 1800 / (1 + 0.09)^3 = \$1389.93$$

           #2: Using the table (S7.1) on page 287 of the text.
$$P = FX = 1800 * .772 = \$1389.93$$

S2.   An investment requires an initial payment of $2500 now. What is the amount worth in ten years? What is the present value if the interest rate is 5%?

Solution:
Step 1:   Identify the following information:
           $PV = 2500$ $I = 5$ $N = 10$

Step 2:   Calculate using a financial calculator.
$$P = FV / (1 + i)^n$$
$$2500 = FV / (1 + 0.05)^{10}$$
$$FV = 2500 * 1.6288946 = \$4072.24$$

S3.   You have been asked to evaluate two investments to determine which is a better option. The following information is known about the two investments.

	Investment A	Investment B
Initial Investment	$10,000	$14,000
Income (cash per year)		
Year 1	5000	4000
Year 2	4000	4000
Year 3	3000	4000
Year 4	2000	4000

The interest rate is 5%, so which is the better criteria?

Solution:

	PV Factor @ 5%	Investment A's PV	Investment B's PV
Year 1	.952	$4760 = .952 x 5000	$4760 = .952 x 5000
Year 2	.907 = 1.859 – .952	3628 = .907 x 4000	4535 = .907 x 5000
Year 3	.864 = 2.723 – 1.859	2592 = .864 x 3000	4320 = .864 x 5000
Year 4	.823 = 3.546 – 2.723	1646 = .823 x 2000	4115 = .823 x 5000
Totals		$12,626	$17,730
Initial Investment		-$10,000	-$14,000
NPV		$2,626	$3,730

Investment B is the best option of the two investments.

S4. Quality Plastics, Inc., is considering two different investment alternatives. Investment A has an initial cost of $25,000, and investment B has an initial cost of $26,000. Both investments have a useful life of 4 years. The cash flows for these investments follow. The cost or the interest rate (i) is 8%. (Factors come from Table S7.1 on pg. 287 of the text).

Investment A's Cash Flow	Investment B's Cash Flow	Year	Present Value Factor at 8%
$10,000	$9,000	1	.926
9,000	9,000	2	.857
8,000	9,000	3	.794
7,000	9,000	4	.735

Solution:
To find the present value of the cash flows for each investment, we multiply the present value factor by the cash flow for each investment for each year. The sum of these present value calculations minus the initial investment is the net present value of each investment. The computations appear in the following table:

Year	Investment A's Present Values	Investment B's Present Values
1	$9,260 = (.926)($10,000)	$8,334 = (.926)($9,000)
2	$7,713 = (.857)($9,000)	$7,713 = (.857)($9,000)
3	$6,352 = (.794)($8,000)	$7,146 = (.794)($9,000)
4	$5,145 = (.735)($7,000)	$6,615 = (.735)($9,000)
Totals	$28,470	$29,808
Minus initial investment	−25,000	-26,000
Net present value	$3,470	$3,808

The net present value criterion shows investment B to be more attractive than investment A because it has a higher present value.

1.   An investment will produce $8,000 eight years from now. What is the amount worth today? What is the present value if the interest rate is 8%?

2.   An investment will produce $100,000 twenty years from now. What is the amount worth today? What is the present value if the interest rate is 6%?

3.   An investment requires an initial payment of $50,000 now. What is the amount worth in thirty years? What is the present value if the interest rate is 8%?

4.   An investment requires an initial payment of $15,000 now. What is the amount worth in ten years? What is the present value if the interest rate is 4%?

5.   You have been asked to evaluate two investments to determine which is the better option. The following information is known about the two investments.

	Investment A	Investment B	Investment C
Initial Investment	$105,000	$140,000	$135,000
Income (cash per year)			
Year 1	54000	56000	80000
Year 2	54000	46000	30000
Year 3	30000	30000	30000
Year 4	20000	20000	30000

The interest rate is 7%, so, which is the better criterion?

6.   You have been asked to evaluate two investments to determine which is a better option. The following information is known about the two investments.

	Investment A	Investment B	Investment C
Initial Investment	$35,000	$50,000	$44,800
Income (cash per year)			
Year 1	18000	20000	16000
Year 2	14000	20000	16000
Year 3	10000	15000	16000
Year 4	6000	15000	16000

The interest rate is 9%, so, which is the better criterion?

8

Location Strategies

I.   **The Strategic Importance of Location**

A. Location decisions greatly affect both fixed and variable costs.

B. It has a major impact on the overall risk and profit of the company.
   1. Example: Depending on the product and type of production or service taking place, transportation costs alone can total as much as 25% of the product's selling price.
   2. One-fourth of a firm's total revenue may be needed just to cover freight expenses of the raw materials coming in and finishing products going out.
   3. Location may also affect taxes, wages, raw material costs, and rents.

C. Location and Costs
   1. Consulting firm McKinsey believes "location ultimately has the power to make (or break) a company's business strategy."
   2. Once management is committed to a specific location, many costs are firmly in place, such as regions with high-energy costs or labor that is expensive, ill-trained, or has poor work ethics.
   3. The general objective of location strategy is to maximize the benefit of location to the firm.
   4. Location options include:
      a. Expanding an existing facility instead of moving.
      b. Maintaining current sites while adding another facility elsewhere.
      c. Closing the existing facility and moving to another location.

Lecture Key: *There are many factors that must be considered before committing to a specific location for your business. Some factors are controllable and others are not. You want to have the best location in order to be successful, but at the same time, you don't want to have high costs to achieve this goal.*

II.   **Factors That Affect Location Decisions**

  A. Steps to decide on a location (as illustrated in the figure below):
     1. Choose the best country.
     2. Focus on a region and a community.
     3. Choose a specific site within a community.

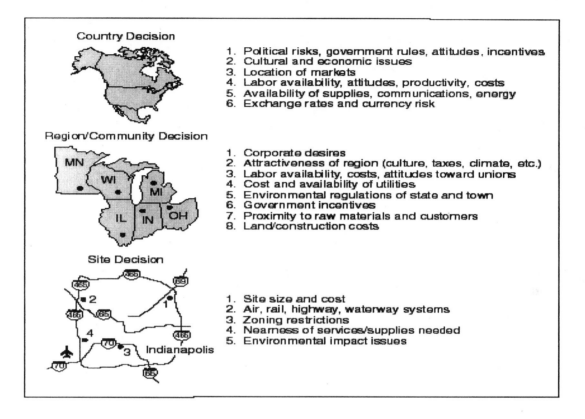

  B. Labor Productivity
     1. Management is interested in the combination of productivity and the wage rate.

        Cost per unit   =   Labor cost per day/Productivity (units per day)

     2. Low wages aren't always beneficial because of employees' poor training, poor education, poor work habits, or lack of transportation.
     3. Labor content of the product   =   labor cost per unit
  C. Exchange Rates and Currency Risk – Values of foreign currencies continually rise and fall in most countries.
  D. Costs
     1. <u>Tangible Costs</u>: readily identifiable costs that can be measured with some precision. Include utilities, labor, materials, taxes, depreciation, transportation of raw materials, transportation of finished goods, site construction, and other costs.
     2. <u>Intangible Costs</u>: a category of location costs that cannot be easily quantified, such as quality of life and government. Include quality of education, public transportation facilities, community attitudes toward the industry and the company, quality and attitude of prospective employees, climate and sports teams.
  E. Attitudes
     1. Governmental attitudes at a time a location decision is made may not last.
     2. Workers' attitudes may differ from country to country, region to region, and small town to city, which can affect a company's decision to relocate.
     3. Foreign firms face challenges because of cultural variations and bribery.

F. Proximity to Markets
1. Service organization's primary location factor is to locate near the customers.
2. Manufacturing firms like to be near the customers when it is expensive or difficult to transport goods.
3. Just-in-time production—suppliers want to locate near users to speed deliveries.
G. Proximity to Suppliers
1. Firms locate near their raw materials and suppliers because of:
   a. Perishability (bakeries and dairy plants)
   b. Transportation costs (steel producers)
   c. Bulk (lumber mills)
H. Proximity to Competitors (Clustering)
1. Clustering: the location of competing companies near each other, often because of a critical mass of information, talent, venture capital, or natural resources.
2. Examples: wine makers in Napa Valley in the U.S. and Bordeaux region in France, software firms in Silicon Valley, and racecar builders in the Huntington/North Hampton region of England.

Lecture Key: Choosing a site location for your business is definitely a challenge (the points above illustrate this). All of these points must be analyzed together, not separately, to make an educated and strategic decision regarding location.

III. **Methods of Evaluating Location Alternatives**

A. The Factor-Rating Method – a location method that instills objectivity into the process of identifying hard-to-evaluate costs.
1. Factors
   a. Labor costs
   b. Labor availability
   c. Proximity to raw materials and suppliers
   d. Proximity to markets
   e. Government fiscal policies
   f. Environmental regulations
   g. Utilities
   h. Site costs
   i. Transportation availability
   j. Quality of life issues in the community
   k. Foreign exchange
   l. Quality of government
2. Six steps:
   a. Develop a list of relevant factors called "critical success factors."
   b. Assign a weight of importance to each factor.
   c. Develop a scale for each factor.
   d. Management score each location for each factor.
   e. Multiply each factor's weight and the total score of each location.
   f. Make recommendation based on the maximum point score.

Five Flags over Florida, a U.S. chain of 10 family-oriented theme parks, has decided to expand overseas by opening its first park in Europe. The rating sheet in table below provides a list of critical success factors that management has decided are important; their weightings and their rating for two possible sites – Dijon, France, and Copenhagen, Denmark – are shown.

Solution:

Critical Success Factor	Weight	Scores (Out of 100)		Weighted Scores	
		France	Denmark	France	Denmark
Labor availability and attitude	.25	70	60	(.25)(70) = 17.5	(.25)(60) = 15.0
People-to-car ratio	.05	50	60	(.05)(50) = 2.5	(.05)(60) = 3.0
Per capita income	.10	85	80	(.10)(85) = 8.5	(.10)(80) = 8.0
Tax structure	.39	75	70	(.39)(75) = 29.3	(.39)(70) = 27.3
Education and health	.21	60	70	(.21)(60) = 12.6	(.21)(70) = 14.7
Totals	1.00			70.4	68.0

The table also indicates use of weights to evaluate alternative site locations. Given the option of 100 points assigned to each factor, the French location is preferable. By changing the points or weights slightly for those factors about which there is some doubt, we can analyze the sensitivity of the decision. For instance, we can see that changing the scores for "labor availability and attitude" by 10 points can change the decision.

> B. Locational Break-Even Analysis
>> 1. Locational Break-Even Analysis
>>> a. The use of cost-volume analysis to make an economic comparison of location alternatives.
>>> b. Can be done mathematically or graphically.
>> 2. Three steps to locational break-even analysis:
>>> a. Determine fixed and variable cost for each location.
>>> b. Plot the costs for each location, with costs on the vertical axis of the graph and annual volume on the horizontal axis.
>>> c. Select the location that has the lowest total cost for the expected production volume.

A manufacturer of automobile carburetors is considering three locations – Akron, Bowling Green, and Chicago – for a new plant. Cost studies indicate that fixed costs per year at the sites are $30,000, $60,000, and $110,000, respectively; and variable costs are $75 per unit, $45 per unit, and $25 per unit, respectively. The expected selling price of the carburetors produced is $120. The company wishes to find the most economical location for an expected volume of 2,000 units per year.

(See Figure 8.2 on pg. 308 of the text. For each of the three, we can plot the fixed costs (those at a volume of zero units) and the total cost (fixed costs + variable costs) at the expected volume of output. These lines have been plotted.)

Solution:

For Akron,

Total Cost = $30,000 + $75(2,000) = $180,000

For Bowling Green,

Total Cost = $60,000 + $45(2,000) = $150,000

For Chicago,

Total Cost = $110,000 + $25(2,000) = $160,000

With an expected volume of 2,000 units per year, Bowling Green provides the lowest cost location. The expected profit is:

Total revenue – Total cost = $120(2,000) – $150,000 = $90,000 per year

The crossover point for Akron and Bowling Green is:

$$30,000 + 75(x) = 60,000 + 45(x)$$
$$30(x) = 30,000$$
$$x = 1,000$$

and the crossover point for Bowling Green and Chicago is:

$$60,000 + 45(x) = 110,000 + 25(x)$$
$$20(x) = 50,000$$
$$x = 2,500$$

Thus, for a volume of less than 1,000, Akron would be preferred, and for a volume greater than 2,500, Chicago would yield the greatest profit.

C. Center-of-Gravity Method
1. Center-of-gravity method – a mathematical technique used for finding the location of a distribution center that will minimize distribution cost.
2. The center of movement in a geographic area based on transport weight and distance.
3. Identifies a set of coordinates designating a central location on a map relative to all other locations. The ideal location is the one that minimizes the weighted distance. The number of containers shipped weights distance.
4. Factors for managers to consider:
   a. Location of market
   b. Volume of goods shipped to the markets
   c. Shipping costs
5. Steps:
   Step 1: Locate the fixed sites (the suppliers) on a grid map and assign location coordinates.
   Step 2: Determine the weights that each supplier ships.
   Step 3: Calculate the centralized location coordinates using the following equations:

$$\text{X-coordinate} = \frac{\sum d_{ix} Q_i}{\sum Q_i}$$

$$\text{Y-coordinate} = \frac{\sum d_{iy} Q_i}{\sum Q_i}$$

Where:
d_{ix} = x-coordinate of location i
d_{iy} = y-coordinate of location i
Q_i = Quantity of goods moved to or from location i

Example: Center-of-Gravity Method
___

Consider the case of Quain's Discount Department Stores, a chain of four large Target-type outlets. The firm's store locations are in Chicago, Pittsburgh, New York, and Atlanta; they are currently being supplied out of an old and inadequate warehouse in Pittsburgh, the site of the chain's first store. Data on demand rates at each outlet are shown in table below.

Demand for Quain's Discount Department Stores	
Store Location	**# of Containers Shipped per Month (Q_i)**
Chicago	2,000
Pittsburgh	1,000
New York	1,000
Atlanta	2,000

The firm has decided to find some "central" location in which to build a new warehouse. Its current store locations are shown in table below (from Figure 8.3 on pg. 310 in the text).

Location:	d_{ix}	d_{iy}
Chicago	30	120
Pittsburgh	90	110
New York	130	130
Atlanta	60	40

Solution:

$$X = \frac{\sum d_{ix} Q_i}{\sum Q_i} = \frac{30(2000) + 90(1000) + 130(1000) + 60(2000)}{2000 + 1000 + 1000 + 2000}$$
$$= 66.7$$

$$Y = \frac{\sum d_{iy} Q_i}{\sum Q_i} = \frac{120(2000) + 110(1000) + 130(1000) + 40(2000)}{2000 + 1000 + 1000 + 2000}$$
$$= 93.3$$

This location (66.7, 93.3) would then be found by overlaying a U.S. map on the exhibit; we find this location is near central Ohio. The firm may well wish to consider Columbus, Ohio, or a nearby city as an appropriate location.

    D. Transportation Model – determines the best pattern of shipment from several points of supply to several points of demand so as to minimize total production and transportation costs.

IV.   Service Location Strategy

    A. Service-sector location analysis focuses on maximizing revenue because service firms find that location often influences revenues more than costs.

    B. There are 8 major components of volume and revenue for the service firm:
        1. Purchasing power of the customer-drawing area.
        2. Service and image compatibility with demographics of the customer-drawing area.
        3. Competition in the area.
        4. Quality of the competition.
        5. Uniqueness of the firms' and competitors' locations.
        6. Physical qualities of facilities and neighboring businesses.
        7. Operating policies of the firm.
        8. Quality of management.

Lecture Key: *Having a good grasp on these eight components will enable an operations manager to have a strong picture of expected revenues. Service firms should understand that the location of their business will directly affect their revenues, and it is often beneficial to locate near competitors because they attract large crowds of customers.*

SERVICE/RETAIL/PROFESSIONAL LOCATION	GOODS-PRODUCING LOCATION
Revenue Focus	**Cost Focus**

Volume / revenue
  Drawing area; purchasing power
  Competition; advertising/pricing
Physical quality
  Parking/access; security/lighting;
    appearance/image
Cost determinants
  Rent
  Management caliber
  Operation policies (hours, wage rates)
	Tangible costs
	  Transportation cost of raw material
	  Shipment cost of finished goods
	  Energy & utility cost; labor; raw material; taxes,
	    and so on
	Intangible and future costs
	  Attitude toward union
	  Quality of life
	  Education expenditures by state
	  Quality of state and local government

Techniques	**Techniques**
Regression models to determine importance of various factors Factor-rating method Traffic counts Demographic analysis of drawing area Purchasing power analysis of area Center-of-gravity method Geographic information systems	Transportation method Factor-rating method Locational break-even analysis Crossover charts
Assumptions	**Assumptions**

Location is a major determinant of revenue
High customer-contact issues are critical
Costs are relatively constant for a given area; therefore,
  the revenue function is critical
	Location is a major determinant of cost
	Most major costs can be identified explicitly for each site
	Low customer contact allows focus on the identifiable
	  costs
	Intangible costs can be evaluated

    C. How Hotel Chains Select Sites
        1. A hotel with an accurate location has a distinct strategic advantage over competitors.
        2. By testing several independent variables and forming a regression model, hotels are able to determine profitability and predict success or failure of a site.
    D. The Telemarketing Industry
        1. Traditional variables, such as location and appearance, are irrelevant when face-to-face contact is not required in an industry such as telemarketing or selling over the Internet.
        2. The cost and availability of labor becomes more important.
    E. Geographic Information Systems (GISs)
        1. GISs help firms make successful, analytical decisions regarding location with geographically coded files that conduct demographic analyses.
        2. Geographic databases available through GISs:
            a. Census data by block, tract, city, county, congressional district, metropolitan area, state, zip code.
            b. Maps of every street, highway, bridge, and tunnel in the U.S.
            c. Utilities such as electrical, water, and gas lines.
            d. All rivers, mountains, lakes and forests.
            e. All major airports, colleges, and hospitals.

3. Airlines use GISs to identify airports where ground services are most effective.
4. Commercial office building developers use GISs to choose cities for future construction by addressing:
    a. Residential areas
    b. Retail shops
    c. Cultural and entertainment centers
    d. Crime incidence
    e. Transportation options
5. GIS software packages
    a. Atlas GIS (from Strategic Mapping)
    b. Hemisphere Solutions (by Unisys Corp.)
    c. Map Info (from MapInfo Corp.)
    d. Arc/Info (by ESRI)
    e. SAS/GIS (by SAS Institute, Inc.)
    f. Market Base (by National Decision Systems, Inc.)
    g. MapPoint 2002 (by Microsoft)

Lecture Key: *When deciding where to place a new company or where to open a new location of an existing company, a Geographic Information System software package would help an operations manager pick the prime location. GIS software packages allow you to search by almost anything: demographics, restaurants, airports, hotels, ATMS, freeway exits; and the information can be mapped by state, county, city, zip code or census tract.*

Location Factor Rating

S1.   Using the following factor ratings, determine the best location alternative.

Factor	Weight	1	2	3
Labor Pool	.30	50	75	80
Traffic	.25	90	85	95
Parking	.20	75	80	70
Shipping Modes	.15	95	88	75
Air Service	.10	80	70	60

Solution:

Step 1:   Calculate the weighted scores for each site. They are computed by multiplying the factor weights by the score for that factor. For example, the weighted score for "labor pool and climate" for site 1 is

Labor Pool: (0.30) (50) = 15 points   Shipping: (0.15) (95) = 14.25 points
Traffic: (0.25) (90) = 22.5 points   Air: (0.10) (80) = 8 points
Parking: (0.20) (75) = 15 points

Step 2:   Calculate the total score for each site 1. This is done by adding the above factor scores together. This would give you 74.75.

Step 3:   Continue these calculations for sites 2 and 3. The weighted scores for each factor for each site and the total scores are summarized as follows:

Location Factor	Site 1	Site 2	Site 3
Labor Pool	15	22.5	24
Traffic	22.5	21.25	23.75
Parking	15	16	14
Shipping Modes	14.25	13.2	11.25
Air Service	8	7	6
	77.5	79.95	79

Step 4:   Make Decision: Site 2 has the highest factor rating (79.95) compared with the other locations; however, this evaluation would have to be used with other information, particularly a cost analysis, before making a decision.

S2.   Using the following factor ratings, determine the best location alternative.

Factor	Weight	1	2	3
Convenience	.30	60	70	80
Traffic	.25	90	80	85
Parking	.25	75	80	75
Real Estate	.20	95	98	95

Solution:

Step 1:   Calculate the weighted scores for each site. They are computed by multiplying the factor weights by the score for that factor. For example, the weighted score for "labor pool and climate" for site 1 is:

Convenience: (0.30) (60) = 18 points   Parking: (0.25) (75) = 18.75 points
Traffic: (0.25) (90) = 22.5 points   Real Estate: (0.20) (95) = 19 points

Step 2:   Calculate the total score for each site 1. This would give you 78.25.

Step 3: Continue these calculations for sites 2 and 3. The weighted scores for each factor for each site and the total scores are summarized below. Make Decision: Site 3 has the highest factor rating (83).

Location Factor	Site 1	Site 2	Site 3
Convenience	18	21	24
Traffic	22.5	20	21.25
Parking	18.75	20	18.75
Real Estate	19	19.6	19
	78.25	80.6	83

S3. Betty's Basket Weaving Company is the largest seller of baskets in the country. They are currently relocating because their building has been declared unsafe and unfit for doing business. The move must take place quickly and the building must already be established. Betty knows she must pick a site selection team and decide within two weeks before too much business is lost. Here is what the site team has found. Which site is the best?

Location Factor	Weight	Site 1	Site 2	Site 3
Proximity to Suppliers	.30	90	85	70
Community Support	.10	65	80	90
Labor Pool	.20	70	75	80
Business Regulations	.10	60	70	75
Taxing Requirements	.05	80	75	85
Area Demand	.20	85	85	90
Facility Size	.05	65	75	70

Solution:

Step 1: Calculate the site scores for the three sites.   Score:

Site 1: $(.30)(90) + (.10)(65) + (.20)(70) + (.10)(60) + (.05)(80) + (.20)(85) + (.05)(65)$ = 77.75
Site 2: $(.30)(85) + (.10)(80) + (.20)(75) + (.10)(70) + (.05)(75) + (.20)(85) + (.05)(75)$ = 80
Site 3: $(.30)(70) + (.10)(90) + (.20)(80) + (.10)(75) + (.05)(85) + (.20)(90) + (.05)(70)$ = 79.25

Step 2: Make Decision: based on this information, recommend site 2.

1. Using the following factor ratings, determine which location alternative should be chosen on the basis on maximum composite score (highest average), 1, 2, or 3.

Location Factor (100 pts. each)	Weight	Site 1	Site 2	Site 3
Convenience	.25	70	60	80
Parking	.20	76	92	82
Operating Costs	.20	90	90	60
Shopper Traffic	.15	86	80	70
Recruiting	.10	90	82	95
Neighborhood	.10	85	75	99

2. John, the manager of a local doctor's office, has received an analysis of several cities being considered for a new office complex. The data (100 points maximum) are:

	Location		
Factor	A	B	C
Hospital Facilities	10	6	4
Business Services	9	5	5
Community Services	6	7	9
Real Estate Costs	3	8	7
Construction Costs	6	5	10
Cost of Living	7	8	8
Taxes	5	4	6
Doctor Recruitment	6	7	8

a. If the manager weights the factors equally, which location would John pick?
b. If business services and construction costs are given weights that are double the weights of the other factors, does this change John's decision?

3. University Mascot is a chain of college bookstores currently managing and operating on campus sites in the west. The CEO, Dan Webb, wants to expand and open new stores in one of four new mall locations in the South. Dan has indicated five factors that are important to its decision, including proximity of a college, community median income, mall vehicle traffic flow and parking, quality and number of stores in the mall, and proximity of other malls or shopping areas. Dan has the company's managers determine the weight of each factor based on importance. A team of managers visited each potential location and rated them according to each factor, as follows.

Location Factor	Weight	Scores (1 to 100)			
		Mall 1	Mall 2	Mall 3	Mall 4
College proximity & success	0.30	90	60	80	85
Median income	0.25	65	80	80	90
Vehicle traffic	0.25	79	90	60	70
Mall quality and size	0.10	80	100	90	60
Proximity of other shopping	0.10	50	30	90	85

Given that all sites have basically the same leasing costs and labor and operating costs, recommend a location based on the rating factors.

4. University Mascot now wants to expand and take over existing college bookstore operations in the South. Dan has indicated five factors that are important to its decision, including proximity of a college, community median income, mall vehicle traffic flow and parking, quality and number of stores in the mall, and proximity of other shopping areas. Dan has the company's managers determine the weight of each factor based on importance. A team of managers visited each potential location and rated them according to each factor, as follows. Dan knows that if he adds more than 6 stores that he will have spread his resources too thin. Using the information in #3, which 6 of 9 stores should Dan expand his operations?

Location Factor	Weight	Scores (1 to 100)				
		Campus 1	Campus 2	Campus 3	Campus 4	Campus 5
College proximity & success	0.30	60	85	85	90	65
Median income	0.25	80	90	75	90	85
Vehicle traffic	0.25	90	70	50	55	65
Mall quality and size	0.10	100	60	95	55	40
Proximity of other shopping	0.10	30	85	85	75	55

Given that all sites have basically the same leasing costs and labor and operating costs, recommend the locations based on the rating factors.

5. University Mascot now wants to expand and take over existing college bookstore operations in the South. Now, Dan knows additional information that requires more analysis – he can add a total of 6 stores with the 3 being college stores and the other 3 being in a mall. Using the information in #3 and #4, which 6 of 9 stores should Dan expand his operations?

6. Sky Computers manufactures computer components such as chips, circuit boards, motherboards, keyboards, and LCD panels, and sells them around the world. It wants to construct a new warehouse / distribution center in Asia to serve emerging Asian markets. Since this is a new market and area from Sky's current operations, they want to be extra careful about identifying important factors. It has identified sites in Shanghai, Hong Kong, and Singapore and has rated the important location factors for each site as follows.

		Scores (1 to 100)		
Location Factor	Weight	Shanghai	Hong Kong	Singapore
Political stability	0.40	60	90	50
Economic growth	0.25	70	75	80
Port facilities	0.10	95	90	70
Container support	0.10	80	90	70
Land & Construction Cost	0.03	20	30	95
Transportation/Distribution	0.03	80	70	95
Duties & Tariffs	0.03	90	90	85
Trade regulations	0.02	95	95	80
Airline service	0.02	80	70	60
Area roads	0.02	70	80	60

Recommend a site based on these location factors and ratings. Can you think of any factors that Sky neglected?

7. Simpleton University is going to construct a new student union that will include a bookstore, post office, theaters, market, mini-mall, meeting rooms, swimming pool, and weight and exercise rooms. The university administration has assembled a group of students and faculty to act as the site selection team to identify the best potential sites on campus for the new facility. The site team has identified five sites on campus and has rated the important location factors for each site as follows.

		Scores (1 to 100)				
Location Factor	Weight	South	West A	West B	North	East
Proximity to housing	0.25	65	85	65	70	70
Student traffic	0.25	60	85	60	75	70
Parking availability	0.15	80	70	80	90	65
Plot size, terrain	0.15	90	75	90	80	95
Infrastructure	0.05	40	60	40	50	95
Off-campus accessibility	0.05	70	70	70	90	45
Proximity to dining facilities	0.05	70	90	70	60	40
Visitor traffic	0.03	65	55	65	70	0
Landscape/aesthetics	0.02	60	70	60	50	25

Recommend a site based on these location factors and ratings.

8. EnviroChem is going to construct a new $1.2 billion plant and has selected four small towns in the west as potential sites. The important location factors and ratings for each town are as follows.

Scores (1 to 100)

Location Factor	Weight	Cove Bay	Robert	Ash	Elling
Labor laws/unions	0.15	60	70	80	90
Education	0.15	85	95	70	80
Labor skill/education	0.10	70	80	85	70
Cost of living	0.10	85	75	85	65
Taxes	0.10	55	60	90	50
Incentive package	0.05	70	80	90	50
Government reg.	0.05	65	55	65	40
Environmental reg.	0.05	70	80	65	40
Work ethic	0.05	70	75	40	55
Infrastructure	0.04	60	70	50	80
Quality of life	0.04	95	90	60	60
Transportation	0.04	95	80	70	60
Space for expansion	0.04	90	90	80	40
Urban proximity	0.04	70	80	90	55

Recommend a site based on these location factors and ratings.

Center of Gravity:

S1. Fred's hot dog stand purchases ingredients from 4 suppliers. The company wants to construct a new central distribution center to process and package ingredients before shipping them to the various ballparks Fred's stands are located in. Using the center of gravity technique, where should the center be located?

Suppliers	A	B	C	D
X	250	100	150	300
Y	150	300	350	500
Weight	80	75	150	120

Solution:

Step 1: Calculate the X coordinate for the Center of Gravity site using the formula below. The X coordinate is at point 186.5.

$$X = \frac{\sum X_i W_i}{\sum W_i} = \frac{250(80) + 100(75) + 150(150) + 300(120)}{80 + 75 + 150 + 120}$$
$$= 186.5$$

Step 2: Calculate the Y coordinate for the Center of Gravity Site using the formula below. The Y coordinate is at point 346.

$$Y = \frac{\sum Y_i W_i}{\sum W_i} = \frac{150(80) + 300(75) + 350(150) + 500(120)}{80 + 75 + 150 + 120}$$
$$= 346$$

Step 3: Locate the coordinate (x=186.5, y = 346) on the grid map. This is the optimal site for the distribution center.

Step 4: Analysis: Further analysis of this area would be required to determine if there is a suitable physical site in that general area. Does it have the infrastructure and other site requirements? Location factor analysis would still have to be conducted at this point.

S2.   Peter's Piping Place is looking to relocate. They have four suppliers to their company. They want to locate near all four, but closer to their two main suppliers. With the following information provided, where should Peter's Piping Place move?

Suppliers	A	B	C	D
X	100	250	200	150
Y	200	100	300	250
Weight	150	60	125	40

Solution:

Step 1:   Calculate the X coordinate for the Center of Gravity site using the formula below. The X coordinate is at point 163.

$$X = \frac{\sum X_i W_i}{\sum W_i} = \frac{100(150) + 250(60) + 200(125) + 150(40)}{150 + 60 + 125 + 40}$$
$$= 163$$

Step 2:   Calculate the Y coordinate for the Center of Gravity site using the formula below. The Y coordinate is at point 346.

$$Y = \frac{\sum Y_i W_i}{\sum W_i} = \frac{100(200) + 100(60) + 300(125) + 250(40)}{150 + 60 + 125 + 40}$$
$$= 223$$

Step 3:   Locate the coordinate (x=163, y = 223) on the grid map. This is the optimal site for the new facility.

Step 4:   Analysis: Further analysis of this area would be required to determine if there is a suitable physical site in that general area. Does it have the infrastructure and other site requirements? Location factor analysis would still have to be conducted at this point.

S3.   Shelley's Spacewalk does birthday parties in 3 areas of town. To increase business, the company wants to build a storage center to place the spacewalks in order to be more efficient for each party. Where should the storage center be located?

Area	A	B	C
X	150	117	103
Y	105	99	116
Weight	75	95	100

Solution:

Step 1:   Calculate the X coordinate for the Center of Gravity site using the formula below. The X coordinate is at point 120.98.

$$X = \frac{\sum X_i W_i}{\sum W_i} = \frac{150(75) + 117(95) + 103(100)}{75 + 95 + 100}$$
$$= 120.98$$

Step 2:   Calculate the Y coordinate for the Center of Gravity site using the formula below. The Y coordinate is at point 106.96.

$$Y = \frac{\sum Y_i W_i}{\sum W_i} = \frac{150(75) + 117(95) + 103(100)}{75 + 95 + 100}$$
$$= 106.96$$

Step 3:   Locate the coordinate (x=120.98, y=106.98) on the grid map. This is the optimal site for the storage area.

Step 4:   Analysis: Further analysis of this area would be required to determine if there is a suitable physical site in that general area. Does it have the infrastructure and other site requirements? Location factor analysis would still have to be conducted at this point.

1. Fish USA raises fish in five locations throughout the country based on the ideal conditions that are needed. The mature fish will be shipped from a new, centralized warehouse whose location is to be determined. The monthly quantities to be shipped to each location are the same. A coordinator system has been established, and the coordinates of each location have been determined as shown. Determine the coordinates of the centralized warehouse.

Location	(X, Y)
A	7, 9
B	2, 8
C	6, 2
D	1, 9
E	5, 5

2. A swimsuit manufacturer produces women's suits at four locations in Europe. The manager plotted the relative locations of the facilities, and they are shown in the table below. The location of a central shipping point for materials must now be determined. Monthly quantities to be shipped to each location are shown below. Determine the coordinates of the location that will minimize distribution costs.

Location	(X, Y)	Monthly Quantity
A	7, 9	1500
B	2, 8	2000
C	6, 2	2550
D	1, 9	3050

3. The local gasoline distributor, LA Fuel Source, wants to minimize the shipping cost for shipments to the five gas stations it operates. Given the locations of the gas stations and the volumes to be shipped daily, determine the location of the distributor's new pump station.

(X, Y)	Monthly Quantity
5, 8	260
4, 10	900
7, 20	250
6, 10	300
8, 15	400

4. Using the center of gravity technique, determine MallCorp's new southeast regional warehouse for the destinations shown on the following map. Bimonthly shipments will be the quantities listed in the table.

Destination	Quantity	(x,y)
D1	450	100, 200
D2	500	300, 100
D3	350	400, 200
D4	250	200, 400
D5	550	500, 300

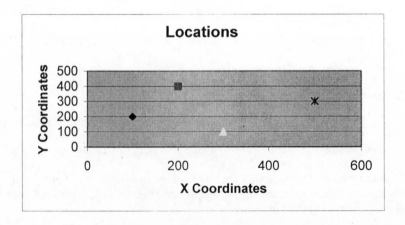

5. EnviroChem wants to build a new storage facility in New Orleans. In order to get materials, people, and parts to the facility economically, the facility needs to be in the vicinity of the Interstate 10 and Interstate 55 interchanges, the Port of New Orleans, and the New Orleans International Airport. The coordinates of these four sites and the number of weekly packages that flow to each are as follows.

	I-10	I-55	Port	Airport
X	10	15	5	30
Y	25	30	16	14
Weight	1000	750	500	220

Determine the best site using the center of gravity technique.

6. The Cajun International restaurant chain uses a packaging plant to prepare the seasoning ingredients it provides its meal packs. The company is attempting to determine the location for a new plant that will service the five major grocery chains in east Texas. The grid-map coordinates of the five warehouses for the chains and the annual numbers of trucks transported to each warehouse are shown.

Coordinates

Restaurant	X	Y	Annual Shipments
1	300	100	300
2	300	300	255
3	150	350	150
4	300	400	200
5	500	100	185

a. Determine the least cost location using the center of gravity method.
b. Plot the five restaurants and the proposed new distribution center on a grid map.

7. Spec Consulting has been hired to develop a location plan for a new hospital. It is attempting to determine the location that is centrally located. The area where the hospital will be constructed includes four cities, which together have a sizable population base. The grid map coordinates for the four towns and the populations of each are given.

Coordinates

Town	X	Y	Population (10,000s)
River Bend	50	30	6.55
Mt. Francis	60	50	4.25
Sertis	80	10	6.50
Bayou Rim	30	40	5.95

a. Determine the least cost location using the center of gravity method.
b. Plot the five restaurants and the proposed new distribution center on a grid map.

8. Simpleton University is attempting to locate the best site for a new athletic complex. The university administration would like to know what the best location is relative to the three main concentrations of student housing and the main access road to campus for visitors. They will use expected use from each area's population per event. The coordinates of these areas (in yards) and event populations are as follows.

Campus Student Concentrations

	Thomas Hall	Bernard Hall	Henry Hall	College Dr.
X	1500	2000	2500	2700
Y	1750	3200	1200	2500
Weight	5500	7500	8500	11500

Determine the best site using the center of gravity method.

9.   SparkIt, a manufacturer of car spark plugs, is going to build a new warehouse facility to serve its stores in six Louisiana cities—Hammond, Denham Springs, LaPlace, New Orleans, Lafayette, and Alexandria. The coordinates of these cities (in miles), using Baton Rouge, La, as the origin (0,0) of a set of coordinates, and the annual truckloads that supply each city are shown as follows.

	Hammond	Denham Springs	LaPlace	New Orleans	Lake Charles	Alexandria
X	20	5	35	55	100	70
Y	55	15	65	75	65	90
Weight	90	125	100	150	100	75

a.   Determine the best site using the center of gravity method.
b.   Look at a map of Louisiana, and identify the closest town to the grid coordinates developed in part (a).

Looking at the map, can you suggest a better location in the vicinity? Explain your answer.

9

Layout Strategy

I. **The Strategic Importance of Layout Decisions**

  A. One of the key decisions that determines the long run efficiency of operations.

  B. The objective of layout strategy is to develop an economic layout that will meet the firm's competitive requirements.

    1. It establishes competitive priorities.

    2. It supports differentiation, low cost, and rapid response strategies.

  C. Layout design considerations include:

    1. Higher utilization of space, equipment, and people.

    2. Improved flow of information, materials, or people.

    3. Improved employee morale and safer working conditions.

    4. Improved customer/client interaction.

    5. Flexibility.

  D. Layout designs must be viewed as flexible in order to keep pace with the ever-changing, dynamic work environment.

    1. Consider using small, flexible equipment.

    2. In order to make quick and easy changes, operations managers must design flexibility into layouts by cross-training workers, maintaining equipment, keeping investments low, and placing work stations close together.

Lecture Key: *Layout is a critical part of efficient operations management. It helps a business to support its competitive strategies and to make decisions about capacity, processes, flexibility, and costs. In addition, a well-planned layout improves the quality of work life, customer contact, and image.*

II. **Types of Layout**

  A. Layout decisions include the best placement of resources.

  B. Six major types of layout design:

    1. Fixed-position – for use with large, bulky projects.

    2. Process-oriented (job shop or intermittent production) – used with low volume, high variety production.

    3. Office – used to facilitate movement of information by positioning workers, their equipment, and spaces.

    4. Retail – allocates shelf space and responds to customer behavior.

    5. Warehouse – addresses trade-offs between space and material handling.

    6. Product-oriented – positioning based on the best utilization of personnel and machines in a repetitive or continuous production.

  C. Design strategy is more of an art than a skill.

D. Good layout requirements determine:
   1. Material handling equipment – decisions regarding the best equipment to use.
   2. Capacity and space requirements.
   3. Environment and aesthetics – concerned about employee and customer comfort.
   4. Flows of information – communication can be facilitated by an effective layout.
   5. Cost of moving between various work areas.

Layout Strategies

Project (Fixed Position)	Job Shop (Process Oriented)	Office	Retail	Warehouse (Storage)	Repetitive/ Continuous (Product Oriented)
Examples					
Ingall Ship Building Corp. Trump Plaza Pittsburgh Airport	Shouldice Hospital Hard Rock Cafes	Allstate Insurance Microsoft Corp.	Kroger's Supermarket Walgreens Bloomingdales	Federal-Mogul's warehouse The Gap's distribution center	Sony's TV assembly line Dodge Caravan minivans
Problem					
Move material to the limited storage areas around the site	Manage varied material flow for each product	Locate workers requiring frequent contact close to one another	Expose customer to high-margin items	Balance low-cost storage with low-cost material handling	Equalize the task time at each workstation

Lecture Key: *An efficient layout strategy focuses on the best methods to integrate the flow of materials, people, and information within and between areas to accomplish the business mission. Choices of layout strategy are generally bound by the nature of the business and its competitive strategy. However, all layout strategies include the five basic decisions outlined above. Since many layouts cannot be mathematically modeled, the decisions concerning layouts have developed into an art.*

III.   Fixed-Position Layout

A. Stationary or large bulky projects (Ex: ships, bridges, houses, oil wells)
   1. Remains in one place.
   2. Workers and equipment come to one work area.
B. Three complications associated with fixed-position layouts:
   1. Limited space.
   2. Different items become critical as the project progresses.
   3. Material needs volume is dynamic.
C. A variety of methods are used to handle complications.
   1. Shift assignment of space to crafts on as needed basis as project progresses.
   2. Complete portions of project off-site.

Lecture Key: *Challenges include the handling of dynamic volumes of materials for multiple crafts and limited storage space. These challenges are often met with less than optimal solutions and require great attention to insure the project is not delayed due to materials logistics. Storage constraints are often resolved by completing portions of the project off-site. Managers will focus on scheduling and coordination of segments within the process.*

IV. Process-Oriented Layout

A. Designed for low-volume, high variety productions
   1. A job-shop environment; each output can undergo a different sequence of operations.
      a. Processes are organized around equipment, skills, and management (Ex. Hospital emergency room).
      b. Most efficient for handling products/services that have a variety of requirements/needs.
   2. Advantages of Process-Oriented Layout
      a. Flexibility in equipment and labor assignments (Ex: A breakdown in one part of the process does not shut down the entire process).
      b. Good for small batch manufacturing operations.
   3. Disadvantages of Process-Oriented Layout
      a. General-purpose use of equipment.
      b. Orders take more time to move through the system due to shifting sequences of operation, materials, and people.
      c. Higher labor skills are required to operate general-purpose equipment.
   4. Common tactic for process-oriented layout is to arrange work processes to minimize costs of material handling
      a. Reduce the number of loads moved between sequences of operation.
      b. Reduce the distance between most frequently used sequences of operation.
      c. Cost formula:

$$\text{Minimize cost} = \sum_{i=1}^{n} \sum_{j=1}^{n} X_{ij} C_{ij} \qquad (9\text{-}1)$$

where
n = total number of work centers or departments
i, j = individual departments
X_{ij} = number of loads moved from department i to department j
C_{ij} = cost to move a load between department i and department j

Example: Process Layout

Walters Company management wants to arrange the six departments of its factory in a way that will minimize interdepartmental material handling costs. They make an initial assumption (to simplify the problem) that each department is 20 x 20 feet and that the building is 60 feet long and 40 feet wide. The process layout procedure that they follow involves six steps:

Solution:
Step 1: Construct a "from-to matrix" showing the flow of parts or materials from department to department. See the from-to matrix below:

Load Summary Chart						
From/To:	**Department**					
Depart.	**1**	**2**	**3**	**4**	**5**	**6**
1	---	50	100	0	0	20
2		---	30	50	10	0
3			---	20	0	100
4				---	50	0
5					---	0
6						---

Step 2: Determine the space requirements for each department as shown in the layout below.

Building Dimensions and a Possible Department Layout

	Room 1	Room 2	Room 3	
	Assembly Department (1)	Painting Department (2)	Machine Shop Department (3)	40'
	Receiving Department (4)	Shipping Department (5)	Testing Department (6)	
	Room 4	Room 5	Room 6	

60'

Step 3: Develop an initial schematic diagram showing the sequence of departments through which parts must move. Try to place departments with a heavy flow of materials or parts next to one another.

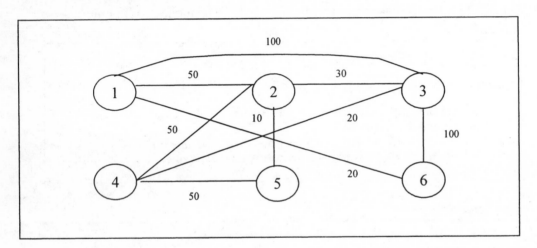

Step 4: Determine the cost of this layout by using the material handling cost equation:

$$Cost = \sum\sum X_{ij} C_{ij}$$

Walters Company assumes that a forklift carries all interdepartmental loads. The cost of moving one load between adjacent departments is estimated to be $1. Moving a load between nonadjacent departments costs $2. Looking at the from-to matrix, we see that the handling cost between departments 1 and 2 is $50 ($1 x 50 loads), $200 between departments 1 and 3 ($2 x 100 loads), $40 between departments 1 and 6 ($2 x 20 loads), and so on. Rooms that are diagonal to one another, such as 2 and 4, are treated as adjacent. The total cost for the layout shown in the diagram above is:

Cost = $50 (1 and 2) + $200 (1 and 3) + $40 (1 and 6) + $30 (2 and 3) + $50 (2 and 4)
  + $10 (2 and 5) + $40 (3 and 4) + $100 (3 and 6) + $50 (4 and 5)
  = $570

Step 5: Using a trial and error approach, try to improve the current layout. Looking at the current layout to determine the most important relationships is the first task. Departments 1 and 3 need to be close together since they have the largest loads between them (100). Also, they are currently non-adjacent, so moving them closer should reduce overall expense.

So, it may be possible to switch departments 1 and 2. You would then redo the department diagram and determine the cost of this arrangement.

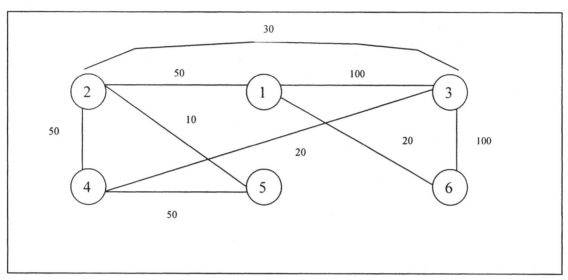

Cost = $50 (1 and 2) + $100 (1 and 3) + $20 (1 and 6) + $60 (2 and 3) + $50 (2 and 4)
    + $10 (2 and 5) + $40 (3 and 4) + $100 (3 and 6) + $50 (4 and 5)
    = $480

Analysis: By moving the positions of 1 and 3, this resulted in a $90 reduction in material handling cost. It should be noted that this is only one of several possible changes. In this particular problem, there are a total of 720 potential combinations.

  B. Computer Software for Process-Oriented Layouts
    1. Much more efficient for larger problems.
    2. Produces good but not always optimal solutions.
    3. Different programs
      a. CRAFT – best known
        i. Computerized Relative Allocation of Facilities Technique
        ii. Good results, not always optimal
      b. ALDEP – Automated Layout Design Program
      c. CORELAP – Computerized Relationship Layout Planning
      d. Factory Flow
  C. Work Cells
    1. A temporary product-oriented arrangement of machines and personnel.
      a. Reorganizes people and machines that would normally be dispersed in different process departments.
      b. Focuses on making a single product or group of related products.
      c. Used in 40% of U.S. plants with less than 100 employees and 74% of large plants.
    2. Used when volume warrants special machinery and equipment arrangements.

3. Advantages:
   a. Reduced work-in-process inventory
   b. Less floor space required
   c. Reduced raw material and finished goods inventories
   d. Reduced direct labor costs
   e. Heightened sense of employee participation
   f. Increased use of equipment and machinery
   g. Reduced equipment and machinery investment
4. Requirements for cellular planning:
   a. Identification of product families
   b. High level of training and flexibility by employees
   c. Staff support or flexible, imaginative employees
   d. Tests at each station in the cell
5. U-shaped cells are used and provide several advantages:
   a. Immediate inspection
   b. Fewer workers needed
   c. Workers can reach more of the work area
   d. Efficiently balanced work
   e. Enhanced communication

Improving Layouts by Moving to the Work Cell Concept

Note in both (a) and (b) that U-shaped work cells can reduce material and employee movement. The U shape may also reduce space requirements, enhance communication, cut the number of workers, and make inspection easier.

(a)

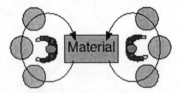

Current layout—workers in small closed areas. Cannot increase output without a third worker.

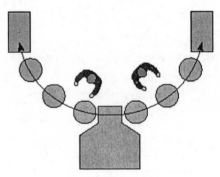

Improved layout—workers can assist each other. May be able to add a third worker.

(b)

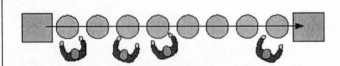

Current layout—straight lines make it hard to balance tasks because workers may not be able to divide tasks evenly.

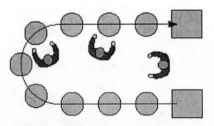

Improved layout—in U shape, workers have better access. Four workers were reduced to three.

188

D. The Focused Work Center and the Focused Factory
   1. Permanent or semi-permanent arrangement of machines and personnel from general-purpose, process-oriented facility to large work cell within a facility.
   2. Used when a firm identifies a large family of similar products that have a large, stable demand.
   3. Advantages include better ability to stay in tune with customers, higher quality of products, and higher margins.
   4. Focused factory is in a separate location.

Lecture Key: *Managers use a process-oriented layout in environments where there is low-volume and high-variety manufacturing or services. Grouping together tasks and the equipment needed to perform those tasks attains efficiency of the work system. Also, by reducing the space between interrelated departments, firms can reduce costs associated with the movement of materials between departments.*

V. **Office Layout**

   A. Importance is placed on the flow and availability of information.
      1. Managers should examine:
         a. Electronic communication patterns.
         b. Conventional communication patterns.
         c. Separation needs.
         d. Other factors affecting effectiveness.
      2. A relationship chart is a useful tool for layout need analysis.
   B. Flexibility
      1. Is important in offices as well as a factory environment.
      2. Is becoming a necessity because of constant technological changes.
   C. General office guidelines
      1. Space per person (not universal):
         a. 100 square feet per office worker
         b. 400 square feet per executive
         c. 25 square feet per person for a conference room
      2. Designers are expanding upwards instead of outwards by making use of the vertical dimensions of workstations. Attempting to keep workstation "footprint" to a minimum.
   D. Two major trends leading to a reduction of employees needed on premises
      1. Increased use of technology – allows for greater flexibility in information movement.
      2. Virtual companies – reduces the necessity for on-site employees.

Office Relationship Chart

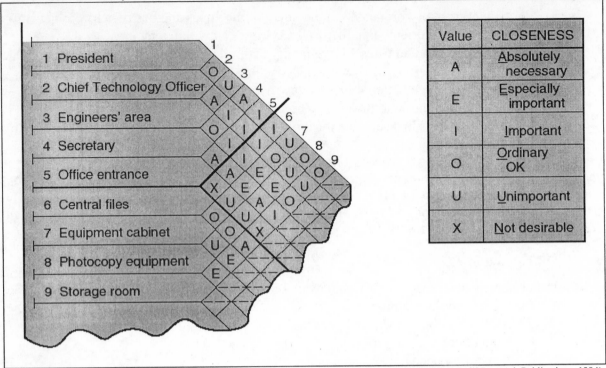

Value	CLOSENESS
A	Absolutely necessary
E	Especially important
I	Important
O	Ordinary OK
U	Unimportant
X	Not desirable

Source: Adapted from Richard Muther, *Simplified Systematic Layout Planning*, 3rd ed. (Kansas City, Mgt. & Ind'l Research Publications, 1994). Used by permission of the publisher.

Lecture Key: *Office layouts are based on creating efficiency through access to information. By analyzing an office through the use of tools such as a relationship chart, managers can prioritize office layouts. Increasing technology is resulting in an increase for both the need and the ability to create more flexible office environments.*

VI.   Retail Layout

   A. Profitability varies directly with customer exposure to products, so it is very important to expose customers to as many products as possible. Main objective is to maximize profitability per square foot of floor space. Increasing the rate of exposure leads to sales and higher return on investment. Addresses flow, allocates space, and responds to customer behavior.

   B. Ideas helpful for determining the overall arrangement of stores:

      1. Locate high-draw items around the periphery of the store.

         Ex: Dairy products and bread on opposite sides of a grocery store.

      2. Use prominent locations for high-impulse and high-margin items.

         Ex: Housewares, beauty aides, and shampoo.

      3. Distribute "power items" to opposite sides of an isle and disperse them to increase the viewing of other items.

        a. Power items – items that dominate a purchasing trip.

      4. Use end-of-aisle locations for items needing high exposure.

      5. Convey the store mission of the store by careful selection of the leadoff department.

        Ex: Wine in front of a liquor store specializing in fine wines.

   C. Slotting fees

      1. Fees paid by manufacturers for prime product placement in stores.

      2. Controversial topic due to questions regarding legality and ethics of such practices. Fees may stifle new products, limit their ability to expand, and cost consumers money.

D. Servicescapes
1. The physical surroundings in which a service takes place and how they have a humanistic effect on customers and employees.
2. Types:
a. Ambient conditions – background characteristics such as lighting, sound, smell, and temperature. Effects can include how much is spent and how long someone stays in the building. Ex: Fine-dining restaurant with tablecloths and candlelight.
b. Spatial layout and functionality – customer circulation, aisle characteristics such as width, direction, angle, shelf-spacing, and product groupings. Ex: High grocery store shelves and long aisles.
c. Signs, symbols, and artifacts – building design characteristics that carry social significance such as carpeted areas that encourage shoppers to slow down and browse. Ex: Wal-Mart's greeters.

Lecture Key: The retail layout strategy is used in settings where it is believed that customer exposure to products is directly related to sales and profitability. Operational managers attempt to design a store layout by determining how they can expose customers to as many products as possible while taking into consideration factors such as customer flow and behavior as well as space allocation. The main objective to this approach is maximizing profitability per square foot of floor space.

VII. **Warehousing and Storage Layouts**

A. Goal of warehousing and storage layouts is to minimize costs by finding the optimum trade-off between handling and warehousing costs.
1. Management tries to maximize the utilization of the warehouse's full volume while maintaining low material handling costs.
2. Material handling costs – all costs related to incoming transport, storage, and outgoing transport of stored materials, including equipment, people, materials, supervision, insurance, and depreciation.
B. Management tries to minimize the sum of resources spent on finding and retrieving material plus any deterioration and damage to the material.
C. Focus of the layout is on the relationship between the receiving/unloading area and the shipping/loading area.
D. Cross docking
1. Received products are immediately processed.
2. Eliminates the need for formal receiving, stocking, storing, and order-selection activities.
3. Requires tight scheduling and shipments need accurate identification.
4. The elimination of storage is a full cost savings.
5. Very similar to JIT in principle.
E. Random stocking
1. Randomly located inventory, which is controlled by automatic identification systems (AISs).
2. Management information systems allow users to locate and track inventory.
3. Space does not need to be reserved for specific items.
4. Computerized random stocking includes:
a. Maintaining a list of open locations.
b. Maintaining accurate records of existing inventory and its locations.
c. Sequencing items on orders.
d. Combining orders.
e. Minimizing travel distance for frequently used items.

F. Customizing
  1. Allows products to be customized at the warehouses where materials are stored.
  2. Allows a competitive advantage in markets with rapidly changing products.
  3. Often located next to major airports or other transportation hubs to facilitate quick delivery.

Lecture Key: *The main goal of warehouse layouts is to minimize total costs by finding the optimum trade-off between handing costs and warehouse space costs. Stacking vertically can maximize space. Through methods such as cross-docking, random stocking, and warehouse customization, businesses can reduce costs and improve efficiency based on their particular needs.*

VIII. Repetitive and Product-Oriented Layout

A. Facility organized around products of similar high volume, low variety products.
B. Goal is to create a smooth, continuous flow along assembly line and minimize idle time between workstations.
C. Assumptions of Product-Oriented Layout
  1. Volume is adequate for high equipment utilization.
  2. Product demand is stable enough to justify high investment in specialized equipment.
  3. Product is standardized or justifies investment in specialized equipment.
  4. Supplies of raw materials and components are adequate and of uniform quality.
D. Types of Product-Oriented Layout
  1. Fabrication Line – Machine-paced, product-oriented facility for building components in a series.
  2. Assembly Line – An approach that puts fabricated parts together at a series of workstations; used in repetitive processes.
E. Assembly Line Balancing
  1. The line must be balanced in both lines.
    a. Fabrication line – time spent to perform work on one machine must equal or balance the time spent to perform work on the next machine.
    b. Assembly line – balance can be achieved by moving tasks from one individual to another.
  2. The central problem is to balance the output at each workstation on the production line while obtaining the desired amount of output.
F. Management's goal is to create smooth, continuous flow along the assembly line with a minimal amount of idle time. A well-balanced assembly line has the advantage of high personnel and facility utilization and equity between employees' workloads.

An Assembly-Line Layout

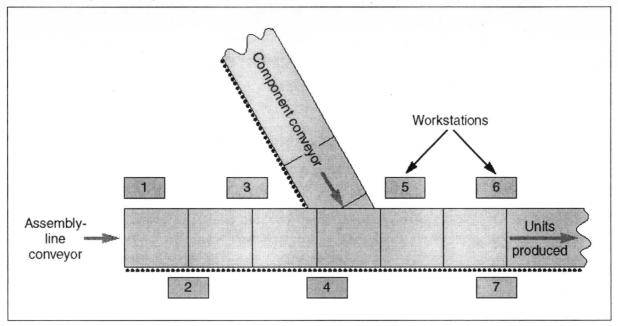

G. Advantages of Product-Oriented Layout:
1. Low variable cost per unit
2. Low material handling costs
3. Reduced work in processing inventories
4. Easier training and supervision
5. Rapid throughput
H. Disadvantages of Product-Oriented Layout:
1. High volume is required
2. Work stoppage at any one point ties up entire operation
3. Lack of flexibility
I. Assembly Line Balancing is used to minimize imbalance between machines or personnel while meeting a required output from the line. To produce at a specified rate, management must know the tools used, equipment used, work methods used, and precedence relationships among activities.
J. Steps for Line Balancing:
1. Determine tasks.
2. Determine sequence.
3. Draw precedence diagram.
4. Estimate task times.
5. Calculate cycle time.

$$\text{Cycle Time} = \frac{\text{production time available per day}}{\text{units required per day}}$$

6. Calculate number of workstations.
7. Assign tasks.
   a. Layout heuristics may be used.
8. Calculate efficiency.

We want to develop a precedence diagram for an electrostatic copier that requires a total assembly time of 66 minutes. The table below gives the tasks, performance times, and precedence relationships.

Task	Performance Time (min.)	Preceding Task
A	10	---
B	11	A
C	5	B
D	4	B
E	12	A
F	3	C, D
G	7	F
H	11	E
I	3	G, H
Total Time:	66	

Solution:

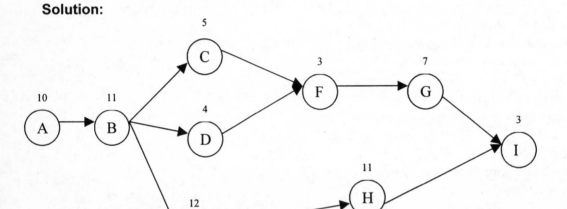

194

On the basis of the precedence diagram and activity times given in the previous example, the firm determines that there are 480 productive minutes of work available per day. Furthermore, the production schedule requires that 40 units be completed as output from the assembly line each day. Thus:

Solution:

Step 1: Calculate the cycle time.

$$\text{Cycle Time (in minutes)} \;=\; 480 \text{ min.} \,/\, 40 \text{ units} \;=\; 12 \text{ minutes / unit}$$

Step 2: Minimum number of workstations.

$$
\begin{aligned}
\text{Minimum number of workstations} \;&=\; \text{total task time / cycle time}\\
&=\; 66 \text{ min.} \,/\, 12 \text{ min. per unit}\\
&=\; 5.5 \text{ or } 6 \text{ stations}
\end{aligned}
$$

Step 3: Use the most following heuristic to assign jobs to workstations.

Station:	Remaining Time	Will Fit	Assign	Idle Time
I	12 min.	A	A (10 min.)	2 min.
II	12 min.	B, E	B (11 min.)	1 min.
III	12 min.	E, C, D	E (12 min.)	0 min.
IV	12 min.	C, D	C (5 min.)	7 min.
		D	D (4 min.)	3 min.
		F	F (3 min.)	0 min.
V	12 min.	G, H	H (11 min.)	1 min.
VI	12 min.	G	G (7 min.)	5 min.
		I	I (3 min.)	2 min.

The table above shows one solution that does not violate the sequence requirements and that groups tasks into six stations. To obtain this solution, activities with the most following tasks were moved into workstations to use as much of the available cycle time of 12 minutes as possible. The first workstation consumes 10 minutes and has an idle time of 2 minutes.

The second workstation uses 11 minutes, and the third consumes the full 12 minutes. The fourth workstation groups 3 small tasks and balances perfectly at 12 minutes. The fifth has 1 minute of idle time, and the sixth (consisting of tasks G and I) has 2 minutes of idle time per cycle. Total idle time for this solution is 6 minutes per cycle.

Example: Assembly Line Efficiency

We can calculate the balance efficiency for the previous example as follows:

Solution:

Efficiency = $\sum$ task times / (actual # of workstations) x (assigned cycle time)

= 66 min. / (6 stations x 12 minutes) = 91.7%

Note that opening a seventh workstation, for whatever reason, would decrease the efficiency of the balance to 78.6%.

Efficiency = 66 min. / (7 stations x 12 minutes) = 78.6%

K. Solved by computers
1. COMSOAL
2. ASYBL

Lecture Key: *Product-oriented layouts are organized around products or families of similar high volume, low variety products. The output at each workstation must be balanced. This helps create a smooth flow while minimizing idle time at each workstation. The ideal layout is found by knowledge of the task and its components along with problem solving, either mathematically or through the use of heuristics.*

CHAPTER 9 PROBLEMS

Process Layouts

S1. Lancing Nursery sells garden and landscape material. The landscape material is stored behind the store in a lot. They also produce soil mixtures for special needs. The arrangement of the five materials is: top soil in bin 1, dirt in bin 2, gravel in bin 3, sand in bin 4, and compost in bin 5. The average number of loads transported between the five bins per week is given in the accompanying load summary chart. The current layout of the facility is shown schematically on the 2 x 3 grid. Notice that there is quite a bit of flexibility in the facility, as indicated by the six possible locations (i.e., intersections) available for five bins. In addition, the front-end loader used in the yard is very flexible, allowing horizontal, vertical, and diagonal movement of material since there is a road down the middle.

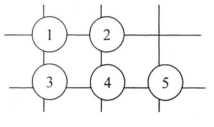

Load Summary Chart					
From/To:	Bin				
Bin	1	2	3	4	5
1	---	20	2	15	10
2	5	---	2	12	15
3			---	4	0
4	7	10	20	---	8
5					---

Lancing wants to determine if this is the best layout by:
a. Evaluating the current layout in terms of nonadjacent loads.
b. If needed, proposing a new layout on a 2 x 3 grid that will minimize the number of nonadjacent loads.

Solution:

Step 1: Calculate the composite movements. These are the back-and-forth movements between bins. For example, the composite movement between bin 1 and bin 2 is the number of movements going from bin 1 to bin 2 (20 loads) plus the number of movements from bin 2 to bin 1 (5 loads). So, the number of composite movements would be 20 + 5, or 25. The remaining composite movements are listed below in the table.

Step 2: Rank the composite movements from highest to lowest. Moving to and from between bin 1 and 2 is the highest rank, so it goes first in the list. The following table contains the results:

Composite Movements			Composite Movements	
1 ------ 2	25 loads		1 ------ 5	10 loads
3 ------ 4	24 loads		4 ------ 5	8 loads
1 ------ 4	22 loads		1 ------ 3	2 loads
2 ------ 5	15 loads		2 ------ 3	2 loads
2 ------ 4	12 loads		3 ------ 5	0 loads

Step 3: Analysis: The higher the composite movements, the closer the work centers need to be.

Step 4: Evaluate the "goodness" of the layout by scoring it in terms of nonadjacent loads. The results are shown visually in grid 1.

Step 5: Identify the adjacent and nonadjacent moves in the layout. The adjacent moves are marked with a solid line and the nonadjacent moves are shown with a curved dashed line to highlight the fact that material is moved farther than we would like. Following our composite movement list, 2 ◄► 3 and 2 ◄► 4 are adjacent moves, but 1 ◄► 5 is not (This is the only nonadjacent move in this layout). Our nonadjacent score is with 10 loads of material from 1 ◄► 5.

197

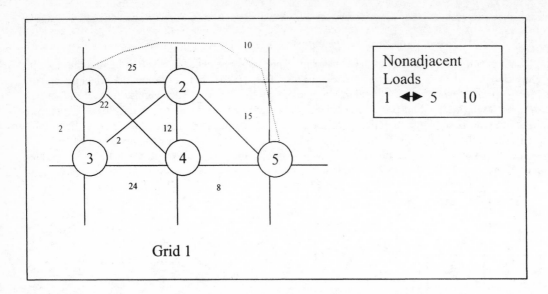

Grid 1

Nonadjacent
Loads
1 ←→ 5   10

Step 6: Try to improve this layout. By looking at the grid and list of composite movements, it can be determined that bins 2 and 4 should be located adjacent to bin 1, and that bins 1 and 2 may be located away from bin 3 without adding to the score of nonadjacent loads. We can improve this layout by switching the positions of bins 3 and 5 and/or moving bin 3 across the road. By doing so, the nonadjacent load score is reduced to 2 since the nonadjacent move is going from bin 3 to bin 1. The grid below represents the optimal layout with a nonadjacent score of 2.

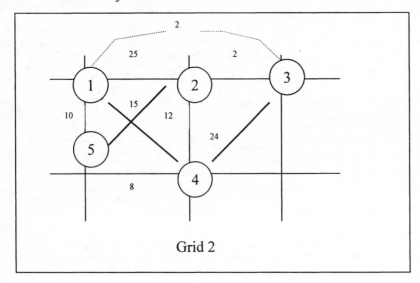

Grid 2

S2.   Griffin International has a sheet metal fabrication facility with a variety of different machines that are used to produce customized products. Each machine is the focus of a different work center. The work centers are assigned to positions within the facility. Work center 1 has a large cutting tool to process large pieces of large material. Due to the nature of the material size, this work center is located near the large roll up door by location A of the facility. The following information will help you in your analysis of how to assign work centers to positions within the facility. What is the best layout for Griffin?

Load Summary Chart						
From/To:	**Department**					
Department	1	2	3	4	5	6
1	---	90	25	23	11	18
2	35	---	8	5	10	16
3	37	2	---	1	0	7
4	41	12	1	---	4	0
5	14	16	0	9	---	3
6	32	38	13	2	2	---

Work Center Positions		
A	B	C
D	E	F

Solution:

Step 1:   Calculate the composite movements. These are the back-and-forth movements between work centers. For example, the composite movement between work center 1 and work center 2 is the number of movements going from work center 1 to work center 2 (90 loads) plus the number of movements from work center 2 to work center 1 (35 loads). So, the number of composite movements would be 90 + 35, or 125. The remaining composite movements are listed below in the table.

Step 2:   Rank the composite movements from highest to lowest. Moving to and fro between work centers 1 and 2 is the highest rank, so it goes first in the list. The following table contains the results:

Composite Movements		Composite Movements	
1 --- 2	125 loads	2 --- 4	17 loads
1 --- 4	64 loads	4 --- 5	13 loads
1 --- 3	62 loads	2 --- 3	10 loads
2 --- 6	54 loads	5 --- 6	5 loads
1 --- 6	50 loads	3 --- 4	2 loads
2 --- 5	26 loads	4 --- 6	2 loads
1 --- 5	25 loads	3 --- 5	0 loads
3 --- 6	20 loads		

Step 3:   Analysis: The higher the composite movements, the closer the work centers need to be.

Step 4:   Evaluate the current location and where the work centers should be assigned. Remember that work center 6 has to go in location A due to the constraint of the door. The grid will visually represent the location and initial assignment.

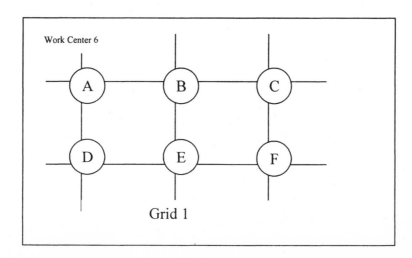

Grid 1

Step 5: Determine the assignment. Looking at the composite movements table, work centers 1 and 2 need to be next to each other due to the high composite movements. Position B and E may be a good fit.

Step 6: See the next highest scores and how they relate to the current assignment and possible assignments. The next highest is 1-3 and 1-4. I want to look at 3-4 to see how it would relate. 3-4 is low, so they don't need to be close, so 3 and 4 would be on either side of work center 1. Suggestion may be if work center is in position E, then D and F may be possibilities.

Step 7: Determine if 3 or 4 should be in position D. Look at the movements between work center 6 and 3 or 4. Movement between 3-6 is 20 loads, and 4-6 is 2 loads. So, it is more important for 3 to be closer to 6, and since 6 is fixed in position A, work center 3 would be assigned to position D.

Step 8: Recap the assignment possibilities in order of assigning work centers.

Position A	Work Center 6
Position E	Work Center 1
Position D	Work Center 3
Position F	Work Center 4
Position B	Work Center 2

Step 9: The only work center remaining is number 5, so it is assigned to the only open position, C. The grid below represents the positioning of the work centers within the facility and the loads between the work centers.

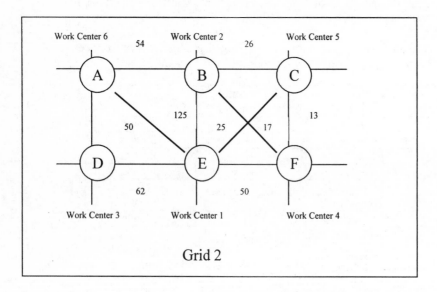

Grid 2

1. Capital City Deli Market is interested in improving its layout to better serve customers and improve its sales and profits. A from-to matrix showing weekly average trips between departments is shown below as well as their current layout. Capital City Deli is looking at the possibility exchanging the locations of the dry groceries department (A) and the health aids department (F). Calculate the load-distance (ld) score for Capital City's current and proposed layouts. Explain which is better.

A	12	20	25	10	50
B		40	25	25	40
C			34	30	20
D				45	15
E					30
F					

A	B	C
D	E	F

Current Layout

F	B	C
D	E	A

Proposed Layout

200

2.   For Problem 1, find an improved layout for the Capital City Deli Market.
      For example, try:

A	C	D
F	B	E

By means of a table, show load-distance calculations for both the current and improved layouts.

3.   Sparkle Manufacturing is a pool part manufacturer and is redesigning its layout. The from-to matrix of the numbers of trips between departments is shown below.

Department	Trips Between Departments					
	1	2	3	4	5	6
1	---	20	25	---	---	50
2		---	---	15	10	35
3			---	40	---	10
4				---	---	25
5					---	
6						---

The current layout is shown below. Find an improved layout using trial and error.

Which departments should you locate close together?

Current layout for Sparkle Manufacturing.

1	2	3
4	5	6

4.   Capital City Hospital serves a local community of about 200,000 in southern Louisiana. Capital City Hospital provides a variety of services: research, radiology, laboratory, examining rooms, surgery, and visitation. The hospital would like to find an improved layout.

A – Radiology	B – Research	C – Examining Rooms
D – Surgery / Recovery	E – Physical Therapy	F – Visitation

From-To Matrix for Capital City Hospital

Department	Patient Moves Between Departments					
	A	B	C	D	E	F
A	---	40	45	---	---	70
B		---	---	35	30	55
C			---	60	---	30
D				---	---	45
E					---	
F						---

5. Fine Body Needs is a specialty store for teenagers and young adult women. The retailer is in the process of assigning storage areas in its warehouse in order to minimize the number of trips made to retrieve items needed. Given below are the departments that need to be located, the number of trips made per week for each department, and the area needed by each department.

Department	Trips To and From Dock	Area Needed
Skin care	270	3
Hair care	160	2
Makeup	120	1
Bath	100	1
Clothing	150	3

	Storage	Storage	Storage	Storage	Storage
Dock	Aisle				
	Storage	Storage	Storage	Storage	Storage

6. Extreme Cold, a manufacturer of equipment that is cold resistant, has plants located in the northwestern part of United States. One of their plants in Salem is having difficulty in coping with the customer's orders. The management wants to improve providing products to its clients and desires to enhance the plant layout and reduce the congestion and wait times some orders experience. The following matrix provides frequency of contacts between financial planners during a typical day.

A		B		C
	D		E	

Frequency of Contacts Between Clients and Financial Planners

Machine	A	B	C	D	E
A	---	10	15	8	7
B		---	9	10	22
C			---	14	11
D				---	15
E					---

7. Snack & Go distribution warehouse is recently having problems in delivering goods to its regional stores. Snack & Go packages quick snacks for convenience. These products have a relatively short shelf life. Frequent delays, especially due to poor layout, is becoming a common occurrence. Both current layout and trips between departments in a typical day is given below.

4		2		1
	3		5	

From-To Matrix for Snack & Go's Warehouse

Department	1	2	3	4	5
1	---	45	35	18	10
2		---	19	20	12
3			---	34	19
4				---	15
5					---

8. Lightforce electronics store sells the latest electronic goods and accessories. The different types of items are stored in departments that take up the same amount of space. Given the available warehouse space specified in the diagram and a from-to matrix showing the number of trips to and from each department in the tables, help Lightforce decide where to store each type of electronic goods and accessories.

	2	4	5
Dock			
	6	1	3

Department	Category	Trips To and From Dock
A	Computers	40
B	Digital Cameras	45
C	DVDs	15
D	Camcorders	30
E	TVs	50
F	Small Electronics	70

Line Balancing

S1. Sleek & Smooth Skincare decided to market a new product. It is a new hydrating lotion with moisturizing beads to help soften the skin. This will be produced in the same fashion as other products that are distributed. It will be produced in an assembly line format. The cycle time is desired to meet a demand of 480 units with an operating time of 480 min/day. Use the most # following as the decision rule. From the information below, construct a network diagram; calculate cycle time, theoretical minimum number of workstations, the total amount of idle time, the percent of idle time, and the efficiency level.

Task	Time	Immediately Preceding
A	.7	---
B	.9	A
C	.2	B
D	.6	---
E	1.0	D
F	.5	C,E
G	.4	F

Step 1: Draw the precedence diagram. Elements A and D have no elements preceding them, so nodes A and D are connected to the Start node (dummy node representing beginning of the project). From the table above, it can be determined that Element A precedes Element B, so the line segment that begins at node A must end at node B. The remaining diagram is represented below.

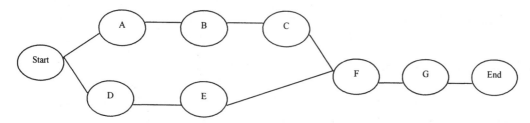

Step 2: Calculate the desired cycle time. To calculate the desired cycle time use the formula, production time (480 minutes per day) divided by the number of units of production. This will be:

$$(C_d) = \frac{\text{production time available}}{\text{desired units of output}} = \frac{480 \text{ min.}}{480 \text{ units}} = 1.0 \text{ minutes}$$

Evaluate if this is a feasible time by seeing if it is equal to or more than the minimum cycle time possible (longest task in process). The minimum is 1.0, so we can continue.

Step 3: Calculate the theoretical minimum number of workstations. Use the formula total element times (4.3 minutes) divided by the desired cycle time (1.0). This gives you 4.3 stations as the minimum possible as illustrated below.

$$N = \frac{\Sigma t_i}{C_d} = \frac{.7 + .9 + .2 + .6 + 1.0 + .5 + .4}{1.0} = \frac{4.3}{1.0} = 4.3 \text{ workstations}$$

Since we cannot have half a workstation (or any portion of a workstation), we round up to 5 workstations. We must group elements into workstations so that the sum of the element time at each workstation is less than or equal to the desired cycle time of 1.0 minute.

Step 4: Assign elements to workstations. To help evaluate the options, a table was set up with the Station number, the remaining time in the station (a element cannot be assigned to a station if its completion time is greater than the remaining time in the station), the elements that will fit (determine all possible elements that are eligible for the station given that their preceding events have been completed and the element time is less than the remaining time in the station, the element that has been assigned, and the idle time in the station after the element was assigned to the station).

Step 5: Open Station I. Before any element is assigned to the station, the remaining time in the station is equal to the desired cycle time (1.0 minutes).

Step 6: Determine the elements that will fit. First look at the precedence diagram.

Elements A and D have no preceding events, so they meet the first criteria (all preceding events have been completed or there are no preceding events). Element B is not eligible, because Element A has not been assigned. Second, A's time (0.7 minutes) is less than the remaining time in the station, so A would go into the Will Fit column. D's time (0.6) is less than the remaining time in the station (1.0), so it would go into the Will Fit column.

Assign Station	Remain Time	Will Fit	Assign	Idle Time
I	1.0	A,D		

Step 7: Assign element to Station 1. The two choices are Elements A and D. You have to make a decision about which to assign first. To help, the problem says to assign tasks using the most number of activities following the element in the diagram. A has 4 activities that have to be completed after it (B, C, F, and G). D has 3 activities after it (E, F, and G). Since A has more, it is assigned first and put in Station 1.

Step 8: Calculate the idle time in the station after Element A has been assigned. This is done by subtracting A's time (0.7) from the remaining time in the station (1.0), so the idle time is 0.3.

Assign Station	Remain Time	Will Fit	Assign	Idle Time
I	1.0	A,D	A	0.3

Step 9: Now, the idle time (0.3) becomes the remaining time in the station.

Assign Station	Remain Time	Will Fit	Assign	Idle Time
I	1.0	A,D	A	0.3
	0.3			

Step 10: Determine if any other activities will fit in Station I by repeating previous steps.

Element D has no preceding events and Element B's predecessor A is assigned, so they meet the first criteria (all preceding events have been completed or there are no preceding events). Second, B's time (0.9 minutes) and D's time (0.6 minutes) are greater than the remaining time in the station (0.3), so neither would go into the Will Fit column. Station I is now closed since no other elements can be added.

Step 11: Continue the assignment of elements. Open Station 2. Element D has no preceding events and Element B's predecessor A is assigned, so they meet the first criteria (all preceding events have been completed or there are no preceding events). Second, B's time (0.9 minutes) and D's time (0.6 minutes) are less than the remaining time in the station (1.0), so both would go into the Will Fit column.

Assign Station	Remain Time	Will Fit	Assign	Idle Time
I	1.0	A,D	A	0.3
	0.3			
II	1.0	D, B		

Step 12: Assign element to Station 2. The two choices are Elements B and D. You have to make a decision about which to assign first. To help, the problem says to assign tasks using the most number of activities following the element in the diagram. B has 3 activities that have to be completed after it (C, F, and G). D has 3 activities after it (E, F, and G). We cannot make a decision based on the number of following. We have to now look at the element time and pick the longest time (B: 0.9; D: 0.6). Since B is longer, it is assigned first and put in Station 2.

Assign Station	Remain Time	Will Fit	Assign	Idle Time
I	1.0	A,D	A	0.3
	0.3			
II	1.0	D, B	B	0.1

Step 13: Calculate the idle time in the station after Element B has been assigned. This is done by subtracting B's time (0.9) from the remaining time in the station (1.0), so the idle time is 0.1.

Step 14: Determine if any other activities will fit in Station 2 by repeating previous steps.

Element D has no preceding events and Element C's predecessor B is assigned, so they meet the first criteria (all preceding events have been completed or there are no preceding events). Second, C's time (0.2 minutes) and D's time (0.6 minutes) are greater than the remaining time in the station (0.3), so neither would go into the Will Fit column. Station 2 is now closed since no other elements can be added.

Step 15: Continue the assignment of elements. Open Station 3. Element D has no preceding events and Element C's predecessor A is assigned, so they meet the first criteria (all preceding events have been completed or there are no preceding events). Second, C's time (0.2 minutes) and D's time (0.6 minutes) are less than the remaining time in the station (1.0), so both would go into the Will Fit column.

Assign Station	Remain Time	Will Fit	Assign	Idle Time
I	1.0	A,D	A	0.3
II	1.0	D, B	B	0.1
III	1.0	C, D	D	0.4
	0.4	C	C	0.2
IV	1.0	E	E	0
V	1.0	F	F	0.5
	0.5	G	G	0.1

Step 16: Analysis: Our assembly line consists of five workstations, arranged as follows:

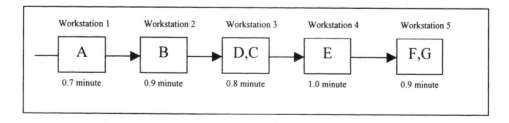

Step 17: Analysis: Since the theoretical minimum number of workstations was five, we know we have balanced the line as efficiently as possible.

Step 18:   Calculate the efficiency of the line. The efficiency is calculated by summing the element times (0.7 + 0.9 + 0.6 + 0.2 + 1.0 + 0.5 + 0.9). Then, divide the total time (4.3) by the product of the number of assigned stations (5) and the cycle time (1.0). The assembly line has an efficiency of :

$$E = \Sigma t_i / n\ (C_a) = (0.7 + 0.9 + 0.6 + 0.2 + 1.0 + 0.5 + 0.4) / (5 * 1.0) = .86\ or\ 86.0\%$$

S2.   Assume the cycle time is to be the minimum length possible. OT = 350 min/day. Use the most number following and then largest cycle time as the decision.

Task	Time	Immediately Preceding	# Following
A	.2	-	3
B	.4	-	3
C	.3	A	2
D	1.3	B	2
E	.1	C,D	1
F	.8	E	0

Solution:

Step 1:   Draw the precedence diagram. Elements A and D have no elements preceding them, so nodes A and D are connected to the Start node (dummy node representing beginning of the project). From the table above, it can be determined that Element A precedes Element B, so the line segment that begins at node A must end at node B. The remaining diagram is represented below.

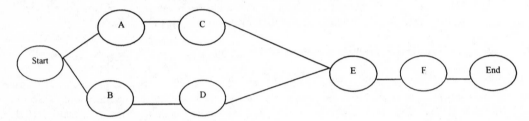

Step 2:   Identify the desired cycle time. The problem says to use the minimum length possible. This is equal to the longest task in the sequence and would maximize output capacity.

   $(C_d) = 1.3$ minutes (Element D)

Step 3:   Calculate the theoretical minimum number of workstations. Use the formula total element times (3.1 minutes) divided by the desired cycle time (1.0). This gives you 2.38 stations as the minimum possible as illustrated below.

$$N = \frac{\Sigma t_i}{C_d} = \frac{.2 + .4 + .3 + 1.3 + 0.1 + .8}{1.3} = \frac{3.1}{1.3} = 2.38\ \text{workstations}$$

   Since we cannot have half a workstation (or any portion of a workstation), we round up to 3 workstations. We must group elements into workstations so that the sum of the element time at each workstation is less than or equal to the desired cycle time of 1.0 minute.

Step 4:   Assign elements to workstations. To help evaluate the options, a table was set up with the Station number, the remaining time in the station (a element cannot be assigned to a station if its completion time is greater than the remaining time in the station), the elements that will fit (determine all possible elements that are eligible for the station given that their preceding events have been completed and the element time is less than the remaining time in the station, the element that has been assigned, and the idle time in the station after the element was assigned to the station).

Step 5:   Open Station I. Before any element is assigned to the station, the remaining time in the station is equal to the desired cycle time (1.3 minutes).

Step 6: Determine the elements that will fit. First, look at the precedence diagram.

Elements A and B have no preceding events, so they meet the first criteria (all preceding events have been completed or there are no preceding events). Second, A's time (0.2 minutes) is less than the remaining time in the station, so A would go into the Will Fit column. B's time (0.4) is less than the remaining time in the station (1.3), so it would go into the Will Fit column.

Assign Station	Remain Time	Will Fit	Assign	Idle Time
I	1.3	A, B		

Step 7: Assign element to Station 1. The two choices are Elements A and B. You have to make a decision about which to assign first. To help, the problem says to assign tasks using the most number of activities following the element in the diagram. A has 3 activities that have to be completed after it (C, E, and F). B has 3 activities after it (D, E, and F). We cannot make a decision based on the number of following. We have to now look at the element time and pick the longest time (A: 0.2; B: 0.4). Since B is longer, it is assigned first and put in Station 1.

Step 8: Calculate the idle time in the station after Element B has been assigned. This is done by subtracting B's time (0.4) from the remaining time in the station (1.3), so the idle time is 0.9.

Assign Station	Remain Time	Will Fit	Assign	Idle Time
I	1.3	A, B	B	0.9

Step 9: Now, the idle time (0.9) becomes the remaining time in the station.

Assign Station	Remain Time	Will Fit	Assign	Idle Time
I	1.3	A, B	B	0.9
	0.9			

Step 10: Determine if any other activities will fit in Station I by repeating previous steps.

Element A has no preceding events and Element D's predecessor B is assigned, so they meet the first criteria (all preceding events have been completed or there are no preceding events). Second, A's time (0.2 minutes) is less than the remaining time (0.9), but D's time (1.3 minutes) is greater than the remaining time in the station (0.9), so only A would go into the Will Fit column. Element A would be assigned to Station 1. Since the remaining time is now 0.7, continue to try to assign elements to Station 1. C is available on the diagram and on time (0.3 < 0.7), so add it to Station 1.

Assign Station	Remain Time	Will Fit	Assign	Idle Time
I	1.3	A, B	B	0.9
	0.9	A	A	0.7
	0.7	C	C	0.4

Note that Element D still is too long to put in Station 1. Also, Element E is not eligible (Will Fit) due to the fact that Element D has not been assigned, even though its time is small enough to be added to Station 1. Close Station 1.

Step 11: Continue the assignment of elements. Open Station 2. Element D's predecessor B is assigned, so they meet the first criteria (all preceding events have been completed or there are no preceding events). Second, D's time (1.3 minutes) is equal to the remaining time in the station (1.3), so it would go into the Will Fit column.

Assign Station	Remain Time	Will Fit	Assign	Idle Time
I	1.3	A, B	B	0.9
	0.9	A	A	0.7
	0.7	C	C	0.4
II	1.3	D	D	0

Step 12: Assign element to Station 2. Element D is your only choice, so assign it to Station 2. Close Station 2 since there is no remaining time (idle = 0).

207

Step 13: Continue the assignment of elements. Open Station 3. Element E's predecessors C and D are assigned, so it meets the first criteria (all preceding events have been completed or there are no preceding events). Second, E's time (0.1 minutes) is less than the remaining time in the station (1.3), so it would go into the Will Fit column. Since it is the only choice, assign to Station 3, and the remaining time is 1.2. See if any other elements can be added to Station 3. Element F is the only remaining element, and its time (0.8) is less than the remaining time, so it will fit. Assign Element F to Station 3 and the remaining time is 0.4.

Assign Station	Remain Time	Will Fit	Assign	Idle Time
I	1.3	A, B	B	0.9
	0.9	A	A	0.7
	0.7	C	C	0.4
II	1.3	D	D	0
III	1.3	E	E	1.2
	1.2	F	F	0.4

Step 14: Analysis: Our assembly line consists of five workstations, arranged as follows:

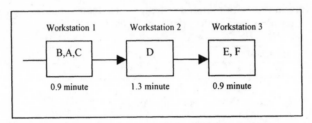

Step 17: Analysis: Since the theoretical minimum number of workstations was three, we know we have balanced the line as efficiently as possible.

Step 18: Calculate the efficiency of the line. The efficiency is calculated by summing the element times (0.4 + 0.2 + 0.3 + 1.3 + 0.1 + 0.8). Then, divide the total time (3.1) by the product of the number of assigned stations (3) and the cycle time (1.3). The assembly line has an efficiency of :

$$E = \sum t_i / n (C_a) = (0.4 + 0.2 + 0.3 + 1.3 + 0.1 + 0.8) / (3 * 1.3) = .795 \text{ or } 79.5\%$$

S3. Yazoo Corporation is planning to launch a new model of lawnmowers and you have been asked to balance the production process. Yazoo estimates demand at 600 units. Given the tasks, times and precedence relationships below (assuming an eight hour work day) compute the following:

a. Maximum cycle time, cycle time based on demand, and largest task.
b. Draw the Precedence Diagram.
c. Assign the elements based on the number of stations needed (based on greatest number of tasks following and largest processing time as the tiebreaker). Use the minimum cycle time possible.
d. Compute the efficiency for this process.

Element	Length (Minutes)	Predecessor
A -- Handle	2.0	Start
B -- Wheels	4.5	A
C -- Regulator	1.0	A
D -- Motor	3.1	Start
E -- Starter	2.1	D
F -- Blade	0.9	C, E
G -- Paint	1.1	B
H -- Inspection	3.5	G, F
	18.2	

208

Solution:

Step 1: Identify the maximum cycle time, cycle time based on demand, and largest task. The maximum cycle time is equal to the sum of all the times of all the elements.

It is equal to 18.2 minutes.

Calculate the desired cycle time. To calculate the desired cycle time, use the formula, production time (8 hrs. x 60 min. = 480 minutes per day) divided by the number of units of production (600 units). This will be:

$$(C_d) = \frac{\text{production time available}}{\text{desired units of output}} = \frac{480 \text{ min.}}{600 \text{ units}} = 0.80 \text{ minutes}$$

The calculated cycle time 0.80 would be considered infeasible since the minimum cycle time is equal to the longest task (Element B – 4.5 minutes) in the sequence. The desired cycle time would have to be revised and the demand of 600 would not be satisfied. Remember that you have ways to change demand by raising the prices. You may have an opportunity, or you need to look for ways to reduce the element times to allow you to meet demand.

Step 2: Draw the precedence diagram for part B.

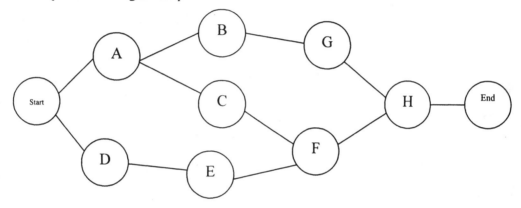

Step 3: Assign elements to workstations. To help evaluate the options, a table was set up with the Station number, the remaining time in the station (an element cannot be assigned to a station if its completion time is greater than the remaining time in the station), the elements that will fit (determine all possible elements that are eligible for the station given that their preceding events have been completed and the element time is less than the remaining time in the station, the element that has been assigned, and the idle time in the station after the element was assigned to the station).

Step 4: Open Station 1. Before any element is assigned to the station, the remaining time in the station is equal to the desired cycle time (4.5 minutes).

Step 5: Determine the elements that will fit. First, look at the precedence diagram.

Elements A and D have no preceding events, so they meet the first criteria (all preceding events have been completed or there are no preceding events). Second, A's time (2.0 minutes) is less than the remaining time in the station, so A would go into the Will Fit column. D's time (3.1) is less than the remaining time in the station (4.5), so it would go into the Will Fit column.

Assign Station	Remain Time	Will Fit	Assign	Idle Time
I	4.5	A, D		

Step 6: Assign element to Station 1. The two choices are Elements A and D. You have to make a decision about which to assign first. To help, the problem says to assign tasks using the most number of activities following the element in the diagram. A has 3 activities (longest path following A) that have to be completed after it (B-G-H or C-F-H). D has 3 activities after it (E, F and H). We cannot make a decision based on the number of following. We have to now look at the element time and pick the longest time (A: 2.0; B: 3.1). Since D is longer, it is assigned first and put in Station 1.

209

Step 7: Calculate the idle time in the station after Element B has been assigned. This is done by subtracting D's time (3.1) from the remaining time in the station (4.5), so the idle time is 1.4.

Assign Station	Remain Time	Will Fit	Assign	Idle Time
I	4.5	A, D	D	1.4

Step 8: Now, the idle time (1.4) becomes the remaining time in the station.

Assign Station	Remain Time	Will Fit	Assign	Idle Time
II	4.5	A, D	D	1.4
	1.4			

Step 9: Determine if any other activities will fit in Station 1 by repeating previous steps.

Element A has no preceding events and Element E's predecessor D is assigned, so they meet the first criteria (all preceding events have been completed or there are no preceding events). Second, A's time (2.0 minutes) is greater than the remaining time (1.4), and E's time (2.1 minutes) is greater than the remaining time in the station (0.9), so neither would go into the Will Fit column. Station 1 is now closed.

Assign Station	Remain Time	Will Fit	Assign	Idle Time
I	4.5	A, D	D	1.4

Step 10: Continue the assignment of elements. The following table represents the assignments.

Assign Station	Remain Time	Will Fit	Assign	Idle Time
I	4.5	A, D	D	1.4
II	4.5	A, E	A	2.5
	2.5	C, E	E	0.4
III	4.5	B, C	B	0
IV	4.5	C, G	C	3.5
	3.5	F, G	G	2.4
	2.4	F, G	F	1.5
V	4.5	H	H	1

Step 11: Calculate the efficiency of the line. The efficiency is calculated by summing the element times (2.0 + 4.5 + 1.0 + 3.1 + 2.1 + 0.9 + 1.1 + 3.5). Then, divide the total time (18.2) by the product of the number of assigned stations (5) and the cycle time (4.5). The assembly line has an efficiency of :

$$E = \sum t_i / n\,(C_a) = (2.0 + 4.5 + 1.0 + 3.1 + 2.1 + 0.9 + 1.1 + 3.5) / (5 * 4.5) = .801 \text{ or } 80.1\%$$

1. The baseball office at your university has asked that you help set up a small assembly line for processing regional ticket sales. Since your team is very good and the university is hosting the regional, demand is expected to be very high. The various tasks, task times, and necessary preceding tasks are listed below:

   a. If demand indicates 10 units are needed in an hour, what is the maximum cycle time allowable?
   b. What is the theoretical number of workstations needed?
   c. Draw the precedence diagram.
   d. Using the "Longest Task" heuristic rule, first to assign tasks to workstations (use the greatest number of followers as the second tiebreaker), what is the actual number of workstations needed to meet demand requirements? What tasks would be assigned to them?
   e. What would be the efficiency of the line?

Activity	Task #	Time (Min.)	Predecessor
Remove forms/checks/money order for mail	1	1	--
Scan form/checks/money order for completeness	2	1	1
Update ticket information on computer	3	2.5	2
Put check/money order into drawer	4	0.5	1
Pull/staple the tickets off printer	5	2.0	3
Pull return envelope from bin	6	0.5	--
Peel return mailing label printed	7	2.0	3
Put return label on return envelope	8	1	6, 7
Insert tickets and order form into return envelope	9	1.5	5
Pull regional schedule	10	0.5	--
Insert regional schedule	11	0.5	10
Seal return envelope	12	1.0	4, 9, 11
Meter the return envelope	13	1.5	8, 12

2. An assembly line with 20 tasks is to be balanced. The longest task is 2.0 minutes, and the total time for all tasks is 30 minutes. The line will operate for 480 minutes per day.

    a. What are the minimum and maximum cycle times?
    b. What range of output is theoretically possible for the line?
    c. What is the minimum number of workstations needed if the maximum output rate is to be sought?
    d. What cycle time will provide an output rate of 125 units per day?

3. A manager wants to assign tasks to workstations as efficiently as possible, and achieve an hourly output of 40 units or 320 units per day. Assume the shop works a 60-minute hour. Assign the tasks shown in the accompanying precedence diagram (times are in minutes) to workstations using the following rules:

    a. In order of most following tasks. Tiebreaker: Longest task.
    b. Longest task. Tiebreaker: In order of most following tasks.

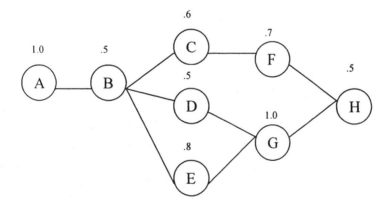

4. Kurt Wayne wants to assign tasks to workstations as efficiently as possible, and achieve an hourly output of 6 units. The department uses a working time of 60 minutes per hour. Assign the tasks shown in the accompanying precedence diagram (times are in minutes) to workstations using the most number following as your first decision rule. Assign tasks and calculate the efficiency.

Activity	Predecessor	Time (min.)
A	---	5
B	A	6
C	B	4
D	---	9
E	D, G	4
F	---	2
G	F	3
H	C, E	7
I	H	5

5. Supplies & More, a large manufacturer of office equipment, is planning to add a new line of label makers, and you have been asked to balance the process, given the following task times and precedence relationships. Assume that cycle time is to be the minimum possible.

Task	Predecessor	Time (min.)
A	---	1.2
B	A	2.4
C	B	1.2
D	---	1.4
E	D	2.2
F	C	3.2
G	E, F	1.0

Do each of the following:

a. Draw the precedence diagram.
b. Determine the maximum cycle time.
c. Determine the maximum number of stations needed.
d. Assign tasks to workstations on the basis of greatest number of following tasks. Use longest processing time as a tiebreaker.
e. Compute the percentage of idle time and efficiency for the assignment in part (d).

6. Twelve tasks, with times and precedence requirements as shown in the following table, are to be assigned to workstations using a cycle time of 1.4 minutes. Two heuristic rules will be tried: longest task times, and most number of following.

Task	Predecessor	Time (min.)
A	---	0.1
B	A	0.2
C	B	0.9
D	C	0.6
E	---	0.1
F	D, E	0.2
G	F	0.4
H	G	0.1
I	H	0.2
J	I	0.7
K	J	0.3
L	K	0.2

a. Draw the precedence diagram for this line.
b. Assign tasks to stations based on the most # of following, then most # proceeding.
c. Compute the percentage of idle time and efficiency for this line.

212

7.   For the set of tasks given below, do the following:

a. Develop the precedence diagram and determine the maximum cycle time in minutes for a desired output of 500 units in a 7-hour day. Why might a manager use a cycle time of .50 minutes?
b. Determine the minimum number of workstations for an output of 500 units per day.
c. Balance the line using the largest # of following tasks. Break ties with the longest tasks. Use a cycle time of .5 minutes. Calculate the percentage of idle time and efficiency for the line to help you.

Task	Predecessor	Time (min.)
A	---	.45
B	A	.11
C	B	.09
D	---	.50
E	D	.26
F	E	.11
G	C	.12
H	C	.10
I	F, G, H	.09
J	I	.10

8.   A shop works a 420-minute day. The manager of the shop wants an output of 210 units per day for the assembly line that has the elemental tasks shown in the table. Do the following:

a. Construct the precedence diagram.
b. Assign tasks according to the most # of following tasks rule.
c. Assign tasks according to the most # of preceding tasks rule.
d. Compute the idle time and efficiency for each rule. Which one yields the better set of assignments in this instance?

Task	Predecessor	Time (min.)
A	---	0.5
B	A	1.4
C	A	1.2
D	B	0.7
E	B, C	0.5
F	D	1.0
G	E	0.4
H	G	0.3
I	F	0.5
J	E, J	0.8
K	H, J	0.9
L	K	0.3

9.   Fashion Extreme is an exclusive producer of female handbags. To ensure high quality, the process has maintained handmade tasks. This laborious process requires the completion of six primary work elements, which are listed here.

Work Element	Precedence	Time (Hr.)
A – Tan leather	---	.50
B – Dye leather	A	.25
C – Shape case	B	.10
D – Mold hinges & fixtures	--	.05
E – Install hinges & fixtures	C, D	.15
F – Assemble case	E	.25

a. Construct a precedence diagram for the manufacture of briefcases.
b. If the demand is 50 cases per 40-hour week, compute the cycle time for the process.
c. Compute the lead-time required for assembly line.
d. How would you balance this assembly line?
e. Compute the line's efficiency and balance delay.
f. Calculate the theoretical minimum number of workstations. Can a better arrangement be determined?

10.   Referring to problem 9, suppose the demand for handbags increases to 100 cases per week.

a. Calculate a new cycle time and rebalance the line.
b. Calculate the efficiency and balance delay of the manufacturing process.
c. Calculate the theoretical minimum number of workstations. Can a better arrangement be determined?

11.   Barbara's YumYum Shop has set a production quota of 1000 party cakes per 40-hour workweek. Use the following information.

a. Draw and label a precedence diagram.
b. Compute the cycle time.
c. Compute the theoretical minimum number of workstations.
d. Balance the assembly line by using the longest task time and heuristic rules.
e. Calculate the efficiency and % of idle time of the assembly line.

Element	Predecessor	Time (min.)
A	---	3
B	A	5
C	B	4
D	A, E	6
E	---	5
F	C, D	4

10

Human Resources and Job Design

I. **Human Resource Strategy for Competitive Advantage**

A. The objective of a human resource strategy is to manage labor and design jobs so people are effectively and efficiently utilized.

B. We need to ensure that people are efficiently utilized within the constraints of other operations management decisions, and have a reasonable quality of work life (reasonably safe, pay is equitable, and achieves an appropriate level of both physical and psychological requirements) in an atmosphere of mutual commitment.

C. Constraints on Human Resource Strategy
  1. Product mix – determines seasonality and stability of employment.
  2. Technology, equipment, and processes – safety and job content. These decisions pose the most substantial constraints because they can be anything from stressful to boring to dangerous to non-stop.
  3. Location – environment in which employees work. This decision may have an impact on the ambient environment in which the employees work.
  4. Layout decisions – job content.

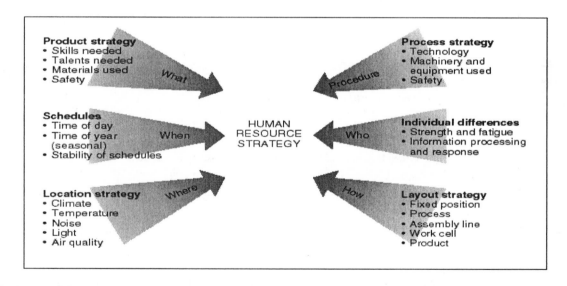

Lecture Key: *The management of employees is critical for competitive advantage. However, Human Resource Strategy can only be effective if there is a mutual commitment in which both management and employee strive to meet common objectives. Managers must enhance performance through optimum job design. It is not difficult to implement if the management has genuine respect for its employees.*

II.   Labor Planning

A. Employment stability deals with the number of employees maintained by an organization at any given time. There are two basic policies dealing with stability.
   1. <u>Following demand exactly</u> keeps direct labor costs tied to production, but incurs other costs, such as hiring and termination costs, unemployment insurance, and premium wages.
   2. <u>Holding employment constant</u> maintains a trained workforce and keeps hiring, termination, and unemployment costs to a minimum.
B. Work Schedules – the standard work schedule in the U.S. is five 8-hour days, but variations do exist.
   1. Flex time allows employees, within limits, to determine their own schedules. This provides the employee with more autonomy and independence.
   2. From an OM perspective, this poses a problem due to production work requiring full staffing for efficient operations. Due to this, many industries cannot give their employees this option.
   3. Flexible work week is a plan that calls for fewer, but longer days, such as four 10-hour days. This may be beneficial for firms with high process start-up times.
   4. Another option is to move employees to part-time status. This is especially attractive in service industries such as banks and restaurants.
C. Job Classifications and Work Rules – many organizations have strict job classifications and work rules, which restrict employee flexibility on the job.
   1. Union pressure restricts what can or cannot be done.
   2. This may, however, give OM more flexibility. This makes staffing and establishing work schedules easier.
      a. Fewer classifications and work-rule constraints can help to build morale and meet staffing requirements.
      b. A flexible workforce may be needed to achieve a competitive advantage through better customer responsiveness.

Lecture Key: Employees are a very key part of a business. It is important to maintain a good relationship with them. In order to do this, firms try to accommodate them with stable employment, flexible work schedules, and flexibility with their job classifications.

III.   Job Design

A. Labor specialization is the division of labor into unique tasks. An example of labor specialization is the assembly line. It is accomplished in three ways.
   1. Development of dexterity and faster learning by the employee because of repetition.
   2. Less loss of time because the employee would not be changing jobs or tools.
   3. Development of specialized tools and the reduction of investment because each employee has only a few tools needed for a particular task.

Lecture Key: Despite the repetitiveness involved in labor specialization, the applicant pool is generally large due to the high wage rate for modest skills. The setback to labor specialization is that the same task is being repeated, so employees only apply those specific skills at the workplace and nothing more.

B. Approaches to job expansion:
  1. Job enlargement occurs when tasks with similar skills are added to an existing job. Job rotation is a version of job enlargement that occurs when the employee is allowed to move from one specialized job to another.
  2. Job enrichment adds planning and control to the job. Employee empowerment is the practice of enriching jobs so employees accept responsibility for a variety of decisions normally associated with staff specialists.

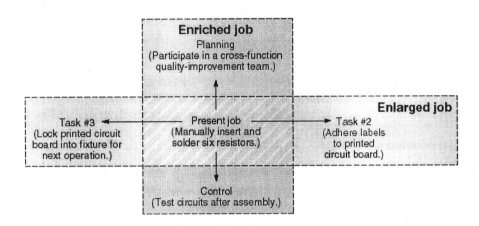

Lecture Key: *It is important for managers to look for opportunities to increase job satisfaction and excitement by adding variety in their jobs by expanding the tasks, responsibilities, and autonomy.*

C. Psychological Components of Job Design
  1. In the 1920's the Hawthorne studies introduced psychology to the workplace. They found that individual differences may be dominant in what an employee expects from the job and what the employee thinks her or his contribution to the job should be.
  2. Hackman and Oldham have incorporated five desirable characteristics of job design:
    a. Skill variety
    b. Job identity
    c. Job significance
    d. Autonomy
    e. Feedback

Lecture Key: *The psychological needs of employees have received increasing focus. These needs are considered along with added job variety to give higher levels of job satisfaction.*

  3. Self-directed teams are a group of empowered individuals working together to reach a common goal. Some limitations to job design are:
    a. Higher capital cost.
    b. Individual differences.
    c. Higher wage rates.
    d. Smaller labor pool.
    e. Increased accident rates.
    f. Current technology may not lend itself to job expansion.

Lecture Key: *Teams may allow employees to have more responsibilities, which helps to increase productivity, product quality, and reduces turnover, tardiness, and absenteeism.*

4. Motivation and Incentive Systems include:
   a. Bonuses, which are a monetary reward, usually in cash or stock options, given to management.
   b. Profit sharing is a system providing some portion of any profit for distribution to the employees.
   c. Gain sharing is a system of rewards to employees for organizational improvements.
   d. Incentive system is an employee award system based on individual or group productivity.
5. Ergonomics and Work Methods
   a. Ergonomics means the study of work, and in the U.S. the term human factors is often substituted for ergonomics.
   b. Operations managers need to be sure that operators have the strength, reflexes, perception, and mental capacity to provide necessary control.
   c. Feedback to operators is provided by sight, sound, and feel; it should not be left to chance.
   d. The work environment is the physical environment in which employees' work affects their performance, safety, and quality of work life. Illumination, noise and vibration, temperature, humidity, and air quality are work environment factors under the control of the organization and the operations manager.
   e. Methods analysis is developing work procedures that are safe and produce quality products efficiently.
      i. Flow diagrams are drawings used to analyze movement of people or material.
      ii. Process charts are a graphic representation that depicts a sequence of steps for a process.

			PROCESS CHART
Present Method ☐			
Proposed Method ☒			
SUBJECT CHARTED _Axle-stand Production_			DATE _6/1/03_
			CHART BY _JH_
			CHART NO. _1_
DEPARTMENT _Work cell for axle stand_			SHEET NO. _1_ OF _1_

DIST. IN FEET	TIME IN MINS.	CHART SYMBOLS	PROCESS DESCRIPTION
50		○ ➡ ☐ D ▽	From press machine to storage bins at work cell
	3	○ ▷ ☐ D ▼	Storage bins
5		○ ➡ ☐ D ▽	Move to machine 1
	4	● ▷ ☐ D ▽	Operation at machine 1
4		○ ➡ ☐ D ▽	Move to machine 2
	2.5	● ▷ ☐ D ▽	Operation at machine 2
4		○ ➡ ☐ D ▽	Move to machine 3
	3.5	● ▷ ☐ D ▽	Operation at machine 3
4		○ ➡ ☐ D ▽	Move to machine 4
	4	● ▷ ☐ D ▽	Operation at machine 4
20		○ ➡ ☐ D ▽	Move to welding
	Poka-yoke	○ ▷ ■ D ▽	Poka-yoke inspection at welding
	4	● ▷ ☐ D ▽	Weld
10		○ ➡ ☐ D ▽	Move to painting
	4	● ▷ ☐ D ▽	Paint
		○ ▷ ☐ D ▽	
97	25		TOTAL

○ = operation; ▷ = transportation; ☐ = inspection; D = delay; ▽ = storage

iii. Activity charts are a way of improving utilization of an operator and a machine or some combination of operators.

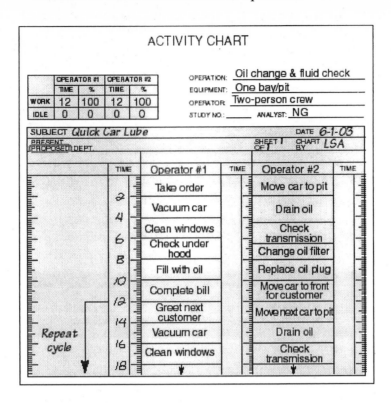

ACTIVITY CHART

OPERATION: Oil change & fluid check
EQUIPMENT: One bay/pit
OPERATOR: Two-person crew
STUDY NO.: _____ ANALYST: NG

	OPERATOR #1		OPERATOR #2	
	TIME	%	TIME	%
WORK	12	100	12	100
IDLE	0	0	0	0

SUBJECT Quick Car Lube   DATE 6-1-03
PRESENT (PROPOSED) DEPT.   SHEET 1 OF 1   CHART BY LSA

	TIME	Operator #1	TIME	Operator #2	TIME
	2	Take order		Move car to pit	
	4	Vacuum car		Drain oil	
	6	Clean windows		Check transmission	
	8	Check under hood		Change oil filter	
	10	Fill with oil		Replace oil plug	
	12	Complete bill		Move car to front for customer	
	14	Greet next customer		Move next car to pit	
Repeat cycle	16	Vacuum car		Drain oil	
	18	Clean windows		Check transmission	

iv. Operations chart is a chart depicting right and left-hand motions.

LEFT-HAND / RIGHT-HAND CHART
SOUTHERN TECHNICAL INSTITUTE
MARIETTA, GEORGIA 30060

PROCESS Bolt-Washer Assembly
STUDY NO.
OPERATOR SRA
ANALYST
DATE 6 /1 /03 SHEET NO. 1 of 1
METHOD (PRESENT) PROPOSED)
REMARKS

SYMBOLS	PRESENT		PROPOSED		DIFFERENCE	
	LH	RH	LH	RH	LH	RH
○ OPERATIONS	5	10				
⇨ TRANSPORTATIONS						
□ INSPECTIONS						
D DELAYS	10	5				
▽ STORAGES						
TOTALS	15	15				

LEFT-HAND ACTIVITY Present METHOD	DIST.	SYMBOLS	SYMBOLS	DIST.	RIGHT-HAND ACTIVITY Present METHOD
1 Reach for bolt		●⇨□D▽	○⇨□■▽		Idle
2 Grasp bolt		●⇨□D▽	○⇨□■▽		Idle
3 Move bolt to		●⇨□D▽	○⇨□■▽		Idle
work area		○⇨□D▽	○⇨□D▽		
4 Hold bolt		○⇨□■▽	●⇨□D▽		Reach for washer
5 Hold bolt		○⇨□■▽	●⇨□D▽		Grasp washer
6 Hold bolt		○⇨□■▽	●⇨□D▽		Move washer to bolt
7 Hold bolt		○⇨□■▽	●⇨□D▽		Place washer on bolt

Lecture Key: *The components of job design comprise a job for an individual or group. These components specify the tasks and how the employees will perform the tasks as well as how to keep the employees motivated. The managers are responsible for the monitoring of any defects of the product. They are also responsible for examining the feedback.*

IV.   The Visual Workplace

A. The visual workplace uses a variety of visual communication techniques to rapidly communicate information to stakeholders.

B. Looks for ways to efficiently share information through low-cost visual devices, which take the place of bulky and tedious paperwork.

C. Faster way to communicate pertinent information about an enterprise to its stakeholders.

D. Visual systems should include all variables that are involved in the organization and should focus on improvement.

E. Tools such as charts and signals may help workers and management.

F. Signals in the workplace:
1. Kanbans – signal to indicate the need for more production.
2. 3-minute clock in Burger King – visual standard indicating the acceptable wait time.
3. Painted symbols – indicate the location of job tools.
4. Quota numbers – indicate the quotas for employees in plain view for all to see.
5. Andon – signal that there is a problem.

Lecture Key: *With the increased speed of the business environment, data in the workplace changes very fast. The visual workplace helps operations managers deal with the need to share up-to-date information. It eliminates waste by making problems visual.*

V.   Labor Standards

A. Labor standards – the amount of time required to perform a job or part of a job.

B. Accurate labor standards are needed for management to know what its labor requirements are, what its costs should be, and what constitutes a fair day's work.

Supplement 10
Work Measurement

I. Labor Standards and Work Measurement

A. At the beginning of the 20th century, a large proportion of work was manual and labor of products was high.

B. Managers initiated studies to improve work methods and understand human effort.

C. Effective operations management requires meaningful standards that can help a firm determine the following:
1. Labor content of items produced (the labor cost).
2. Staffing needs (how many people it will take to meet required production).
3. Cost and time estimates prior to production (to assist in a variety of decisions, from cost estimates to make-or-buy decisions).
4. Crew size and work balance (who does what in a group activity or on an assembly line).
5. Expected production (so that both manager and worker know what constitutes a fair day's work).
6. Basis of wage-incentive plans (what provides a reasonable incentive).
7. Efficiency of employees and supervision (a standard is necessary against which to determine efficiency).

D. Labor standards – represent the amount of time it should take an average employee to perform specific job activities. Labor standards are set in four ways:
1. Historical experience
2. Time studies
3. Predetermined time standards
4. Work sampling

Lecture Key: The efforts to improve work methods and understand human effort continue to this day. Labor standards remain important and continue to play a major role in both service and manufacturing organizations.

II. Historical Experience

A. How many labor hours were required to do a task the last time it was performed?

B. Historical standards have an advantage of being inexpensive and easy to obtain.

C. Not objective (historical standards) however, and accuracy is not known, whether they represent a good or bad work pace, and whether unusual occurrences are included.

D. Time studies, predetermined time standards, and work sampling are preferred.

III. Time Studies

A. Originally proposed in 1881 by Frederick W. Taylor, time study is still the most widely used time-study method.

B. Time-study procedures: timing a sample of a worker's performance and using it as a basis for setting a standard time.

C. Using these 8 steps, a trained person can establish a standard:

1. Define the task to be studied (after methods analysis has been conducted).

2. Divide the task into precise elements (parts of a task that often take no more than a few seconds).

3. Decide how many times to measure the task (the number of cycles or samples needed).

4. Time and record elemental times and ratings of performance.

5. Compute the average observed cycle time. The average observed cycle time is the arithmetic mean of the times for *each* element measured, adjusted for unusual influence for each element:

$$\text{Average observed cycle time} = \frac{\Sigma(\text{times to perform each element})}{\text{number of cycles observed}}$$

6. Determine performance rating and then compute the normal time for each element.
   Normal time = (average observed cycle time) / (performance rating factor).

   a. The performance rating adjusts the observed time to what a normal worker could expect to accomplish.

   b. For example, a normal worker should be able to walk 3 miles per hour. He or she should also be able to deal a deck of 52 cards into 4 equal piles in 30 seconds. A performance rating of 1.05 would indicate that the observed worker performs the task slightly faster than average. Numerous videos specify work pace on which professionals agree, and benchmarks have been established by the Society for the Advancement of Management. Performance rating, however, is still something of an art.

7. Add the normal times for each element to develop a total normal time for the task.

8. Compute the standard time. This adjustment to the total normal time provides for allowances such as *personal* needs, unavoidable work *delays*, and worker *fatigue*:
   Standard time = total normal time / 1 – allowance factor
   *The adjustment to standard time provides allowances for personal needs, unavoidable work delays, and fatigue.

D. Personal time allowances – often established in the range of 4-7%. Depends on nearness to restrooms, drinking fountains, etc. Delay allowances – set as a result of actual studies. Fatigue allowances – based on growing knowledge of human expenditure.

Example: Performing a Time Study and Developing a Standard Time

The time study of a work operation yielded an average observed cycle time of 4.0 minutes. The analyst rated the observed worker at 85%. This means the worker performed at 85% of normal productivity when the study was made. The firm uses a 13% allowance factor. We want to compute the standard time.

Solution:
It is given that the average observed time and the rating time of the worker are:

Average observed time   = 4.0 min.
Rating factor   = .85

Calculate the Normal time using the following formula:

Normal time   = (average observed cycle time) (rating factor)
              = (4.0) (0.85)
              = 3.4 min.

Compute the standard time using the following formula and values calculated above.

Standard time = normal time/1-allowance factor
              = 3.4 / 1 – 0.13
              = 3.9 min.

Example: Performing a Time Study and Developing a Standard Time

Management Science Associates promotes its management development seminars by mailing thousands of individually composed and typed letters to various firms. A time study has been conducted on the task of preparing letters for mailing. On the basis of the observations below, Management Science Associates wants to develop a time standard for this task. The firm's personal, delay, and fatigue allowance factor is 15%.

Time Study Observation Sheet							
		Cycles (in minutes)					Performance
		1	2	3	4	5	Rating
A	Compose and type letter	8	10	9	21*	11	120%
B	Type envelope address	2	3	2	1	3	105%
C	Stuff, stamp, seal, and sort envelopes	2	1	5*	2	1	110*

Solution:

Step 1: Delete unusual or nonrecurring observations such as those marked with an asterisk (*).

Step 2: Compute the average element times as (for remaining observations):

$$\bar{t} = \Sigma t \,/\, n =$$

For element A, the average time is:

$$\bar{t} = 8 + 10 + 9 + 11 \,/\, 4 = 9.5 \text{ min.}$$

For element B, the average time is:

$$\bar{t} = 2 + 3 + 2 + 1 + 3 \,/\, 5 = 2.2 \text{ min.}$$

For element C, the average time is:

$$\bar{t} = 2 + 1 + 2 + 1 \,/\, 4 = 1.5 \text{ min.}$$

Step 3: Compute the normal time for each job element:

Normal time = (average observed time) x (rating)

$$Nt_A = (\bar{t})(RF) = (9.5)(1.2) = 11.4 \text{ min.}$$

$$Nt_B = (\bar{t})(RF) = (2.2)(1.05) = 2.31 \text{ min.}$$

$$Nt_C = (\bar{t})(RF) = (1.5)(1.10) = 1.65 \text{ min.}$$

Step 4: Add the normal times for each element to find the total normal time:

Total normal time = 11.4 + 2.31 + 1.65 = 15.36 min.

Step 5: Compute the standard time for the job:

The standard time is computed by adjusting the normal cycle time by an allowance factor using the following formula:

$$ST = (\text{Total normal time}) \,/\, (1 - AF)$$
$$ST = (15.36) \,/\, (1 - 0.15) = 18.07 \text{ min.}$$

Analysis: 18.07 minutes is the time standard for this job. Beware of abnormally short and long observed times. This may result in errors if used in the time study.

E. Time study requires sampling process. You must consider variability of each element. For adequate sample size, consider three items:
1. How accurate we want to be.
2. Desired level of confidence.
3. How much variation exists within the job elements.
4. Formula for finding sample size given these three variables:

   Required sample size = n = $[(zs) / (h * x\text{-}bar)]^2$

   Where:

   h = accuracy level desired in percent of the job element, expressed as a decimal (5% = .05)

   z = number of standard deviations required for desired level of confidence (90% confidence = 1.65; see Table S10.1 or Appendix I for the more common z values)

   s = standard deviation of the initial sample

   x = mean of the initial sample

   n = required sample size

5. Formula for finding standard deviation (s):

   $$s = \sqrt{\Sigma(x_i - \bar{x})^2 / n - 1}$$

   Where:

   x_i = value of each observation

   $\bar{x}$ = mean of the observations

   n = number of observations in the sample

Example: Determining the Sample Size

Thomas W. Jones Manufacturing Co. has asked you to check a labor standard prepared by a recently terminated analyst. Your first task is to determine the correct sample size. Your accuracy is to be within 5% and your confidence level is 95%. The standard deviation of the sample is 1.0 and the mean 3.0.

Solution:
Determine the given parameters:

Accuracy Level:	h	= 0.05
Mean of sample:	$x\text{-}bar$	= 3.00
Standard deviation:	s	= 1.0

Number of standard deviations for given confidence level: $z = 1.96$

Calculate the sample size (n) using the following formula:

$$n = [(zs) / (h * x\text{-}bar)]^2$$
$$n = [(1.96 * 1.0) / (0.05 * 3)]^2 = 170.74 = 171 \text{ samples}$$

Analysis: Therefore, you recommend a sample size of 171.

IV.   Predetermined Time Standards

A. Divide manual work into small basic elements that already have established times; in order to estimate time, factors for each element of task are added together.

B. Most common predetermined time standard is methods time measurement, or MTM

C. Predetermined Time Standards based on Therbligs – basic physical elements of motion.
1. Coined by Frank Gilbreth.
2. Stated in terms of time measurement units (TMUs), which are equal to .00001 hours or .0006 minutes.

Example: Using Predetermined Time Standards

Pouring a tube specimen in a hospital lab is a repetitive task for which the MTM data in Figure S10.2 may be used to develop standard times. The sample tube is in a rack and the centrifuge tubes are in a nearby box. A technician removes the sample tube from the rack, uncaps it, gets the centrifuge tube, pours and places both tubes in the rack. The first work element involves getting the tube from the rack. Suppose the conditions for GETTING the tube and PLACING it in front of the technician are:

- Weight (less than 2 pounds)
- Conditions of GET (easy)
- Place accuracy (approximate)
- Distance range (8 to 20 inches)

Solution:

Then the MTM element for this activity is AA2 (as in Figure S10.2 on pg. 398 of the text). The rest of Table S10.2 below is developed from similar MTM tables. Most MTM calculations, by the way, are computerized, so the user need only key in the appropriate MTM codes, such as AA2 in this example. One of Gilbreth's techniques was to use cameras to record movement by attaching lights to an individual's arms and legs. In that way they could track the movement of individuals while performing various jobs.

Element Description	Element	Time
Get tube from rack	AA2	35
Get stopper, place on counter	AA2	35
Get centrifuge tube, place at sample tube	AD2	45
Pour (3 sec.)	PT2	83
Place tubes in rack (simo)	PC2	40
		Total TMU = 238
0.0006 * 238 = Total standard minutes = 0.14		

D. Advantages of predetermined time standards over direct time studies
  - a. May be established in laboratory, which won't disturb actual production activities.
  - b. Can be used for planning since standard can be set before task is performed.
  - c. No performance rations are necessary.
  - d. Unions accept as fair means of setting standards.
  - e. Very effective in firms that do substantial numbers of studies of similar tasks.

Lecture Key: In addition to historical experience and time studies, production standards can be set by using predetermined time standards. The most common predetermined time standard is methods time measurement (MTM).

V. Work Sampling

  A. Estimates the percent of time a worker spends on various tasks.
  B. Requires random observations to record the activity a worker is performing.
  C. Knowledge of allocation may lead to staffing changes, reassignment of duties, estimates of activity costs, and setting of delay allowances for labor standards.
  D. Work sampling procedures can be summarized with 5 steps:
  1. Take a preliminary sample to obtain an estimate of the parameter value.
  2. Compute the sample size required.
  3. Prepare a schedule for observing the worker at appropriate times. The concept of random numbers is used to provide for random observation.
  4. Observe and record worker activities.
  5. Determine how workers spend their time.
  E. Management must select desired confidence level and accuracy. Analysts must select a preliminary value for the parameter under study.

  Formula: $n = z^2 p(1 - p) / h^2$

  Where: n = required sample size

  z = standard normal deviation for the desired confidence level

  p = estimated value of sample proportion
  (of time worker is observed busy or idle)

  h = acceptable error level, in percent

Example: Determining the Number of Observations

The manager of Wilson County's welfare office, Madeline Thimmes, estimates her employees are idle 25% of the time. She would like to take a work sample that is accurate within 3% and wants to have 95.45% confidence in the results.

Solution:
Determine the given information:

$z = 2$ for 95.45% confidence level
$p = 25\%$ (.25) is estimated idle sample proportion
$h = 3\%$ (.03) is acceptable error level

Using the following formula, calculate the number of observations:

$$n = z^2 p(1 - p) / h^2$$
$$= 2^2 (.25) (.75) / .03^2 = 833 \text{ observations}$$

Analysis: At a 95.45% confidence level and 3% error rate, the number of observations needed is 833 observations. If the percent of idle time observed is not close to 25% as the study progresses, then the number of observations may have to be recalculated and increased or decreased as appropriate.

F. The focus of work sampling is to determine how workers allocate time among activities.

Example: Evaluating Employees in Previous Problem

Madeline Thimmes, the operations manager of Wilson County's state welfare office, wants to be sure her employees have adequate time to provide prompt, helpful service. She believes that service to welfare clients who phone or walk in without an appointment deteriorates rapidly when employees are busy more than 75% of the time. Consequently, she does not want her employees to be occupied with client service activities more than 75% of the time.

Solution:
1. From the previous study, 833 observations are needed.
2. Observations are to be made in a random, nonbiased way over a period of 2 weeks to ensure a true sample.
3. Define the activities that are "work." Work is defined as all of the activities that are necessary to take care of the client (filing, meetings, data entry, discussions with the supervisor, etc.).
4. Personal time is to be included in the 25% of nonwork time.
5. Observations are made in a nonintrusive way so as not to distort the normal work patterns.

Results at the end of 2 weeks after 833 observations:

Number of Observations	Activity
485	On the phone or meeting with a welfare client
126	Idle
62	Personal time
23	Discussions with supervisor
137	Filing, meeting, and computer data entry
833	

G. Work sampling offers several advantages over time-study methods.
   1. Single observer can observe several workers simultaneously.
   2. Observers usually do not require much training and no timing devices are needed.
   3. Study can be temporarily delayed at any time.
   4. Because work sampling uses instantaneous observations, the worker has little chance of affecting outcome.
   5. Procedure is less intrusive and therefore less likely to generate objections.
H. Disadvantages of work sampling
   1. Does not divide work elements as completely as time studies.
   2. Can yield biased or incorrect results if observer does not follow random routes of travel and observation.
   3. Less intrusive and tends to be less accurate.

Performing a Time Study and Developing a Standard Time

S1.   Lawn Tractor is attempting to streamline its production schedule and normalize its three shifts so that each worker has a standard time. A time study for a shift worker is authorized by the manager, and the times needed to complete the workers' tasks are recorded in the table below. The manager sets the allowance factor for the elements at 10%. Calculate the normal time, standard time, and determine how many units could be produced in a three-hour period.

Element	Rating Factors	Observation				
		1	2	3	4	5
1	100	1.0	1.4	1.2	1.2	1.3
2	90	2.0	2.6	1.8	2.2	2.3
3	115	3.0	3.2	3.2	3.4	3.3
4	100	1.9	1.8	1.7	1.8	1.7

Solution:

Step 1:   Compute average element times. The average element time is computed by summing the individual observation times and dividing by the number of observations. For Element 1, the average element time is:

$$\bar{t} = \Sigma t / 10 =$$
$$\bar{t} = (1.0 + 1.4 + 1.2 + 1.2 + 1.3) = 6.1/5 = 1.22$$

Step 2:   Compute the normal elemental times. The normal time is computed by adjusting the average time, t, by the performance-rating factor, RF. Use the formula average time multiplied by the rating factor.

For Element 1, the normal time is:

$$Nt = (\bar{t})(RF) = (1.22)(1.0) = 1.22$$

For Element 2, the normal time is:

$$Nt = (\bar{t})(RF) = (2.18)(0.90) = 1.962$$

Step 3:   Compute the normal time for operation. The normal cycle time, NT, is computed by summing the normal times for all elements, which for this example is 0.387.

The normal cycle time, NT, is:

$$NT = \Sigma(\bar{t}) = (1.22 + 1.962 + 3.703 + 1.78) = 8.665$$

Step 4:   The standard time is computed by adjusting the normal cycle time by an allowance factor:

$$ST = (NT)(1 + AF) = (8.664)(1 + 0.10) = 9.53 \text{ min.}$$

Step 5:   Compute the number of units that can be completed in a 3-hour period. Divide the standard time into 180 minutes (3 hours x 60 minutes) as illustrated below:

Number units in 3 hours = 180 min. / 9.53 min. per unit = 18.88 or 18 units

Element	Rating Factors (%)	Observation					Average	Normal Time
		1	2	3	4	5		
1	100	1.0	1.4	1.2	1.2	1.3	1.22	1.22
2	90	2.0	2.6	1.8	2.2	2.3	2.18	1.962
3	115	3.0	3.2	3.2	3.4	3.3	3.22	3.703
4	100	1.9	1.8	1.7	1.8	1.7	1.78	1.78
								8.665

S2.   ComTech, an electronics company, is attempting to streamline its production schedule and normalize its two shifts so that each worker has a standard time. A time study for each workstation is authorized by the manager, and the times needed to complete the workers' tasks are recorded in the table below. The manager sets the allowance factor for the elements at 15%. Calculate the normal time, standard time, and determine how many units could be produced in a three-hour period.

Workstation	Rating Factors	Observation				
		1	2	3	4	5
1	115	5.0	5.1	5.8	5.2	5.0
2	85	6.0	5.5	6.2	6.1	6.2
3	95	1.2	1.4	1.2	1.2	1.5
4	85	3.2	3.1	3.0	3.3	3.1

Solution:

Step 1:   Compute average element times. The average element time is computed by summing the individual observation times and dividing by the number of observations. For Element 1, the average element time is:

$$\bar{t} = \Sigma t \: / \: 10 =$$
$$\bar{t} = (5.0 + 5.1 + 5.8 + 5.2 + 5.0) = 26.1/ 5 \; = \; 5.22$$

Step 2:   Compute the normal elemental times. The normal time is computed by adjusting the average time, t, by the performance-rating factor, RF. Use the formula average time multiplied by the rating factor.

For Element 1, the normal time is:

$$\text{Normal time} = (\bar{t})(RF) = (5.22)(1.15) \; = \; 6.003$$

For Element 2, the normal time is:

$$\text{Normal time} = (\bar{t})(RF) = (6.0)(0.85) \; = \; 5.1$$

Step 3:   Compute the normal time for operation. The normal cycle time, NT, is computed by summing the normal times for all elements, which for this example is 15.007.

The normal cycle time, NT, is:

$$\text{Normal time} = \Sigma(\bar{t}) = (6.003 + 5.1 + 1.235 + 2.669) \; = \; 15.007$$

Step 4:   The standard time is computed by adjusting the normal cycle time by an allowance factor:

$$\text{Standard Time} = (\text{Normal Time})(1 + AF) = (15.007)(1 + 0.15) \; = \; 17.26 \text{ min.}$$

Step 5:   Compute the number of units that can be completed in a 3-hour period. Divide the standard time into 120 minutes (2 hours x 60 minutes) as illustrated below:

Number units in 3 hours = 120 min. / 17.26 min. per unit = 6.95 or 6 units

Element	Rating Factors (%)	Observation					Average	Normal Time
		1	2	3	4	5		
1	115	5.0	5.1	5.8	5.2	5.0	5.22	6.003
2	85	6.0	5.5	6.2	6.1	6.2	6.0	5.1
3	95	1.2	1.4	1.2	1.2	1.5	1.3	1.235
4	85	3.2	3.1	3.0	3.3	3.1	3.14	2.669
								15.007

Step 6:   Analysis: The manager can expect to produce 6 units in a two-hour period. If the company is running 2 ten-hour shifts, then that is 10 two-hour periods during a day. The production should be 60 units per day (10 periods x 6 units per period). If the manager wants to produce more, then he should concentrate on workstations 2, 3, and 4 since they are operating below 100% performance (85%, 95%, and 85% respectively).

1. Using the data below from a recent time study, determine the average time for each task, normal time for each task, the normal time for the operation, and the standard time if the allowance rate is 20%.

Task	Rating Factors	Observation				
		1	2	3	4	5
1	.80	1.2	.95	1.1	1.0	1.05
2	.95	2.1	2.05	2.1	2.2	2.15
3	1.0	.65	.65	.70	.70	.65
4	.85	1.1	1.05	1.08	.95	1.0

2. Using the data below from a recent time study, determine the average time for each task, normal time for each task, the normal time for the operation, and the standard time if the allowance rate is 10%.

Task	Rating Factors	Observation				
		1	2	3	4	5
1	1.10	10.25	11	10.5	10.0	10.25
2	1.05	20.75	20.0	19.5	21.0	20.5
3	.95	2.65	2.65	1.70	2.20	2.35
4	.90	5.50	5.15	5.65	5.80	5.25

3. Using the data below from a recent time study, determine the average time for each task, normal time for each task, the normal time for the operation, and the standard time if the allowance rate is 15%.

Task	Rating Factors	Observation				
		1	2	3	4	5
1	.95	3.2	3.15	3.0	3.85	3.75
2	.90	2.5	2.0	3.0	2.25	2.75
3	1.10	3.0	3.10	3.10	3.30	3.15
4	1.05	4.0	4.12	4.25	4.02	4.10

Incentive Piece-Rate System

S1. If Lawn Tractor pays workers a piece rate of $3.00 per unit, what would an average worker be paid per hour, and what would the subject of the time study in the Time Study example expect to be paid?

Solution:

Step 1: Determine the average units produced by a worker during an hour. The average worker would produce the following number of units in an hour:

Number of units per hour = 60 minutes per hour / standard time per unit
(calculated in S1 of time study problems)
= 60 min. / 9.53 min per unit
= 6.3 units or 6 units

Step 2: Compute the hourly wage. The hourly wage rate would be calculated by the number of units per hour (6 units) multiplied by the rate per unit ($3.00).

Hourly wage = (6 units per hour) x ($3.00) = $18.00

S2. If ComTech pays workers a piece rate of $2.25 per unit, what would an average worker be paid per hour, and what would the subject of the time study in the Time Study example expect to be paid?

231

Solution:

Step 1:   Determine the average units produced by a worker during an hour. The average worker would produce the following number of units in an hour:

$$\text{Number of units per hour} = 60 \text{ minutes per hour} / \text{standard time per unit}$$
$$\textit{(calculated in S1 of time study problems)}$$
$$= 60 \text{ min.} / 17.26 \text{ min per unit}$$
$$= 3.48 \text{ units or 3 units}$$

Step 2:   Compute the hourly wage. The hourly wage rate would be calculated by the number of units per hour (6 units) multiplied by the rate per unit ($3.00).

$$\text{Hourly wage} = (3 \text{ units per hour}) \times (\$2.25) = \$6.75$$

Determining the Number of Cycles

S1.   In the Time Study example, Lawn Tractor conducted a time study for 5 cycles of a job assembling a unit of output, which we will consider to be a sample. The average cycle time, T, for the job was 8.4 minutes. The standard deviation of the sample was 0.485 minutes. The company wants to determine the number of cycles for a time study such that it can be 90 percent confident that the average time computed from the time study is within 7 percent of the true average cycle time.

Solution:

Step 1:   Identify the information needed.

Z score: Z = 1.65 (at 90% confidence level)
Standard Deviation: s = .485 (from time study problem and above write up)
Percent within the average: e = 7% or 0.07
Average Cycle Time (not adjusted): T = 8.4 (from time study problem and above write up)

Step 2:   Calculate the sample size, N, using the formula below:

$$n = \left[\frac{zs}{eT} \right]^2 = \left[\frac{(1.65)(0.485)}{(0.07)(8.4)} \right]^2 = 1.85 \text{ or } 2$$

Step 3:   Analysis: The time study should include 2 cycles to be 90 percent confident that the time-study average job cycle time is within 7 percent of the true average job cycle time. The 5 cycles that were used in our time study were a few more than were needed.

What is the confident level (as a percent) at 5 cycles (N = 5) and the mean time from the time study is within 3 percent of the true mean?

Step 4:   Solve for the z score in the formulas below if N = 5 and e = 0.03. T and s remain the same.

$$n = \left[\frac{zs}{eT} \right]^2$$

$$5 = \left[\frac{(z)(0.485)}{(0.03)(8.4)} \right]^2 = 1.16 \text{ or } 2$$

$$z = 1.16 \quad P[z = 1.16] = 0.3770$$

Step 5:   Analysis: The confident level would be .754 or 75.4%. Since this is a two-tail test (half of the tail on the right of the center line and half on the left of the center line), you must find the probability of a z score at 1.16, which is 0.377. Then, multiply by two to account for the half of the probability that is on the right and the half that is on the left. This is how 75.4% is determined.

S2.   Determine the sample size for a time study so there is 97% confidence that the average time computed from time study is within 2% of the actual average cycle time. The average cycle time is 2.2, and the standard deviation is 0.30.

Solution:

Step 1:   Identify the information needed.

Z score: Z = 2.17 (at 97% confidence level)
Standard Deviation: s = .30 (from above write up)
Percent within the average: e = 2% or 0.02
Average Cycle Time (not adjusted): T = 2.2 (from above write up)

Step 2:   Calculate the sample size, N, using the formula below:

$$n = \left[\frac{zs}{eT} \right]^2 = \left[\frac{(2.17)(0.30)}{(0.02)(2.2)} \right]^2 = 218.9 \text{ or } 219$$

Step 3:   Analysis: The time study should include 219 cycles to be 97 percent confident that the time-study average job cycle time is within 2 percent of the true average job cycle time.

1.   Huntington Industries conducted a time study for 10 cycles of a job assembling a unit of output, which we will consider being a sample. The average cycle time, T, for the job was 11.4 minutes. The standard deviation of the sample was 1.85 minutes. The company wants to determine the number of cycles for a time study such that it can be 95 percent confident that the average time computed from the time study is within 4 percent of the true average cycle time. What is the confident level (as a percent) at 20 cycles (N = 20) and the mean time from the time study is within 2 percent of the true mean?

2.   Sparkle Inc. conducted a time study for 20 cycles of a job assembling a unit of output, which we will consider being a sample. The average cycle time, T, for the job was 18.2 minutes. The standard deviation of the sample was 2.15 minutes. The company wants to determine the number of cycles for a time study such that it can be 85 percent confident that the average time computed from the time study is within 5 percent of the true average cycle time.

3.   Maverick Building Supplies conducted a time study for 10 cycles of a job assembling a unit of output, which we will consider to be a sample. The average cycle time, T, for the job was 6.45 minutes. The standard deviation of the sample was 0.75 minutes. The company wants to determine the number of cycles for a time study such that it can be 97 percent confident that the average time computed from the time study is within 8 percent of the true average cycle time.

4.   A time study determined an average cycle time of 6.5 minutes, with a standard deviation of 1.35 minutes. These were determined by a sample of 100 cycles. Is the sample size of 100 large enough that the confident level of 98% is reached for the standard time within 5% of the true value?

Number of Observations in the Work Sample

S1.   The manager on a data entry lab on campus is worried that the students entering reports for the state are idle a large portion of the time that they are there. The delivery of the reports has been delayed for days at a time, and students will show up and have no work. Since this is a budgeted project, the manager worries about running out of money before all reports have been entered. The manager thinks that the students are idle as much as 30% of the time. The manager wants to accurately determine the percentage of idle time within 5% of the true average and to have a 99% confidence level before the manager's next meeting with the state. How many observations are needed to meet these requirements?

Solution:

Step 1: Determine the information needed.

z score: z = 2.57 (at a 99% confidence level)
Percent within the average: e = 5% or 0.05
Probability that the students are idle: 30% or 0.30
Probability that the students are not idle: 70% or 1 − 0.30 = 0.70

Step 2: Calculate the number of observations using the following formula:

$$n = (z/e)^2 * p(1 - p)$$
$$= (2.57/0.05)^2 * (0.3) * (0.7) = 10.8 \text{ or } 11 \text{ observations}$$

Step 3: Analysis: A total of 11 observations are needed.

S2. A computer technician is conducting a work sampling study of a lab of computers to determine the portion of the time the computers are being used. The technician believes that the computers are being used 80% of the time. The technician is concerned that the lab is reaching its capacity and more computers will be needed. (The computer's capacity is set at 85%.) The technician wants to accurately determine the percentage of usage within 10% of the true average and to have a 90% confidence level. How many observations are needed to meet these requirements?

Solution:

Step 1: Determine the information needed.

z score: z = 1.65 (at a 90% confidence level)
Percent within the average: e = 6% or 0.06
Probability that the computers are being used: 85% or 0.85
Probability that the students are not idle: 15% or 1 − 0.15 = 0.85

Step2: Calculate the number of observations using the following formula:

$$n = (z/e)^2 * p(1 - p)$$
$$= (1.65/0.06)^2 * (0.8) * (0.2) = 121 \text{ observations}$$

Step 3: Analysis: A total of 121 observations are needed.

1. A work sampling study of a group of machines is being performed to determine the portion of the time the machines are being used. The manager believes that the machines are being used 85% of the time. The manager is concerned that the process is reaching its capacity and more machines will be needed. (The computer's capacity is set at 90%.) The technician wants to accurately determine the percentage of usage within 5% of the true average and to have a 95% confidence level. How many observations are needed to meet these requirements?

2. A work sampling study of workers is being performed to determine the portion of the time the workers are busy. The manager believes that the workers are busy only 65% of the time. The manager will have to reduce the workforce if the idle time for the workers is 40% of the time or greater. The manager wants to accurately determine the percentage of time busy within 8% of the true average and to have a 99% confidence level. How many observations are needed to meet these requirements?

3. A work sampling study of a group of machines is being performed to determine the portion of the time the machines are being used. The manager believes that the machines are being used 80% of the time. The manager is concerned that the process is reaching its capacity and more machines will be needed. The technician wants to accurately determine the percentage of usage within 3% of the true average and to have a 98% confidence level. How many observations are needed to meet these requirements?

11

Supply Chain Management

I. **The Strategic Importance of the Supply Chain**

A. Supply-chain management is the integration of the activities that obtain materials and services, transform them into intermediate goods and final products, and deliver them to customers (i.e., purchasing and outsourcing activities, and many other activities that are important to the supplier-distributor relationship).

B. Supply-chain management includes determining:
1. Transportation vendors
2. Credit and cash transfers
3. Suppliers
4. Distributors and banks
5. Accounts payable and receivable
6. Warehousing and inventory levels
7. Order fulfillment
8. Sharing customer, forecasting, and production information.

C. Objective of supply-chain management is to use suppliers who ultimately want to give the most value to the customer.

D. Emphasis is placed on the supply chain when firms wish to increase their competitiveness.

E. In order to satisfy a dynamic marketplace, the firm should make the suppliers "partners" in the firm's strategy.

F. The supply chain is intended to assist the OM strategy.

G. Different strategies should be reflected up and down the supply chain.

H. There should also be an expectation that strategy should be distinct for different products and altered as products move through their product life cycle.

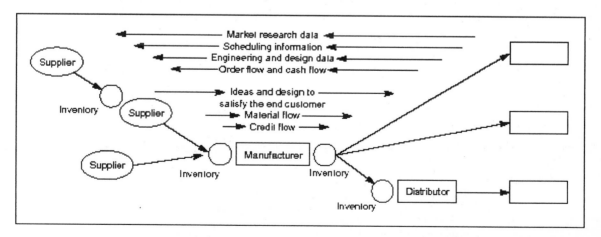

II. Global Supply-Chain Issues

A. When companies "go global," expanding their supply chains becomes a strategic challenge (i.e., quality production in the area you are working with might be poor or tariffs and quotas may block non-local companies from doing business).

B. Supply chains in a global environment must be:

1. Flexible enough to react to sudden changes in parts availability, distribution or shipping channels, import duties, and currency rates.

2. Able to use the latest computer and transmission technologies to schedule and manage the shipment of parts in and finished products out.

3. Staffed with local specialists to handle duties, trade, freight, customs, and political issues.

Lecture Key: The supply chain involves every aspect of making a product and getting it to the customers, from start to finish. This includes deciding which suppliers to use, getting the supplies to the factory, making the product, putting the products onto trucks and shipping them to the customer. As stated above, the supply chain is intended to assist the OM strategy. If the OM strategy is to cut costs and save money, then up and down the supply chain, the firm should be looking for ways to cut costs and save money.

III. Supply Chain Economics

A. The supply chain plays a vital part in a firm's strategy and is the most costly activity firms incur.

B. A huge portion of revenue is devoted to the supply chain; therefore, an effective strategy is crucial.

C. The supply chain offers a major opportunity to cut costs and increase contribution margins.

Example

The Goodwin Company spends 50% of its sales dollars in the supply chain. The firm has a net profit of 4%. Of the remaining 46%, 23% is fixed and the remaining 23% is variable. Solution: The dollar value of sales needed to generate the same profit that results from $1 of supply chain savings would be $3.70. See Table 11.3 on pg. 416 of the text.

D. Make-Or-Buy Decisions

1. Unlike wholesalers or retailers, manufacturers don't buy everything that they sell.

2. Make-or-Buy decisions means choosing between producing a component or a service in-house or purchasing it from an outside source.

3. Examples of reasons for making would be to maintain a lower core competence or to have lower production costs. Examples of reasons for buying would be that there is a lower acquisition cost and it would reduce inventory costs. See Table 11.4 for considerations for the make or buy decision.

4. Whether the firm chooses to buy or make, supply-chain performance should be reviewed periodically because vendor competence and costs change, as do a firm's own strategy, production capabilities, and costs.

5. Table 11.4: Considerations for the Make-or-Buy Decision

a. Reasons for Making

i. Maintain core competence

ii. Lower production cost

iii. Unsuitable suppliers

iv. Assure adequate supply (quantity or delivery)

v. Utilize surplus labor or facilities and make a marginal contribution

   vi. Obtain desired quality
   vii. Remove supplier collusion
   viii. Obtain unique item that would entail a prohibitive commitment for a supplier
   ix. Protect personnel from a layoff
   x. Protect proprietary design or quality
   xi. Increase or maintain size of the company (management preference)
  b. Reasons for Buying
   i. Frees management to deal with its primary business
   ii. Lower acquisition cost
   iii. Preserve supplier commitment
   iv. Obtain technical or management ability
   v. Inadequate capacity
   vi. Reduce inventory costs
   vii. Ensure alternative sources
   viii. Inadequate managerial or technical resources
   ix. Reciprocity
   x. Item is protected by a patent or trade secret
 E. Outsourcing
  1. Transfers some of what are traditional internal activities and resources of a firm to outside vendors, making it slightly different than the traditional make-or-buy decision.
  2. Through outsourcing, another supplier provides resources to the firm in order to let the firm focus on its own core competencies.
  3. For example, Waste Management might outsource their finances to an accounting firm, their legal problems to a law firm, and their computer problems to a technology firm.

Lecture Key: *The supply chain is a very important aspect of any firm. There are several ways that a firm can reduce costs by merely inspecting their supply chain. There may be a certain method that could be altered to reduce costs or another supplier could sell the same product for less.*

IV. Supply Chain Strategies

 A. A firm that has a many supplier strategy forces the suppliers to compete with each other by choosing the supplier with the lowest offer on its proposed demands.
 B. A strategy with a few suppliers allows the supplier to form a long-term relationship with a company, and therefore will be more dedicated and knowledgeable about that company.
 C. A company that uses the vertical integration strategy can choose to produce its goods or services that were once purchased (forward integration) or it can actually buy the supplier or distributor (backward integration).
 D. The Keiretsu strategy is used when the firm helps to financially support the supplier, which allows the supplier to become part of the company coalition.
 E. A virtual company remains flexible by relying on a variety of supplier relationships that it uses on an as needed basis to provide service on demand.

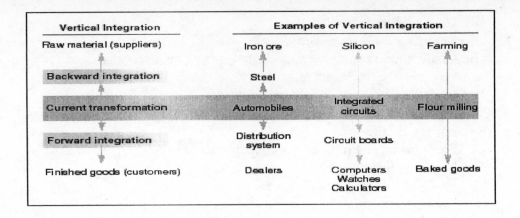

Vertical Integration	Examples of Vertical Integration		
Raw material (suppliers)	Iron ore	Silicon	Farming
Backward integration	Steel		
Current transformation	Automobiles	Integrated circuits	Flour milling
Forward integration	Distribution system	Circuit boards	
Finished goods (customers)	Dealers	Computers Watches Calculators	Baked goods

Lecture Key: *In order to obtain its outside resources, a company must decide on which supply chain strategy it is going to use. In deciding, the firm must carefully analyze both the advantages and disadvantages of each strategy and then choose which strategy best suits the mission and goals for the company.*

V.   Managing the Supply Chain

A. Each functional entity of an organization must have an agreement on the goals, a strong trust in the suppliers, and compatible organizational cultures.

B. In an integrated supply chain, there are several issues that arise because it is so crucial that the information about the company's current inventory is accurate.
   1. Local optimization distorts information about what is really happening in the supply chain because the focus is put on maximizing profit and decreasing costs.
   2. Sales incentives, quality discounts and promotions all create fluctuations that end up being costly to members of the supply chain.
   3. Large lots reduce unit costs but often fail to reflect the actual size of the inventory.

C. Distortion and fluctuation cause what is known as the bullwhip effect.

D. Opportunities for effective management in the supply chain include the following 10 items:
   1. Accurate pull data about the current inventory is necessary so that the order that is sent to the supplier is correct.
   2. Lot size reductions can be accomplished by providing economic shipments, reducing cost of the order, and providing discount based on size of individual shipment.
   3. Single stage control is used when one member is assigned to monitor and manage the inventory for the retailer.
   4. Vendor managed inventory permits the supplier to maintain the inventory for the buyer.
   5. Postponement will delay the customization or modifications that need to be done to a product for as long as possible.
   6. Channel assembly sends the individual parts of a product to the distributor, instead of the finished product, and allows the distributor to assemble it.
   7. Drop shipping and special packaging is simply shipping the product directly from the supplier to the consumer.
   8. Blanket orders are contracts that allow a company to purchase certain items from the vendor.
   9. Standardization will reduce the number of variations that have to be done to a certain product.
   10. Electronic data interchange is a computerized way of communicating and transmitting data between organizations.

VI.   Internet Purchasing

A. Internet purchasing is for the use of employees of the purchasing firm that involves everything from order releases to ordering a vendor catalog with the simple click of a button.
B. Internet purchasing reduces ordering lead-time and purchasing costs are controlled.
C. Other additional benefits include comparison-shopping, rapid ordering, and reduction in inventory.

VII.   Vendor Selection

A. Decision regarding from whom to buy goods or services.
B. Factors such as strategic fit, vendor competence, delivery, and quality performance have to be considered.
C. Three-stage process: Vendor Evaluation, Vendor Development, and Negotiations.
   1. Vendor Evaluation
      a. Develop evaluation criteria, such as those in Example 2, in order to determine the likelihood of potential vendors becoming good suppliers.
      b. Criteria and weights selected depend on the supply-chain strategy to be achieved.
      c. If good suppliers are not selected, then all other supply-chain efforts are wasted.

Example: Vendor Selection

Hau Lee, president of Creative Toys in Palo Alto, is interested in evaluating suppliers who will work with him to make non-toxic, environmentally friendly paints and dyes for his line of children's toys. This is a critical strategic element of his supply chain, and he desires a firm that will contribute to his product. He begins his analysis of one potential supplier, Faber Paint and Dye.

Solution:
Hau first reviews the supplier differentiation attributes in Table 11.1 and develops the list of selection criteria shown on the top of the next page. He then assigns the weights shown to help him perform an objective review of potential vendors. His staff assigns the scores shown and computes the total weighted score.

Criteria	Weights	Scores (1-5) (5 Highest)	Weight X Score
Engineering/research/innovation skills	.20	5	1.0
Production process capacity (flexibility/technical assistance)	.15	4	.6
Distribution/delivery capability	.05	4	.2
Quality systems and performance	.10	2	.2
Facilities/location	.05	2	.1
Financial and managerial strength (stability and cost structure)	.15	4	.6
Information systems capability (E-commerce, Internet)	.10	2	.2
Integrity (environmental compliance/ethics)	.20	5	1.0
	1.00		3.9 Total

*Faber Paint and Dye receives an overall score of 3.9. Hau now has a basis for comparison to other potential vendors, selecting the one with the highest overall rating.

2. Vendor Development
   a. Integrate supplier into the firm
   b. Include everything from training, to engineering and production help, to procedures for information transfer.
   c. Procurement policies need to be established.
3. Negotiations
   a. Approaches taken by supply-chain personnel to develop contractual relationships with suppliers.
   b. Negotiations often focus on quality, delivery, payment, and cost.
   c. Three classic types of negotiation strategies: the cost-based model, the market-based price model, and competitive bidding.
      i. Cost-based model – requires that the supplier open its books to the purchaser. The contract price is then based on time and materials or on a fixed cost with an escalation clause to accommodate changes in the vendor's labor and materials cost.
      ii. Market-based price model – price is based on a published, auction, or index price. Many commodities (agriculture products, paper, metal, etc.) are priced this way.
      iii. Competitive Bidding:
         aa. Appropriate when suppliers are not willing to discuss costs or where near-perfect markets do not exist.
         bb. Typical policy for purchases, may determine initial cost, and may also make difficult the communication and performance that are vital for engineering changes, quality, and delivery.
         cc. A disadvantage of this method is that the development of long-term relations between buyer and seller are hindered.
         dd. A fourth approach is to combine one or more of the preceding negotiation techniques.

Lecture Key: *When a business has to select vendors, many factors have to be taken into consideration because vendor selection can have a significant effect on the supply-chain strategy. The strategy determines what criteria and weights will be used to evaluate potential vendors. If a poor vendor is chosen, then all other efforts made by the supply-chain are useless. Once a vendor has been chosen, they need to be integrated into the company and then a negotiation strategy needs to be applied in order to establish the contractual relationship.*

VIII. Logistics Management

A. Seeks efficiency of operations through the integration of all material acquisition, movement, and storage activities.

B. Needed when transportation and inventory costs are substantial on both the input and output sides of the production process.

C. Distribution Channels – Five major distribution channels have to be evaluated when the total distribution costs are high.
1. Trucking
2. Railroads
3. Airfreight
4. Waterways
5. Pipelines

D. Cost of Shipping Alternatives
1. The longer a product is in transit, the longer a firm has money invested.
2. Faster shipping tends to cost more than slow shipping.
3. Example 3 evaluates this trade-off system by comparing carrying costs to shipping costs.

Example

A shipment of new connectors for semiconductors needs to go from San Jose to Singapore for assembly. The value of the connectors is $1,750.00 and holding cost is 40% per year. One airfreight carrier can ship the connectors 1 day faster than its competitor, at an extra cost of $20.00.

Solution:
Step 1: Determine the daily holding cost.

Daily $ of holding the product $= $ (annual holding cost × product value)/365
$= (.40 \times \$1,750.00)/365 = \$1.92$

Step 2: Analysis: Since the cost of saving one day is $20.00, which is much more than the daily holding cost of $1.92, we decide on the less costly of the carriers and take the extra day to make the shipment. This saves $18.08 ($20.00 – $1.92).

Note: The solution becomes radically different if the 1-day delay in getting the connectors to Singapore delays delivery (making a customer mad) or delays payment of a $150,000.00 final product. (Even 1 day's interest on $150,000.00 or a mad customer makes a savings of $18.08 insignificant.) For the operations or logistics manager there are many other considerations, including coordinating shipments to maintain a schedule, getting a new product to market, and keeping a customer happy. There is no reason why estimates of these other costs cannot be added to the estimate of daily holding cost. Determining the impact and cost of these many other considerations is what makes the evaluation of shipping alternatives interesting.

Lecture Key: Logistics Management evaluates means of distribution and costs of shipping alternatives. It tries to measure, obtain efficiency of operations, and to gain a competitive advantage.

IX.   **Benchmarking Supply-Chain Management**

   A. Firms setting benchmarks result in well-managed supply chain relationships. See table below.
   B. Benchmarking firms have driven down costs, lead times, late deliveries, and shortages, all while improving quality.
   C. Effective supply chain management aids firms in their response to demand in global marketplace, therefore providing them with a competitive advantage.

Table: Supply-Chain Performance Compared

	Typical Firms	Benchmark Firms
Administrative costs as % of purchases	3.3%	.8%
Lead time (weeks)	15	8
Time spent placing an order	42 minutes	15 minutes
% of late deliveries	33%	2%
% of rejected material	1.5%	.0001%
Number of shortages per year	400	4

Lecture Key: Benchmarking is necessary for businesses wanting to establish well-managed supply chain relationships, reducing money spent in the supply chain, and on gaining a competitive advantage.

Vendor Selection

S1.   Associated Foods is searching for a new vendor for their chain of grocery stores. They have the choice between Brooke Corp. and Stacie Enterprises. The factors the two were compared on consisted of company, service, product, and sales and the rating scale consisted of 1-4 with a 1 being poor and a 4 being excellent. The company, service, and sales categories were weighted at 20% respectively, and the product category was weighted at 40%.

Company	4 (excellent)	3 (good)	2 (fair)	1 (poor)
Financial strength		B	S	
Manufacturing range	SB			
Research facilities		S	B	
Geographical locations	S	B		
Management		SB		
Labor relations			B	S
Trade relations		B	S	

Products	4 (excellent)	3 (good)	2 (fair)	1 (poor)
Quality	SB			
Price	B	S		
Packaging		SB		

Sales	4 (excellent)	3 (good)	2 (fair)	1 (poor)
Product knowledge		SB		
Sales calls	S	B		
Sales service		SB		

Service	4 (excellent)	3 (good)	2 (fair)	1 (poor)
Deliveries on time	SB			
Handling of problems		S	B	
Technical assistance		B		S

Brooke Corporation= B   Stacie Enterprises= S

Solution:

Step 1:   Multiply the weight of each category times the given rating.

Category one: Company

Brooke Corp.:		Stacie Enterprises:	
Factor one	(3)(.20) = .60	Factor one	(2)(.20) = .40
Factor two	(4)(.20) = .80	Factor two	(4)(.20) = .80
Factor three	(2)(.20) = .40	Factor three	(3)(.20) = .60
Factor four	(3)(.20) = .60	Factor four	(4)(.20) = .80
Factor five	(2)(.20) = .40	Factor five	(3)(.20) = .60
Factor six	(3)(.20) = .60	Factor six	(1)(.20) = .20
	(2)(.20) = .40	Factor seven	(2)(.20) = .40
	3.7		3.8

Step 2:

Category two: Products

Brooke Corp.:		Stacie Enterprises:	
Factor one	(4)(.40) = 1.6	Factor one	(4)(.40) = 1.6
Factor two	(4)(.40) = 1.6	Factor two	(3)(.40) = 1.2
Factor three	(3)(.40) = 1.2	Factor three	(3)(.40) = 1.2
	4.4		4.0

Step 3:

Category three: Sales

Brooke Corp.:
Factor one   (3)(.20) = .60
Factor two   (3)(.20) = .60
Factor three (3)(.20) = .60
                      1.8

Stacie Enterprises:
Factor one   (3)(.20) = .60
Factor two   (4)(.20) = .80
Factor three (3)(.20) = .60
                      2.0

Step 4:

Category four: Service

Brooke Corp.:
Factor one   (4)(.20) = .80
Factor two   (2)(.20) = .40
Factor three (3)(.20) = .60
                      1.8

Stacie Enterprises:
Factor one   (4)(.20) = .80
Factor two   (3)(.20) = .60
Factor three (1)(.20) = .20
                      1.6

Step 5:   Overall, Associated Foods should choose Brooke Corp. because they had the highest scores in each of the categories.

S2.   Working for the purchasing department of CDC construction in Baton Rouge, La, you ask a customer to evaluate three suppliers as "good," "fair," or "bad." Products should be weighted 30%, Service 25%, Sales 25%, and Company 20%. The following was established.

Company	Good (3)	Fair (2)	Bad (1)
Financial Strength	H,L	P	
Supplier	P	H, L	
Locations	H, L		P
Management	P	H, L	

Sales	Good (3)	Fair (2)	Bad (1)
Product Knowledge	P		H, L
Advertisements	H, L	P	
Sales Service	P		H, L

Service	Good (3)	Fair (2)	Bad (1)
Deliveries			
Problem Handling			
Technical Assistance			

Products	Good (3)	Fair (2)	Bad (1)
Quality			
Price			

L – Lowery Supplies   H – Home Supplies   P – E.D. Price

244

Solution:

Step 1: Analyze Ranking

Lowery

Company	= (.2 x 3) + (.2 x 2) + (.2 x 3) + (.2 x 2) + (.2 x 2) =	2.4
Service	= (.25 x 3) + (.25 x 2) + (.25 x 1) =	1.5
Sales	= (.25 x 1) + (.25 x 3) + (.25 x 1) =	1.25
Products	= (.30 x 2) + (.30 x 2) =	1.2
Total		6.35

Home

Company	= (.2 x 3) + (.2 x 2) + (.2 x 3) + (.2 x 2) + (.2 x 2) =	2.4
Service	= (.25 x 3) + (.25 x 2) + (.25 x 1) =	1.5
Sales	= (.25 x 1) + (.25 x 3) + (.25 x 1) =	1.25
Products	= (.30 x 2) + (.30 x 2) =	1.2
Total		6.35

E.D. Price

Company	= (.2 x 2) + (.2 x 3) + (.2 x 1) + (.2 x 3) + (.2 x 3) =	2.4
Service	= (.25 x 3) + (.25 x 3) + (.25 x 3) =	2.25
Sales	= (.25 x 3) + (.25 x 2) + (.25 x 3) =	2.0
Products	= (.30 x 3) + (.30 x 2) =	1.5
Total		8.15

Step 2: Choose Best Supplier

P – E.D. Price with a score of 8.15

S3. Develop a vendor-rating form that represents your comparison of the education offering by universities in which you considered enrolling. Using the information in the table below, identify the "best" choice. Are you attending that "best" choice? If not, why not?

Solution:

Step 1: Develop a rating system.

Rating: 1-5 with a 1 being poor and a 5 being excellent. Tuition was weighted at 40% and the other two were weighted at 30% respectively.

Step 2: Using the chart to represent your findings, determine the best selection.

	Tuition	Campus Atmosphere	Housing	Total
LSU	5	4	3	12
Loyola	4	2	1	7
UNO	4	1	1	6
Tulane	1	3	3	7

Step 3: Multiply the weight of each category times the given rating.

Category One: Tuition	Weight	Rating	Score
LSU	.40	5	2.0
Loyola	.40	4	1.6
UNO	.40	4	1.6
Tulane	.40	1	.40

Category Two: Campus Atmosphere	Weight	Rating	Score
LSU	.30	4	1.2
Loyola	.30	2	.60
UNO	.30	1	.30
Tulane	.30	3	.90

Category Three: Housing	Weight	Rating	Score
LSU	.30	3	.90
Loyola	.30	1	.30
UNO	.30	1	.30
Tulane	.30	3	.90

Step 4: Analysis:

From the table constructed above, the best choice in a college based on our three factors would be to attend LSU because this school has the highest cumulative total of 12. Yes, we are currently attending the "best" choice...LSU.

1. Develop a vendor-rating form that represents your comparison of the education offered by High Schools in which you considered enrolling. Fill in the necessary data, and identify the "best" choice. Did you attend your best choice?

The three High School choices are Mount Carmel, Dominican, and Chapelle.

Academics are weighted 40% and the other three are 20%. The ranking is 1-4 with 1 being poor and 4 being excellent:

High School	Academics	Athletics	Extra Curricular Activities	Tuition
Mount Carmel	4	3	3	2
Dominican	4	2	3	3
Chapelle	3	2	3	3

Shipping Alternatives

S1. Your options for shipping $200,000 of products from New Orleans, Louisiana to Hong Kong: are (a) a ship that will take 20 days at a cost of $4,000 or (b) truck the products to San Francisco, then ship them at a total cost of $4,800. The second option (b) will take 15 days. You're paid via a letter of credit the day the products arrive. Your holding cost is estimated at 40% of the value per year. Which option is most economical?

Solution:

Step 1: Find the daily cost of holding the product:

Option (a): (.40 x 4,000)/365 = $4.38
Option (b): (.40 x 4,800)/365 = $5.26

Step 2: Choose option (a) because the holding cost is less than option (b).

What customer issues are not presented in the data above?

Step 3: Answer: Coordinating shipments and getting the new products to market are not mentioned in the data given.

S2.   Stacie Enterprises is the logistics vendor for Brooke Manufacturing Company. Brooke has daily shipments of car doors from its New Orleans plant to an auto assembly line in Mississippi. The value of the standard shipment is $300,000. Stacie Enterprises has two options: (a) its standard two-day shipment or (b) a subcontractor who will team drive overnight with an effective delivery of one day. The extra driver costs $150. Brooke's holding cost is 25% annually for this kind of inventory. Which option is most economical?

Solution:

Step 1:   Find the daily cost of holding the product:

Option (a): (.25 x 300,000)/365 =$205.40
Option (b): (.25 x 150)/365 =

Step 2:   Choose option (b) because the holding cost is more than the extra cost for the driver.

What production issues are not included in the data presented above?

Step 3:   Answer: Coordinating shipments and getting the new products to market are not mentioned in the data given.

Supplement 11
E-Commerce and
Operations Management

I. The Internet

A. The Internet is revolutionary for management because it connects people around the world, tying design, manufacturing, delivery, sales, and after-service activities together.

B. The Intranet is a spin off of the Internet and is used to connect departments within the office together.

C. The Internet has vastly changed operations management and its application can be limited only by our imagination and creativity.

Lecture Key: *The Internet and Intranet together have a very large impact on operations management. They allow for easier communication within the company, as well as with the customers and suppliers.*

II. Electronic Commerce

A. E-Commerce refers to the use of the Internet (or another computer network) to buy and sell products and services and to relay information, leading to lower prices.

B. The business activities range from marketing tools to product design to speeding accounting functions.

C. There are four types of E-Commerce.
1. Business to Business is when businesses are on both sides of transactions.
2. Business to Consumer is when the buyer is an individual customer.
3. Consumer to Consumer is when the consumers sell through electronic advertisements or auctions to other consumers.
4. Consumer to Business is when individuals sell goods or services to a business.

Lecture Key: *Using the Internet to buy and sell goods and services is very useful and efficient for businesses. However, it is not just business to business exchanges that benefit from the new e-commerce, consumers who sell to business and to other consumers benefit as well.*

III. Economics of E-Commerce

A. E-Commerce greatly reduces the costs of operations management by improving communication and spreading economically valuable information.

B. The e-commerce provider is the middle-man in the exchange of goods, services and information and it matches the buyers and sellers.

C. E-commerce is so efficient, it is pushing the envelope towards "perfect markets."

D. Time constraints that were once a huge factor in some exchanges is no longer a problem because of the convenience of transferring information via e-commerce.

Lecture Key: *E-Commerce is so efficient, cheap, practical and innovative that anyone not using this avenue is left out in the dirt. This process will be perfected in a matter of time and it continues to be the most economical way to exchange goods, services and information.*

IV. Product Design

A. Products need to be developed much faster to be competitive and e-commerce helps processes to go much faster at a lower cost.

B. Operations managers can monitor product data over the Internet leading to more accurate data for suppliers, subcontractors, and strategic planners.

C. This also allows for input from people around the world instead of everyone being in one place at one time, which is not as efficient and costs more.

Lecture Key: In order for e-commerce to work at the highest efficiency, the product needs to be designed in the fastest yet most economical way. The Internet allows for tracking of customer trends and the relaying of up-to-date information to others involved in the production process.

V. E-Procurement

A. E-procurement is purchasing or order release done over the Internet or via approved online vendor catalogs.

B. An Online Catalog is usually integrated into a company's sales and service agenda, allowing for easy to use, current information.
1. These systems allow for customized pricing and 24 hour ordering.
2. They also allow for more attention to the small accounts that may have been overlooked if this system was not in place.

C. Intermediaries are companies that host a site where buyers and sellers can meet, which keeps costs very low since the overhead of faxing, copies, and long distance phone calls are at a minimum.

D. An online exchange provided by the buyer is helpful because everything can be bought in one place, leading to better service, higher efficiency, and lower prices.

E. The cost of providing quotes and bids can be very high, so many quoting services are moving toward the Internet. The presentations can be done on the Internet and sent via the Internet.

F. Internet Outsourcing is when a company sends their taxes, payroll, human resources and other internal services within their company to an external company, often times using the Internet.

G. Online Auctions can be maintained by buyers, sellers or intermediaries and can help move inventory where it is needed for the best markets.
1. Finding a large base of potential bidders is the way to be successful in Online Actions.
2. Since firms spend most of their money on purchases, this will reduce the costs because of the competitive environment.

Lecture Key: E-procurement can speed up the process of buying and selling goods and services. This also allows for a competitive market and people being able to specialize their company a lot. They no longer need to keep a staff for bookkeeping or pay the expenses of sending people to market to purchase inventory.

VI. Inventory Tracking

A. Fed Ex was the first to track shipments from pick-up to delivery, which most operations managers use now.

B. Now operations managers use data collection, bar code technology, radio frequency, and electronic communication to track inventory in all areas of the production, shipping and delivery process.

C. In the movement towards every customer getting exactly what he or she wants, there is more room for error, however operations management adjusts for that through inventory tracking.

Lecture Key: *Operations managers have revolutionized the high variety of orders that many companies deal with by tracking everything that is made and comes and goes from the company. This process is electronic and it reduces human error dramatically.*

VII. Inventory Reduction

A. There are no longer huge warehouses where inventory is kept; it is more like a "pass through facility."
B. Also, everything is delivered "Just-in-Time" where one place handles the testing, packing, assembly, and delivery so the process is more efficient.
C. The inventory and purchasing systems for many large companies are integrated into a delivery company so that orders can go out immediately.

Lecture Key: *When there is a consistent company that handles every part of ordering, shipping, and delivering, the process is more efficient and, once mastered, needs little changing.*

VIII. Scheduling and Logistics Improvements

A. Large shipping companies can interface their computer systems with their clients and know where their entire inventory is at a given time.
B. This process allows for inventory to never go to a warehouse, getting it where it needs to be fast and for lower costs.
C. It is proven that trucking capacity is not being utilized, therefore there is a lot of room for improvement, which is something operations managers are looking into.

Lecture Key: *An operations manager must weigh the pros and cons of their inventory system and delivery of products. Many find that connecting their computer systems with the supplier is very efficient because it bypasses the cost of sitting in a warehouse.*

12

Inventory Management

I.   **Functions of Inventory**

A. Inventory Adds Function to Operations
1. Decouple parts of the production process.
2. Separate the functions in demand.
3. Take advantage of quality discounts.
4. Hedge against inflation.

B. Types of Inventory
1. Raw material inventory – has been purchased but not processed.
   Example: Wood needed to build table
2. Work in process inventory – raw materials that are currently undergoing change.
   Example: Wood being cut at the shop
3. Maintenance, Repair, and Operating Supply – materials, tools in charge of keeping other processes productive.
   Example: Oil and grease to keep wood cutter running smoothly
4. Finished goods inventory – finished product that is ready for shipping.
   Example: Wood table

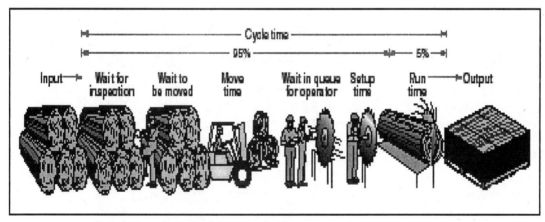

FIGURE 12.1 ■ The Material Flow Cycle

Most of the time that work is in process (95% of the cycle time) is not productive time.

251

II.   Inventory Management

    A. ABC Analysis – a method of dividing on-hand inventory by annual dollar volume into three classifications.

    B. We determine annual dollar volume by multiplying annual demand times cost per unit.

        $Volume = Annual Demand x Cost per unit

        1. Class A – items where annual dollar is high.

        2. Class B – items where annual dollar is medium.

        3. Class C – items where annual dollar is low.

Example: ABC Analysis

Silicon Chips, Inc., maker of super fast DRAM chips, has organized its 10 inventory items on an annual dollar-volume basis. Shown below are the items (identified by stock number), their annual demand, unit cost, annual dollar volume, and the percentage of the total represented by each item. In the table below, we show these items grouped into ABC classifications:

Solution:

Item Stock Number	% of Number of Items Stocked	Annual Volume (Units) x	Unit Cost =	Annual Dollar Volume	% of Annual Dollar Volume		Class
#10286	20%	1,000	$90.00	$90,000	38.8%	72%	A
#11526		500	154.00	77,000	33.2%		A
#12760	30%	1,550	$17.00	26,350	11.3%	23%	B
#10867		350	42.86	15,001	6.4%		B
#10500		1,000	12.50	12,500	5.4%		B
#12572	50%	600	$14.17	8,502	3.7%	5%	C
#14075		2,000	.60	1,200	.5%		C
#01036		100	8.50	850	.4%		C
#01307		1,200	.42	504	.2%		C
#10572		250	.60	150	.1%		C

FIGURE 12.2 ■

Graphic Representation of ABC Analysis

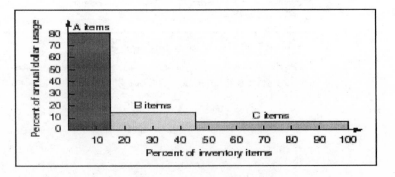

C. Policies Based on ABC Analysis
   1. Purchasing resources expended on supplier development should be much higher for item A than item B.
   2. A items should have higher inventory control, belonging in a secure area, and accuracy of records should be verified more frequently.
   3. Forecasting A items should warrant more care.
D. Record Accuracy
   1. Critical ingredient in production and inventory systems.
   2. Allows organization to focus on items that are demanded the most.
E. Cycle Counting
   1. Continuing reconciliation of inventory with inventory records.
   2. Records must be verified through a series of controls within a continuous audit of the operations.

Example: Cycle Counting

Cole's Trucks, Inc., a builder of high-quality refuse trucks, has about 5,000 items in its inventory. After hiring Matt Clark, a bright young OM student, for the summer, the firm determined that it has 500 A items, 1,750 B items, and 2,750 C items. Company policy is to count all A items every month (every 20 working days), all B items every quarter (every 60 working days), and all C items every 6 months (every 120 working days). How many items should be counted each day?

Solution:

Item Class	Quantity	Cycle Counting Policy	# of Items Counted/Day
A	500	Each month (20 working days)	500/20 = 25/day
B	1,750	Each quarter (60 working days)	1,750/60 = 29/day
C	2,750	Every 6 months (120 working days)	2,750/120 = 23/day
			77/day

Seventy-seven items are counted each day.

F. Control of Service Inventories
   1. Shrinkage – retail inventory that is unaccounted for between receipt and sale.
   2. Pilferage – a small amount of theft.
   3. Control techniques include:
      a. Good personnel selection, training, and discipline. These are never easy, but very necessary in food-service, wholesale, and retail operations, where employees have access to directly consumable merchandise.
      b. Tight control of incoming shipments. This task is being addressed by many firms through the use of bar-code and radio frequency ID systems that read every incoming shipment and automatically check tallies against purchase orders. When properly designed, these systems are very hard to defeat. Each item has its own stock keeping unit (SKU), pronounced "skew."
      c. Effective control of all goods leaving the facility. This job is done with bar codes on items being shipped, magnetic strips on merchandise, or via direct observation. Direct observation can be personnel stationed at exits (as at Costco and Sam's Club wholesale stores) and in potentially high-loss areas, or can take the form of one-way mirrors and video surveillance.

III. Inventory Models

A. Independent vs. Dependent Demand
1. Demand for refrigerators is independent of the demand for toaster ovens.
2. Demand for toaster oven components is dependent on the requirements of toaster ovens.

B. Holding, Ordering, and Setup Costs
1. Holding costs are the costs associated with holding or "carrying" inventory over time. Therefore, holding costs also include obsolescence and costs related to storage, such as insurance, extra staffing, and interest payments. Table 12.1 shows the kinds of costs that need to be evaluated.
2. Ordering cost includes costs of supplies, forms, order processing, clerical support, and so forth. When orders are being manufactured, ordering costs also exist, but they are a part of what is called setup cost.
3. Setup cost is the cost to prepare a machine or process for manufacturing an order. This includes time and labor to clean and change tools or holders. Operations managers can lower ordering costs by reducing setup costs and by using such efficient procedures as electronic ordering and payment. In many environments, setup cost is highly correlated with setup time.

DETERMINING INVENTORY HOLDING COSTS	
Category	Cost (and Range) as a % of Inventory Value
Housing $ (building rent or depreciation, operating $, taxes, insurance)	6% (3 – 10%)
Material handling $ (equipment lease or depreciation, power, operating $)	3% (1 – 3.5%)
Labor $	3% (3 – 5%)
Investment $ (borrowing $, taxes, and insurance on inventory)	11% (6 – 24%)
Pilferage, scrap, and obsolescence	3% (2 – 5%)
Overall carrying cost	26%

IV. Inventory Models for Independent Demand

A. Basic economic order quantity (EOQ) model – oldest and most commonly used inventory control technique.
1. Based on several assumptions, which must be fulfilled in order to use:
    a. Demand for the inventory is known, constant, and independent.
    b. Lead time (time between placement of an order and receipt) must be constant and known.
    c. Receipt of the order is instantaneous and complete (one batch at one time).
    d. Quantity discounts are not possible.
    e. The only variable cost is the cost of placing an order (setup cost) and holding cost or carrying cost.
    f. Stockouts can be avoided if orders are placed at the right time.

B. Inventory usage over time:

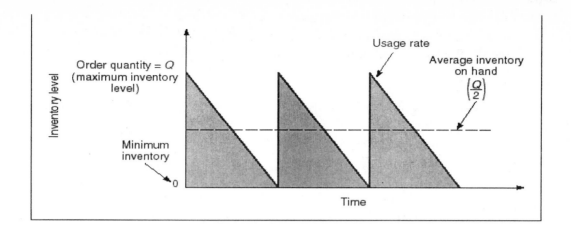

C. The graph displays a sawtooth shape because given the assumptions of EOQ when the inventory level reaches zero, a new order is placed bringing inventory back to Q. This process is able to continue indefinitely over time due to the constant demand and lead time assumptions of the model.
   1. An integral objective in most inventory control models, including EOQ, is the objective to minimize total cost. Variable costs according to the EOQ are setup and holding costs. Whereas the cost of the actual inventory along with all other costs are constant.
   2. By minimizing these variable costs, one may reduce total cost.
D. The optimal order size, Q*, the quantity that minimizes cost.

Graphical display of cost:

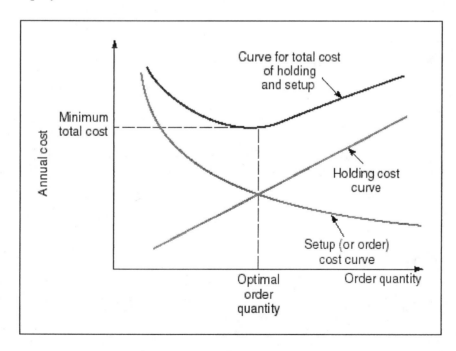

E. The nature of both variable costs gives rise to a trade-off between the two; for example, one may reduce the set-up cost by ordering larger lots, but that would (assuming a constant demand) increase holding cost. And vice versa, hence we are interested in solving for the optimal order size.

F. Solving for Q* occurs at the intersection of holding and carrying cost. Steps for solving for Q*:
1. Develop an expression for setup costs (ordering cost).
2. Develop an expression for carrying costs (holding cost).
3. Set the setup cost equal to the holding cost.
4. Solve the equation for the optimal order quantity.

G. Variables used in equation:
Q = number of pieces in the order
$Q*$ = optimal number (EOQ)
D = annual demand in units
S = setup cost per order
H = holding cost per unit per year

H. Determination of the equation:
1. The total annual setup cost is:
   Annual setup cost = $(D/Q) * S$
2. The total annual carrying cost is:
   Annual carrying cost = $(Q/2) * H$
3. The total annual inventory cost is:
   $TC = [(D/Q) * S] + [(Q/2) * H]$
4. The optimal value of Q is:
   $Q_{opt} = \sqrt{(2*D*S)/H}$
5. Expected Number Orders:
   $N = D / Q*$
6. Expected Time Between Orders:
   $T = \dfrac{\text{Work Days/Yr}}{N}$
7. Daily demand:
   $d = \dfrac{D}{\text{Work Days/Yr}}$
8. Reorder Point:
   $ROP = d * L$

Example: EOQ Model

Sharp, Inc., a company that markets painless hypodermic needles to hospitals, would like to reduce its inventory cost by determining the optimal number of hypodermic needles to obtain per order. The annual demand is 1,000 units; the setup or ordering cost is $10 per order; and the holding cost per year is $.50. Using these figures, we can calculate the optimal number of units per order:

Solution: EOQ Model
Step 1: Identify cost:

Holding cost: H = $0.50 per unit
Setup cost: S = $10 per order
Annual Demand: D = 1,000 units

Step 2: Calculate the optimal order size:

$$Q_{opt} = \sqrt{(2*D*S)/H}$$
$$Q_{opt} = \sqrt{[2\,(10)(1000)]}\,/\,0.50$$
$$= 200 \text{ units}$$

Example: Number of Orders and Time Between Orders

Using the data from Sharp, Inc., in the previous example, and assuming a 250-day working year, we find the number of orders (N) and the expected time between orders (T) as:

Step 3: Calculate the number of orders per year.

$$N = D / Q*$$
$$= 1000 / 200 = 5 \text{ orders per year}$$

Step 4: Calculate the order cycle given the store is open 311 days annually.

$$T = \frac{\text{Work Days/Yr}}{N}$$
$$= 250 / 5 = 50 \text{ days between orders}$$

Example: Total Annual Inventory Cost

Again using the Sharp, Inc., data from Examples 3 and 4, we determine that the total annual inventory costs are:

Step 5: Calculate the total annual inventory cost using Q_{opt} of 2000.

$$TC = [(D/Q) * S] + [(Q/2) * H]$$
$$= [(1000/200) * 10] + [(200/2) * 0.50]$$
$$= \$100$$

I. Using this model we are able to write an equation for total cost of inventory. By adding the price of the inventory itself as a fixed cost as follows:

$$TC = [(D/Q) \times S] + [(Q/2) \times H] + PD$$

V. Robust Model
   A. A benefit of EOQ is that it is robust, that is, it gives satisfactory answers even with substantial variation in its parameters.
   B. Variations in holding, setup, demand, or EOQ make very modest changes in TC. Therefore errors do not cost very much. This is attractive since we have limits on our ability to forecast demand, holding costs, and ordering cost.

If management in the Sharp, Inc., examples underestimated total demand by 50% (say demand is actually 1,500 needles rather than 1,000 needles) while using the same Q, the annual inventory cost increases only $25 ($100 versus $125), or 25%. Here is why.

If demand in the earlier example is actually 1,500 needles rather than 1,000, but management uses an order quantity of Q = 200 (when it should be Q = 244.9 based on D = 1,500), the sum of holding and ordering cost increases 25%:

Solution:

$$Annual\ cost\ = [(D/Q) * S] + [(Q/2) * H]$$
$$= [(1500/200) * 10] + [(200/2) * 0.50] = \$125$$

C. Reorder Points
1. After finding how much to order, we now need to know when to order.
2. Although the EOQ model assumes receipt of the order is instantaneous, in real life there is lead time (time between order and receipt)
3. ROP = (demand per day) x (lead time in days per order)
   = D x L
4. Because we assume demand to be constant, in real life we must add safety stock in case of an increase in D.
5. Demand per day is found:
   D / # of working days per year

Graph of Reorder Point

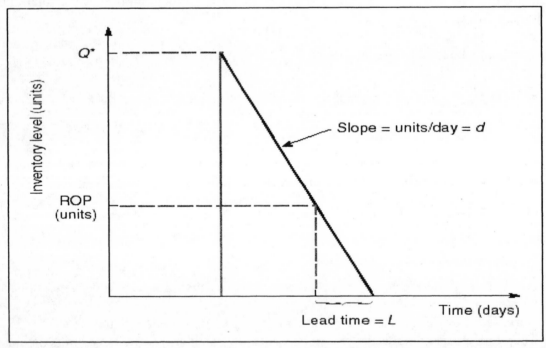

Lecture Key: *The optimum order quantity and lead time represent the time between placing and receiving an order. Also the amount of safety stock added depends on the nature of the business and lead time.*

Electronic Assembler, Inc., has a demand for 8,000 VCRs per year. The firm operates a 250-day working year. On average, delivery of an order takes 3 working days. We calculate the reorder point as:

Solution:

Step 1: Determine the daily demand:

$$d = D / \text{\# of working days per year}$$
$$= 8000 / 250 = 32 \text{ units per day}$$

Step 2: Determine the ROP:

$$\text{ROP} = d \times L$$
$$= 32 \text{ units/day} \times 3 \text{ days} = 96 \text{ units}$$

Analysis: Thus, when inventory stock drops to 96, an order should be placed. The order will arrive 3 days later, just as the firm's stock is depleted.

VI.   Production Order Quantity Model

   A. This is an economic order quantity technique applied to production orders. The model is useful in two situations:
      1. When inventory continuously builds up over a period of time after an order has been placed.
      2. When units are produced and sold simultaneously.
   B. In order to derive this model, you must set the ordering cost equal to the holding cost. This enables you to come up with the optimal ordering size. The following letters make up the model:
      Q = Number of pieces per order
      H = Holding cost per unit per year
      p = daily production rate
      d = daily demand rate (usage rate)
      t = length of the production run in days
   C. Production Order Quantity Model Equations:
      1. Annual inventory holding cost
         = (Avg. inventory level) X (holding cost per unit per year)
      2. Avg. Inventory level
         = (Maximum inventory level) / 2
      3. Maximum inventory level
         = (Total produced during production run) – (Total used during prod. run)
         = $pt - dt$

         or

         = $Q(1 - d/p)$

D. Annual inventory holding cost
   = (Q/2) * [1 – (d/p)] * H
E. Annual inventory setup cost
   = (D / Q) * S
F. Production Order Quantity (POQ; Q_p*)
   Q_p* = √[2*D*S] / [H * (1 – d/p)]

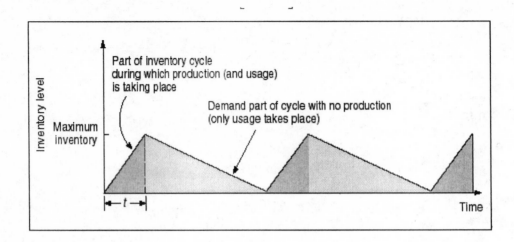

Lecture Key: *The production Order Quantity Model is unlike the EOQ model in the fact that the holding costs are reduced in the production order quantity model.*

Example: POQ Model

Nathan's Manufacturing, Inc., makes and sells specialty hubcaps for the retail automobile market. Nathan's forecast for its wire-wheel hubcap is 1,000 units next year, with an average daily demand of 4 units. However, the production process is most efficient at 8 units per day. So the comp. Produces 8 per day but only uses 4. Given the following values, solve for the optimum number of units per order.

Solution:
Step 1: Determine the variables.

Annual demand:	D = 1,000 units
Setup costs:	S = $10
Holding cost:	H = $0.50 per unit per day
Daily production rate:	p = 8 units per day
Daily demand rate:	d = 4 units per day

Step 2: Calculate the POQ:

$$Q_p* = \sqrt{[2*D*S]/[H*(1-d/p)]}$$

$$= \sqrt{[2*1,000*10]/[0.50*(1-1/2)]}$$

$$= 282.8 \text{ or } 283 \text{ hubcaps}$$

Quantity Discount Models

A. Quantity discounts are placed on particular items when they are:
   1. Ordered in large quantities.
   2. A Quantity Discount Schedule.

Discount Number	Discount Quantity	Discount (%)	Discount Price
1	0 to 999	No discount	$5.00
2	1,000 to 1,999	4	$4.80
3	2,000 and over	5	$4.75

   3. The main job for the manager is to reduce total cost. He/she may do this by ordering the product at the lowest unit cost, (#3), but they also have to look at the inventory cost if they order such a large quantity. Using the formula for this:

   Total Cost = Setup cost + Holding cost + Product Cost
   TC = [(D/Q) * S] + [(Q/2) * H] + PD
      Where:
         Q = Quantity ordered
         D = Annual demand in units
         S = Ordering or setup cost per order or per setup
         P = Price per unit
         H = Holding cost per unit per year

B. 4 steps of Quantity Discount Problems:
   Step 1: Calculate a value for the optimal order size using:
      $Q_{opt} = \sqrt{(2*D*S)/IP}$
      Where: IP = Item Price
   Step 2: Adjust the order quantity upward to the lowest quantity that will qualify for the discount. This is finding break points for each price discount. For example, price breaks occur at 1,000 units and 2,000 units.
   Step 3: Compute a total cost for every Q* determined in Steps 1 and 2.
   Step 4: Select the Q* that has the lowest total cost computed in Step 3.

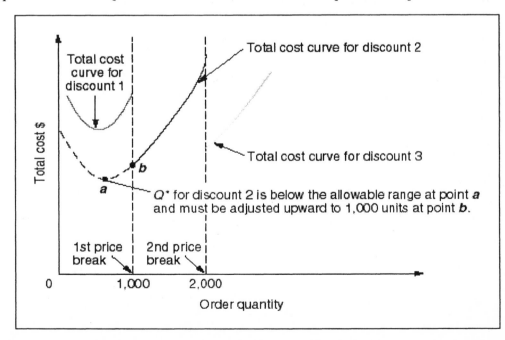

261

Example: Quantity Discount Problems
_____

Wohl's Discount Store stocks toy race cars. Recently, the store has been given a quantity discount schedule for these cars. This quantity schedule was shown in the table below.

Discount Number	Discount Quantity	Discount (%)	Discount Price
1	0 to 999	No discount	$5.00
2	1,000 to 1,999	4	$4.80
3	2,000 and over	5	$4.75

Thus, the normal cost for the toy race cars is $5.00. For orders between 1,000 and 1,999 units, the unit cost drops to $4.80; for orders of 2,000 or more units, the unit cost is only $4.75. Furthermore, ordering cost is $49.00 per order, annual demand is 5,000 race cars, and inventory carrying charge, as a percentage of cost, I, is 20%, or .2. What order quantity will minimize the total inventory cost?

Solution:
Step 1: Calculate a value for the optimal order size using:

$$Q_1^* = \sqrt{(2 * 5,000 * 49)/(.2 * 5.00)} \qquad = 700 \text{ car orders}$$
$$Q_2^* = \sqrt{(2 * 5,000 * 49)/(.2 * 4.80)} \qquad = 714 \text{ car orders}$$
$$Q_3^* = \sqrt{(2 * 5,000 * 49)/(.2 * 4.75)} \qquad = 718 \text{ car orders}$$

Step 2: Adjust the order quantity upward to the lowest quantity that will qualify for the discount. Since Q_1^* is between 0 and 999, it need not be adjusted. Because Q_2^* is below the allowable range of 1,000 to 1,999, it must be adjusted to 1,000 units. The same is true for Q_3^*. It must be adjusted to 2,000 units.

$$Q_1^* = 700$$
$$Q_2^* = 1,000 \text{ (adjusted from 714)}$$
$$Q_3^* = 2,000 \text{ (adjusted from 718)}$$

Step 3: Compute a total cost for every Q* determined in Steps 1 and 2.

$$TC_{700} = [(5,000/700) * 49] + [(700/2) * (.2 * 5.00)] + 5.00 \qquad = \$25,700$$
$$TC_{1,000} = [(5,000/1000) * 49] + [(1000/2) * (.2 * 4.80)] + 4.80 \quad = \$24,725$$
$$TC_{2,000} = [(5,000/2000) * 49] + [(2000/2) * (.2 * 4.75)] + 4.75 \quad = \$24.822.50$$

Step 4: Select the Q* that has the lowest total cost computed in Step 3.

The order quantity of 1,000 toy racecars will minimize the total cost ($24,725). If the discount on 2,000 units is slightly lowered, then it would be better to adjust the order quantity to 2,000 units.

VIII. Probabilistic Models With Constant Lead Time

A. Probabilistic models provide a probability distribution when the product demand is unknown.
1. The service level is the complement of the probability of a stockout, which occurs when you run out of stock.
2. The equation to find the reorder point :
   Reorder point (ROP) = Daily demand x Order lead time
   $$= d \times L$$
3. Safety stock, extra stock that makes sure you don't run out, must also be figured into the equation:
   ROP = (d x L) + ss
   Where: ss = safety stock
4. When determining the safety stock, you must consider the cost of incurring a stockout and the cost of holding the extra inventory. Using the following formula, you can compute the annual stockout cost:
   Annual Stockout Cost = Sum of the units short x probability
   x stockout cost/unit x # of orders per year

B. This graph shows that quantity needed at the reorder point is 350, but because of safety stock you will actually need 366.5.

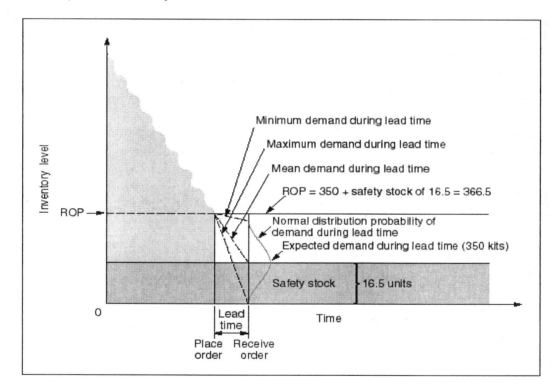

Example: Safety Stock

David Rivera Optical has determined that its reorder point for eyeglass frames is 50 (d x L) units. Its carrying cost per frame per year is $5, and stockout (or lost sale) cost is $40 per frame. The store has experienced the following probability distribution for inventory demand during the reorder period. The optimum number of orders per year is six.

Number of Units	Probability
30	.20
40	.20
50 – ROP	.30
60	.20
70	.10
	1.0

How much safety stock should David Rivera keep on hand?

Solution:

The objective is to find the amount of safety stock that minimizes the sum of the additional inventory holding cost and stockout costs. The annual holding cost is simply the holding cost per unit multiplied by the units added to the ROP. For example:

> Safety Stock (ss)　　　　 = 20 frames
> New ROP　　　　　　　 = 70 frames (50 frames + 20 ss frames)
> Additional carrying cost　= $5 x 20 extra frames = $100

For any level of safety stock, stockout cost is the expected cost of stocking out. We can compute it by multiplying the number of frames short by the probability of demand at that level, by the stockout cost, by the number of times per year the stockout can occur (which in our case is the number of orders per year). Then we add stockout costs for each possible stockout level for a given ROP. For zero safety stock, for example, a shortage of 10 frames will occur if demand is 60, and a shortage of 20 frames will occur if the demand is 70. Thus the stockout costs for zero safety stock are:

> Annual Stockout Costs　 = Sum of the units short x probability
> 　　　　　　　　　　　　　　 x stockout cost/unit x # of orders per year
> 　　　　　　　　　　　 = (10 frames short) x (.20 probability)
> 　　　　　　　　　　　　　　 x ($40 per stockout) x (6 possible stockouts per year)
> 　　　　　　　　　　　 = $960

Summary

Safety Stock	Additional Holding Cost	Stockout Cost	Total Cost
20	(20) ($5) = $100	$ 0	$100
10	(10) ($5) = $50	(10) (.1) ($40) (6) = $240	$290
0	$ 0	(10) (.2) ($40) (6) + (20)(.1)($40)(6) = $960	$960

The safety stock with the lowest total cost is 20 frames. Therefore, this safety stock changes the reorder point to 50 + 20 = 70 frames.

Lecture Key: It should be noted that in some situations it may be impossible to determine the cost of running out of stock. In these situations, a manager may decide to keep enough safety stock in order to meet customer demand.

Lecture Key: Exactly how much stock should you have at any given time and when you will need to reorder? This information is extremely beneficial to any manager as he or she manages his or her inventory. The process and numbers are not difficult, but if computed incorrectly, disaster could loom for the company.

Example: How Much Safety Stock?

Memphis Regional Hospital stocks a "code blue" resuscitation kit that has a normally distributed demand during the reorder period. The mean (average) demand during the reorder period is 350 kits, and the standard deviation is 10 kits. The hospital administrator wants to follow a policy that results in stockouts occurring only 5% of the time.

    a. What is the appropriate value of Z?
    b. How much safety stock should the hospital maintain?
    c. What reorder point should be used?

Solution:
    a. Determine the z score needed to stockout only 5% of the time. This is the same as a 95% service level $(1 - .05)$. Using the normal distribution table (Appendix I), find the z value at 1.65 standard deviations from the mean.
    b. Safety stock = z x σ
                      = 1.65 x 10 = 16.5 kits
    c. Calculate the ROP
           ROP = Expected demand during the lead time + safety stock
                   = 350 kits + 16.5 kits of safety stock = 366.5 or 367 kits

IX.   Fixed-Period (P) Systems

    A. In a fixed period system, inventory is ordered at the end of a certain period. This point is the only time that inventory is counted. The period for ordering is fixed, but quantity is not. Only the amount needed to bring inventory to a targeted level should be ordered.
    B. Fixed-period systems are like the fixed-quantity systems in three ways:
        1. The only relevant costs are the ordering and holding costs.
        2. Lead times are known and constant.
        3. Items are independent of one another.

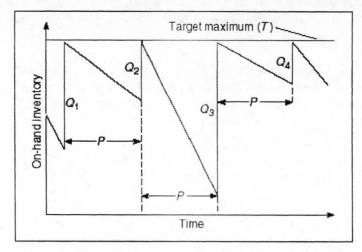

C. This graph shows that whenever this company did reorder, they always ordered exactly enough to meet their target maximum. It also shows how this method is not fixed on quantity in order to reorder. Three different amounts of inventory were reached before they reordered.

Example: Fixed-Period (P) Systems

Hard Rock London has a back order for three leather bomber jackets in its retail shop. There are no jackets in stock, none are expected from earlier orders, and it is time to place an order. The target value is 50 jackets. How many bomber jackets should be ordered?

Solution:
Order Amount
= Target (T) − On-hand inventory − Earlier orders not yet received + Back orders
= 50 − 0 − 0 + 3 = 53 jackets

D. There are advantages and disadvantages for using the fixed-period system.
1. Advantages: It allows vendors to make routine orders and also to save on ordering and transportation costs.
2. Disadvantages: Since a vendor may order inventory on the same schedule, there is possibility of a stock out. This can be detrimental to any business because then they do not have products to sell. To compensate for these, managers may carry too much safety stock, which can prove to be costly.

CHAPTER 12 PROBLEMS

ABC Classification System

S1.   The manager of a small manufacturing firm has responsibility for maintaining an inventory of items used in production. The parts inventory, unit cost, and annual usage are as follows:

Item #	Unit Cost	Annual Vol. (Units)	Total Dollar Value
286	$90	1000	$90,000
2526	154	500	77,000
3760	17	1600	27,200
4867	43	300	12,900
5500	13	1000	13,000
572	14	600	8,400
75	.50	2000	1,000
36	9	100	900
9307	.40	1200	480
10572	.50	250	125

The manager wants to classify the inventory parts according to the ABC system to determine which stocks of parts should most closely be monitored.

Solution:

Step 1:   Rank the items according to their total value. Item 286 has the highest total value at $90,000, so it is ranked first.

Step 2:   Compute each item's percentage of total value by dividing the total value of an item by the total value of all items. For Item 286, it would be 90,000 / 214, 205 = 39.0%.

Step 3:   Calculate the cumulative total as each item is added to the inventory. The cumulative total begins at 0. After Item 286 is added, the cumulative total is 0 + 39.0 or 39.0. After Item 2526 is added, the cumulative total is 39.0 + 33.3 or 72.3. You would continue through the entire list. The last item should have a cumulative total of 100.0%.

Part	Total Value	% of Total Value	% Cumulative	Classification
286	$90,000	39.0	39.0	A
2526	77,000	33.3	72.3	A
3760	27,200	11.8	84.1	B
4867	12,900	5.6	89.7	B
5500	13,000	5.6	95.3	B
572	8,400	3.6	98.9	C
75	1,000	0.4	99.3	C
36	900	0.4	99.7	C
9307	480	0.2	99.9	C
10572	125	0.1	100.0	C
	$214,205			

Step 4:   Determine the classification of each item based on the cumulative ranking. The first 80% of the cumulative total are class A items. The next 10% to 15% (or cumulative percentage of 90% to 95%) are class B items. The final 5% (or cumulative percentage of 95% to 100%) are class C items. The last column in the chart above shows the classification of items. The cutoffs are judgment, but you want them to be close to the percentages. We will make a cut after Item 2526 or 72.3% and another cut after Item 572 or 95.3%.

Analysis: You would want to ensure accurate forecasting and security of items 286 and 2526 since they are the most important. This doesn't mean that you neglect the other items, but you don't put as much emphasis on them. The only exception could be if the B or C item is an important complement to one of your A items.

S2.   The manager of a small manufacturing firm has responsibility for maintaining an inventory of items used in production. The parts inventory, unit cost, and annual usage are as follows:

Item #	Unit Cost	Annual Vol. (Units)	Total Dollar Value
305	$771	3325	$2,565,000
1873	$1,320	713	$940,500
2737	$146	2280	$332,229
3512	$369	1283	$472,693
3955	$111	1425	$158,786
505	$120	855	$102,600
158	$30	23200	$696,000
130	$77	14250	$1,099,286
6620	$3	85500	$293,143
7505	$429	356	$152,679

The manager wants to classify the inventory parts according to the ABC system to determine which stocks of parts should most closely be monitored.

Solution:

Step 1:   Rank the items according to their total value. Item 305 has the highest total value at $2,565,000, so it is ranked first. Item 130 is second at $1,099,286.

Step 2:   Compute each item's percentage of total value by dividing the total value of an item by the total value of all items. For Item 305, it would be 2,565,000/ 6,812,914 = 39.0%.

Step 3:   Calculate the cumulative total as each item is added to the inventory. The cumulative total begins at 0. After Item 305 is added, the cumulative total is 0 + 37.6 or 3.6. After Item 130 is added, the cumulative total is 37.6 + 16.1 or 53.8. You would continue through the entire list. The last item should have a cumulative total of 100.0%.

Item #	Total Dollar Value	% of Total Value	Cumulative %	Classification
305	$2,565,000	37.6%	37.6%	A
130	$1,099,286	16.1%	53.8%	A
1873	$940,500	13.8%	67.6%	A
158	$696,000	10.2%	77.8%	A
3512	$472,693	6.9%	84.7%	B
2737	$332,229	4.9%	89.6%	B
6620	$293,143	4.3%	93.9%	B
3955	$158,786	2.3%	96.3%	C
7505	$152,679	2.2%	98.5%	C
505	$102,600	1.5%	100.0%	C
	$6,812,914			

Step 4:   Determine the classification of each item based on the cumulative ranking. The last column in the chart above shows the classification of items. The cutoffs are judgment, but you want them to be close to the percentages. We will make a cut after Item 158 or 77.8% and another cut after Item 6620 or 93.9%.

Analysis: You would want to ensure accurate forecasting and security of items 305, 130, 1873, and 158 since they are the most important. This doesn't mean that you neglect the other items, but you don't put as much emphasis on them. The only exception could be if the B or C item is an important complement to one of your A items.

1.   Kurt Wayne has been asked to complete an ABC Analysis for a small set of inventory. Please help Kurt complete his analysis. Explain what this analysis means.

Item	Annual Demand	Unit Cost
1	150	50
2	60	150
3	75	100
4	200	150
5	150	75

2.   Lawn Trimmer has 10 items that it keeps in inventory. The manager has asked you to evaluate these items and recommend which items are the most important based on ABC Analysis.

Item	Annual Demand	Unit Cost
D1	300	500
D2	400	120
D3	150	450
E4	600	100
E5	100	200
R6	50	5000
R7	30	15,000
R8	60	200
T9	175	100
T10	250	50

3.   Using ABC Analysis, decide which of the following products need a forecasting system developed.

SKU #	Annual Demand	Unit Cost
A	80	40.00
B	120	80.00
C	70	30.00
D	100	20.00
E	50	60.00
F	150	10.00
G	80	70.00
H	150	40.00
I	120	10.00
J	20	80.00

Cycle Counting

S1.   Tiger Electronics, a small manufacturer, has approximately 10,000 items in its inventory and wants to know how many items need to be counted each day based on the following facts: 10% are classified as A items, 40% are B items, and 50% are C items. Also, they want A items counted every month, B items counted every quarter, and C items counted semiannually.

Solution:

Step 1:   List the items and the information known for each.

Total Items	% of Each Category	Total Items per Category
10,000 total items	x .10 (A)	1000
	x .40 (B)	4000
	x .50 (C)	5000

Step 2:   Divide the quantity for each one by the cycle counting policy to get the number of items counted per day.

Item Class	Items / Category	Cycle Counting Policy	# of Items Counted per Day
A	1000	÷ 20 days (working days per month)	50 items
B	4000	÷ 60 days (working days per quarter)	67 items
C	5000	÷ 120 (working days semiannually)	42 items

Step 3:   Add these up and you will set the number of items to be counted each day.

Item Class	# of Items Counted per Day
A	50 items
B	67 items
C	42 items
	159 items per day

Decision: 159 items are counted each day.

S2.   Brad's mower, a small manufacturing and repair shop, has approximately 100,000 items in its inventory and have hired Jim Beam to manage its inventory. Jim has determined that 15% of the items in inventory are A items, 40% are B items, and 45% are C items. He would like to set up a system in which all A items are counted monthly (every 25 working days), all B items are counted quarterly (every 75 working days), and all C items are counted semiannually (every 150 days). How many items need to be counted each day?

Solution:
Step 1:   List the items and the information known for each.

Total Items	% of Each Category	Total Items per Category
100,000 total items	x .15 (A)	15000
	x .40 (B)	40000
	x .45 (C)	45000

Step 2:   Divide the quantity for each one by the cycle counting policy to get the number of items counted per day.

Item Class	Items / Category	Cycle Counting Policy	# of Items Counted per Day
A	15000	÷ 25 days (working days per month)	600 items
B	40000	÷ 75 days (working days per quarter)	534 items
C	45000	÷ 150 (working days semiannually)	300 items

Step 3:   Add these up and you will set the number of items to be counted each day.

Item Class	# of Items Counted per Day
A	600 items
B	534 items
C	300 items
	1434 items per day

Decision: 1434 items are counted each day.

Economic Order Quantity (EOQ)

Note: For the purpose of clarity, the problems will use H to represent the Holding Cost and S to represent the Setup Cost.

S1.   The Crawfish Kitchen sells 1200 pounds of crawfish a week. Each pound costs $10 to hold. The ordering cost and carrying cost is $50. Due to seasonal production, the kitchen is open only 40 weeks of the year. The manager wants to determine the following items.
   a. EOQ.
   b. The holding cost for crawfish.
   c. The setup cost for placing an order.
   d. The total inventory cost for using the EOQ.

Solution:

Step 1:   Determine all the annual demand. Demand per week multiplied by the number of weeks of operation (1200 * 40 =48,000). Other costs are given such as: carrying cost is $50 and holding cost is $10 per pound.

Step 2:   Using the EOQ formula, calculate the economic order quantity.

   a. $Q* = \sqrt{(2*D*S)/H} = \sqrt{(2*48{,}000*50)/10} = 692.82$ pounds

Step 3:   The annual holding cost is calculated by multiplying the holding cost per pound by the average pounds held in inventory. The average is calculated by dividing the EOQ by 2.

   b.   Annual Holding Cost $= 10 * (692.82 / 2) = \$3464.10$

Step 4:   The annual ordering cost is calculated by multiplying the ordering cost per pound by the number of annual orders. The number of orders per year is calculated by dividing the annual demand by the EOQ.

   c.   Annual Ordering Cost $= 50 * (48{,}000 / 692.82) = \$3464.10$

Step 5:   The total annual inventory cost is calculated by adding the ordering cost to the cost of holding the pounds in inventory. These costs were calculated in parts b. and c.

   d. Total Cost $=$ Annual Holding Cost $+$ Annual Ordering Cost
   $= \$3464.10 + \$3464.10 = \$6928.20$

Analysis: The EOQ could be rounded up or down depending upon the objectives of the company. If the objective were to minimize inventory holding, then you would round down to 692. If your objective were to maximize customer service, then you would round up to 693.

S2.   Pelican Landing stocks and sells fishing gear. It costs the firm $450 each time it places an order with the manufacturer for the fishing gear. The cost of carrying a complete set of fishing gear in inventory for a year is $170. The store manager estimates that total annual demand for the fishing gear will be 1,200 units, with a constant demand rate throughout the year. Orders are received within minutes after placement from a local warehouse maintained by the manufacturer. The store policy is never to have stockouts of the gear. The store is open for business every day of the year except Christmas Day. Determine the following:

   a. Optimal order quantity per order.
   b. Minimum total annual inventory costs.
   c. The number of orders per year.
   d. The time between orders (in working days).

Solution:

Step 1: Determine all the annual demand and other costs:

Order costs = $450/order
Holding costs = $170/year
D = 1200 units/year
364 days year

Step 2: Using the EOQ formula, calculate the economic order quantity.

a. $Q^* = \sqrt{(2*D*S)/H} = \sqrt{(2*1200*450)/170} = 79.7$ units

Step 3: Using the total cost formula, calculate the total cost at the economic order quantity.

b. Annual Cost = [(Q*/2)*H] + [(D/Q*) * S]
    = [(80/2)*170] + [(1200/80) * 450] = $13,550

Step 4: Calculate the number of orders per year by dividing the annual demand by the EOQ.

c. The number of orders per year = N = 1200 / 80 = 15

Step 5: Calculate the time between orders (in working days) by dividing the total number of days of operations annually by the number of orders per year (N = 15 for part c.).

d. The time between orders = T = 364/15 = 14.27 days between orders

S3. Lagneaux's Country Store stocks and sells wooden chairs. It costs the store $120 each time it places an order with the carpenter for the chairs. The cost of carrying the chair in inventory for a year is $20. The store manager estimates the total annual demand for the chairs to be 110 chairs, with a constant demand rate throughout the year. The store is open 240 days out of the year. Determine the following:

a. Optimal order quantity per order.
b. Total annual inventory costs.
c. Optimal number of orders per year.
d. The time between orders (in working days).

Solution:

a. $Q^* = \sqrt{((2*D*S)/H)} = \sqrt{((2*110*120)/20)} = 36.33$
b. TC – [H * (Q/2)] + [S * (D/Q)] = [20 * (36.33/2)] + [120 * (110/36.33)] = 726.64
c. N = D/Q = 110/36.33 = 3.03
d. T = Working Days/N = 240/3.03 = 79.21 → 79 days

1. Lawn Trimmer stocks and distributes lawn equipment. It costs the firm $650 each time it places an order with the production department for the large lawn tractor. The cost of holding the tractor in inventory is $2000 for a year. The store manager estimates that total annual demand for the computers will be 50,000 tractors, with a constant demand rate throughout the year. Orders are received within minutes after placement by the production department. The company operates shifts every day of the year except Christmas Day. Determine the following:

a. Optimal order quantity per order.
b. Minimum total annual inventory costs.
c. The number of orders per year.
d. The time between orders (in working days).

2. Bonnie Woo is developing an inventory system on one of her most popular products. Annual demand for this product is 25,000 units, the unit cost is $200; holding cost is considered to be approximately 20% of the unit price. Order costs for this item are approximately $30.00 per order and lead-time is 10 days. The company has operations open 365 days per year.

    a. What is the economic order quantity?
    b. What is the reorder point?
    c. What is the total annual inventory cost?
    d. What is the optimal number of orders per year?
    e. What is the optimal number of days between any two orders?

3. Barb's Bakery purchases sugar in 20 pound sacks. The bakery uses an average of 6,000 sacks a year. Preparing an order and receiving a shipment of sugar involves a cost of $5 per order. Annual holding costs are $20 per sack.

    a. What is the economic order quantity?
    b. What is the average number of sacks on hand?
    c. What is the total annual inventory cost?
    d. What is the optimal number of orders per year?
    e. If the annual ordering cost were to increase to $10 per order, how much would that change your previous answer?

4. The A-Z Tax Service operates on average 300 days per year. The manager wants to optimize the order quantity for reams of paper. He has compiled the following cost and demand data. The company averages 12,000 reams of paper annually. The holding cost is $2 per ream annually, and it costs approximately $5 to order a ream of paper. What is the optimal order quantity?

5. A local pipe manufacturer has contacted a consultant to help determine the costs associated with making an order for a 6" stock pipe. The costs are approximately $350 per order. The consultant has also determined that the costs of carrying the item in inventory amount to approximately $15 per running foot of pipe per year. Demand for the item is reasonably constant over time, and the forecast is for 120,000 running feet per year. When an order is placed for the pipe, the supplier immediately delivers the entire order to the firm. The firm operates 6 days a week plus a few Sundays, or approximately 340 days per year. Determine the following:

    a. Optimal order quantity per order.
    b. Total annual inventory costs.
    c. Optimal number of orders to place per year.
    d. Number of operating days between orders, based on Optimal ordering.

6. Fabric Discount purchases denim from a supplier in the southeast region of the US. Fabric Discount produces material that includes 800,000 yards of denim per year to make their various patterns. The cost of ordering the denim from the supplier company is $75 per order. It costs $0.10 per yard annually for Fabric Discount to hold a yard of denim in inventory. Determine the EOQ for yards of denim. What is the minimum total inventory for Fabric Discount?

EOQ Model with Noninstantaneous Receipt (POQ)

S1.   Cedar Key Citrus makes orange juice to supply to stores in its area. The mill can make 550 pounds of orange juice per day, and the demand at the area stores is 400 gallons per day. Each time the mill makes orange juice, it costs $225 to set up the production process. The annual cost of carrying a gallon of orange juice in a refrigerated storage area is $30. The mill operates 365 days/year. Determine the optimal order size and the minimum total inventory cost.

Solution:

Step 1:   Identify cost.

H = $30 per pound d = 400 pounds per day
S = $225 per order p = 550 pounds per day
D = 400 x 365 = 146,000 pounds

Step 2:   Calculate the optimal order size.

$Q_{opt} = \sqrt{[(2* S *D)]/ [H *(1 - (d/p)]}$
$Q_{opt} = \sqrt{[2\ (225)(146,000)] / [30*(1 - (400/550)]} =$ 2,833.73 pounds

Step 3:   Calculate the total annual inventory cost using Q_{opt} of 2,833.73 pounds.

$TC = [(S *(D/Q)] + [(H *(Q/2)) * (1 - (d/p))]$
$= [(225)(146,000 / 2,833.73)] + [((30) * (2,833.73 / 2) *(1 - (400/550))] =$ $23183.87

S2.   Vermilion Dairy produces milk to supply stores in the parish. The dairy can produce 200 gallons of milk per day, and the demand at the stores is 160 per day. Each time the dairy produces milk it costs $100 to set up the production process. The annual cost of carrying a gallon of milk in a refrigerated storage area is $20. The dairy operates 365 days a year. Determine the optimal order size and the total annual inventory cost.

Solution:

Step 1:   Identify cost.

H = $20 per gallon d = 160 gallons per day
S = $100 per order p = 200 gallons per day
D = 160 x 365 = 58,400 gallons

Step 2:   Calculate the optimal order size.

$Q_{opt} = \sqrt{[(2* S *D)]/ [H *(1 - (d/p)]}$
$Q_{opt} = \sqrt{[2\ (100)(58,400)] / [20*(1 - (160/200)]} =$ 1708.8 gallons

Step 3:   Calculate the total annual inventory cost using Q_{opt} of 1708.8 gallons.

$TC = [(S *(D/Q)] + [(H *(Q/2)) * (1 - (d/p))]$
$= [(100)(58,400 / 1708.8)] + [((20) * (1708.8 / 2) *(1 - (160/200))] =$ $6,835.20

Step 4:   Calculate the setup cost for an order.

$SC = D/Q * S = (58400/1708.8) * 100 = 3,417.6$

Step 5:   Calculate the holding cost per gallon.

$HC = .5 * H * Q * (1 - d/p) = .5 * 20 * 1708.8 * (1 - 160/200) = 3417.6$

Step 6:   Calculate the maximum inventory level.

Maximum Inventory $= Q * (1 - d/p) = 1708.8 * (1 - 160/200) = 341.76$

1.   Madeline Craig, owner of Kitchen Edge, wants to decide the optimal production quantity for its top seller, Economy Chopper. The company produces 10,000 Choppers per year, and Madeline estimates that capacity for production is 200 choppers per day. Daily demand has been determined from sales records to be 75 per day. The cost of ordering a production run is $80, and the chopper has a holding cost of $1.50 per chopper. What is the optimal order quantity? What is the minimum inventory cost?

2.   Lawn Trimmer receives wheel assemblies for its products from a supplier. The supplier has an annual demand of 150,000 assemblies. The company operates 300 days per year for production. The daily demand is 460 units per day. The ordering and holding costs have been estimated at $30 per order and $0.50 per assembly, respectively.

3.   Sparkle Pool Chemicals is looking to optimize its production inventory quantities for chlorine. The company has an annual demand of 50,000 gallons of chlorine annually and produces 350 days per year. The daily demand for Sparkle's products is 75 gallons per day. The inventory carrying cost is 10% of the purchase price of $10.00 per gallon. The ordering cost is $60 per order. Determine the optimal order quantity. Sparkle must make decisions regarding inventory space for the chlorine and needs to know the most that will be on hand at one time.

4.   Hammond Honey makes honey to supply to stores in its area. The mill can make 550 pounds of honey per day, and the demand at the area stores is 400 pounds per day. Each time the mill makes honey, it costs $225 to set up the production process. The annual cost of carrying a pound of honey in a refrigerated storage area is $30. The dairy is operated 365 days per year. Determine the optimal order size and the minimum total annual inventory cost.

5.   The Healthy Medical Supply fills 1-liter bottles with antiseptic solution, which it stores in plastic bottles in its warehouse and supplies nationally to hospitals on demand. It costs $800 to set up a production run for the filling machine. Once it is filled into containers, the solution is stored in a sterile environment at an annual cost of $20 per bottle. The demand for the solution is 600 bottles of solution per day. The company can produce 1200 bottles per day. Determine the economic order quantity and the minimum total annual inventory cost.

6.   You are the supply manager for Huntington Tools. Huntington makes 25,000 hand scrapers per year. Demand is 75 scrapers per day and production is 200 per day. The setup cost is estimated to be $100 per order and the carrying cost is $1.00 per scraper. What is the optimal order quantity, annual inventory cost, and maximum inventory levels?

Quantity Discount

S1.   Kid Play Manufacturers produces and stocks dolls. They have been given a quantity discount schedule for the dolls. This quantity list is given below. The ordering cost is $49 per order and the holding cost is 20% of the cost. If annual demand is 5,000 dolls, what order quantity would be optimal to minimize cost?

Quantity	Price
1 – 999	$5.00
1,000 – 1,999	4.80
2,000+	4.75

Solution:

Step 1:   Determine the optimal order size and total cost with the basic EOQ model.

$S = \$49$ $H = \text{Cost} \times 0.20 \text{ per doll}$ $D = 5{,}000 \text{ dolls per year}$

$$Q_{opt} = \sqrt{(2 * S * D)/ H}$$
$$= \sqrt{(2 * 5000 * 49)/ (.20*5)} = 700 \text{ dolls}$$

Step 2:   Using $Q = 700$, this gives us a price of $5.00. Calculate the total cost.

$$TC = [S*(D/Q)] + [H*(Q/2)] + (P*D)$$
$$= [(49 * (5000/700)] + [1 * (700/2)] + [5*5000] = \$25{,}700$$

Step 3: Compare the total cost calculated with the total cost at the higher discount level. The next cost break is at Q = 1000.

$$TC_{1000} = [S*(D/Q)] + [H*(Q/2)] + (P*D)$$
$$= [(49 * (5000/1000)] + [0.96 * (1000/2)] + [4.80*5000] = \$24,725$$

The next cost break is at Q = 2000.

$$TC_{2000} = [S*(D/Q)] + [H*(Q/2)] + (P*D)$$
$$= [(49 * (5000/2000)] + [0.95 * (2000/2)] + [4.75*5000] = \$24,822.5$$

Step 4: Make the decision.

The costs are lower at Q = 1000. The maximum discount price should be taken, and 1000 units should be ordered since this will result in the maximum discount.

S2. A hospital needs 10,000 surgical instruments annually and the holding cost for those instruments is 10% of the cost of the instruments. It costs the hospital $40 per order. If the normal price is $100 per instrument, then what amount should the hospital order each time it places an order to minimize inventory cost? What price should the hospital expect to pay for each item? What is the annual cost for the optimal order quantity? Below represents the ordering discount agreement.

Quantity	Price
1 – 1,999	$100.00
2,000 – 4,999	90
5,000+	80

Solution:

Step 1: Determine the optimal order size and total cost with the basic EOQ model.

S = $40   H = Cost x 0.10 per instrument   D = 10,000 instruments per year

$$Q_{opt} = \sqrt{(2* S * D)/ H}$$
$$= \sqrt{(2* 40 * 10,000)/ (.10*100)} = 282.84 \text{ instruments}$$

Step 2: Using Q = 283, this gives us a price of $100. Calculate the total cost.

$$TC = [S*(D/Q)] + [H*(Q/2)] + (P*D)$$
$$= [(40 * (10000/283)] + [10 * (283/2)] + [100*10000] = \$1,002,828.40$$

Step 3: Compare the total cost calculated with the total cost at the higher discount level. The next cost break is at Q = 2000.

$$TC_{2000} = [S*(D/Q)] + [H*(Q/2)] + (P*D)$$
$$= [(40 * (10000/2000)] + [10 * (2000/2)] + [90*10000] = \$910,200$$

The next cost break is at Q = 5000.

$$TC_{5000} = [S*(D/Q)] + [H*(Q/2)] + (P*D)$$
$$= [(40 * (10000/5000)] + [10 * (5000/2)] + [80*10000] = \$825,080$$

Step 4: Make the decision.

The costs are lower at Q = 5000. The maximum discount price should be taken, and 5000 units should be ordered since this will result in the maximum discount. The hospital should expect to pay $80 per instrument and have an annual inventory cost of $825,080.

1.   Extreme Laces, Inc. sells shoestrings at the rate of 3000 pairs per year. The ordering cost is $10 per order and the holding cost is 10% of the purchase price per unit per year. The cost of the shoestrings varies with the quantity ordered as follows:

0 – 999	$0.22
1000 – 1499	$0.20
1500 or above	$0.18

How many pairs of shoestrings should Extreme Laces order?

2.   The manager of a chemical plant has asked the project manager to determine the optimal quantity size for valve bolts to order based on the following information. The annual demand for all projects in the plant is 4,000 bolts. The cost per order is $20.00, and the carrying cost is 40% of the unit cost. The following chart represents the discount levels for the bolts.

0 – 1499	$2.00
1500 – 2999	$1.80
3000 or above	$1.60

How many pairs of shoestrings should Extreme Laces order?

3.   Copy Express offers discounts for bulk job contracts. The Marketing Specialist wants to determine the number of pages to include in the companies annual contract with Copy Express. Copy Express will order and store the entire annual need for paper for The Marketing Specialist, but they also pass storage cost to the company. The manager of the company realizes that last year that they used Copy Express to produce 500,000 sheets of copies. The ordering cost for setting up the runs is $10 and the carrying cost is $.05 per sheet. What is the optimal order quantity and minimum inventory cost?

Annual Order	Cost per Sheet
0 – 149,999	$0.15
150,000 – 299,999	$0.12
300,000 – 449,999	$0.09
450,000 or above	$0.05

Reorder Point for Variable Demand

S1.   Goldfish Jones provides goldfish for decorative ponds at homes. Jones' daily demand for goldfish is normally distributed with a mean of 3000 fish and a standard deviation of 300 fish. Lead-time is 20 days. Determine the reorder point if Goldfish Jones wants to limit the probability of a stockout and work stoppage to 6 percent.

Solution:

Step 1:   Determine the model information.

Average Demand per day = 3000 fish per day
$L = 20$ days
$\sigma_d = 300$ fish per day

Step 2:   Determine the z score for a 94% service level (1-tail test).

$Z = 1.555$

Step 3:   Determine the safety stock at 94%.

$SS_{.96} = z\sigma\sqrt{L} = 1.555 * 300 * \sqrt{20} = 2086.25$ fish

Step 4:   Calculate the reorder point at 94%.

$R = dL + z\sigma\sqrt{L} = 3000 (20) + [(1.555)(300)(\sqrt{20})] = 62,086.25$ fish

S2.   The local newsstand wants to determine the optimal order quantity for newspapers. The daily demand during the week is 500 newspapers per day (normally distributed) with a standard deviation of 60 newspapers. On the weekend, demand drops to 300 newspapers with a standard deviation of 50. The lead-time for orders is a half a day (or .5). Any newspapers that are not sold will be trash, so the stand is willing to service few people to ensure no loss of money due to waste. The stand will set the service level at 90%. What is the reorder point for newspapers during the week? Should the newsstand use a different order point for the weekend if on the weekend they want to service 96% of their normal customers?

Solution:

Step 1:   Determine the model information.

Average Demand per day = 500 newspapers per day   L = 0.5 days
σ_d = 60 newspapers per day

Step 2:   Determine the z score for a 90% service level (1-tail test).

Z = 1.285

Step 3:   Determine the safety stock at 90%.

$SS_{.96} = z\sigma\sqrt{L}$ = 1.285 * 60 * $\sqrt{.5}$ = 54.5 newspapers

Step 4:   Calculate the reorder point at 90%.

$R = dL + z\sigma\sqrt{L}$ = 500 (0.5) + [(1.285)(60)($\sqrt{0.5}$)] = 304.5 or 305 newspapers

Step 5:   Calculate the reorder point for the weekend at 96%.

$R = dL + z\sigma\sqrt{L}$ = 300 (0.5) + [(1.75)(50)($\sqrt{0.5}$)] = 211.8 or 212 newspapers

Decision: Due to the potential loss by wasting 93 newspapers, you would want to use two different ordering policies.

1.   Jim Ware produces concrete products for landscape and garden use. Jim's daily demand for concrete statues is normally distributed with a mean of 50 statues and a standard deviation of 9 statues. Lead-time is 25 days. Determine the reorder point if the quarry company wants to limit the probability of a stockout and work stoppage to 10 percent.

2.   The Lake Arena, home of the new professional basketball team, agreed to buy soft drinks from Sports Concession Inc. for its customers. The daily demand for soft drinks is normally distributed with an average of 250 liters of drinks and a standard deviation of 30 cases. The lead-time required to receive an order from the local distributor is 3 days. Determine the safety stock and reorder point if the arena wants to maintain a 95 percent service level. What would be the increase in the safety stock if a 98 percent service level were desired?

3.   A pipe manufacturer that specialized in plumbing pipes made of copper wants to determine the reorder point necessary to keep the stockout rate at 10%. The monthly demand for the copper alloy used in the pipes is normally distributed with an average of 5000 linear feet and a standard deviation of 75 feet. The lead-time is set at 20 days, but it could take as long as 30 days to receive the shipment. Determine the safety stock and reorder point to keep the stockout rate at the target. What happens to the reorder point if the lead-time has shifted to 30 days?

4.   A fence contractor uses a special aluminum wire to attach the fences to the post. The contractor uses approximately 50 boxes of precut wire per week with a normally distributed standard deviation of 2 boxes. The lead-time to receive the wire is 2 weeks. The annual demand is estimated at 2500 boxes. If the contractor wants to maintain a 90% service level, what safety stock level and reorder point should he use?

5.   Using the following information, determine when the item should be reordered and where the safety stock should be set if the service level is 90%, 95%, or 99%. (Determine the demand during the reorder period assuming a constant demand rate for the 12-month period.)

Annual Demand: 12,000 gallons
Standard deviation during lead-time: 50 gallons
Lead-time: 1 month

Order Size for Fixed Period Model with Variable Demand

S1.   Superdome Athletic Complex stocks sports drinks it purchases from a regional distributor in another city. The daily demand for drinks at the complex is normally distributed with a mean of 180 bottles and a standard deviation of 20 bottles. The distributor sends a representative to check the complex's inventory every 30 days, and during a recent visit there were 25 bottles in stock. The lead-time to receive and order is 10 days. The concessions manager has requested an order size that will enable him to limit the probability of a stockout to 4 percent.

Solution:
Step 1:   Identify all model information.

d = 180 bottles per day t_b = 30 days Z = 1.75
L = 10 days σ_d = 20 bottles I = 25 bottles

Step 2:   Calculate safety stock for a 96% service level.

$$SS_{.96} = \{1.75 * 20 [\sqrt{(30+10)}]\} = 220.5$$

Step 3:   Calculate the reorder point for a 96% service level.

$$Q = d(t_b + L) + [z\sigma_d(\sqrt{(t_b + L)})] - I$$
$$Q = [180 * (30 + 10)] + [1.75*(20)*(\sqrt{(30+10)})] - 25 = 7395.5 \text{ bottles}$$

S2.   The Ice Shoppe distributes bags of ice to convenience stores in the immediate area. The daily demand for the bags of ice in the area is normally distributed with a mean of 200 bags and a standard deviation of 30 bags. The Ice Shoppe sends a representative to check the area's inventory every 7 days, and during a recent visit there were no bags of ice in stock. The lead time to receive an order is 2 days. The convenience stores requested an order size that will enable them to limit the probability of a stockout to 4 percent. Determine the order size for this period. There is no inventory on hand.

Solution:
Step 1:   Identify all model information.

d = 200 bottles per day t_b = 7 days I = 0 bags
L = 2 days σ_d = 30 bags Z = 1.75 (Service Level = $1 - .04 = .96$)

Step 2:   Calculate safety stock for a 96% service level.

$$SS_{.96} = z\sigma_d\sqrt{(t_b + L)} = [1.75 * 30 [\sqrt{(7 + 2)}]] = 157.2 \text{ bags}$$

Step 3:   Calculate the reorder point for a 96% service level.

$$Q = d(t_b + L) + [z\sigma_d(\sqrt{(t_b + L)})] - I$$
$$Q = [200 * (7 + 2)] + [1.75*(30)*(\sqrt{(7 + 2)})] - 0 = 1957.5 \text{ bags}$$

1.   Cost Less Discount Drugstore is responsible for the inventory of its store. The store carries a full line of over the counter sinus medication. The most popular product has a demand rate of 50 boxes per week with a standard deviation of 3 boxes that exhibits normally distributed characteristics. The lead-time is seven days and the supplier visits to check the shelf every two weeks. What is the reorder point if the drugstore only wants to accept a 2% chance of stocking out? What is the safety stock required? What is the annual cost of maintaining the safety stock if the holding cost is $0.50 per box per week?

2.   Spark It, an auto parts retailer, has a variety of spark plugs in its stores. Since not every vehicle requires the same type, inventory levels must be monitored to ensure customer service. For its model XRZ101, the manager has determined that the annual demand is 12,000 units and has a constant demand rate over the course of the 12-month period. It is normally distributed with a standard deviation of 20 units per week (remember to convert to consistent units). The store is inventoried once every month and the lead-time to receive the order is 1 month. What is the reorder point at 90% and 94% customer service levels?

3.   Lake Arena also stocks cotton candy ingredients from its local food supplier. The weekly demand for the ingredients at the arena is normally distributed with a mean of 150 pounds and a standard deviation of 30 pounds. The supplier sends a customer service rep to visit and inventory the arena's supplies every 14 days, and during a recent visit there were 10 pounds in stock. The lead-time to receive an order is 7 days. The restaurant manager has requested an order size that will enable him to limit the probability of a stockout to 10 percent.

4.   The Peanut Gallery vendor stocks peanuts in a vendor cart. The average daily demand for the peanuts is normally distributed with a mean of 25 pounds of nuts and a standard deviation of 2 pounds. A vendor for a food distributor calls to check with the Peanut Gallery about its inventory every Friday; it is assumed that the gallery has no inventory since the peanuts will go bad if not used. The order is received on Monday of every week (the lead-time is 3 days). Determine the order size for this order period that will result in a 94 percent service level.

5.   A local ice cream store is trying to determine when to place an order and how much safety stock to hold for its top seller, Creamy Home Made. The demand is normally distributed throughout the week with an average demand rate of 40 gallons per week and a standard deviation of 10 gallons. Orders must be placed with the distributor two weeks in advance of delivery and the store is checked every week. What safety stock is required to service 90% of the customers who want to purchase Creamy Home Made? Given the 90% service level, when should an order be placed for more Creamy Home Made?

13

Aggregate Planning

I. Aggregate Planning (also known as aggregate scheduling)

A. Aggregate planning is concerned with determining quantity and timing of production for the intermediate future, often from 3 to 18 months ahead.

B. The objective of aggregate planning is to minimize cost over the planning period.

C. Four things are needed for aggregate planning:

1. A logical overall unit for measuring sales and output, such as air-conditioning units at GE or cases of beer at Anheuser-Busch.

2. A forecast of demand for a reasonable intermediate planning period in these aggregate terms.

3. A method for determining the costs that we discuss in this chapter.

4. A model that combines forecasts and costs so that scheduling decisions can be made for the planning period.

II. The Planning Process

A. Demand forecasting can address short-, medium-, and long-range problems.

B. Scheduling decisions address the problem of matching productivity to fluctuating demands.

C. Diagram below illustrates the time horizons and features for short-, intermediate-, and long-range planning.

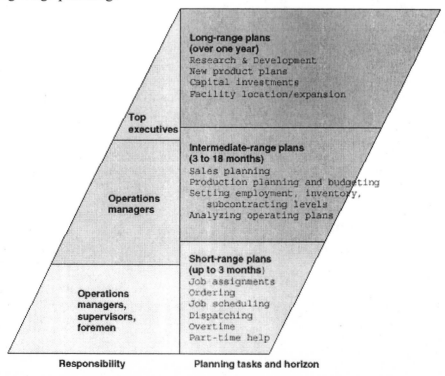

| Responsibility | Planning tasks and horizon |

Lecture Key: Top management is responsible for long-term decisions such as strategic and policy related issues. The operations manager uses top management's plans as a source of direction and works with the resources allocated by strategic planners. Operations personnel help dealing with short-term planning involving loading, expediting, dispatching and other short-term decisions.

III. The Nature of Aggregate Planning

   A. An aggregate plan means combining appropriate resources into general, or overall, terms.

   B. Disaggregation involves the process of breaking the aggregate plan into greater detail as shown in the illustration below.

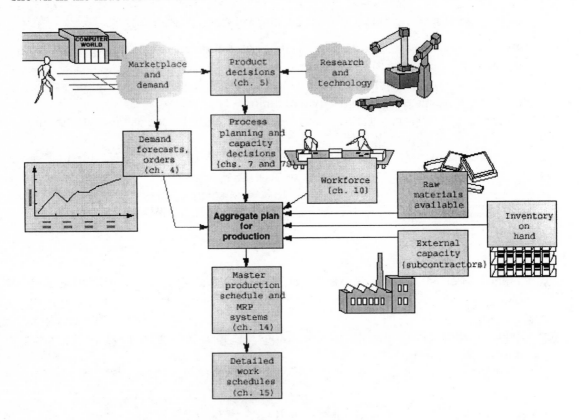

   C. Dissaggregation results in a master production schedule, which is a timetable that specifies what is to be made and when.

Lecture Key: Aggregate planning works with the demand forecast, facility capacity, inventory levels, and workforce size. This explains why aggregate planning looks at production and not a product-by-product breakdown. Since aggregate planning is part of a larger production system, the understanding of the interactions between the plan and several internal and external factors are useful.

IV. Aggregate Planning Strategies

   A. When generating an aggregate plan, the operations manager must answer several questions:

      1. Should inventories be used to absorb changes in demand during the planning period?

      2. Should changes be accommodated by varying the size of the workforce?

      3. Should part-timers be used, or should overtime and idle time absorb fluctuations?

      4. Should subcontractors be used on fluctuating orders so a stable workforce can be maintained?

      5. Should prices or other factors be changed to influence demand?

B. A firm can choose from 5 basic capacity or production options:
  1. Changing inventory levels.
  2. Varying the workforce size by hiring or layoffs.
  3. Varying production rules through overtime or idle time.
  4. Subcontracting.
  5. Using part-time workers.
C. There are three basic demand options:
  1. Influencing demand by advertising, promotions, personal selling, and price cuts.
  2. Back ordering during high-demand periods.
  3. Counterseasonal product and service mixing.
D. Operations managers use a mixture of capacity options and demand options to develop a strategy.
  1. Chase strategy – attempts to achieve output rates for each period that match the demand forecast for that period.
  2. Level strategy (level scheduling) – is an aggregate plan in which daily production is uniform from period to period.

Aggregate Planning Options: Advantages and Disadvantages

OPTION	ADVANTAGES	DISADVANTAGES	SOME COMMENTS
Changing inventory levels.	Changes in human resources are gradual or none; no abrupt production changes.	Inventory holding costs may increase. Shortage may result in lost sales.	Applies mainly to production, not service, operations.
Varying workforce size by hiring or layoffs.	Avoids the costs of other alternatives.	Hiring, layoff, and training costs may be significant.	Used where size of labor pool is large.
Varying production rates through overtime or idle time.	Matches seasonal fluctuations without hiring/training costs.	Overtime premiums; tired workers; may not meet demand.	Allows flexibility within the aggregate plan.
Subcontracting.	Permits flexibility and smoothing of the firm's output.	Loss of quality control; reduced profits; loss of future business.	Applies mainly in production settings.
Using part-time workers.	Is less costly and more flexible than full-time workers.	High turnover/training cost; quality suffers; scheduling difficult.	Good for unskilled jobs in areas with large temporary labor pools.
Influencing demand.	Tries to use excess capacity. Discounts draw new customers.	Uncertainty in demand. Hard to match demand to supply exactly.	Creates marketing ideas. Overbooking used in some businesses.
Back ordering during high-demand periods.	May avoid overtime. Keeps capacity constant.	Customer must be willing to wait, but goodwill is lost.	Many companies back order.
Counterseasonal product and service mixing.	Fully utilizes resources; allows stable workforce.	May require skills or equipment outside firm's areas of expertise.	Risky finding products or services with opposite demand patterns.

Lecture Key: *Aggregate Planning Strategies involve the manipulation of inventory, production rates, labor levels, capacity, and other controllable variables. Aggregate planning also contains capacity and demand options. In capacity options, they attempt to absorb fluctuations in demand. In addition, demand options try to smooth out changes in the demand pattern over the planning period.*

V.   Methods for Aggregate Planning

A. A mixed strategy is a planning strategy that uses two or more controllable variables to set a feasible production plan.

B. Graphical and charting techniques are aggregate planning techniques that work with a few variables at a time to allow planners to compare projected demand with existing capacity. The five steps in the graphical method are:
1. Determine the demand in each period.
2. Determine capacity for regular time, overtime, and subcontracting each period.
3. Find labor costs, hiring and layoff costs, and inventory holding costs.
4. Consider company policy that may apply to the workers or to stock levels.
5. Develop alternative plans and examine their total costs.

Example: Average Requirement

A Juarez, Mexico, manufacturer of roofing supplies has developed monthly forecasts for an important product and presented the 6-month period January to June in the table below.

Month	Expected Demand	Production Days	Demand per Day (Computed)
Jan.	900	22	41
Feb.	700	18	39
Mar.	800	21	38
Apr.	1,200	21	57
May	1,500	22	68
June	1,100	20	55
	6,200	124	55

Solution:
Compute the demand per day using the following formula:

d = expected demand / # of production days each month
$d_{Jan.}$ = 900 / 22 = 41 units per day during Jan.
$d_{Feb.}$ = 700 / 18 = 39 units per day during Feb.
$d_{Mar.}$ = 800 / 21 = 38 units per day during March

Compute the average requirement using the following formula:

Average requirement = Total expected demand / # of production days
                     = 6,200 / 124 = 50 units per day

One possible strategy (Plan 1) for the manufacturer described in the previous example is to maintain a constant workforce throughout the 6-month period. A second (Plan 2) is to maintain a constant workforce at a level necessary to meet the lowest demand month (March) and to meet all demand above this level by subcontracting. Both Plans 1 and 2 have level production and are, therefore, called level strategies. Plan 3 is to hire and layoff workers as needed to produce exactly monthly requirements – a chase strategy. The table below provides cost information necessary for analyzing these three alternatives:

Cost Information

Inventory carrying cost	$5 per unit per month
Subcontracting cost per unit	$10 per unit
Average pay rate	$5 per hour ($40 per day)
Overtime pay rate	$7 per hour (above 8 hours/day)
Labor-hours to produce a unit	1.6 hours per unit
Cost of increasing daily production rate (hiring & training)	$300 per unit
Cost of decreasing daily production rate (layoffs)	$600 per unit

Solution:

Analysis of Plan 1: When analyzing this approach, which assumes that 50 units are produced per day, we have a constant workforce, no overtime or idle time, no safety stock, and no subcontractors. The firm accumulates inventory during the slack period of demand, January through March, and depletes it during the higher-demand warm season, April through June. We assume beginning inventory = 0 and planned ending inventory = 0:

Step 1: Compute the average requirement using the following formula:

$$\text{Average requirement} = \text{Total expected demand / \# of production days}$$
$$= 6,200 / 124 = 50 \text{ units per day}$$

Step 2:

Month	Production at 50 Units Per Day	Demand Forecast	Monthly Inventory Change	Ending Inventory
Jan.	1,100 = 50 x 22 days	900	+200 = 1100 – 900	200 = 0 + 200
Feb.	900 = 50 x 18 days	700	+200 = 900 – 700	400 = 200 + 200
Mar.	1,050 = 50 x 21 days	800	+250 = 1050 – 800	650 = 400 + 250
Apr.	1,050 = 50 x 21 days	1,200	-150 = 1050 – 1200	500 = 650 – 150
May	1,100 = 50 x 22 days	1,500	-400 = 1100 – 1500	100 = 500 – 400
June	1,000 = 50 x 20 days	1,100	-100 = 1000 – 1100	0 = 100 – 100
				$\Sigma = 1,850$

Step 3: Calculate the total units of inventory held during the period.

Total = 200 (Jan. Inv.) + 400 (Feb. Inv.) + 650 (Mar. Inv.)
        + 500 (Apr. Inv.) + 100 (May Inv.) + 0 (June Inv.) = 1,850 units

Workforce required to produce 50 units per day = 10 workers

Each unit requires 1.6 labor-hours to produce, each worker can make 5 units in an 8 hour day. To produce 50 units, 10 workers are needed.

8 hours / 1.6 hours per unit = 5 units per day
50 units per day / 5 units per worker = 10 workers

Step 4: Calculate costs.

Costs		Calculations
Inventory carrying	$9,250	(=1,850 units carried x $5 per unit)
Regular-time labor	49,600	(=10 workers x $40 per day x 124 days)
Other costs (overtime, hiring, layoffs, subcontracting)	0	
Total Cost	$58,850	

Example: Analysis of Plan 2

Although a constant workforce is also maintained in Plan 2, it is set low enough to meet demand only in March, the lowest month. To produce 38 units per day in-house, 7.6 workers are needed. (You can think of this as 7 full-time workers and 1 part-timer.) All other demand is met by subcontracting. Subcontracting is thus required in every other month. No inventory holding costs are incurred in Plan 2.

Because 6,200 units are required during the aggregate plan period, we must compute how many can be made by the firm and how many must be subcontracted:

Solution:
Step 1: Compute the demand per day using the following formula:

d = expected demand / # of production days each month
$d_{Jan.}$ = 900 / 22 = 41 units per day during Jan.
$d_{Feb.}$ = 700 / 18 = 39 units per day during Feb.
$d_{Mar.}$ = 800 / 21 = 38 units per day during March (lowest daily demand)

Step 2: Compute the in-house production.

In-house production = production per day (lowest) x production days
Production days = 124 production days
= 22 (Jan.) + 18 (Feb.) + 21 (Mar.) + 21 (Apr.) + 22 (May) + 20 (June)
In-house production = 4,712 units
= 38 units per day in March x 124 production days
Subcontract units = Total units needed − In-house production units
= 6,200 units − 4,712 units = 1,488 units

Step 3: Calculate costs.

Costs		Calculations
Regular-time labor	$37,696	(= 7.6 workers x $40 per day x 124 days)
Subcontracting	14,880	(= 1,488 units x $10 per unit)
Total Cost	$52,576	

Example: Analysis of Plan 3

The final strategy, Plan 3, involves varying the workforce size by hiring and firing as necessary. The production rate will equal the demand, and there is no change in production from the previous month, December. The table below shows the calculations and the total cost of Plan 3. Recall that it costs $600 per unit produced to reduce production from the previous month's daily level and $300 per unit change to increase the daily rate of production through hirings:

Solution:

Month	Forecast	Daily Production Rate	Basic Production Cost (Demand x 1.6 hrs per unit x $5 per hr.)	Extra Cost of Increasing Production (Hiring Cost)	Extra Cost of Decreasing Production (Layoff Cost)	Total Cost
Jan.	900	41	$7,200	---	---	$7,200
Feb.	700	39	5,600	---	$1,200 (=2 x $600)	6,800
Mar.	800	38	6,400	---	$600 (=1 x $600)	7,000
Apr.	1,200	57	9,600	$5,700 (=19 x $300)	---	15,300
May	1,500	68	12,000	$3,300 (=11 x $300)	---	15,300
June	1,100	55	8,800	---	$7,800 (=13 x $600)	16,600
	6,200		$49,600	$9,000	$9,600	$68,200

Analysis: The total cost is $68,200 for production, hiring, and layoff for Plan 3.

Summary of Plans:

Cost	Plan 1 (Constant workforce of 10 workers)	Plan 2 (Workforce of 7.6 workers plus subcontract)	Plan 3 (Hiring and layoffs to meet demand)
Inventory carrying	$9,250	$0	$0
Regular labor	49,600	37,696	49,600
Overtime labor	0	0	0
Hiring	0	0	9,000
Layoffs	0	0	9,600
Subcontracting	0	14,880	0
Total Cost	$58,850	$52,576	$68,200

C. Mathematical Approaches to Planning
   1. The transportation method of linear programming is not a trial-and-error approach like charting, but rather produces an optimal plan for minimizing costs.
   2. The management coefficients model is a formal planning model built around a manager's experience and performance.
   3. APP – by Transportation Method
      a. Decision to change the size of workforce has already been made or is prohibited.
      b. Used to develop aggregate production plan.

c. Not used when hiring and firing.
d. Gathers all cost information into one matrix and plans production based on the lowest-cost alternatives.
e. Cost of production plan can be determined by multiplying the total units produced in each production category or held in inventory by their respective costs and summing them.

PERIOD PRODUCTION		Period of Use				Unused Capacity	Capacity
		1	2	3	4		
	Beginning Inventory	i	$i + h$	$i + 2h$	$i + 3h$		I
1	Regular	r	$r + h$	$r + 2h$	$r + 3h$		R_1
	Overtime	o	$o + h$	$o + 2h$	$o + 3h$		O_1
	Subcontract	s	$s + h$	$s + 2h$	$s + 3h$		S_1
2	Regular	$r + b$	r	$r + h$	$r + 2h$		R_2
	Overtime	$o + b$	o	$o + h$	$o + 2h$		O_2
	Subcontract	$s + b$	s	$s + h$	$s + 2h$		S_2
3	Regular	$r + 2b$	$r + b$	r	$r + h$		R_3
	Overtime	$o + 2b$	$o + b$	o	$o + h$		O_3
	Subcontract	$s + 2b$	$s + b$	s	$s + h$		S_3
4	Regular	$r + 3b$	$r + 2b$	$r + b$	r		R_4
	Overtime	$o + 3b$	$o + 2b$	$o + b$	o		O_4
	Subcontract	$s + 3b$	$s + 2b$	$s + b$	s		S_4
	Demand	D_1	D_2	D_3	D_4		

Example: Transportation Method of Linear Programming

Farnsworth Tire Company developed data that related to production, demand, capacity, and cost at its West Virginia plant. These data are shown in the table below:

	Sales Period		
	March	**April**	**May**
Demand	800	1,000	750
Capacity:			
Regular	700	700	700
Overtime	50	50	50
Subcontracting	150	150	130
Beginning inventory	100 tires		

Costs:

Regular Production Cost per Unit:	$40 per tire
Overtime Production Cost per Unit:	$50 per tire
Subcontracting Cost per Unit:	$70 per tire
Inventory Holding Cost per Unit per Period:	$2 per tire per month

		Period of Use				
PERIOD PRODUCTION		**1**	**2**	**3**	**Unused Capacity**	**Capacity (Supply)**
	Beginning Inventory	0 — 100	2 — -----	4 — ----	0 — ----	100
1	Regular	40 — 700	42 — -----	44 — ----	0 — ----	700
	Overtime	50 — ----	52 — 50	54 — ----	0 — ----	50
	Subcontract	70 — ----	72 — 50	74 — ----	0 — 100	150
2	Regular		40 — 700	42 — ----	0 — ----	700
	Overtime		50 — 50	52 — ----	0 — ----	50
	Subcontract		70 — 150	72 — ----	0 — ----	150
3	Regular			40 — 700	0 — ----	700
	Overtime			50 — 50	0 — ----	50
	Subcontract			70 —	0 — 130	130
	Demand	800	1000	750	230	2780

Solution: The transportation tableau illustrates the solution

1. To set up the tableau, demand requirements for each quarter are listed on the bottom row and capacity constraints for each type of production (i.e., regular, overtime, or subcontracting) are placed in the far right column.

2. Next, cost figures are entered into the small square at the corner of each cell. Reading across the first row, inventory on hand in period 1 that is used in period 1 incurs zero cost. Inventory on hand in period 1 that is not used until period 2 incurs $2 holding cost. If the inventory is held until period 3, the cost is $2 more, or $4.

3. Interpreting the cost entries in the second row, if a unit is produced under regular production in period 1 and used in period 1, it costs $40. If a unit is produced under regular production in period 1 but is not used until period 2, it incurs a production cost of $40 plus an inventory cost of $2, or $42. If the unit is held until period 3, it will cost $2 more, or $44. The cost calculations continue in a similar fashion for overtime and subcontracting, beginning with production costs of $50 and $70, respectively.

4. The costs for production in periods 2 and 3 are determined in a similar fashion, with one exception. Half of the remaining transportation tableau is blocked out as infeasible. This occurs because no backordering is allowed for this problem, and production cannot take place in one period to satisfy demand that occurs in previous periods.

5. Now that the tableau is set up, we can begin to allocate units to the cells and develop our production plan. The procedure is to assign units to the lowest cost cells in a column so that demand requirements for the column are met; yet capacity constraints of each row are not exceeded. Beginning with the first demand column for period 1, we have 100 units of beginning inventory available to us at no cost. If we use all 100 units in period 1, there is no inventory left for use in later periods. We indicate this fact by putting a dash in the remaining cells of the beginning inventory row. We can satisfy the remaining 700 units of demand for period 1 with regular production at a cost of $40 per unit.

6. In period 2, the lowest cost alternative is regular production in period 2. We assign 700 units to that cell and, in the process, use up all the capacity for that row. Dashes are placed in the remaining cells of the row to indicate that they are no longer feasible choices. The remaining units needed to meet demand in period 2 are taken from overtime production in period 2, which is 50 units at a cost of $50. That brings the total to 750, so you are still 250 short. Then, the next cheapest cost is period 1 overtime that would be held until period 2. This provides an additional 50 units. Then, subcontracting from period 2 at $70 is used for the next 150 units. This leaves 50 units from period 1 subcontracting at a cost of $72. Note that this would leave 100 units unused in period 1 subcontracting.

7. Continuing to the third period's demand of 750 units, we fully utilize the 700 units available from regular production in the same period and 50 units of overtime production. As noted by the dashed line, period 1's regular production has reached its capacity and it is no longer an alternative source of production.

8. The unused capacity column is filled in last. In period 1, 100 units of subcontracting capacity are available but unused. This information is valuable because it tells us the flexibility the company has to accept additional orders.

The cost of the production plan can be determined directly from the transportation tableau by multiplying the units in each cell times the cost in the corner of the cell and summing them. Alternatively, the cost can be determined from the production plan by multiplying the total units produced in each production category or held in inventory by their respective costs and summing them, as follows:

$(2100 \times \$40) + (150 \times \$50) + (100 \times \$70) + (100 \times \$2) = \$92,400$

| Period | Demand | PRODUCTION PLAN | | | Ending Inventory |
		Regular Production	Overtime	Subcontract	
1	800	700	50	50	100
2	1000	700	50	50	0
3	750	700	50	0	0
Total	2550	2100	150	1250	100

Lecture Key: Methods for aggregate planning range from widely used charting (or graphical) methods to a series of more mathematical approaches. Mathematical models and linear programming have gained some acceptance in the industry. However, operations managers need to make decisions quickly based on the changing dynamics of the workplace, and building good, reliable models is time-consuming.

VI. Aggregate Planning in Services

A. Controlling the cost of labor in service firms is critical and involves the following:
  1. Close scheduling of labor-hours to assure quick response to customer demand.
  2. Some form of on-call labor resource that can be added or deleted to meet unexpected demand.
  3. Flexibility of individual worker skills that permits reallocation of available labor.
  4. Individual worker flexibility in rate of output or hours of work to meet expanded demand.
B. Examples:
  1. In restaurants, aggregate scheduling is directed toward smoothing the production rate and finding the size of the workforce to be employed.
  2. Hospitals face aggregate planning problems in allocating money, staff, and supplies to meet the demands of patients.
  3. National chains of small service firms.
  4. Aggregate planning for miscellaneous services deals mainly with planning for human resource requirements and managing demand.
  5. In the airline industry, aggregate planning consists of tables or schedules for:
    a. The number of flights in and out of each hub.
    b. The number of flights on all routes.
    c. The number of passengers to be serviced on all flights.
    d. The number of air personnel and ground personnel required at each hub and airport.

Klasson and Avalon, a medium-sized Tampa law firm of 32 legal professionals, has developed a 3-month forecast for 5 categories of legal business it anticipates (see table below). Assuming a 40-hour workweek and that 100% of each lawyer's hours are billed, about 500 billable hours are available from each lawyer this fiscal quarter. Hours of billable time are forecast and accumulated for the quarter by the 5 categories of skill (column 1), then divided by 500 to provide a count of lawyers needed to cover the estimated business. Between 30 and 39 lawyers will be needed to cover the variations in level of business between worst and best levels of demand. (For example, best-care scenario is 19,500 total hours, divided by 500 hours per lawyer, equals 39 lawyers needed.)

Because all 32 lawyers at Klasson and Avalon are qualified to perform basic legal research, this skill area has maximum scheduling flexibility (column 6). The most highly skilled (and capacity-constrained) categories are trial work and corporate law. In these areas, the firm's best-care forecast just barely covers trial work with 3.6 lawyers needed (see column 5) and 4 qualified (column 6). Meanwhile, corporate law is short 1 full person. Overtime can be used to cover the excess this quarter, but as business expands, it might be necessary to hire or develop talent in both of these areas. Real estate and criminal practice are adequately covered by available staff, as long as other needs do not use their excess capacity.

Solution:

(1) Category of Legal Business	Labor Hours Required			Capacity Constraints	
	(2) Best Case (hours)	(3) Likely Case (hours)	(4) Worst Case (hours)	(5) Maximum Demand in People	(6) Number of Qualified Personnel
Trial work	1800	1500	1200	3.6	4
Legal research	4500	4000	3500	9.0	32
Corporate law	8000	7000	6500	16.0	15
Real estate law	1700	1500	1300	3.4	6
Criminal law	3500	3000	2500	7.0	12
Total hours	19500	17000	15000		
Lawyers needed	39	34	30		

With its current legal staff of 32, Klasson and Avalon's best-care forecast will increase the workload by 20% (assuming no new hires). This represents one extra day of work per lawyer per week. The worst-case scenario will result in about 6% underutilization of talent. For both of these scenarios, the firm has determined that available staff will provide adequate service.

Lecture Key: *Aggregate planning in services also has to deal with capacity and demand issues, but management takes a more active role in demand. In actuality, industries such as banking, trading, and fast foods, aggregate planning may be easier.*

VII.   Yield Management

A. Yield, or revenue, management is the aggregate planning process of allocating resources to customers at prices that will maximize yield or revenue.

Example: Yield Management

The Cleveland Downtown Inn is a 100-room hotel that has historically charged one set price for its rooms, $150 per night. The variable cost of a room being occupied is low. Management believes the cleaning, air-conditioning, and incidental costs of soap, shampoo, and so forth, are $15 per room per night. Sales average 50 rooms per night. Figure 13.5 illustrates the current pricing scheme. Net sales are $6,750 per night with a single price point.

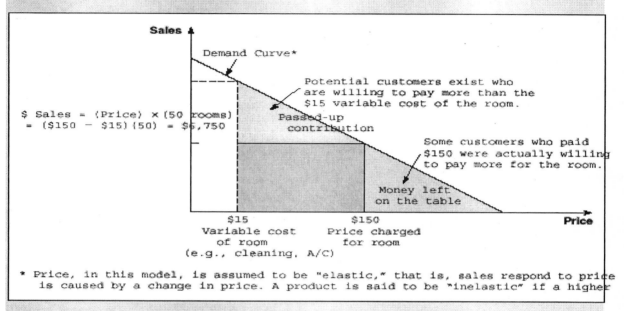

B. To make yield management work, the company needs to manage three issues:
1. Multiple pricing structures must be feasible and appear logical (and preferably fair) to the customer.
2. Forecasts of the use and duration of the use.
3. Changes in demand.

CHAPTER 13 PROBLEMS

Pure Production Planning Strategies

S1.   Osteen Fish Company ships a variety of seafood worldwide. Its line of shellfish exhibits a highly seasonal demand pattern with peaks in the fall months. Given costs and quarterly sales forecasts, determine whether a level production or Chase demand production strategy would more economically meet the demand for shellfish.

Quarter	Sales Forecast (lb)
Spring	60,000
Summer	75,000
Fall	150,000
Winter	120,000

Hiring cost	=	$100 per lb/period
Firing cost	=	$500
Inventory carrying cost	=	$3.50 unit
Production per employee	=	1,000 lbs /period
Beginning workforce	=	100 workers

Solution:
Level Production Strategy:

Step 1:   Calculate the production per period.

Total demand for the year (60,000 + 75,000 + 150,000 + 120,000 = 400,000).

Divide the total demand by the number of periods (400,000 / 4 = 100,000) to get the production amount per period.

Step 2:   Calculate the inventory for each period by subtracting the production amount by the sales forecast (100,000 – 60,000 = 40,000) for period 1.

Step 3:   Calculate a cumulative total inventory for each period (40,000 [period 1] + 25,000 [period 2 excess] = 65,000). This is the total inventory level at the end of period 2.

Quarter	Sales Forecast	Production Plan	Inventory
Spring	60,000	100,000	40,000
Summer	75,000	100,000	65,000
Fall	150,000	100,000	15,000
Winter	120,000	100,000	0
	400,000		120,000

Step 4:   Calculate the total inventory held for the year (40,000 + 65,000 + 15,000 + 0 = 120,000).

Step 5:   Calculate the cost for the level plan. The only cost is the inventory holding cost.

Cost = 120,000 lb/inventory * $3.50 per pound holding cost = $420,000

Chase Demand Strategy:

Step 1:   Calculate the production amount for each period. Since this is a chase plan, the production will equal the sales forecast (60,000 [Sales forecast for period 1] = 60,000 [Production planned for period 1]).

Step 2:   Calculate the number of workers needed for each period. Take the production amount for the spring quarter and divide it by the amount each worker can produce (60,000 / 1,000). You will need 60 workers for the spring to meet demand and production requirements.

Step 3:   Calculate the number of workers that must be hired or fired during each period. The beginning workforce at the end of the previous winter is 100. Take the number of workers needed and subtract it from the previous workforce (100 – 60 = 40 fired). You will need to reduce the workforce by 40 workers. For the summer, you need 75 workers and have 60 workers at the end of the spring. So, 15 workers will need to be hired.

Quarter	Sales Forecast	Production Plan	Workers Needed	Workers Hired	Workers Fired
Spring	60,000	60,000	60	--	40
Summer	75,000	75,000	75	15	--
Fall	150,000	150,000	150	150	--
Winter	120,000	120,000	120	--	30
				165	70

Step 4: Calculate the cost of the chase plan. The cost for this plan is for hiring ($100 per employee) and firing ($500 per employee) workers.

Cost = (165 workers hired * $100) = (70 workers fired * $500) = $515,000

Decision: Recommend using the Level Production Strategy.

S2.   Coffee, Etc. produces a line of specialty coffee that exhibits a varying demand pattern. Given the following demand forecasts and costs, design a production plan for Coffee, Etc. using the pure strategies for level and chase production planning.

Period	Demand
Jan.	500
Feb.	600
March	800
April	700

Inventory holding cost	$3 per unit per month
Begin inventory	0
Production per employee	70 units per month
Hiring costs	$50 per employee
Firing costs	$90 per employee
Beginning workforce	10 employees

Solution:
Level Production Strategy:

Step 1: Calculate the production per period (2600 / 4 = 650).

Step 2: Calculate the inventory for each period.

(500 – 650 = 150 for January)
(600 – 650 = 50 for February)
(800 – 650 = –150 for March)
(700 – 650 = –50 for April)

Step 3: Calculate a cumulative total inventory for each period.

(150 + 50 – 150 – 50 = 0)

Month	Sales Forecast	Production Plan	Inventory
Jan.	500	650	150
Feb.	600	650	200
March	800	650	50
April	700	650	0
	2600	2600	400

Step 4: Calculate the total inventory held for the year (150 + 200 + 50 + 0 = 400).

Step 5: Calculate the cost for the level plan. The only cost is the inventory holding cost.

Cost = 400 lb/inventory * $3.00 per pound holding cost = $1,200

Chase Demand Strategy:

Step 1: Calculate the production amount for each period. Since this is a chase plan, the production will equal the sales forecast (500 [Sales forecast for period 1] = 500 [Production planned for period 1]).

Step 2: Calculate the number of workers needed for each period (500 / 70 = 8).

Step 3: Calculate the number of workers that must be hired or fired during each period. The beginning workforce at the end of the previous winter is 10 (10 – 8 = 2 fired).

Month	Sales Forecast	Production Plan	Workers Needed	Workers Hired	Workers Fired
Jan.	500	500	8	--	2
Feb.	600	600	9	--	1
March	800	800	12	5	--
April	700	700	10	--	2
				5	5

Step 4: Calculate the cost of the chase plan. The cost for this plan is for hiring ($50 per employee) and firing ($90 per employee) workers.

Cost = (5 workers hired * $50) = (5 workers fired * $90) = $700

Decision: Recommend using the Chase Production Strategy.

S3.   At Water Sports Unlimited, the managers decided that it is more cost effective for them to produce their own tubes. Yet with the varying production levels, they have forecasted the following information to use for their decisions. They want to decide whether a pure level strategy or a pure chase strategy would be the most economical.

Period	Demand
Winter	2500
Spring	4000
Summer	5000
Fall	3750

Inventory holding cost	$10 per unit per month
Begin inventory	0
Production per employee	75 units per month
Hiring costs	$500 per employee
Firing costs	$200 per employee
Beginning workforce	70 employees

Solution:
Level Production Strategy

Step 1: Calculate the production per period (15250 / 4 = 3810).

Step 2: Calculate the inventory for each period.

Step 3: Calculate a cumulative total inventory for each period.

Quarter	Sales Forecast	Production Plan	Inventory
Winter	2500	3810	1312.5
Spring	4000	3810	1120
Summer	4500	3810	437.5
Fall	4250	3810	0
	15250	15250	3610

Step 4: Calculate the total inventory held for the year.

Step 5: Calculate the cost for the level plan. The only cost is the inventory holding cost.

Cost = 3610 lb/inventory * $10.00 per pound holding cost = $36,100

Chase Demand Strategy
Step 1: Calculate the production amount for each period.

Step 2: Calculate the number of workers needed for each period.

Step 3: Calculate the number of workers that must be hired or fired during each period.

Quarter	Sales Forecast	Production Plan	Workers Needed	Workers Hired	Workers Fired
Winter	2500	2500	30	--	40
Spring	4000	4000	57	17	--
Summer	4500	4500	65	8	--
Fall	4250	4250	61	--	4
	15250	15250		25	44

Step 4: Calculate the cost of the chase plan. The cost for this plan is for hiring ($50 per employee) and firing ($125 per employee) workers.

Cost = (25 workers hired * $500) = (44 workers fired * $200) = $21,300

Decision: Recommend using the Chase Production Strategy.

1. Champs On the Run produces a line of specialty athletic gear that exhibits a varying demand pattern. Given the following demand forecasts and costs, design a production plan for Champs On the Run using the pure strategies for level and chase production planning.

Quarter	Demand
1	4500
2	6500
3	8500
4	9800

Inventory holding cost	$5/unit/quarter
Beginning inventory	0
Production per employee	50-units/quarter
Hiring cost	$100 per employee
Firing cost	$200 per employee
Beginning workforce in Dec.	1800 employees

2. Authentic produces athletic uniforms for the college/professional sports market. The demand for professional uniforms is high during the beginning of each fall, and then drops off after Christmas. The unavailability of the uniform gear could be detrimental to the survival of the stores since the demand will find another provider, but the cost of storing gear and their dependence on a successful team must also be considered. Given the demand and cost factor shown here, use the pure strategies (level and chase) to determine the most economical production plan. There is no backordering! Any unmet demand is considered lost sales, so once you run out, inventory is zero.

Months	Demand Forecast
May – July	300,000
Aug – Oct	600,000
Nov – Jan	400,000
Feb – April	50,000

No Beginning inventory

Inventory holding cost	$1.50 per unit
Production per employee	1000 per quarter
Beginning workforce	45 workers
Cost of hiring	$75 per employee
Cost of firing	$150 per employee

297

3. Fabric Discount produces a line of economy fabrics that exhibits a varying demand pattern for bolts of cloth. Given the following demand forecasts and costs, design a production plan for Fabric Discount using the pure strategies for level and chase production planning.

Quarter	Demand (bolts)
1	15
2	25
3	45
4	20

Inventory holding cost	$15/unit/quarter
Beginning inventory	0
Production per employee	3 bolts/quarter
Hiring cost	$40 per employee
Firing cost	$80 per employee
Beginning workforce in Dec.	7 employees

4. Fun & Sun produces recreation and leisure products. Given the demand and cost factor shown here, use the pure strategies (level and chase) to determine the most economical production plan. There is no backordering! Any unmet demand is considered lost sales, so once you run out, inventory is zero.

Month	Demand Forecast
1	150
2	200
3	400
4	500
5	800
6	1000
7	1200
8	900
9	750
10	350
11	100
12	50

No beginning inventory

Inventory holding cost	$10.50 per unit/month
Production per employee	15 units per month
Beginning workforce	6 workers
Cost of hiring	$125 per employee
Cost of firing	$200 per employee

298

5. Fun & Sun wants to develop a production plan for its line of water fountains. Given the demand and cost factor shown here, use the pure strategies (level and chase) to determine the most economical production plan. There is no backordering! Any unmet demand is considered lost sales, so once you run out inventory is zero.

Month	Demand Forecast
1	120
2	135
3	140
4	120
5	125
6	125
7	140
8	135

No beginning inventory

Inventory holding cost	$2.50 per unit/month
Production per employee	2 units per month
Beginning workforce	65 workers
Cost of hiring	$250 per employee
Cost of firing	$275 per employee

6. Log Furniture Inc. produces a line of rustic furniture that exhibits a varying demand pattern. Given the following demand forecasts and costs, design a production plan for Log Furniture Inc. using the pure strategies for level and chase production planning.

Month	Demand
May	25
June	30
July	35
August	45
September	40
October	35

Inventory holding cost	$50/unit/month
Beginning inventory	0
Production per employee	5 units/month
Hiring cost	$140 per employee
Firing cost	$180 per employee
Beginning workforce in Dec.	7 employees

Mixed Production Planning Strategies

S1. Andree's All-American manufactures fashionable tennis wear and needs help planning production for next year. Demand for tennis gear is fairly stable, but has peaks during the summer months. Given the following costs and demand forecasts, test these three strategies for meeting demand: (a) level production with overtime and inventory, (b) level production with subcontracting, (c) chase plan. Which strategy would you recommend?

Month	Demand Forecast
January	500
February	300
March	200
April	1500
May	2500
June	3500
July	4500
August	2500
September	500
October	300
November	300
December	2500

Beginning workforce	80 workers
Production /day	6 units per employee
Production rate during regular time	$15 per unit
Production rate during overtime	$25 per unit
Subcontracting cost	$30 per unit
Increasing production	$100 per worker
Decreasing production	$200 per worker
Inventory holding cost	$0.50 per unit/period
No beginning inventory	

Solution:
Level Production with Overtime and Inventory

Step 1: Calculate the level production quantity for each month by dividing the total forecasted demand for the production period by the total number of periods.

Production Per Day = Forecasted Demand / total periods = 19100 /365 = 52.33 units per day

Step 2: Calculate the number of workers.

Workers = Production per Period / Production per Employee
= 52.33 / 6 = 8.33

Step 3: Calculate the inventory and overtime for each period.

Analysis is in the following table.

Step 4: Calculate the total cost for the strategy.

Total $ = (Total production x $/regular production) + (Total overtime x $/overtime production) + (Total Inventory x Inventory Holding $)
= (19,100 * $15) + (2784.1 * $25) (24679.7 * $0.50) = $368,443

				Units Produced		
Production/day = 19,100/365 = 52.33				**# workers = 53/6=8.8**		**8.83**
Month	**Days**	**Forecast**	**Regular**	**Overtime**	**Subcontract**	**Inventory**
JAN	31	500	1622.2			1122.2
FEB	28	300	1465.2			2287.4
MAR	31	200	1622.2			3709.6
APRIL	30	1500	1569.9			3779.5
MAY	31	2500	1622.2			2901.6
JUNE	30	3500	1569.9			971.5
JULY	31	4500	1622.2	1906.3		0.0
AUG	31	2500	1622.2	877.8		0.0
SEPT	30	500	1569.9			1069.9
OCT	31	300	1622.2			2392.1
NOV	30	300	1569.9			3661.9
DEC	31	2500	1622.2	---		2784.1
	365	19100	19100	2784.1	0	24679.7
			$15.00	$25.00	$30.00	$0.50
			$286,500	$69,603	$0	$12,340

Cost = $286,200 + 69,603 + 12,340 = $368,443

Level Production with Subcontracting

Step 1: Calculate the minimum daily requirements for each month by dividing the forecast by the number of days of production in each month.

Production Per Day for Jan. = Forecasted Demand / total periods
= 500 /31 = 16.1 units per day
Production Per Day for Feb. = Forecasted Demand / total periods
= 300 /28 = 10.7 units per day
Production Per Day for Jan. = Forecasted Demand / total periods
= 200 /31 = 6.5 units per day

Step 2: Determine the minimum for all months. March has the lowest for all months. Illustrated by the table below. The production per day will be 6.5 units per day.

Step 3: Calculate the number of workers.

Workers = Production Per Period / Production per Employee
= 6.5 / 6 = 1 worker

Step 4: Calculate the regular production for each period by multiplying the days of production during each month by the production per day. For Jan., there are 31 days of production, and production per day is 6.5 units. The regular production is 201.5 units. Further analysis is in the table below for all periods.

Step 5: Any demand not met during regular production will be made up by subcontracting.

Calculate the units subcontracting by regular production period from the forecast. For January, 500 units of demand – 201.5 units of regular production. You would subcontract a total of 298.5 units during January.

Step 6: Calculate the total regular and subcontracted units. See the table.

Step 7: Calculate the total cost for the strategy.

Total $ = (Total production x $/regular production) + (Subcontracted units x Subcontracting $)
= (2372.5* $15) + (16727.5* $30) = $537,456

Production per day per month = 200 / 31 = 6.5 units for March.			6.5 units is minimum	# of Workers = Prod. / Prod. Per Employee		1 worker
Month	Days	Minimum daily requirement per month		Forecast	Regular	Subcontract
JAN	31	16.1		500	201.5	298.5
FEB	28	10.7		300	182	118
MAR	31	6.5		200	201.5	-1.5
APRIL	30	50.0		1500	195	1305
MAY	31	80.6		2500	201.5	2298.5
JUNE	30	116.7		3500	195	3305
JULY	31	145.2		4500	201.5	4298.5
AUG	31	80.6		2500	201.5	2298.5
SEPT	30	16.7		500	195	305
OCT	31	9.7		300	201.5	98.5
NOV	30	10.0		300	195	105
DEC	31	80.6		2500	201.5	2298.5
				19100	2372.5	16727.5
					$15.00	$30.00
					$35,640	$501,825.00

Chase Production Strategy (Hiring/Firing Workers)

Step 1: Determine the production per period.

Production per period = Demand per period
January Demand Forecast (500) = January Production (500)

Step 2: Calculate the number of workers needed per period.

Workers per period = Regular production / Production per employee
= 500 / 6 = 83 workers needed in January

Step 3: Calculate the change in workers (hiring/firing) between periods. Beginning workforce is 80 workers during the previous December. 83 workers needed – 80 workers presently = 3 workers hired. Illustrated in the table below.

Step 4: Calculate the total cost for the strategy.

Total $ = (Reg. Production x Reg. Production $) + (# of employees hired x Hiring $ per employee)
+ (# of employees fired x Firing $ per employee)
= (19100 x 15) + (720 x 100) + (1117 x 200) = $581,900

Month	Forecast	Regular	# of Workers	Workers Hired	Workers Fired
JAN	500	500	83	3	
FEB	300	300	50		33
MAR	200	200	33		17
APRIL	1500	1500	250	217	
MAY	2500	2500	417	167	
JUNE	3500	3500	583	166	
JULY	4500	4500	750	167	
AUG	2500	2500	417		333
SEPT	500	500	83		334
OCT	300	300	50		33
NOV	300	300	50		0
DEC	2500	2500	417	----	367
	19100	19100		720	1117
		$15.00		$100	$200
		$286,500		$72,000	$223,400

Cost = $286,500 + 72,000 + 223,400 = $581,900

Decision: Pick the alternative with the lowest cost. Recommend a level production plan using inventory and overtime.

1. Champs On the Run, manufacturer of their famous "1" tennis racket, needs help planning production for next year. Demand for race gear follows a seasonal pattern, as shown here. Given the following costs and demand forecasts, test these three strategies for meeting demand: a.) Level production with overtime and inventory, b.) Level production with subcontracting, c.) Chase plan. Which strategy would you recommend?

Month	Days of Production	Demand Forecast
January	25	500
February	20	300
March	27	200
April	25	1500
May	28	2500
June	30	3500
July	30	4500
August	30	2500
September	20	500
October	25	300
November	20	300
December	20	2500

Beginning workforce	8 workers
Production rate during regular time	$15 per unit
Production rate during overtime	$25 per unit
Subcontracting cost	$30 per unit
Increasing production	$100 per unit
Decreasing production	$200 per unit
Inventory holding cost	$0.50 per unit/period
Production in Dec. of previous year	2600 units
No beginning inventory	

2. Loans for Homes prepares mortgage loans for customers year round. However, demand is heaviest during August, September, and October. Loans for Homes increases its workforce several times over during those months and uses as much overtime as is available. In rare cases, Loans for Homes subcontracts out some work, but that practice really eats into profits. The average cost to prepare a mortgage loan is $550. Customers whose closing is delayed pay $100 less per week late. Use the following data to help Loan for Homes design an economical service strategy with the following mix options (a.) Overtime, (b.) Subcontracting, and (c.) Chase strategy.

Month	Days of Production	Demand Forecast
January	25	60
February	20	50
March	27	30
April	25	45
May	28	50
June	30	60
July	30	100
August	30	300
September	20	700
October	25	500
November	20	60
December	20	50

Regular production cost	$550 per customer
Overtime production cost	$750 per customer
Subcontracting	$900 per customer
Increase production	$50 per loan
Decrease production	$75 per loan
Beginning workforce (capacity)	12 workers (50 loans per month)

3. Using the demand in Problem 4 of the Pure Strategies, determine if Fun & Sun should explore any of the mixed strategies to meet demand. There is no beginning inventory, but inventory should be used before all other sources. Given the following costs and previous demand forecasts, test these three strategies for meeting demand: a.) Level production with overtime and inventory, b.) Level production with subcontracting, c.) Chase plan. Which strategy would you recommend?

Regular production cost	$80 per unit
Overtime production cost	$120 per unit
Subcontracting cost	$140 per unit
Inventory holding cost	$10 per unit/month
Production per employee	15 units per month
Beginning workforce	5 workers
Cost of increasing work	$25 per unit
Cost of decreasing work	$20 per unit
Number of days of production in month	25

4. Using the demand in Problem 5 of the Pure Strategies section, determine if there are better alternatives to consider for Fun & Sun and its line of water fountains. There is no beginning inventory, but inventory should be used before all other sources. Given the following costs and previous demand forecasts, test these three strategies for meeting demand: a.) Level production with overtime and inventory, b.) Level production with subcontracting, c.) Chase plan. Which strategy would you recommend?

Regular production cost	$10 per unit
Overtime production cost	$16 per unit
Subcontracting cost	$18 per unit
Inventory holding cost	$2 per unit/month
Production per employee	15 units per month
Beginning workforce	5 workers
Cost of increasing work	$20 per unit
Cost of decreasing work	$50 per unit
Number of days of production in month	25

5.   Using the demand from Problem 6 in the Pure Strategies section, determine if Log Furniture Inc. should consider any of the mixed strategies to meet demand. There is no beginning inventory, but inventory should be used before all other sources. Given the following costs and previous demand forecasts, test these three strategies for meeting demand: a.) Level production with overtime and inventory, b.) Level production with subcontracting, c.) Chase plan. Which strategy would you recommend?

Regular production cost	$200 per unit
Overtime production cost	$300 per unit
Subcontracting cost	$500 per unit
Inventory holding cost	$50 per unit/month
Production per employee	15 units per month
Beginning workforce	5 workers
Cost of increasing work	$75 per unit
Cost of decreasing work	$150 per unit
Number of days of production in month	24

Transportation Method

S1.   ABC Company uses overtime, inventory, and subcontracting to absorb fluctuations in demand for its playgrounds for children. An aggregate production plan is devised annually and updated quarterly. Cost data, expected demand, and available capacities in units for the next four quarters are given here. Demand must be satisfied in the period it occurs; that is, no backordering is allowed. Design a production plan that will satisfy demand at minimum cost.

Quarter	Expected Demand	Regular Capacity	Overtime Capacity	Subcontract Capacity
1	650	750	100	500
2	1250	950	150	500
3	1350	1050	200	500
4	2750	1050	200	500

Regular production cost per unit	$200
Overtime production cost per unit	$250
Subcontracting cost per unit	$300
Inventory holding cost per unit per period	$30
Beginning inventory	300 units

Solution:

Step 1:   To set up the tableau, demand requirements for each quarter are listed on the bottom row and capacity constraints for each type of production (i.e., regular, overtime, or subcontracting) are placed in the far right column.

Step 2:   Next, cost figures are entered into the small square at the corner of each cell. Reading across the first row, inventory on hand in period 1 that is used in period 1 incurs zero cost. Inventory on hand in period 1 that is not used until period 2 incurs $30 holding cost. If the inventory is held until period 3, the cost is $30 more, or $60. Similarly, if the inventory is held until period 4, the cost is an additional $30, or $90.

Step 3:   Interpreting the cost entries in the second row, if a unit is produced under regular production in period 1 and used in period 1, it costs $200. If a unit is produced under regular production in period 1 but is not used until period 2, it incurs a production cost of $200 plus an inventory cost of $30, or $230. If the unit is held until period 3, it will cost $30 more, or $260. If it is held until period 4, it will cost $290. The cost calculations continue in a similar fashion for overtime and subcontracting, beginning with production costs of $250 and $280, respectively.

Step 4:   The costs for production in periods 2, 3, and 4 are determined in a similar fashion, with one exception. Half of the remaining transportation tableau is blocked out as infeasible. This occurs because no backordering is allowed for this problem, and production cannot take place in one period to satisfy demand that occurs in previous periods.

	PERIOD PRODUCTION	1	2	3	4	Unused Capacity	Capacity
	Period of Use						
	Beginning Inventory	0 / 300	30 / ---- ----	60 / ---- ----	90 / ---- ----		300
1	Regular	200 / 350	230 / 300	260 / 100	290 / ---- ----		750
	Overtime	250	280	310	340 / 100		100
	Subcontract	300	330	360	390		500
2	Regular		200 / 950	230 / ---- ----	260 / ---- ----		950
	Overtime		250	280	310 / 150		150
	Subcontract		300	330	360 / 250	250	500
3	Regular			200 / 1050	230 / ----		1050
	Overtime			250 / 200	280 / ----		200
	Subcontract			300	330 / 500		500
4	Regular				200 / 1050		1050
	Overtime				250 / 200		200
	Subcontract				300 / 500		500
	Demand	650	1250	1350	2750	250	

Step 5: Now that the tableau is set up, we can begin to allocate units to the cells and develop our production plan. The procedure is to assign units to the lowest cost cells in a column so that demand requirements for the column are met, yet capacity constraints of each row are not exceeded. Beginning with the first demand column for period 1, we have 300 units of beginning inventory available to us at no cost. If we use all 300 units in period 1, there is no inventory left for use in later periods. We indicate this fact by putting a dash in the remaining cells of the beginning inventory row. We can satisfy the remaining 350 units of demand for period 1 with regular production at a cost of $200 per unit.

Step 6: In period 2, the lowest cost alternative is regular production in period 2. We assign 950 units to that cell and, in the process, use up all the capacity for that row. Dashes are placed in the remaining cells of the row to indicate that they are no longer feasible choices. The remaining units needed to meet demand in period 2 are taken from regular production in period 1 that is not inventoried until period 2, at a cost of $230 per unit. We assign 300 units to that cell.

Step 7: Continuing to the third period's demand of 1350 units, we fully utilize the 1050 units available from regular production in the same period and 200 units of overtime production. The remaining 100 units are produced with regular production in period 1 and held until period 3, at a cost of $260 per unit. As noted by the dashed line, period 1's regular production has reached its capacity and it is no longer an alternative source of production.

Step 8: Of the fourth period's demand of 2750 units, 1050 come from regular production, 200 from overtime, and 500 from subcontracting in the same period. 150 more units can be provided at a cost of $310 per unit from overtime production in period 2 and 500 from subcontracting in period 3. The next-lowest alternative is $340 from overtime in period 1 or subcontracting in period 2. At this point, we can make a judgment call as to whether our workers want overtime or whether it would be easier to subcontract out the entire amount. As shown in the table, the decision was to use overtime to its full capacity of 100 units and fill the remaining demand of 250 from subcontracting.

Step 9: The unused capacity column is filled in last. In period 2, 250 units of subcontracting capacity are available but used. This information is valuable because it tells us the flexibility the company has to accept additional orders.

The optimal production plan, derived from the transportation tableau, is given in the table below. The values in the production plan are taken from the transportation tableau one row at a time. For example, the 750 units of regular production for period 1 is the sum of 350 + 300 + 100 from the second row of the transportation tableau. Ending inventory is calculated by summing beginning inventory and all forms of production for that period, then subtracting demand. For example, the ending inventory for period 1 is:

$$(300 + 750 + 100) - 650 = 500$$

The cost of the production plan can be determined directly from the transportation tableau by multiplying the units in each cell times the cost in the corner of the cell and summing them. Alternatively, the cost can be determined from the production plan by multiplying the total units produced in each production category or held in inventory by their respective costs and summing them, as follows:

$$(3800 \times \$200) + (650 \times \$250) + (1250 \times \$300) + (2100 \times \$30) = \$1,360,500$$

| Period | Demand | PRODUCTION PLAN | | | Ending Inventory |
		Regular Production	Overtime	Subcontract	
1	650	750	100	0	500
2	1250	950	150	250	600
3	1350	1050	200	500	1000
4	2750	1050	200	500	0
Total	6000	3800	650	1250	2100

1. The Bayou Motor Company is the south's largest producer of motors for offshore fishing boats. As you might suspect, the need for fishing boats exhibits a highly seasonal demand pattern, with peaks during the summer months and valleys during the winter months. To use their resources optimally, Bayou forecasts annual demand to set the master production schedule, and then they adjust the demand on a 2-month demand period. Given the following costs and period sales forecasts, use the transportation method to design a production plan that will economically meet demand. What is the cost of the plan?

Monthly Periods (2-months)	Sales Forecast
Jan.–Feb.	10000
March–April	14000
May–June	24000
July–Aug.	28000
Sept.–Oct.	18000
Nov. –Dec.	8000

Inventory carrying cost	$150.00 per motor per period
Production per employee	500 motors per period
Regular workforce	15 workers
Overtime capacity	5000 motors per period
Subcontracting capacity	4000 motors per period
Cost of regular production	$750 per motor
Cost of overtime production	$1000 per motor
Cost of subcontracting	$1150 per motor

2. Using the demand in Problem 4 of the Pure Strategies, develop a production plan for Fun & Sun using the transportation method. There is no beginning inventory, but inventory should be used before all other sources. Given the following costs and previous demand forecasts, determine the most economical plan to meet demand. What is the cost of the plan?

Regular production cost	$80 per unit
Overtime production cost	$120 per unit
Regular capacity	40 units per month
Overtime capacity	8 units per month
Subcontracting cost	$140 per unit
Subcontracting capacity	12 units per month
Inventory holding cost	$10 per unit/month
Production per employee	15 units per month
Beginning workforce	5 workers

3. Fun & Sun wants to see if there are optimal levels of inventory, overtime, and subcontracting. Determine if there are better alternatives to consider for Fun & Sun and its line of water fountains. There is no beginning inventory, but inventory should be used before all other sources. Given the following costs and quarter demand forecasts, determine the most economical plan to meet demand. What is the cost of the plan?

Quarter	Demand Forecast
1	2000
2	9000
3	9000
4	4000

Regular production cost	$10 per unit
Regular capacity	6000 units per quarter
Overtime production cost	$16 per unit
Overtime capacity	3000 units per quarter
Subcontracting cost	$18 per unit
Subcontracting capacity	2000 units per quarter
Inventory holding cost	$2 per unit/month
Production per employee	15 units per month
Beginning workforce	5 workers

4. Using the demand from Problem 6 in the Pure Strategies section, develop a production plan for Log Furniture Inc. to meet demand. There is no beginning inventory, but inventory should be used before all other sources. Given the following costs and previous demand forecasts, determine the most economical plan to meet demand. What is the cost of the plan?

Regular production cost	$200 per unit
Regular capacity	35 units per month
Overtime production cost	$300 per unit
Overtime capacity	5 units per month
Subcontracting cost	$500 per unit
Subcontracting cost	5 units per month
Inventory holding cost	$50 per unit/month
Production per employee	15 units per month
Beginning workforce	5 workers

Yield Management

S1.   The manager of Rustic Adventures is tired of customers who make reservations then don't show up. Cabins rent for $250 a night and cost $15 to maintain per day. Overflow customers are sent to a local motel for $110 a night. The manager has kept records of no-shows over the past 3 years, and they are given below. Should the Lucky Traveler start overbooking? If so, how many rooms should be overbooked? It is also important to remember that Rustic Adventures has a seasonal demand pattern, so having all available cabins rented is important.

No-Shows	Probability
0	0.25
1	0.35
2	0.20
3	0.10
4	0.10

Solution:

Step 1:   Calculate the expected number of no-shows. Using the data from the probability table, multiply the number of no shows by its probability of occurrence. For example, multiply 0 no shows by its probability of 0.25. Do this for all possible occurrences. Then add all the products together to determine the expected value of no-shows. The expected value is 1.45.

$$0 (0.25) + 1 (0.35) + 2 (0.20) + 3 (0.10) + 4 (0.10) = 1.45$$

Step 2:   Calculate the contribution per cabin. Take the contribution of renting a cabin ($250) minus the cost of maintaining the cabin ($15/day). So, the result would be $250 – 15 = $235.

Step 3:   Calculate the average cost of no-shows per night by multiplying the expected number of no-shows (1.45) by the profit per night ($235). Thus, the average is (1.45) ($235) = $340.75 a night. To reduce the loss, we can try overbooking the rooms.

Step 4:   Calculate the optimal probability of no-show as:

$$P (n < x) \le \frac{C_u}{C_u + C_o} = \frac{235}{235 + 110} = 0.68$$

Step 5:   Set up the cumulative probability table from the original probabilities. To do this, we can determine $P(n < x)$ by taking the cumulative probability and adding the probability of the previous occurrence. For example, the cut off for 0 no-shows is .00 since no no-shows can occur. For 1 no-show, you would take zero's cut off (0.00) and add the probability of 0 no-shows (0.25), so the cumulative probability is 0.25. For 2 no-shows, you would take one's cut off (0.25) and add the probability of 1 no-show (0.35), so the cumulative probability is 0.60. All probabilities are listed below.

No-Shows	Probability	$P (n < x)$
0	0.25	.00
1	0.35	0.25
2	0.20	0.60
3	0.10	0.80
4	0.10	0.90

Step 6:   Determine the optimal number of no-shows. The optimal probability of no-show falls between .60 and .80. Since we are concerned with no-shows less than or equal to .68, we choose the next lowest value, or .60. Following across the table, the manager should overbook by 2 cabins.

Step 7:   Determine the cost of bumping customers. Take all occurrences below the overbooking number and multiply by their probabilities. If everyone shows, the two people will be bumped and everyone shows up 25% of the time, so the result would be 2(.25) or .50. One no-show occurs 35% of the time, so one person would be bumped. So, the cost of bumping customers would be [2(.25) + 1(.35)] $110 = $93.50.

Step 8: Determine the cost of lost revenue for no-shows. Take all occurrences above the overbooking Number (3 and 4) and multiply by their probabilities. If there are three no-shows, then two can be filled with overbooked people and only one empty cabin will result. This happens 10% of the time, so the result would be 1(.10) or .10. Four no-shows occurs 10% of the time, so two cabins would be left empty. So, the cost of lost revenue would be [1(.10) + 2(.10)] $235 = $70.50.

Step 9: Calculate the cost of the overbooking policy. The cost as shown below is calculated by taking the cost of bumping customers and adding the cost of lost revenue, so the cost of overbooking by 2 cabins is $163.50.

Step 10: Calculate the expected savings per night. You can determine this by taking the profit per night minus the total cost of overbooking cabins (235 – 163.50). The savings is $71.50 a night.

1. The manager of the Born Again Spa has experienced many no-shows for scheduled appointments. She usually filled these openings with walk-in customers, but this practice has been shown to cause considerable delay and poor customer service. She has decided to start overbooking the appointments. The average profit from the services provided by the Spa is $35. If a customer arrives that has an appointment and can't be served, then they are given a Rain Check for their next visit. The Rain Check is worth $50. The manager has the following data on the no-shows over the past 6 months. How many appointments should the manager overbook? How much money overbooking would save?

No-Shows	Frequency
0	40
1	60
2	35
3	10

2. The manager of the local gym has experienced many no-shows for scheduled appointments. As a promotional attraction, the manager has included one appointment for each new member with a fitness instructor. The fitness instructors have other paying clients, but this service has proven to be a big draw. He is concerned with the high number of no-shows for these appointments since the fitness instructors had to pass on full pay versus the hourly wage that he pays. He has decided to start overbooking the appointments. To remedy the problem, the manager will only offer a few new member appointments per day, which he has assigned a rate of $10 per visit. The average rate for regular customers is $25 per visit. There are 30 appointments available per day. How many regular appointments should the manager have available per day? The following represents the number of times regular appointments were scheduled for each day last month.

Regular Customers	Frequency
0	2
10	10
20	15
30	3

3. The manager of Wild River Rides is concerned about customers who make reservations then don't show up. Wild River Rides has guided tours of the Snake River. Spots on the raft are sold for $50 and each spot has a cost of $5 to maintain the raft and pay the guide. Overflow customers can be sent to another company for $40 per spot. The manager has kept records of no-shows over the past 3 years, and they are given below. Should Wild River start overbooking? If so, how many spots should be overbooked? It is also important to remember that Wild River has a seasonal demand pattern, so having all available spots sold is important. The raft contains 8 spots. If less than 4 show, then the trip is cancelled and the people moved to other trips.

No-Shows	Probability
0	0.15
1	0.15
2	0.20
3	0.40
4	0.10

14

Material Requirements Planning (MRP) and ERP

I.   MRP Provides a Competitive Advantage for Collins Industries

A. General
   1. Collins Industries is the largest manufacturer of ambulances in the world.
   2. They insist that four tasks need to be performed properly.
      a. The material plan must meet both the requirements of the master schedule and the capabilities of the production facility.
      b. The plan must be executed as designed.
      c. Effective material, consignment inventories and a constant review of purchase methods reduce inventory investment.
      d. Maintain excellent record integrity.

B. Benefits
   1. Better response to customer orders.
      a. Due to adherence to schedules.
      b. Wins orders and market shares.
   2. Faster response to market changes.
   3. Improved utilization of facilities and labor yields higher productivity and return on investment.
   4. Reduced inventory levels frees up capital and floor space.

C. Dependent Demand
   1. Complements:
      a. The demand of one item influences the demand of another item.
      b. For all products, demand for the parts or components are dependent on the actual product.
   2. Preferred to the EOQ products
      a. The dependent techniques used in a production environment are called material requirements planning (MRP).

II.   Dependent Inventory Model Requirements

A. Master Production Schedule
   1. Specifies what is to be made.
   2. The plan includes a schedule, variety of inputs, customer demand, engineering capabilities, labor availability, inventory fluctuations, supplier production plan, and financial plans.
   3. MRP will help determine precise feasibility of the schedule.

FIGURE 14.1 ■

The Planning Process

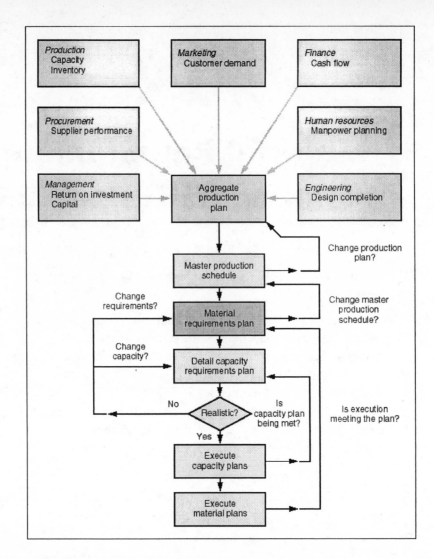

Regardless of the complexity of the planning process, the production plan and its derivative, the master production schedule, must be developed.

4. The master production schedule tells us what is required to satisfy demand and meet the production plan.
5. This is set up in specific products as opposed to the aggregate production plan.

FIGURE 14.2 ■

The Aggregate Production Plan Provides the Basis for Development of the Detailed Master Production Schedule

Months	January				February			
Aggregate Production Plan (Shows the total quantity of amplifiers)	1,500				1,200			
Weeks	1	2	3	4	5	6	7	8
Master Production Schedule (Shows the specific type and quantity of amplifier to be produced)								
240 watt amplifier	100		100		100		100	
150 watt amplifier		500		500		450		450
75 watt amplifier			300				100	

312

6. The near-term portion of the plan, a.k.a. the "fixed" schedule, cannot be altered. (The Wheeled Coach division of Collins Industries is set up this way.) The rest of the schedule is the "rolling" schedule.
7. The master schedule can be expressed in either a make-to-order, assemble-to-stock or make-to-stock company.

This relationship of the master production schedule to the processes is shown in Figure 14.3.

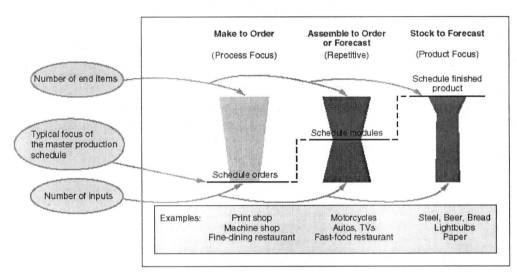

FIGURE 14.3 ■ Typical Focus of the Master Production Schedule in Three Process Strategies

A master production schedule for two of Nancy's Specialty Foods' products, crabmeat quiche and spinach quiche, might look like Table 14.1.

TABLE 14.1 ■

Master Production Schedule for Crabmeat Quiche and Spinach Quiche at Nancy's Specialty Foods

GROSS REQUIREMENTS FOR CRABMEAT QUICHE										
Day	6	7	8	9	10	11	12	13	14	and so on
Amount	50		100	47	60		110	75		
GROSS REQUIREMENTS FOR SPINACH QUICHE										
Day	7	8	9	10	11	12	13	14	15	16	and so on
Amount	100	200	150			60	75		100		

B. Bill of Material
1. Manufactured items are defined with these lists of quantities of components, ingredients, and material required to make a product.
2. Errors or complete loss of these bills are not good due to the fact that they can cause engineering change notices (ECN's), which are engineering corrections and can be very confusing.
3. A bill of material defines products through structure. This example shows this through parent or upper structures and components/children or lower structures.

Speaker Kits, Inc., packages high-fidelity components for mail order. Components for the top-of-the-line speaker kit, "Awesome" (A), include standard 12-inch speaker kits (Bs) and 3 speaker kits with amp-boosters (Cs).

Each B consists of 2 speakers (Ds) and 2 shipping boxes, each with an installation kit (E). Each of the three 300-watt stereo kits (Cs) has 2 speaker boosters (Fs) and 2 installation kits (Es). Each speaker booster (F) includes 2 speakers (Ds) and 1 amp-booster (G). The total for each Awesome is 4 standard 12-inch speakers and twelve 12-inch speakers with the amp-booster. (Most purchases require hearing aids within 2 years, and at least one court case is pending because of structural damage to a men's dormitory.) As we can see, the demand for B, C, D, E, F, and G is completely dependent on the master production schedule for A – the Awesome speaker kits. Given this information, we can construct the following product structure:

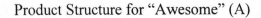

Product Structure for "Awesome" (A)

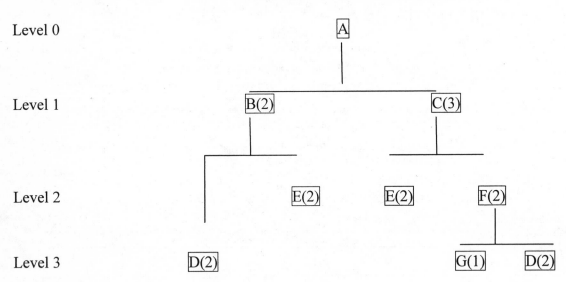

Solution:
This structure has four levels: 0, 1, 2, and 3. There are four parents: A, B, C, and F. Each parent item has at least one level below it. Items B, C, D, E, F, and G are components because each item has at least one level above it. In this structure, B, C, and F are both parents and components. The number in parentheses indicates how many units of that particular item are needed to make the item immediately above it. Thus, B(2) means that it takes two units of B for every unit of A, and F(2) means that it takes two units of F for every unit of C.

Once we have developed the product structure, we can determine the number of units of each item required to satisfy demand for a new order of 50 Awesome speaker kits. This information is displayed below:

Part B:	2 x number of As	= (2) x (50)	= 100
Part C:	2 x number of As	= (3) x (50)	= 150
Part D:	2 x number of Bs + 2 x number of Fs =	(2) x (100) + (2) x (300) =	800
Part E:	2 x number of Bs + 2 x number of Cs =	(2) x (100) + (2) x (300) =	500
Part F:	2 x number of Cs	= (2) x (150)	= 300
Part F:	1 x number of Fs	= (1) x (300)	= 300

Thus, for 50 units of A, we will need 100 units of B, 150 units of C, 800 units of D, 500 units of E, 300 units of F, and 300 units of G.

    4. These bills of material also show costing and items to production or assembly personal. They are usually called "pick list" when used this way.

    5. Modular bills
       a. Bills of material organized by major subassemblies or by product options.
       b. This is used to limit scheduling and production by organizing around relatively few modules rather than a multitude of final assemblies.
       c. This allows the MPS to be prepared for a reasonable number of items and to postpone assembly.

    6. Planning bills and phantom bills
       a. Planning bills (a.k.a. kits) are material groupings created in order to assign an artificial parent to the bill of material.
       b. Planning bills are used when we want to group subassemblies and issue kits into the project.
       c. Phantom bills are bills of material for components that exist only temporarily and are never inventoried.

    7. Low-level coding
       a. Low-level coding is a number that identifies items at the lowest level at which they occur.
       b. This resource allows easy computing of the requirements of an item.

C. Accurate Inventory Records – good inventory management is needed for MRP to work (99% accuracy needed).

D. Purchase Orders Outstanding – knowledge of outstanding orders is necessary for MRP and well-managed purchasing and inventory control departments.

E. Lead Times for Each Component
    1. Lead time is the time to purchase, produce or assemble an item.
    2. In production systems it is the order, wait, move, queue, setup and run times for each component.

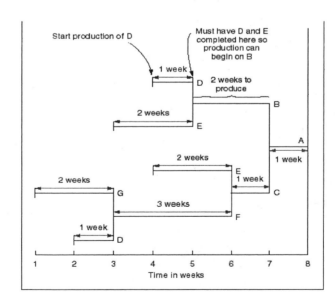

TABLE 14.2 ■ Lead Times for Awesome Speaker Kits (As)

COMPONENT	LEAD TIME
A	1 week
B	2 weeks
C	1 week
D	1 week
E	2 weeks
F	3 weeks
G	2 weeks

III. MRP Structure

A. General
1. The MRP procedure is straightforward and can be done by hand.
   a. Include: a master production schedule, a bill of material, inventory and purchase record, and lead times for each item.
   b. Once the ingredients are accurate, the next step is to construct a gross material requirements plan.

Example: MRP Structure – Gross Requirements Planning

Each Awesome speaker kit (item A of the previous example) requires all the items in the product structure for A. Lead times are shown in the table below.

Item	Lead Time
A	1 week
B	2 weeks
C	1 week
D	1 week
E	2 weeks
F	3 weeks
G	2 weeks

Solution:

Using this information, we construct the gross material requirements plan and draw up a production schedule that will satisfy the demand of 50 units of A by week 8.

		Week								Lead Time
		1	2	3	4	5	6	7	8	
A	Required date								50	
	Order release date							50		1 week
B	Required date							100		
	Order release date					100				2 weeks
C	Required date							150		
	Order release date						150			1 week
D	Required date					200	300			
	Order release date			200	300					2 weeks
E	Required date						300			
	Order release date			300						3 weeks
F	Required date			600	200					
	Order release date		600		200					1 week
G	Required date			300						
	Order release date	300								2 weeks

Step 1: If you want 50 units of A at week 8, you must start assembling A in week 7 (since A takes 1 week to complete).

Step 2: Thus, in week 7, you will need 100 units of B and 150 units of C to complete the 50 units of A. These two items take 2 weeks and 1 week, respectively, to produce. Production of B, therefore, should start in week 5, and production of C should start in week 6 (lead time subtracted from the required date for these items).

Step 3: Working backward, we can perform the same computations for all of the other items.

Step 4: Because D and E are used in two different places in Awesome speaker kits, there are two entries in each data record.

Analysis: So, it takes 8 weeks to complete each Awesome speaker kit.

  2. Gross material requirements plan is shown in the example above.
     a. It shows when an item must be ordered from suppliers if there is no inventory on hand.
     b. When the production of an item must be started in order to satisfy demand for the finished product by a particular date.
  3. Net requirements plan
     a. Prepare when there is inventory on hand.
     b. Consider subassemblies and parts.
     c. Requirements for parent item and components decrease because each kit contains lower level items.

Example: Net Requirement Planning

In the example of the product structure tree, we developed a product structure from a bill of material, and in the previous example, we developed a gross requirements plan. Given the following on-hand inventory, we now construct a net requirement plan.

Item	On Hand
A	10
B	15
C	20
D	10
E	10
F	5
G	0

Solution:
A net material requirements plan includes gross requirements, on-hand inventory, net requirements, planned order receipt, and planned order release for each item. We begin with A and work backward through the components. Shown in the following chart is the net material requirements plan for product A.

ITEM: A	LLC: 0	PERIOD							
LOT SIZE: L4L	LT: 1	1	2	3	4	5	6	7	8
Gross Requirements									50
Scheduled Receipts									
Projected on Hand	10	10	10	10	10	10	10	10	10
Net Requirements									40
Planned Order Receipts									40
Planned Order Releases								40	
								x 2	

ITEM: B	LLC: 1	PERIOD							
LOT SIZE: L4L	LT: 2	1	2	3	4	5	6	7	8
Gross Requirements								80	
Scheduled Receipts									
Projected on Hand	15	15	15	15	15	15	15	15	
Net Requirements								65	
Planned Order Receipts								65	
Planned Order Releases						65			
								x 3	

ITEM: C	LLC: 1	PERIOD							
LOT SIZE: L4L	LT: 1	1	2	3	4	5	6	7	8
Gross Requirements								120	
Scheduled Receipts									
Projected on Hand	20	20	20	20	20	20	20	20	
Net Requirements								100	
Planned Order Receipts								100	
Planned Order Releases							100		
					x 2		x 2		

ITEM: E	LLC: 2	PERIOD							
LOT SIZE: L4L	LT: 2	1	2	3	4	5	6	7	8
Gross Requirements						130	200		
Scheduled Receipts									
Projected on Hand	10	10	10	10	10	10			
Net Requirements						120	200		
Planned Order Receipts						120	200		
Planned Order Releases				120	200				
									x 2

ITEM: F	LLC: 2	PERIOD							
LOT SIZE: L4L	LT: 3	1	2	3	4	5	6	7	8
Gross Requirements							200		
Scheduled Receipts									
Projected on Hand	5	5	5	5	5	5	5		
Net Requirements							195		
Planned Order Receipts							195		
Planned Order Releases				195					
				x 2					x 2

ITEM: D	LLC: 3	PERIOD							
LOT SIZE: L4L	LT: 1	1	2	3	4	5	6	7	8
Gross Requirements				390		130			
Scheduled Receipts									
Projected on Hand	10	10	10	10					
Net Requirements				380		130			
Planned Order Receipts				380		130			
Planned Order Releases			380			130			

From F
/ x 1

ITEM: G	LLC: 3			PERIOD					
LOT SIZE: L4L	LT: 2	1	2	3	4	5	6	7	8
Gross Requirements				195					
Scheduled Receipts									
Projected on Hand	0			0					
Net Requirements				195					
Planned Order Receipts				195					
Planned Order Releases		195							

To complete A, A needs 2 Bs. As shown above, its gross requirements are calculated by multiplying the planned order releases of each parent times the quantity per assembly contained in the bill of material. This process is called explosion. Since 2 Bs are needed for every A, period 7 gross requirements are (40 x 2) = 80 to satisfy the one-week need for final assembly of the 50 As in week 8. Notice that 10 are on-hand, so only 40 more As are needed, which results in only 80 Bs. Since the assemblies are needed in week 7 and the lead-time is 1 week, the order for 40 As is released in week 7.

We have now completed the MRP calculations. To summarize the results, we construct a planned order report from the planned order release row of each matrix, as follows:

Planned Order Report

	Period							
Item	1	2	3	4	5	6	7	8
A								40
B					65			
C						100		
D			120	200				
E			195					
F		380		130				
G	195							

Constructing a net requirements plan is similar to constructing a gross requirements plan. Starting with item A, we work backward to determine net requirements for all items. To do these computations, we refer to the product structure, on-hand inventory, and lead times. The gross requirement for A is 50 units in week 8. Ten items are on hand; therefore, the net requirements and the scheduled planned order receipt are both 40 items in week 8. Because of the 1-week lead-time, the planned order release is 40 items in week 7. Referring to week 7 and the product structure in the first example, we can see that 80 (2 x 40) items of B and 120 (3 x 40) items of C are required in week 7 in order to have a total of 50 items of A in week 8. The letter A to the right of the gross figure for items B and C was generated as a result of the demand for the parent, A. Performing the same type of analysis for B and C yields the net requirements for D, E, F, and G. Note the on-hand inventory in row E in week 6 is zero. It is zero because the on-hand inventory (10 units) was used to make B in week 5. By the same token, the inventory for D was used to make F.

FIGURE 14.6 ■

Several Schedules
Contributing to a Gross
Requirements Schedule
for B

*One "B" is in each A and
one "B" is in each S;
additionally, 10 Bs sold
directly are scheduled in
week 1 and 10 more that
are sold directly are
scheduled in week 2.*

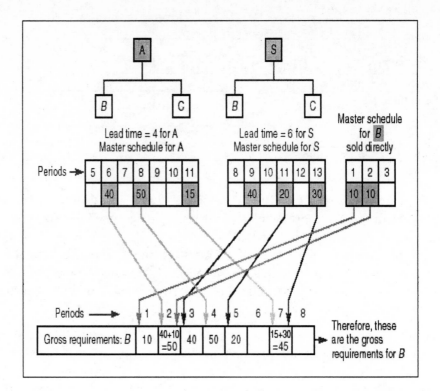

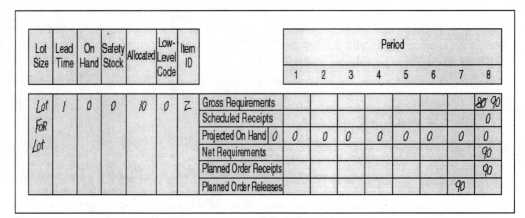

FIGURE 14.7 ■ Sample MRP Planning Sheet for Item Z

The allocated quantity has the effect of increasing the requirements (or, alternatively, reducing the quantity on hand). The logic, then, of a net requirements MRP is

$$\underbrace{\left[\left(\begin{array}{c} \text{gross} \\ \text{requirements} \end{array}\right) + \left(\text{allocations}\right)\right]}_{\text{total requirements}} - \underbrace{\left[\left(\begin{array}{c} \text{on} \\ \text{hand} \end{array}\right) + \left(\begin{array}{c} \text{scheduled} \\ \text{receipts} \end{array}\right)\right]}_{\text{available inventory}} = \begin{array}{c} \text{net} \\ \text{requirements} \end{array}$$

IV.   MRP Management

A. The material requirement plan is not static.
B. MRP Dynamics
   1. Changes in material requirements
      a.   Changes in design, schedules, and production processes alter the material requirements plans and bill of materials.
      b.   Changes occur in the MRP whenever the master production schedule is modified.
   2. Frequent changes
      a.   System nervousness
      b.   Time Fences – A way of allowing a segment of the master schedule to be designated as "not to be rescheduled."
      c.   Pegging – tracing upward in the BOM from the component to the parent item.

V.   MRP and JIT

A. MPR
   1.   MPR is a planning and scheduling technique with fixed lead times.
   2.   Provides a good master schedule and an accurate picture of requirements.
B. JIT (Just-in-Time)
   1.   A way to move material expeditiously.
   2.   Reduces work-in-process inventory.
C. Small bucket approach
   1.   Tool for resource and scheduling management in processed-focused facilities.
   2.   MRP can be integrated with JIT through the following steps:
      Step 1:   Reduce MRP "buckets" from weekly to daily to perhaps hourly. Buckets are time units in an MRP system. Although the examples in this chapter have used weekly time buckets, many firms now use daily or even fraction-of-a-day time buckets. Some systems use a bucketless system in which all time-phased data have dates attached rather than defined time periods or buckets.
      Step 2:   The planned receipts that are part of a firm's planned orders in an MRP system are communicated to the work areas for production purposes and used to sequence production.
      Step 3:   Inventory is moved through the plant on a JIT basis.
      Step 4:   As products are completed, they are moved into inventory (typically finished goods inventory) in the normal way. Receipt of these products' inventory reduces the quantities required for subsequent planned orders in the MRP system.
      Step 5:   A system known as back flush is used to reduce inventory balances. Back flushing uses the bill of materials to deduct component quantities from inventory as each unit is completed.
   3. Schedules are confirmed, updated, or changed every 15 to 20 minutes.
D. Balanced Flow Approach
   1.   The planning portion of MRP is combined with JIT execution.
   2.   Execution is achieved by maintaining a carefully balanced flow of material to assembly areas with small lot sizes.

VI.　Lot Sizing Techniques

How much to order is determined by a lot-sizing decision. There are a variety of ways to determine lot sizes.

    A.　Lot-for-Lot
        1.　A way of producing exactly what is required (dependent demand).
        2.　A system that should produce units only as needed.
            a.　No safety stock
            b.　No anticipation of further orders
        3.　A system that is efficient for frequent, economical orders and just-in-time inventory techniques.

Example: Lot Sizing with the Lot-for-Lot Technique

Speaker Kits, Inc., wants to compute its ordering and carrying cost of inventory on lot-for-lot criteria. Speaker Kits has determined that, for the 12-inch speaker/booster assembly, setup cost is $100 and holding cost is $1 per period. The production schedule, as reflected in net requirements for assemblies, is as follows:

Solution:

ITEM:	LLC:	PERIOD									
LOT SIZE:	LT:	1	2	3	4	5	6	7	8	9	10
Gross Requirements		35	30	40	0	10	40	30	0	30	55
Scheduled Receipts											
Projected on Hand　35		35	0	0	0	0	0	0	0	0	0
Net Requirements		0	30	40	0	10	40	30	0	30	55
Planned Order Receipts			30	40		10	40	30		30	55
Planned Order Releases		30	40		10	40	30		30	55	

Holding cost	=	$1 per unit per week
Setup cost	=	$100 per order
Gross Requirements Average per week	=	27
Lead time	=	1 week

Analysis: The cost associated with this technique is the 7 setup for the 7 order releases. This gives you a total cost of $700.

    B.　Economic Order Quantity (EOQ) – A way of producing what is needed when relatively constant independent demand exists.

With a setup cost of $100 and a holding cost per week of $1, Speaker Kits, Inc., examines its cost with lot sizes based on an EOQ criteria. Using the same requirements as in the previous example, the net requirements and lot sizes follow:

Solution:

ITEM:	LLC:	PERIOD									
LOT SIZE:	LT:	1	2	3	4	5	6	7	8	9	10
Gross Requirements		35	30	40	0	10	40	30	0	30	55
Scheduled Receipts											
Projected on Hand 35		35	0	43	3	3	66	26	69	69	39
Net Requirements		0	30	0	0	7	0	4	0	0	16
Planned Order Receipts			73			73		73			73
Planned Order Releases		73			73		73			73	

Holding cost	= $1 per unit per week
Annual holding ($1 x 52 weeks)	= $52 per unit on an annual basis
Setup cost	= $100 per order
Gross requirements average per week	= 27
Lead time	= 1 week

Ten-week usage equals gross requirement of 270 units; therefore, weekly usage equals 27, and 52 weeks (annual usage) equals 1,404 units. From Chapter 12, the EOQ model is:

$$Q^* = \sqrt{[(2*D*S)]/(H)} \qquad \text{Where: } D = \text{annual usage} = 1,404$$

$$Q^* = \sqrt{[(2*1404*100)]/(52)} = 73 \text{ units}$$

Setups:	1404 / 73	=	19 per year
Setup cost:	19 setups x $100 per setup	=	$1,900
Holding cost:	(73 / 2) * ($1 x 52 weeks)	=	$1,898
Total cost:	$1,900 + $1,898	=	$3,798

The EOQ solution yields a computed 10-week cost of $730
[$3,798 x (10 weeks / 52 weeks) = $730]

Analysis: You should note that the actual cost may be different as in the case above since usage from demand is not constant.

C. Part Period Balancing (PPB)
  1. An inventory ordering technique that balances setup and holding costs by changing the lot size to reflect requirements of the next lot size in the future.
  2. A technique that develops an economic part period (the ratio of setup cost to holding cost).

Once again, Speaker Kits, Inc., computes the costs associated with a lot size by using a $100 setup cost and a $1 holding cost. This time, however, part period balancing is used. The data are shown in the following table:

Solution: PPB Calculations

Periods Combined	Trial Lot Size (Cum. Net Req.)	Part Periods	Costs Setup	Holding	Total
2	30	0			
2,3	70	40 = 40 x 1			
2,3,4	70	40			
2,3,4,5	80	70 = 40 x 1 + 10 x 3	100	+ 70	= 170
2,3,4,5,6	120	230 = 40 x 1 + 10 x 3 + 40 x 4			
6	40	0			
6,7	70	30 = 30 x 1			
6,7,8	70	30 = 30 x 1 + 0 x 2			
6,7,8,9	100	120 = 30 x 1 + 30 x 3	100	+ 120	= 220
10	55	0	100	+ 0	= 100

MRP Lot-Sizing Problem: PPB Technique

ITEM:	LLC:	PERIOD									
LOT SIZE:	LT:	1	2	3	4	5	6	7	8	9	10
Gross Requirements		35	30	40	0	10	40	30	0	30	55
Scheduled Receipts											
Projected on Hand	35	35	0	50	10	10	0	60	30	30	0
Net Requirements		0	30	0	0	0	40	0	0	0	55
Planned Order Receipts			80				100				55
Planned Order Releases		80				100				55	

Holding cost = $1 per unit per week
Annual holding ($1 x 52 weeks) = $52 per unit on an annual basis
Setup cost = $100 per order
Gross requirements average per week = 27
Lead time = 1 week

EPP is 100 (setup cost divided by holding cost = $100/$1). The first lot is to cover periods 1, 2, 3, 4, and 5 and is 80.

The total costs are $490, with setup costs totaling $300 and holding costs totaling $190.

D. Wagner-Whitin Algorithm
   1. A technique for lot-size computation that assumes a finite time horizon beyond which there are no additional net requirements to arrive at an ordering strategy.
   2. The technique provides good results.
   3. The technique is seldom used in practice due to lack of understanding.
E. Lot-Sizing Summary
   1. The technique should be used whenever economical.
   2. The technique has the ability to be modified.
   3. Any of the discussed techniques should provide satisfactory results, although a correct lot size can only be determined after the fact.

Lot-for-lot	$700
EOQ	$730
Part period balancing	$490

VII.   Extensions of MRP

A. Closed Loop MRP – A system that provides feedback to the capacity plan, master production schedule, and production plan so planning can be kept valid at all times.
B. Capacity Planning
   1. An integral part of the closed loop system.
   2. Planning that utilizes a load report – a load report is for showing the requirements in a work center for all work currently assigned there, as well as all planned or expected orders.

FIGURE 14.8 ■

Closed-Loop Material Requirements Planning

Source: Adapted from *Capacity Planning and Control Study Guide* (Alexandria, VA: American Production and Inventory Control Society). Reprinted by permission.

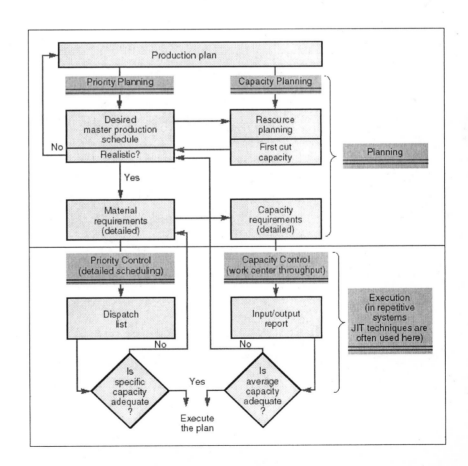

FIGURE 14.9 ■

(a) Initial Resource
Requirements Profile for
a Milling Center (b)
Smoothed Resource
Requirements Profile for
a Milling Center

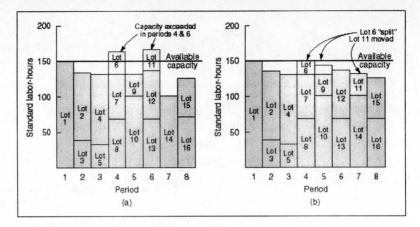

C. Material Requirements Planning II (MRP II)

4. A system that allows inventory data to be augmented by other resource variables.
5. MRP is implemented as the basis and when incorporating MRP II, becomes material resource planning.

		Week			
		5	6	7	8
A	Units (lead time 1 week)				100
	Labor: 10 hours each				1,000
	Machine: 2 hours each				200
	Payable: $0 each				0
B	Units (lead time 2 weeks, 2 each required)			200	
	Labor: 10 hours each			2,000	
	Machine: 2 hours each			400	
	Payable: Raw material at $5 each			1,000	
C	Units (lead time 4 weeks, 3 each required)	300			
	Labor: 2 hours each	600			
	Machine: 1 hour each	300			
	Payable: Raw material at $10 each	3,000			

VIII. MRP in Services

Demand for services can be classified as dependent when it is directly related to the demand for other services.

    a. Example: Restaurants = components of a meal

    b. Example: Hospitals = supplies for surgical inventory

FIGURE 14.10 ■

Product Structure Tree, Bill of Material, and Bill of Labor for Veal Picante

Source: Adapted from John G. Wacker, "Effective Planning and Cost Control for Restaurants," *Production and Inventory Management* (first quarter 1985): 60. Reprinted by permission of American Production and Inventory Control Society.

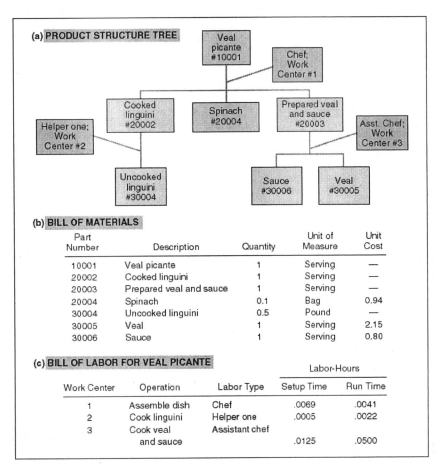

(a) PRODUCT STRUCTURE TREE

(b) BILL OF MATERIALS

Part Number	Description	Quantity	Unit of Measure	Unit Cost
10001	Veal picante	1	Serving	—
20002	Cooked linguini	1	Serving	—
20003	Prepared veal and sauce	1	Serving	—
20004	Spinach	0.1	Bag	0.94
30004	Uncooked linguini	0.5	Pound	—
30005	Veal	1	Serving	2.15
30006	Sauce	1	Serving	0.80

(c) BILL OF LABOR FOR VEAL PICANTE

Work Center	Operation	Labor Type	Labor-Hours Setup Time	Labor-Hours Run Time
1	Assemble dish	Chef	.0069	.0041
2	Cook linguini	Helper one	.0005	.0022
3	Cook veal and sauce	Assistant chef	.0125	.0500

IX. Distribution Resource Planning (DRP)

    A. A time phased stock-replenishment plan for all levels of a distribution network.

    B. Requirements for DRP:

        1. Gross requirements, which are the same as expected demand or sales forecasts.

        2. Minimum levels of inventory to meet customer-service levels.

        3. Accurate lead time.

        4. Definition of the distribution structure.

    C. DRP pulls inventory through the system.

    D. The goal is small and frequent replenishment within the bounds of economical ordering and shipping.

X. Enterprise Resource Planning (ERP)

A. ERP is an information system for identifying and planning the enterprise-wide resources needed to take, make, ship and account for customer orders.

B. The objective of an ERP system is to coordinate a firm's whole business.
1. Because objective is seldom achieved, secondary systems are implemented.
   a. Supply Chain Management (SCM)
   b. Customer Relationship Management (CRM)
   c. Human Resource management (HR)
2. Other options
   a. The use of third-party software in the form of modules called "solution" packages that are called business application-programming interfaces (BAPI).

FIGURE 14.11 ■

MRP and ERP Information Flows, Showing Customer Relationship Management (CRM), Supply Chain Management (SCM), and Finance/Accounting

Other functions such as human resources are often also included in ERP systems.

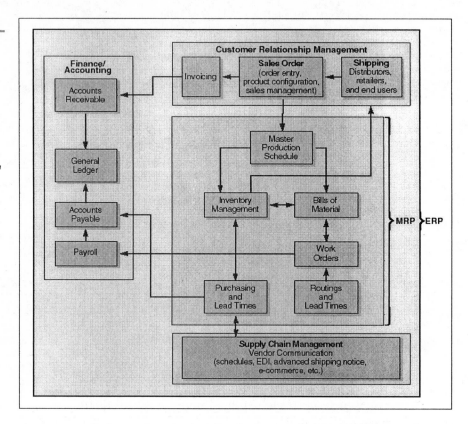

C. Advantages and Disadvantages of ERP
  1. Advantages
     a. Provides integration of the supply chain, production, and administrative process.
     b. Creates commonality of databases.
     c. Can incorporate improved, reengineered, "best processes."
     d. Increases communication and collaboration between business units and sites.
     e. Has a software database that is off-the-shelf coding.
     f. May provide a strategic advantage over competitors.
  2. Disadvantages
     a. Is very expensive to purchase, and even more costly to customize.
     b. Implementation may require major changes in the company and its processes.
     c. Is so complex that many companies cannot adjust to it.
     d. Involves an ongoing process for implementation, which may never be completed.
     e. Expertise in ERP is limited, with staffing an ongoing problem.
D. ERP in the Service Sector
  1. ERP is more common in the manufacturing sector versus the service sector.
  2. Efficient Consumer Response (ECR) is supply chain management systems in the grocery industry; they tie sales to buying, to inventory, to logistics, and to production.

CHAPTER 14 PROBLEMS

Enterprise Resource Planning

S1.   Don's Furniture and Crafts produces a number of products including computer desk chairs. Don's manager is interested in determining the net requirements and supporting information for the production of computer chairs. The master production schedule, abbreviated product structure diagrams, and inventory information are given below.

Master Production Schedule:

	1	2	3	4	5	6
Computer chairs	500		400	400		500

Product Structure Record

- Chair — Level 0
- Seat (1), Base (1), Back (1) — Level 1
- Legs (4), Brace Sub (1), Outer Back Supports (2), Upper Back Supports (1), Middle Back Supports (5) — Level 2

Solution:

We begin with the level 0 item, the chair. Since this is a finished product, the gross requirements row is simply copied from the master production schedule for this item.

ITEM: Chair	LLC: 0	PERIOD					
LOT SIZE: L4L	LT: 1	1	2	3	4	5	6
Gross Requirements		500		400	400		500
Scheduled Receipts		500					
Projected on Hand	100	100	100	0	0	0	0
Net Requirements		0	0	300	400	0	500
Planned Order Receipts				300	400		500
Planned Order Releases			300	400		500	

In period 1 we have 100 units on hand, and 500 scheduled to be received. That gives us (100 + 500) = 600 units available. We use 500 of them to satisfy demand, leaving (600 – 500) = 100 units in inventory at the end of period 1. In period 2, there is no activity, but we still have the 100 units in inventory at the end of the period. In period 3, the 100 units on hand is not enough to cover our demand of 400 units. We need to make 300 more. Thus, our net requirements are 300 units. Since the lot sizing rule is lot-for-lot, we order exactly what we need, 300 units. Recall that our lead-time is 1 week. If we wish to receive our order for 300 units in period 3, we must place the order 1 week in advance, in period 2. To meet demand in period 4, we order 400 units in week 3, 1 week in advance of when we need them. To meet demand in period 6, we order 500 units in week 5, 1 week in advance of when we need them.

Now consider that 500 chairs are needed in week 9, the manager wants to know when base assembly's component parts must be completed to finish the chairs. Final assembly takes 1 week, so an order of 500 is released in week 8. Below are the following lead-times for the component parts.

Component	Lead-time (weeks)
Base Assembly	2
Legs	1
Brace Subassembly	2
Braces	1

ITEM: Chair	LLC: 0	PERIOD					
LOT SIZE: L4L	LT: 1	3	4	5	6	7	8
Planned Order Releases							500
							x 1

ITEM: Base Assembly	LLC: 1	PERIOD					
LOT SIZE: L4L	LT: 2	3	4	5	6	7	8
Gross Requirements							500
Scheduled Receipts							
Projected on Hand 0							0
Net Requirements							500
Planned Order Receipts							500
Planned Order Releases						500	

x 4   x 1

ITEM: Legs	LLC: 2	PERIOD					
LOT SIZE: L4L	LT: 1	3	4	5	6	7	8
Gross Requirements					2000		
Scheduled Receipts							
Projected on Hand 0							
Net Requirements					2000		
Planned Order Receipts					2000		
Planned Order Releases				2000			

ITEM: Brace Assembly	LLC: 1	PERIOD					
LOT SIZE: L4L	LT: 2	3	4	5	6	7	8
Gross Requirements					500		
Scheduled Receipts							
Projected on Hand 0					0		
Net Requirements					500		
Planned Order Receipts					500		
Planned Order Releases			500				

x 4

ITEM: Braces	LLC: 1	PERIOD					
LOT SIZE: L4L	LT: 1	3	4	5	6	7	8
Gross Requirements			2000				
Scheduled Receipts							
Projected on Hand 0							
Net Requirements			2000				
Planned Order Receipts			2000				
Planned Order Releases		2000					

To complete the chairs, the chairs need 1 base assembly. As shown above, its gross requirements are calculated by multiplying the planned order releases of each parent times the quantity per assembly contained in the bill of material. This process is called explosion. Since one base assembly is needed for every chair, period 8 gross requirements are (500 x 1) = 500 to satisfy the one-week need for final assembly of the 500 chairs in week 9. Since the assemblies are needed in week 8 and the lead-time is 2 weeks, the order for 500 base assemblies is released in week 6.

To complete the base assembly, the assembly needs 4 legs. As shown above, its gross requirements are calculated using the same procedure. Since 4 legs are needed for every base assembly, period 6 gross requirements are (500 x 4) = 2000. Since the legs are needed in week 6 and the lead-time is 1 week, the order for 2000 legs is released in week 5. The explosions for the brace assemblies and braces are shown in the above tables.

We have now completed the MRP calculations. To summarize the results, we construct a planned order report from the planned order release row of each matrix, as follows:

Planned Order Report

Item	Period						
	3	4	5	6	7	8	9
Chairs						500	
Base Assembly				500			
Legs			2000				
Brace Assembly		500					
Braces	2000						

1. Product X12Z00 is made of three units of X1 and four units of Y2. X1 is made of one unit of R10 and three units of S20. Y2 is made of two units of R10 and four units of T30. Lead time for X12Z00 is one week; X1, two weeks; Y2, three weeks; R10, two weeks; S20, one week; and T30, three weeks. Draw the product structure tree for X12Z00.

2. Using the information in Problem 1, and if 200 units of X12Z00 are needed in week 10, develop the gross requirements for each of the components. Calculate the gross requirements for each of the components when the firm plans to build 200 units of X12Z00 and also inventories of 50 for X1 and 80 for Y2.

3. Draw a product structure diagram from the Bill of Materials for the Hill Topper Bike. Assuming a 15% profit margin, how should the Hill Topper be priced given the following materials and prices?

Level	Item	Quantity	Price
0	Bike	1	
1	Seat	1	5.00
1	Frame	1	25.00
1	Wheel assembly	2	---
1	Gear assembly	1	---
1	Nuts & Bolts	4	2.50
2	Wheels	2	10.00
2	Bearings	4	5.00
2	Tire	2	4.00
2	Chain	1	12.00
2	Gears	2	10.00

4. Let us say, the company has redesigned Product RAW14 and it is now made of two units of A22 and four units of B33. A is made of three units of C1 and four of D23. D23 is made of two units of E2. Lead times for purchase and assembly of each unit to the end product RAW14 are: RAW14 takes two weeks; A22, B33, C1, and D23 take one week each; and E2 takes three weeks. One hundred units are required in Period 10. (Assume that there is currently no inventory on hand of any of these items.)

Show the product structure tree.

Develop MRP requirements schedule.

5. Log Furniture Inc., a furniture manufacturer, makes one of a kind bed rails for children. The rails are made of the following major components: 1.) four runners, 2.) one bottom support, 3.) and four post legs. They are made in such a way that each part can fit in snugly without major joints, bolts, and nuts. The master schedule and inventory information for the chair assembly is noted below.

Week	Bed Production
1	100
2	0
3	100
4	0
5	100
6	0
7	100
8	0
9	100
10	0

Initial inventories are as follows: runners, 80; bottom support, 50; and bed post, 60.

The assembly of bed takes one week; rail system, 2 weeks; and bed post, 1 week.

Draw the product structure tree for the chair assembly.

Show the MRP record of chair assembly for 10 weeks with the foregoing data and calculate the gross requirements for each of the components.

6. Complete the MRP matrix shown below.

ITEM: Frame12	LLC: 1	PERIOD				
LOT SIZE: L4L	LT: 2	1	2	3	4	5
Gross Requirements			200	100	50	150
Scheduled Receipts			75			
Projected on Hand	25					
Net Requirements						
Planned Order Receipts						
Planned Order Releases						

7. Complete the MRP matrix shown below.

ITEM: TAB20	LLC: 1	PERIOD				
LOT SIZE: Min100	LT: 2	1	2	3	4	5
Gross Requirements		140	70	100	100	120
Scheduled Receipts			100			
Projected on Hand	125					
Net Requirements						
Planned Order Receipts						
Planned Order Releases						

8. Complete the MRP matrix shown below.

ITEM: XEX1	LLC: 1	PERIOD					
LOT SIZE: Min50	LT: 1	1	2	3	4	5	6
Gross Requirements		25	20	30	90	80	50
Scheduled Receipts							
Projected on Hand	75						
Net Requirements							
Planned Order Receipts							
Planned Order Releases							

9.	Lawn Trimmer manufactures and distributes lawn equipment. Assembly instructions include metal poles, plastic trays, and wheel assemblies that are received preformed. It takes three metal poles to build the handle. The Garden Fertilizer consists of 1 handle and 2 wheel assemblies that are fastened to the plastic tray. Two holes are drilled into the plastic tray, and the handle is then inserted into the handles. Then, two pins are inserted through the handle and the tray. Construct a multilevel bill of materials for the Garden Fertilizer.

10.	ZigZag produces a variety of athletic training products. Two of the products, the Accelerator and the Bungee Propeller are made from three basic parts, the bungee, harness, and swivel. Given the following product structures, master scheduling requirements, and inventory information, determine when orders should be released for the Accelerator, the Bungee Propeller, the bungees, harnesses, and swivels and the size of those orders.

Item	On Hand	Scheduled Receipts	Lot Size	MPS
Accelerator	20	0	L4L	200, period 6
Bungee Propeller	10	0	L4L	400, period 5
Bungee	280	0	Mutl300	---
Harness	400	250, period 2	Mutl500	---
Swivel	600	150, period 1	Mult400	---

15

Short-Term Scheduling

I. **The Strategic Importance of Short-Term Scheduling**

   A. Companies use assets more effectively and create capacity per dollar invested, which lowers cost by scheduling effectively.

   B. This added capacity and related flexibility provides faster delivery and better customer service.

   C. Good scheduling is a competitive advantage because it contributes to dependable delivery.

Lecture Key: *Scheduling is a critical factor in the success of a business in that it aids the company in achieving effective throughput for the customer. It provides the business with high profitability, satisfied customers, competitive advantage, and efficiency. Other operational aspects of business must keep in mind the company's scheduling capacities before making decisions and promises to the customers.*

II. **Scheduling Issues**

   A. Scheduling deals with timing of operations.

   B. Scheduling begins with capacity planning, which involves facility and equipment acquisition.

   C. It then moves into aggregate planning, where decisions are made regarding the use of facilities, inventory, people, and outside contractors.

   D. The master schedule breaks down the aggregate plan and develops an overall schedule for outputs.

   E. Short-term schedules then translate capacity decisions, intermediate planning, and master schedules into job sequences and special assignments of personnel, materials, and machinery.

   F. Forward and Backward Scheduling:

      1. Forward Scheduling – schedule that begins as soon as requirements are known.

         a. Used in variety of organizations (i.e., hospitals, clinics, etc.).

         b. Jobs are performed to customer order and delivery is ASAP.

         c. Designed to produce a schedule that can be accomplished even if it means not meeting due date.

         d. Causes buildup of work-in-process inventory.

         e. Works well in firms whose suppliers are usually behind in meeting schedules.

      2. Backward Scheduling – begins with due date and schedules the final operation first and the other job steps in reverse order.

         a. By subtracting lead time for each item, the start time is obtained.

         b. Resources necessary to accomplish schedule may not exist.

         c. Used in many manufacturing and service environments.

Lecture Key: Both of these scheduling methods are used so that the company can determine what the manufacturing department is capable of achieving and what dates the manager can promise the good or service to the customer. Internal communication within the company is vital to customer satisfaction. Management must determine the best scheduling method for every good and service. They must be reliable because the company's reputation rests on these schedules.

    G. Scheduling Criteria
       1. 4 scheduling criteria –
          a. Minimize Completion Time – criterion evaluated by determining average completion time.
          b. Maximize Utilization – evaluated by determining percent of time facility is utilized.
          c. Minimize WIP Inventory – evaluated by determining average number of jobs in system. The relationship between number of jobs in system and WIP inventory will be high. Therefore, fewer numbers of jobs in system, lower the inventory.
          d. Minimize Customer Waiting Time – evaluated by determining average number of late days.
       2. The objective of scheduling is to optimize the use of resources so that production objectives are met.

III. Scheduling Process-Focused Work Centers

    A. Process-Focused Facilities (a.k.a., intermittent; job-shop facilities) – high-variety, low volume systems commonly found in manufacturing and service organizations.
    B. Examples include printers, paint shops, etc.
    C. Production systems where products are made to order.
    D. Items made usually differ in terms of materials used, order of processing, time of processing, setup requirements; scheduling can be complex.
    E. Planning files – item master file, routing file, and work-center file in material requirements planning system.
       1. Item Master File – contains information about each component firm produces or purchases.
       2. Routing File – indicates each flow through shop.
       3. Work-Center Master File – contains information about work center (i.e., capacity and efficiency).
       4. Control Files – track each work order's actual progress against plan.

IV. Loading Jobs in Work Centers

    A. Loading – assigning of jobs to work or processing centers.
    B. OM assigns jobs to work centers so that costs, idle time, and completion time are kept to a minimum.
    C. 2 forms of loading work centers –
       1. Capacity oriented
       2. Assigning specific jobs to work centers
    D. Input-Output Control
       1. Effective scheduling depends on matching schedule to performance.
       2. Input-Output Control – system that allows operations personnel to manage facility work flows by tracking work added to work center and its work completed.
       3. Overloading causes crowding in facility, leading to inefficiencies and quality problems.
       4. Underloading results in idle capacity and wasted resources.

5. 3 options for operations to manage facility work flow –
   a. Correcting performances.
   b. Increasing capacity.
   c. Increasing or reducing input to work center by (a) routing work to or from other work centers, (b) increasing or decreasing subcontracting, (c) producing less (or producing more).

Example: Input-Output Control

The figure below shows the planned capacity for the DNC Milling work center for 5 weeks (weeks 6/6 through 7/4). The planned input is 280 standard hours per week. The actual input is close to this figure, varying between 250 and 285. Output is scheduled at 320 standard hours, which is the assumed capacity. A backlog of 300 hours (not shown in the figure) exists in the work center. However, actual output (270 hours) is substantially less than planned.

Solution:
Neither the input plan nor the output plan is being achieved. Indeed, the backlog of work in this work center has actually increased by 5 hours by week 6/27. This increases work-in-process inventory, complicating the scheduling task and indicating the need for manager action.

Cumulative Change in Backlog = $\sum$ Actual Inputs − $\sum$ Actual Outputs

Work Center DNC Milling (in standard hours)						
Week Ending	6/6	6/13	6/20	6/27	7/4	7/11
Planned Input	280	280	280	280	280	
Actual Input	270	250	280	285	280	
Cumulative Deviation	-10	-40	-40	-35		

Planned Output	320	320	320	320		
Actual Output	270	270	270	270		
Cumulative Deviation	-50	-100	-150	-200		

Cumulative Change in Backlog	0	-20	-10	+5		

Lecture Key: *This process prevents operations from overloading and over scheduling the production process. This type of process control allows the department to run its operations more effectively and efficiently, therefore, meeting or exceeding customers' perceptions of quality and service.*

E. Gantt Charts
   1. Gantt Charts – planning charts used to schedule resources and allocate time.
   2. Visual aids that are useful in loading and scheduling:
      a. When used in loading, they show the loading and idle times of several departments, machines, or facilities.
      b. Display relative workloads in system so management knows what adjustments are appropriate.
      c. Gantt load chart major limitation – it does not account for production variability (i.e., unexpected breakdowns or human errors that require reworking job).
   3. Consequently, chart must be updated regularly to account for new jobs and revised time estimates.
   4. Gantt schedule chart used to monitor jobs in progress.
   5. Indicates which jobs are on schedule and which are ahead of or behind schedule.

Example: Load Gantt Chart

A New Orleans washing machine manufacturer accepts special orders for machines to be used in such unique facilities as submarines, hospitals, and large industrial laundries. The production of each machine requires varying tasks and durations. The figure below shows the load chart for the week of March 8.

Work Center	Day				
	Monday	Tuesday	Wednesday	Thursday	Friday
Metalworks	Job 349	----------------		Job 350	
Mechanical	++++++++++	Job 349		Job 408	++++++++++
Electronics	Job 408	++++++++++	++++++++++	Job 349	++++++++++
Painting	Job 295		Job 408	----------------	Job 349

Processing	
Unscheduled	++++++++++
Center not available	----------------

Solution:

The four work centers process several jobs during the week. This particular chart indicates that the metalworks and painting centers are completely loaded for the entire week. The mechanical and electronic centers have some idle time scattered during the week. We also note that the metalworks center is unavailable on Tuesday and the painting center is unavailable on Thursday, perhaps for preventive maintenance.

Example: Schedule Gantt Chart

First Printing and Copy Center in Winter Park, Florida, uses the Gantt chart in the figure below to show the scheduling of three orders, jobs A, B, and C.

Solution:

Job	Day 1	Day 2	Day 3	Day 4	Day 5	Day 6	Day 7	Day 8
A								
B								
C								

Each pair of brackets on the time axis denotes the estimated starting and finishing of a job enclosed within it. The solid bars reflect the actual status or progress of the job. Job A, for example, is about one-half day behind schedule at the end of day 5. Job B was completed after equipment maintenance. Job C is ahead of schedule.

F. Assignment Method
  1. A special class of linear programming models that involves assigning tasks of jobs to resources.
  2. The objective is to minimize total costs or time required to perform the task at hand.
  3. Only one job per resource.
  4. The assignment method uses a table, and adding or subtracting numbers in the table, in order to find the lowest opportunity cost for each assignment.
  5. Assignment problems can also be used to analyze maximum profit effectiveness or payoff of an assignment.

Example: Assignment Method

The cost table shown earlier in this section is repeated here. We find the minimum total cost assignment of jobs to typesetters by applying steps 1 through 4.

Job	Typesetter		
	A	B	C
R-34	$11	$14	$6
S-66	$8	$10	$11
T-50	$9	$12	$7

Solution:

Step 1a: Using the previous table, subtract the smallest number in each row from every number in the row. The result is shown below.

Job	Smallest	Results after Step 1a		
		A	B	C
R-34	6	5	8	0
S-66	8	0	2	3
T-50	7	2	5	0

Step 1b: Using the previous table, subtract the smallest number in each column from every number in the column. The result is shown below.

Job (Smallest)	Results after Step 1b		
	A (0)	B (2)	C (0)
R-34	5	6	0
S-66	0	0	3
T-50	2	3	0

Step 2: Draw the minimum number of vertical and horizontal straight lines needed to cover all zeros. Because two lines suffice, the solution is not optimal.

Job	Results after Step 2		
	A	B	C
R-34	5	6	0
S-66	0	0	3
T-50	2	3	0

From T-50 Machine A cell, 2 is the smallest uncovered number.

Step 3: Subtract the smallest uncovered number (2 in this table) from every other uncovered number and add it to numbers at the intersection of two lines.

Job	Results after Step 2		
	A	B	C
R-34	3	4	0
S-66	0	0	5
T-50	0	1	0

Return to Step 2 by covering the zeros with straight lines again.

Job	Results after Step 2		
	A	B	C
R-34	3	4	0
S-66	0	0	5
T-50	0	1	0

Analysis: Since 3 lines are necessary, an optimal assignment can be made.

Assign R-34 to person C
S-66 to person B
T-50 to person A

Referring to the original cost table, we see that:

Minimum Cost   =   \$6 (R-34 to C) + \$10 (S-66 to B) + \$9 (T-50 to A) = \$25

If S-66 were assigned to A, then T-50 would be without a zero location.

V.   Sequencing Jobs in Work Centers

   A. Sequencing determines the order in which jobs should be done at each center.
   B. Priority rules are the methods for dispatching jobs to work centers.
      1. FCFS: First Come First Served. The first job to arrive at a work center is the first processed.
      2. SPT: Shortest Processing Time. The shortest jobs are handled first and completed.
      3. EDD: Earliest Due Date. The job with the earliest due date is selected first.
      4. LPT: Longest Processing Time. The longer, bigger jobs are often important and are selected.

Five architectural rendering jobs are waiting to be assigned at Ajax, Tarney and Barnes Architects. Their work (processing) times and due dates are given in the following table. We want to determine the sequence of processing according to (1) FCFS, (2) SPT, (3) EDD, and (4) LPT rules. Jobs are assigned a letter in the order they arrived.

Job	Job Work (Processing) Time (Days)	Job Due Date (Days)
A	6	8
B	2	6
C	8	18
D	3	15
E	9	23

Solution:

1.   The FCFS sequence shown in the next table is simply A-B-C-D-E. The "flow time" in the system for this sequence measures the time each job spends waiting plus time being processed. Job B, for example, waits 6 days while job A is being processed, then takes 2 more days of operation time itself; so it will be completed in 8 days – which is 2 days later than its due date.

Job Sequence	Job Work (Processing) Time	Flow Time	Job Due Date	Job Lateness
A	6	6	8	0
B	2	8	6	2
C	8	16	18	0
D	3	19	15	4
E	9	28	23	5
	28	77		11

The first-come, first-served rule results in the following measures of effectiveness:

a. Average completion time
$$= \sum \text{Total flow time / Number of jobs}$$
$$= 77 \text{ days} / 5 \text{ jobs} = 15.4 \text{ days}$$

b. Utilization
$$= \text{Total job work (processing) time} / \sum \text{Total flow time}$$
$$= 28 \text{ days} / 77 \text{ days} = 36.4\%$$

c. Average # of jobs in system
$$= \sum \text{Total flow time / Total job work (processing) time}$$
$$= 77 \text{ days} / 28 \text{ days} = 2.75 \text{ jobs}$$

d. Average job lateness
$$= \text{Total late days / Number of jobs}$$
$$= 11 \text{ days} / 5 \text{ jobs} = 2.2 \text{ days}$$

2.   The SPT rule shown in the next table results in the sequence B-D-A-C-E. Orders are sequenced according to processing time, with the highest priority given to the shortest job.

Job Sequence	Job Work (Processing) Time	Flow Time	Job Due Date	Job Lateness
B	2	2	6	0
D	3	5	15	0
A	6	11	8	3
C	8	19	18	1
E	9	28	23	5
	28	65		9

The first-come, first-served rule results in the following measures of effectiveness:

a. Average completion time   = $\sum$ Total flow time / Number of jobs
                             = 65 days / 5 jobs = 13 days

b. Utilization   = Total job work (processing) time / $\sum$ Total flow time
                             = 28 days / 65 days = 43.1%

c. Average # of jobs in system = $\sum$ Total flow time / Total job work (processing) time
                             = 65 days / 28 days = 2.32 jobs

d. Average job lateness   = Total late days / Number of jobs
                             = 9 days / 5 jobs = 1.8 days

3.   The EDD rule shown in the next table gives the sequence B-A-D-C-E. Note that jobs are ordered by earliest due date first.

Job Sequence	Job Work (Processing) Time	Flow Time	Job Due Date	Job Lateness
B	2	2	6	0
A	6	8	8	0
D	3	11	15	0
C	8	19	18	1
E	9	28	23	5
	28	68		6

The first-come, first-served rule results in the following measures of effectiveness:

a. Average completion time   = $\sum$ Total flow time / Number of jobs
                             = 68 days / 5 jobs = 13.6 days

b. Utilization   = Total job work (processing) time / $\sum$ Total flow time
                             = 28 days / 68 days = 41.2%

c. Average # of jobs in system = $\sum$ Total flow time / Total job work (processing) time
                             = 68 days / 28 days = 2.43 jobs

d. Average job lateness   = Total late days / Number of jobs
                             = 6 days / 5 jobs = 1.2 days

4. The LPT rule shown in the next table results in the order E-C-A-D-B.

Job Sequence	Job Work (Processing) Time	Flow Time	Job Due Date	Job Lateness
E	9	9	23	0
C	8	17	18	0
A	6	23	8	15
D	3	26	15	11
B	2	28	6	22
	28	103		48

The first-come, first-served rule results in the following measures of effectiveness:

a. Average completion time $=$ Σ Total flow time / Number of jobs
$=$ 103 days / 5 jobs $=$ 20.6 days

b. Utilization $=$ Total job work (processing) time / Σ Total flow time
$=$ 28 days / 103 days $=$ 27.2%

c. Average # of jobs in system $=$ Σ Total flow time / Total job work (processing) time
$=$ 103 days / 28 days $=$ 3.68 jobs

d. Average job lateness $=$ Total late days / Number of jobs
$=$ 48 days / 5 jobs $=$ 9.6 days

Summary:

Rule	Avg. Completion Time (Days)	Utilization (%)	Avg. # of Jobs in System	Avg. Lateness (Days)
FCFS	15.4	36.4	2.75	2.2
SPT	13.0	43.1	2.32	1.8
EDD	13.6	41.2	2.43	1.2
LPT	20.6	27.2	3.68	9.6

Lecture Key: *No one priority rule is better than another. They all have aspects about them that make them more appropriate in a given circumstance. While SPT has the shortest job flow time and average number of jobs in the system, its drawback is that longer projects get pushed back. Customers may view this unfavorably. FCFS does not score well on any category but will appear fair to customers. EDD will minimize tardiness, which is good for jobs with crucial deadlines.*

B. Critical Ratio
1. The Critical Ratio is an index number computed by dividing the time remaining until the due date by the work time remaining.
2. The CR gives priority to jobs that must be done to keep shipping on schedule.
    a. CR less than 1.0 is behind schedule.
    b. CR equal to 1.0 is on schedule.
    c. CR greater than 1.0 is ahead of schedule.

Today is Day 25 on Zyco Medical Testing Laboratories' production schedule. Three jobs are on order, as indicated here:

Job	Due Date	Workdays Remaining
A	30	4
B	28	5
C	27	2

Solution:
We compute the critical ratios, using the formula for CR.

CR = (Due Date – Today) / Workdays Remaining

Job	Due Date	Priority Order
A	(30 – 25) / 4 = 1.25	3
B	(28 – 25) / 5 = 0.60	1
C	(27 – 25) / 2 = 1.00	2

Job B has a critical ratio of less than 1, meaning it will be late unless expedited. Thus, it has the highest priority. Job C is on time and Job A has some slack. Once Job B has been completed, we would recompute the critical ratios for Jobs A and C to determine whether their priorities have changed.

Lecture Key: The critical ratio helps determine the status of a specific job and establish relative priority among jobs on a common basis. It relates both stock and make-to-order jobs, adjusts priority for changes in demand and job progress.

    C. Sequencing N Jobs on Two Machines: Johnson's Rule
        1. Johnson's Rule minimizes the processing time for sequencing a group of jobs through two work centers and minimizes total idle time on machines.
        2. Four Steps:
            a. Jobs are listed, and the time each requires on a machine is shown.
            b. Shortest activity time is selected. If the shortest time lies with the first machine, that job is scheduled first. If the shortest time lies with the second machine, schedule the job last.
            c. Once a job is scheduled, eliminate it.
            d. Use steps 2 and 3 for remaining jobs, working toward center of sequence.

Five specialty jobs at a Fredonia, New York, tool and die shop must be processed through 2 work centers (drill press and lathe). The time for processing each job follows:

Work (Processing) Time for Jobs (in hours)		
Job	Work Center 1 (Drill Press)	Work Center 2 (Lathe)
A	5	2
B	3	6
C	8	4
D	10	7
E	7	12

Solution:

1. We wish to set the sequence that will minimize the total processing time for the five jobs. The job with the shortest processing time is A, in work center 2 (with a time of 2 hours). Because it is at the second center, schedule A last. Eliminate it from consideration.

				A

2. Job B has the next shortest time (3 hours). Because that time is at the first work center, we schedule it first and eliminate it from consideration.

B				A

3. The next shortest time is Job C (4 hours) on the second machine. Therefore, it is placed as late as possible.

B			C	A

4. There is a tie (at 7 hours) for the shortest remaining job. We can place E, which was on the first work center, first. Then D is placed in the last sequencing position.

B	E	D	C	A

This sequence will complete these jobs faster than any other sequence.

Work Center 1	3	7	10	8	5
Work Center 2	6	12	7	4	2

The following bar charts are used to determine the makespan or final completion time for the set of five jobs. Notice that the sequence of jobs (B, E, D, C, A) is the same for both processes and that a job cannot begin at process 2 until it has been completed at process 1. Also, a job cannot begin at process 2 if another job is currently in process. Time periods during which a job is being processed are labeled with the job's letter. The gray shaded areas represent idle time.

Center 1	B	E	D	C	A	
Center 2		B	E	D	C	A
Time	3	9 10	22	29	33 35	

Idle

The completion time for the set of five jobs is 35 hours. Note that although Johnson's rule minimizes makespan and idle time, it does not consider job due dates in constructing a sequence, so there is no attempt to minimize job tardiness.

VI.   Limitations of Rule-Based Disbatching Systems

A. Rule-based systems have limitations:
1. Rules need to be revised to adjust to changes in process, equipment, product mix, etc.
2. Rules do not look upstream or downstream; idle resources and bottleneck resources in other departments may not be recognized.
3. Rules do not look beyond due dates. Must decide which order is more important.
B. Schedulers use sequencing rules like SPT, EDD, or critical ratio.
C. Rules are modified manually or with finite scheduling software.

VII.   Finite Scheduling

A. Finite scheduling is the computerized short-term scheduling that overcomes the disadvantages of rule-based systems by providing the user with graphical interactive computing.
1. Schedule changes based on up-to-the-minute information.
2. Displayed in Gantt chart form.
B. Delivery needs are balanced against efficiency based on today's conditions and orders.
C. Ability to work interactively with the scheduling system to create a realistic schedule.
D. Leaves it up the scheduler to determine what constitutes a "good" schedule.
E. Examples of software Preactor, Asprova, and Jobplan; not all systems are successful.

Lecture Key: Finite scheduling is easier than the rule-based system in that it offers graphical interactive computing services. This scheduling system allows schedulers to create what they consider a "good," realistic schedule. Although finite scheduling is an improvement from rule-based systems, not all are successful because many firms that use it do not use a fully integrated finite scheduling system.

VIII.   Theory of Constraint (TOC)

A. Theory of constraint is that body of knowledge that deals with anything that limits an organization's ability to achieve its goals.
B. Physical Constraints
1. Personnel availability
2. Raw materials
3. Supplies

C. Nonphysical Constraints
 1. Procedures
 2. Morale
 3. Training
D. Steps to recognize and manage constraints:
 1. Identify constraints.
 2. Develop a plan to overcome constraints.
 3. Focus resources on completing step 2.
 4. Reduce the effects on the constraints by off-loading work or by expanding capability. Make constraints known to all who are affected by them.
 5. Once constraints are overcome, repeat step 1 and identify new constraints.

Lecture Key: *The theory of constraint states that managers need to recognize those operations that impede a company's capability to attain goals. There are physical and nonphysical constraints that must be identified. Managers should develop strategies to make these constraints known to all and overcome them.*

IX. **Bottleneck Work Centers**

A. Bottleneck is an operation that limits output in the production sequence.
B. Less capacity; constrain throughput.
C. Changing products, product mixes, and volumes create bottlenecks.
D. Techniques to deal with bottlenecks:
 1. Increase capacity.
 2. Ensure that well-trained employees are available to operate and maintain the work center causing the constraint.
 3. Develop alternative routings, processing procedures, or subcontractors.
 4. Moving inspections and tests to a position just before the bottleneck.
 5. Scheduling throughput to match the capacity of the bottleneck.

Lecture Key: *A bottleneck is a limitation on output caused by a procedure in the production process. Bottlenecks restrict throughputs and take place in almost all process-focused facilities. Dealing with bottlenecks takes skilled employees that can work the area caused by the constraint and also establish other routes, processing procedures and subcontractors. Managers should transfer inspections and tests to a section before the bottleneck occurs.*

X. **Repetitive Manufacturing**

A. Level material use is the use of frequent, high-quality, small lot sizes that contribute to just-in-time production.
B. Advantages:
 1. Lower inventory levels, which release capital for other uses.
 2. Faster product throughput.
 3. Improved component quality and hence, improved product quality.
 4. Reduced floor-space requirements.
 5. Improved communication among employees.
 6. Smoother production processes.

XI. Scheduling for Service

A. Scheduling emphasis is on staffing levels.
B. Service systems seldom store inventories.
C. Services are labor-intensive and demand for labor is highly variable.
D. An appointment system is the schedule for lawyers' and doctors' offices.
E. First-come, first-served schedule is common in retail shops and restaurants.
F. Reservation systems work in rental car agencies, hotels and some restaurants.
G. Hospitals
   1. Very complex scheduling system.
   2. Schedule products (such as surgeries).
H. Banks
   1. Cross training of the workforce allows loan officers and managers to provide short-term help for tellers if there is a surge in demand.
   2. Hire part-time personnel.
I. Airlines
   1. Two constraints:
     a. A complex set of FAA work-time limitations.
     b. Union contracts that guarantee crew pay for some number of hours each day or trip.
   2. Must build crew schedules that meet or exceed crews' guarantees.
   3. Schedules built using linear programming models.
J. 24/7 Operations
   1. Part-time workers can be employed.
   2. Most use computerized scheduling systems.

XII. Scheduling Service Employees with Cyclical Scheduling

A. Cyclical Scheduling has seven steps:
   1. Plan a schedule equal to the number of people being scheduled.
   2. Determine how many of each of the least desirable off-shifts must be covered each week.
   3. Begin the schedule for one employee by scheduling the days off during the planning cycle.
   4. Assign off-shifts for that employee using step 2.
   5. Repeat this pattern for each employee.
   6. Allow each employee to pick his/her "slot" or "line" in order of seniority.
   7. Mandate that any changes from a chosen schedule are strictly between the personnel wanting to switch.

CHAPTER 15 PROBLEMS

Assignment Method of Loading

S1.   Fabric Discount wishes to assign its fabric patterns to different automated sheering machines. Due to the programming time, only one pattern can be assigned to a machine. The following table represents the yards of materials each machine can complete of a particular pattern per hour. How do you suggest assigning patterns to the machines?

Pattern	Threading Machine			
	A	B	C	D
#A18C	120	72	42	160
#B98E	100	62	180	160
#R41W	160	42	84	200
#M10M	200	58	65	120

Solution:

Step 1:   Row Reduction: Identify the smallest number in each row (42 for row 1). Then, subtract each number in the row by the smallest. For example,

Row 1: Smallest = 42, so (120-42; 72-42; 42-42; 160-42)
Row 2: Smallest = 52, so (100-42; 72-42; 42-42; 160-42)

78	30	0	118
58	0	118	98
118	0	42	158
142	0	7	62

Step 2:   Column Reduction: Identify the smallest number in each column (58 for column 1). Then, subtract each number in the column by the smallest. For example,

Column 1: Smallest = 58, so (58-58; 58-58; 118-58; 142-58)
Column 2: Smallest = 52, so (30-0;0-0; 0-0; 0-0)

20	30	0	56
0	0	118	36
60	0	42	96
84	0	7	0

Step 3:   Cover all zeroes and see if the number of column lines is equal to the number of rows highlighted.

20	30	0	56
0	0	118	36
60	0	42	96
84	0	7	0

Step 4: Since the number of lines equals the number of rows, we have reached the final solution. Make assignments:

Pattern	Threading Machine			
	A	B	C	D
#A18C	20	30	0	56
#B98E	0	0	118	36
#R41W	60	0	42	96
#M10M	84	0	7	0

The first row has only one zero, so #A18C is assigned to Machine C. The third row has only one zero, so #R41W is assigned to Machine B. The second row has two zeros, but Machine B is already occupied, so #B98E is assigned to Machine A. That leaves Machine D for #M10M.

Step 5: Referring back to our original matrix, Machine A can produce 120 yards of Pattern #A18C per hour, Machine B can produce 42 yards of #B98E per hour, Machine C can produce 42 yards of #R41W per hour, and Machine D can produce 42 yards of #M10M per hour.

Pattern	Threading Machine			
	A	B	C	D
#A18C	100	72	42	160
#B98E	120	62	180	160
#R41W	160	42	84	200
#M10M	200	58	65	120

1. Jim Wayne owns a concrete mixing plant that produces a variety of concrete products suitable for different conditions. Some products have more liquid for longer drying times, some are dryer so that they will hold a shape, some are fire resistant, and some have colorants in them. Jim has four source mixtures for his products that require different processing times relative to the speed of the mixing machines. The following represent the number of hours to process each product given the mixer being used. Only one job can be assigned to a mixer per day. How do you suggest assigning the products to the mixer to ensure the least amount of time?

Product	Mixer			
	A	B	C	D
#1	7	9	8	8
#2	9	11	5	10
#3	11	5	9	6
#4	9	11	5	6

2. Fabric Discount wishes to assign its fabric patterns to different automated threading machines. Due to the programming time, only one pattern can be assigned to a machine. The following table represents the yards of materials each machine can complete of a particular pattern per hour. How do you suggest assigning patterns to the machines?

Pattern	Threading Machine			
	A	B	C	D
#110	10	8	2	18
#112	12	6	18	18
#114	16	2	14	20
#116	24	15	5	12

350

3. Three plants could be used to produce the products. The plants can only produce one product at a time. Determine the most efficient plant for each product. The following is the information regarding the cost required to produce each product at a plant.

Product	Plant		
	#1	#2	#3
#801	100	175	250
#11201	50	315	125
#89	300	75	75

4. The project planner at a local manufacturing plant has five jobs that can be completed on any of five machines. Determine the allocation of jobs to machines that will result in a minimum time given the respective times to complete on each job on a machine.

Job	Machine				
	#1	#2	#3	#4	#5
51-A	30	34	60	60	22
55-B	22	58	29	55	16
63-C	15	28	42	30	32
70-D	45	25	30	42	18
81-E	44	57	50	60	48

Simple Sequencing Rules

S1. The manager of a local manufacturing company has 6 jobs waiting to enter the system. He has estimated the processing times and due dates, and he is assuming that the jobs arrive in the system in the order below. Determine if FCFS or SPT would be the best way to process the jobs using the information below.

Job (in arriving order)	Processing Time (Days)	Due Date (Days)
A	6	36
B	8	24
C	14	16
D	16	32
E	4	20
F	12	27

Solution:
Using FCFS
Step 1: Calculate the Flow Time and Job Lateness.

Flow Time = Flow time of the previous job + processing time of current activity
= 0 + 6, or 6 for job A
= 6 + 8, or 14 for job B

Job Lateness = Flow Time of Job – Due Date of Job
= 6 – 36, or –30 for job A. This is rounded up to 0.
= 14 – 24, or –10 for job B. This is rounded up to 0.
= 28 – 16, or 12 for job C. This is rounded up to 0.

Job (in sequence)	Processing Time (Days)	Flow Time	Due Date	Job Lateness
A	6	6	36	0
B	8	14	24	0
C	14	28	16	12
D	16	44	32	12
E	4	48	20	28
F	12	60	27	33
	48	200		85

Step 2:   Calculate performance averages for this technique.

Average completion time = Total Flow Time (200) / # of jobs (6) = 200/6 =33.33
Average job lateness = Total Job Lateness (85) / # of jobs (6) = 85/6 =14.16 days

Using SPT
Step 3:   Calculate the Flow Time and Job Lateness.

Flow Time = Flow time of the previous job + processing time of current activity
Job Lateness = Flow Time of Job – Due Date of Job

Job (in sequence)	Processing Time (Days)	Flow Time	Due Date	Job Lateness
E	4	4	20	0
A	6	10	36	0
B	8	18	24	0
F	12	30	27	0
C	14	44	16	28
D	16	60	32	28
	48	166		56

Step 4:   Calculate performance averages for this technique.

Average completion time = Total Flow Time (166) / # of jobs (6)
= 166/6 =27.66
Average job lateness = Total Job Lateness (56) / # of jobs (6)
= 56/6 =9.33 days

Step 5:   Compare the two techniques. Clearly using the shortest processing times is the best since it has the shortest completion time and average job lateness. So, it would be optimal to sequence the jobs using SPT.

1.   In what sequence would the following jobs be sequenced through the same workstation using the following decision rules: FCFS, SLACK, CR, SPT, LPT, and EDD? All jobs arrive at the workstation on the same day (October 1st). Which decision is optimal?

Job	Due Date	Duration (days)
A	Nov. 10	18
B	Nov. 8	25
C	Dec. 1	40
D	Nov. 14	24
E	Nov. 12	10

2.   Natural Hardwood Inc. has five jobs that have been started. Today is June 1st, and the table includes the job with its due date and remaining processing times. Determine the best sequence using one of the following decision rules: FCFS, SLACK, CR, SPT, LPT, and EDD.

Job	Due Date	Duration (days)
010	July 10	10
215	July 18	25
86	July 2	20
9912	July 12	18
154	July 15	15

3. The project manager wants to determine the best way to complete his marketing research. The following includes the tasks that must be completed and their estimated completion times. Using the average completion time and average tardiness, determine the best way to sequence the task. You should attempt to use one of the decision rules to help you. Today is day 200 in the work year.

Task	Completion Time	Due Date
Hire survey takers	15 days	225
Interview client	3 days	220
Develop the survey	4 days	225
Write computer program	10 days	230

4. Ronnie's Lawn Service has been delayed by the recent rainstorms and now has a backlog. Ronnie has 10 small yards all in the same neighborhood that must be worked, but each has a different time to work. Using the decision rules based on the average completion time and average tardiness, determine the best way to sequence the task. Ronnie plans to start working at 6:00 in the morning (running on 24 hours).

Yard	Due Date (Hour of day)	Duration (minutes)
1	12	10
2	18	25
3	16	50
4	10	18
5	11	20
6	20	60
7	15	40
8	15	10
9	11	20
10	18	25

Sequencing Through Two Serial Processes

S1. Using Johnson's Rule to determine the optimal sequence of jobs through the workstations. The times are given in days.

Job	Workstation 1	Workstation 2
A	16	22
B	13	17
C	28	19
D	25	24
E	26	18
F	20	25

Solution:

Step 1: Determine the smallest processing time. The smallest processing time, 13 days, occurs at Workstation 1 for Job B.

Step 2: Assign the job to a position. If the job is at the first station, then we place the job at the beginning of the sequencing. If the job were located at the second station, then we would place it as far to the back of sequence as possible. Since the shortest time is 13 days for Job B, we can determine that it is in the first workstation, therefore, it should be placed as near the beginning of the sequence as possible. B is now eliminated from the job list.

B					

Step 3: Determine the next smallest and continue assigning process. The next smallest time is 16 days. It occurs at Workstation 1 for Job A, so we place Job A as near to the beginning of the sequence as possible. This would be next to B. Job A is eliminated from the job list.

B	A				

353

Step 4: Determine the next smallest. The next smallest time is 18 days (the smallest is actually 17 days, but Job B has already been eliminated). It occurs at Workstation 2 for Job E. Thus, we place Job E as near the end of the sequence as possible since it is located in Workstation 2. Job E is eliminated from the job list.

B	A				E

Step 5: Continue the previous steps until all jobs are assigned. The next smallest time is 19 days. It occurs at Workstation 2 for Job C. Thus, we place Job C as near the end of the sequence as possible. Job C is eliminated from the job list.

B	A			C	E

Step 6: Continue the previous steps until all jobs are assigned. The next smallest time is 20 days. It occurs at Workstation 1 for Job F. Thus, we place Job F as near the beginning of the sequence as possible, which is position 3. Job F is eliminated from the job list.

Step 7: The only remaining job is D, and it is assigned to the only available position, position 4.

B	A	F	D	C	E

Step 8: Analysis: This sequence will complete these jobs faster than any other sequence. The following bar charts are used to determine the makespan or final completion time for the set of six jobs. Notice that the sequence of jobs (B, A, F, D, C, E) is the same for both processes and that a job cannot begin at process 2 until it has been completed at Workstation 1. Also, a job cannot begin at process 2 if another job is currently in process. Time periods during which a job is being processed are labeled with the job's letter. The shaded areas represent idle time.

Workstation 1   **Idle Time**

B	A	F	D	C	E	Idle
13	29	49	74	102	128	

Workstation 2

	B	A	F	D		C		E
	30	51	76	100		119		137

The completion time for the set of six jobs is 137 days. Note that although Johnson's rule minimizes makespan and idle time, it does not consider job due dates in constructing a sequence, so there is no attempt to minimize job tardiness.

1. A step process involving two operations is used to resurface concrete drives. The manager has six jobs waiting to be completed. The operations are listed in the natural sequence in that operation 1 has to be complete before operation 2 can begin. Given the following processing times (in hours), determine the order in which the jobs should be processed so that the rush order can be completed as soon as possible.

Job	Operation 1	Operation 2
A	12	7
B	9	6
C	7	9
D	5	10
E	4	8
F	6	5

2. Michael Smith is a local industrial painter. He uses a three-step process to paint large storage tanks for a local chemical plant. Since the tanks may have residual chemicals on the surface, a thorough cleaning process with a pressure washer is needed to start preparing the surface. After that step, a grinder is used to remove any old paint or loose material. Now, the surface is properly prepared for the new paint. The following table represents the hours needed to complete each operation. The plant has 4 tanks that need to be painted. Determine the best sequence using the shortest processing time and least remaining work.

Tank	Pressure Wash	Grinding	Painting
1	2	6	4
2	6	15	10
3	10	30	20
4	3	5	5

3. Cindy's Candies, a processing plant for hard candy treats, has a two-step process to wrap and package their candies. To ensure freshness, no candies are processed before an order is placed. On Friday of last week, five customer orders were received and now the manager must determine a proper sequencing of the orders. The table contains the hours needed to complete the process and prepare for delivery.

Customer Order	Wrap	Package
1	1.5	.75
2	1.0	.5
3	2.5	2.0
4	3.0	1.0
5	1.0	1.0

4. Mark Dees is a mechanic in a small assembly plant that specializes in cutting and welding soft metal alloys. Mark has just received a project that has six tasks that require the automated cutting and welding machines. Sequence the following jobs using the shortest processing time and least remaining work.

Tasks	Cutting (in min.)	Welding (in min.)
1	20	30
2	15	45
3	10	20
4	20	40
5	30	45

Input/Output Control

S1.   The following information has been compiled in an input/output report for work center 3. Complete the report and interpret the results.

Input/Output Report

PERIOD	1	2	3	4	TOTAL
Planned input	65	65	70	75	
Actual input	60	60	65	65	
Deviation					
Planned output	75	75	75	75	
Actual output	70	70	65	65	
Deviation					
Backlog: 30					

Input/Output Report

PERIOD	1	2	3	4	TOTAL
Planned input	85	85	105	105	
Actual input	90	90	90	90	
Deviation					
Planned output	95	95	95	95	
Actual output	90	90	85	85	
Deviation					
Backlog: 30					

Solution:

Step 1:   Determine the output level of the center. This was given in the input/output report. The center has planned a level production of 90 units per period for work center 3. This is to be accomplished by working off the backlog of work and steadily increasing the input of work.

Step 2:   Calculate the deviation between planned input and actual input. The report is completed by first calculating the deviation between inputs. To do this, use the formula: Deviation equals (actual – planned). For period 1, this would be 90 – 85, or +5. This means that we put in more than we planned.

Step 3:   Calculate the deviation for outputs using the same method as with the inputs. For period 1, this would be 90 – 95, or –5. This means that we produced 5 less units than we planned. This would work to increase the backlog.

Step 4:   Sum the values in the respective planned, actual, and deviation rows.

Step 5:   Calculate the backlog. The initial backlog is 30 units. The following period backlogs are calculated by subtracting each period's actual output from the sum of its actual input and previous backlog. For period 1, backlog equals the sum of the actual input (90) and the previous backlog (30) minus the actual output (90). So, backlog for period 1 is (90 + 30) – 90, or 30. This means that we have not improved the position. We still have 30 units on backlog. We would use this backlog of 30 (in period 1) to calculate the backlog for period 2.

PERIOD	1	2	3	4	TOTAL
Planned input	85	85	105	105	380
Actual input	90	90	90	90	360
Deviation	+5	+5	-15	-15	-20
Planned output	95	95	95	95	380
Actual output	90	90	85	85	350
Deviation	-5	-5	-10	-10	-30
Backlog: 30	30	30	35	40	

Step 6: Analysis: The completed input/output report shows that work center 3 did not process all the jobs that were available during the four periods; therefore, the desired output rate was not achieved. Also, rather than reducing the backlog, the backlog increased to 40 units. This can be attributed to a lower-than-expected input of work from feeding work centers. The I/O reports from those work centers need to be examined to locate the source of the problem.

1. Given the following information on the planned and actual inputs and outputs for a machine shop, complete an input/output report for the shop. The beginning backlog is 12 hours of work.

INPUT						
PERIOD	1	2	3	4	5	TOTAL
Planned input	20	24	24	24	24	
Actual input	24	22	20	27	25	
Deviation						
OUTPUT						
Planned output	23	24	24	24	24	
Actual output	24	24	23	22	24	
Deviation						

2. Given the following information on the planned and actual inputs and outputs for Workstation 12, complete an input/output report for the shop. The beginning backlog is 20 hours of work.

INPUT						
PERIOD	1	2	3	4	5	TOTAL
Planned input	40	45	55	60	60	
Actual input	35	45	50	55	60	
Deviation						
OUTPUT						
Planned output	45	50	55	60	60	
Actual output	45	45	50	55	60	
Deviation						

3.   Given the following information on the planned and actual inputs and outputs for workstation A, complete an input/output report for the shop. The beginning backlog is 40 hours of work.

PERIOD	1	2	3	4	5	TOTAL
INPUT						
Planned input	60	65	70	75	75	
Actual input	60	60	65	70	75	
Deviation						
OUTPUT						
Planned output	75	75	75	75	75	
Actual output	70	70	70	70	70	
Deviation						

Employee Scheduling

S1.   Milk Shake Express employs six workers to operate its store. Demand for service each week (in terms of minimum number of workers required) is given in the following table. Create an employee schedule that will meet the demand requirements and guarantee each worker 2 days off per week.

Day of Week	M	T	W	Th	F	Sat.	Sun.
# of workers	4	4	5	4	5	6	4
Thomas							
Sims							
Savelle							
Abbot							
Davis							
Nixon							

Solution:

Step 1:   Set up the matrix. The completed employee schedule matrix is shown next. The O's represent an off employee, and the X's represent a working employee.

Day of Week	M	T	W	Th	F	Sat.	Sun.
# of workers	4	4	5	4	5	6	4
Thomas	O	X	X	O	X	X	X
Sims	O	X	X	X	O	X	X
Savelle	X	O	X	X	X	X	O
Abbot	X	O	X	X	X	X	O
Davis	X	X	O	X	X	X	X
Nixon	X	X	X	X	X	X	X

Step 2: Using the heuristic, compute the number of workers off. The heuristic rules are the number of employees (N) minus the demand on a working day (D_i), or $N - D_i$.

Step 3: Complete your calculations starting with Monday as D_1.

$N - D_1$ = # of workers off. $6 - 4 = 2$ workers off, so Thomas and Sims off.

Tues: $N - D_2 = 6 - 4 = 2$ workers off, so the next two workers off on Tuesday.
So, Savelle and Abbot are off on Tuesday.

Wed: $N - D_3 = 6 - 5 = 1$ workers off, so the next two workers off on Wednesday.
So, Davis is off on Wednesday.

Thurs: $N - D_4 = 6 - 4 = 2$ workers off, so you would assign Nixon and then starting back at the top, Thomas off on Thursday.

Fri: $N - D_5 = 6 - 5 = 1$ worker off, so Sims off on Friday.

Sat: $N - D_6$ = # of workers off on Saturday. $6 - 6 = 0$ workers off on Saturday.

Sun: $N - D_7$ = # of workers off on Sunday. $6 - 4 = 2$ workers, Savelle and Abbot off on Sunday.

Step 4: Analysis: The resulting schedule meets demand, but each employee does not have his/her 2 days off per week under this schedule. In order to meet that requirement, more workers would be needed. You should be able to look at the schedule and see the constraint. Saturday's demand does not allow for scheduling time off for any employees.

1. Barbara's Bakery is open 7 days per week with peak times on Friday and Saturday. The manager wants a minimum of 3 days per week except during the peak days, on which she thinks 6 people will be needed. She is inclined only to use full-time employees and requires that each employee have 2 consecutive days off each week. Create an employee schedule that will meet the demand requirements determined by the manager, including having 2 consecutive days off.

Day of Week	M	T	W	Th	F	Sat.	Sun.
# of workers	3	3	3	3	6	6	3
Jim Stone							
Peter Blank							
Chris Henry							
Tom Neel							
Mike Carlson							
Scott Peterson							

2.   The Pottery Store is planning a 4-day sale (Thursday – Sunday), and the manager has to develop an employee schedule for the sale. The manager has to have 5 employees for each day of the sale. Also, since the manager knows that Saturday and Sunday are difficult days, he determines that anyone that works either day will have Monday off. On the following days of the week, the manager will need a normal staff of 3 employees with each employee receiving 2 days off each week. Create a schedule that satisfies the manager's requirements. What is the minimum number of employees needed to meet these requirements?

Day of Week	M	T	W	Th	F	Sat.	Sun.
# of workers	3	3	3	5	5	5	5
#1							
#2							
#3							
#4							
#5							
#6							
#7							
#8							
#9							
#10							

3.   Bill's House of Fun is an amusement park that has activities that are family oriented. The amusement park is open every day with Saturday being the busiest day. Bill also knows that Mondays through Wednesdays are slow. The table below is the estimate of normal employees needs. The manager doesn't want any full-time employees, so no one can work more than 3 days per week. Create a schedule that satisfies the manager's requirements. Does Bill need all 15 employees to meet his needs?

Day of Week	M	T	W	Th	F	Sat.	Sun.
# of workers	2	2	2	5	7	8	5
#1							
#2							
#3							
#4							
#5							
#6							
#7							
#8							
#9							
#10							
#11							
#12							
#13							
#14							
#15							

16

Just-in-Time and Lean Production Systems

I. Just-In-Time and Lean Production

A. Just-in-Time (JIT) – a philosophy of continuous and forced problem solving that drives out waste. Lean production – a way to eliminate waste through a focus on exactly what the customer wants. Lean production is driven by a "pull" customer's order. JIT is a key ingredient of lean production.

B. With JIT, suppliers and components are "pulled" through a system to arrive where and when they are needed.

C. Waste Reduction – waste is anything that does not add value to the product from the customer's perspective. Example: product being stored, inspected, or delayed, products waiting in queues, and defective products.

D. Variability Reduction – any deviation from the optimum process that delivers a perfect product on time, every time. Variability occurs because:
   1. Employees, machines, and suppliers produce units that do not conform to standards, are late, or not the proper quantity.
   2. Engineering drawings or specifications are inaccurate.
   3. Production personnel try to produce before drawings or specifications are complete.
   4. Customer demands are unknown.
   5. JIT removes variability.

E. Pull versus Push
   1. Pull system is a system that pulls a unit to where it is needed just as it is needed.
   2. Push is a system that dumps orders on the next downstream workstation regardless of timeliness and resource availability.

Lecture Key: Remember that the purpose of JIT is to add value by remove waste and unwanted variability to eliminate costs that are associated with unneeded inventory. Also remember that the less variability, the less waste and therefore the better the system.

II. Supplier

A. Fours Goals of JIT Partnership:
   1. Elimination of unnecessary activities.
   2. Elimination of in-pant inventory.
   3. Elimination of in-transit inventory.
   4. Elimination of poor supplier.

B. Characteristics of JIT Partnership:
 1. Suppliers
 2. Quantities
 3. Quality
 4. Shipping
B. Concerns of Suppliers:
 1. Desire for diversification
 2. Poor customer scheduling
 3. Engineering changes
 4. Quality assurance
 5. Small lot sizes
 6. Proximity

Lecture Key: The purpose of JIT partnerships is removing waste and driving down cost and it exists when supplier and purchaser work together.

III. **JIT Layout**

A. Distance Reduction – Reducing distance is a major contribution of work cells, work centers, and focused factories.
B. Increase Flexibility – Layout flexibility aids the changes that result from product and process improvements that are inevitable with a philosophy of continuous improvement.
C. Impacts on Employee – Employees working together are cross-trained, so they can bring flexibility and efficiency to the work cell.
D. Reduced Space and Inventory – JIT layouts reduce travel distance, and they also reduce inventory by removing space for inventory.

Lecture Key: Another kind of waste is movement waste, and JIT layouts are used to reduce movement waste. JIT layouts move material directly to the location where needed to reduce distance, save space and eliminate potential areas from unwanted inventory.

IV. **Inventory: Just-in-Time Inventory – the minimum inventory necessary to keep a perfect system running**

A. Reduce Variability
 1. The concept of JIT is to eliminate inventory that hides variability in the production system.
 2. This variability could represent problems such as late deliveries, machine breakdowns, and poor personnel performance.
B. Reduce Inventory
 1. Removing inventory is the first step needed in moving towards JIT.
 2. By reducing inventory, current variability and problems that are being tolerated are uncovered.
 3. Management then eliminates the problems one by one that are exposed by reducing the inventory.
 4. This is done until there is virtually no inventory and no problems (variability).
C. Reduce Lot Sizes
 1. The key to JIT is to produce good products in small lot sizes.
 2. Inventory, and thus inventory costs, can be cut by reducing the size of batches.
 3. When a lot size has been determined, the EOQ production order quantity model can be modified to determine the desired setup time.

4. The Production Order Quantity Model:

$$Q* = \sqrt{[(2DS) / (H(1 - (d/p)))]}$$

Where:
- D = Annual demand
- S = Setup cost
- H = Holding cost
- d = Daily demand
- p = Daily production

Example: Setup Time & Cost

Crate Furniture's production analyst, Aleda Roth, determined that a 2-hour production cycle would be acceptable between two departments. Further, she concluded that a setup time that would accommodate the 2-hour cycle time should be achieved. Roth developed the following data and procedure to determine optimum setup time analytically:

Annual Demand:	D =	400,000 units
Daily Demand:	d =	400,000 per 250 days = 1,600 units per day
Daily Production Rate:	p =	4,000 units per day
EOQ desired:	Q =	400 (which is the 2-hour demand; that is 1,600 per day per four 2-hour periods)
Holding Cost:	H =	$20 per unit per year
Setup Cost:	S =	(to be determined)

Solution:
Roth determines that the cost, on an hourly basis, of setting up equipment is $30. Further, she computes that the setup cost per setup should be:

$$Q = \sqrt{(2 * D * S) / [H * (1 - d/p)]}$$
$$Q^2 = (2 * D * S) / [H * (1 - d/p)]$$
$$S = [(Q^2)(H)(1 - d/p)] / (2 * D)$$
$$S = [(400^2)(20)(1 - 1,600/4,000)] / (2 * 400,000)$$
$$= [(3,200,000)(0.60)] / (800,000) = \$2.40$$

Setup Time = $2.40 / (hourly labor rate)
= $2.40 / ($30 per hour) = 0.08 hour, or 4.8 minutes

Now, rather than producing components in large lots, Crate Furniture can produce in a 2-hour cycle with the advantage of an inventory turnover of four per day.

5. Changes needed for small-lot material flow to work:
   a. Improve material handling and work flow
   b. Radical reduction in setup times

D. Reduce Setup Costs
 1. More frequent orders require reducing setup costs; otherwise, inventory costs will rise.
 2. As the setup costs are lowered, inventory costs also fall (see figure below).

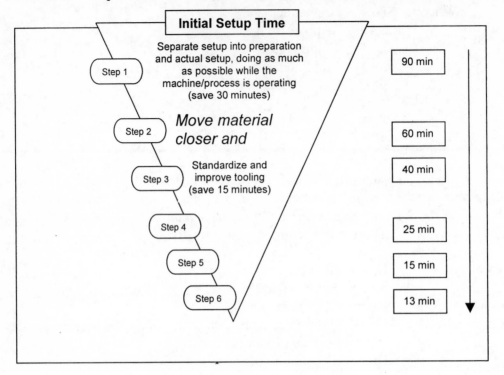

 3. Setup costs are highly correlated with setup times.
 4. Reduced lot sizes must be accompanied by reduced setup times; otherwise, the setup cost must be assigned to fewer units.
 5. Setup times can be reduced substantially (see figure below).

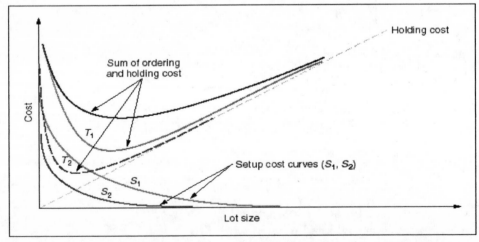

 6. Reducing setup time (and cost) is an excellent way to reduce inventory investment and to improve productivity.

Lecture Key: *There are many JIT inventory tactics that are being implemented in manufacturing to improve quality, drive down inventory investment, and reduce other costs. Also, by reducing inventory, you are able to expose and correct problems that would have normally been hidden with large lot sizes.*

V. Scheduling

A. Schedules must be communicated both within and outside an organization to its suppliers.

B. There are two techniques to scheduling:
1. Level Schedules – process small batches rather than a large-lot approach.
2. Kanban – uses signals between different areas to communicate need for material. There are many characteristics of this technique:
   a. It "pulls" inventory through production process as it is needed, rather than forcing it through, which leads to...
   b. Reduced Inventory.
   c. Containers are usually very small, maybe a few hours worth of production.
   d. This leads to an increased emphasis on meeting tight schedules.
3. Advantages to using Kanban:
   a. Limited amount of faulty or delayed material.
   b. Problems are immediately evident.
   c. Standardized quantities are moved in reusable containers, reducing waste, freeing up floor space, and reducing labor and packing.

Example: Determining the Number of Kanbans

Hobbs Bakery produces short runs of cakes that are shipped to grocery stores. The owner, Ken Hobbs, wants to try to reduce inventory by changing to a kanban system. He has developed the following data and asked you to finish the project by telling him the number of kanbans (containers) needed.

Daily demand	=	500 cakes
Production lead time	=	2 days
Safety stock	=	½ day
Container size (determined on a production order size EOQ basis)	=	250 cakes

Solution:
Demand during lead time (= lead time x daily demand = 2 days x 500 cakes) = 1,000

Safety Stock = 250

\# of kanbans (containers) needed
= Demand during lead time + Safety Stock / Container Size
= (1,000 + 250) / 250 = 5 kanbans

Lecture Key: *Scheduling is essential to an efficient, cost-effective effort in production. The Kanban technique creates the best situation for JIT systems of inventory because small amounts are used at a time and demand for components is easier to recognize. The fact that problems are immediately noticed also reduces the time to fix the problem.*

VI. Quality

  A. Good quality is closely related to a JIT system.

  B. There are three major reasons for this:

    1. Because JIT drives down inventory, the cost of rework, scrap and holding inventory is cut. JIT exposes bad inventory and remedies it quickly.

    2. Since JIT cuts lead times, errors are caught quickly and it reduces the amount of sources of error. Fewer bad units are produced because JIT creates an early warning system for errors.

    3. Consistent good quality allows JIT to function best, since all inventory costs are reduced.

Lecture Key: JIT almost forces good quality out of a process because of the error catching mechanisms, such as the short lead times. Because little inventory is kept, there can be little source of error. Good quality and a JIT system make inventory very cost-effective.

VII. Employee Empowerment

  A. Since no one knows the work better than the employee, it is beneficial to empower them to be able to make decisions regarding their work.

  B. Enriched jobs not only increase the investment of a worker by a firm but also result in improvements in the workplace from employees who see their jobs as meaningful.

VIII. Lean Production

  A. Lean production is essentially the end result of OM.

  B. Emphasis is on understanding the customer and relies more on those external factors, such as customer wants, input and feedback.

  C. "Toyota Production System" is another name for lean production.

  D. Organizations that implement continuous production (JIT), quality to the customer (lean production) and employee empowerment and learning (TPS) tend to drive out activities that do not add value to their product. They also tend to be benchmark performers.

Lecture Key: A healthy combination of all three systems puts organizations on the right track to make excellent returns. Lean production companies' goals are set at perfection: no defects, no inventory and cut out activities that do not add value. In this way they don't just set the standard, they are the standard.

IX. JIT in Services – All techniques from JIT are used in the service industries as well

  A. Suppliers – If a restaurant is NOT on a JIT basis with its supplier, the results are evident: bad food and upset customers.

  B. Layouts – Speed is everything, and the layout out of a restaurant can shave time off serving a customer, making good business.

  C. Inventory – The same techniques and advantages of reducing inventory in other industries are utilized in services as well.

  D. Scheduling – Not only is production on a JIT basis, so is personnel. This helps keep costs down by meeting specific demand at specific times.

Lecture Key: It is easy to see how JIT systems can benefit a service type organization such as a restaurant. While scheduling is the driving force of services, it will not reap any benefits without good suppliers, a strategic layout of the firm and well-designed operations management.

Setup Time & Cost

S1.   Janelle Marie, maker of a specialty line of make-up, has an average inventory turnover 20 times per year. She has determined that she will reduce the lot size. She has determined the following information regarding the base pigments.

Annual Demand:	D	=	800,000 gallons
Daily Demand:	d	=	800,000 per 250 days	= 3,200 gallons per day
Daily Production Rate:	p	=	6,000 gallons per day
EOQ Desired:	Q	=	800 gallons
Holding Cost:	H	=	$10 per gallon per year
Setup Labor Cost:		=	$15 labor cost per hour

Solution:

Step 1:   Calculate the Setup Cost using the POQ equation.

$$Q = \sqrt{(2 * D * S) / [H * (1 - d/p)]}$$
$$Q2 = (2 * D * S) / [H * (1 - d/p)]$$
$$S = [(Q2)(H)(1 - d/p)] / (2 * D)$$
$$S = [(800^2)(10)(1 - 3,200/6,000)] / (2 * 800,000)$$
$$= [(6,400,000)(0.53)] / (1,600,000) = \$2.12$$

Step 2:   Calculate the Setup Time:

Setup Time   = $2.12 / (hourly labor rate)
              = $2.12 / ($15 per hour)   =   0.14 hour, or 8.47 minutes

1.   Stanton Michaels has a manufacturing plant that produces drum sets. Stanton needs a reduced lot size. Stanton has figured out the following numbers:

Annual Demand:	D	=	11,500 units
Daily Demand:	d	=	50 units per day
Daily Production Rate:	p	=	300 units per day
EOQ Desired:	Q	=	200 units
Holding Cost:	H	=	$50 per unit per year
Setup Labor Cost:		=	$75 labor cost per hour

2.   PLASTIKS produces plastic pellet guns for young adults. The production plant has an average inventory turnover of 26 times per year. PLASTIKS has decided to reduce component lot size for the chamber. With the following data figures, determine how many minutes of setup time they should aim for in production.

Annual Demand:	D	=	46,000 units
Daily Demand:	d	=	95 units per day
Daily Production Rate:	p	=	580 units per day
EOQ Desired:	Q	=	190 units (2 hours of production)
Holding Cost:	H	=	$5 per unit per year
Setup Labor Cost:		=	$9 labor cost per hour

Kanbans

S1.   Huntington Industries makes picture frames. One of the workers is responsible for attaching the wire leads and wire used to hang the frames. He is asked to process an average of 70 frames per hour through his work cell. If one kanban is attached to every container, a container holds 50 leads, it takes 10 minutes to receive new frames from the previous workstation, and the factory uses a safety stock factor of 10 percent, how many kanbans are needed for the wire lead process?

Solution:

Step 1:   Determine the given information.

Demand   = 70 bottles per hour
Lead-time   = 10 min. (convert to hours – 10 min. / 60 min. in hr. = 0.166 hour)
Safety Stock   = 0.10 (70 x 0.166) = 1.162 – (safety factor* (demand x lead time))
Container Size = 50 wire leads

Step 2:   Calculate kanbans.

$$N = \frac{d * L + S}{C} = \frac{70 * 0.166 + 1.162}{50} = 0.255 \text{ kanbans}$$

Step 3:   Make your decision.

You would need 0.255 kanbans for the process.

S2.   Another worker at Huntington Industries is responsible for building the frames. He uses special finishing staples to attach the wood to each other. He is asked to process an average of 100 frames per hour through his work cell (each frame needs 8 staples). If one kanban is attached to every container, a container holds 150 staples, it takes 45 minutes to receive new frames from the previous workstation, and the factory uses a safety stock factor of 10 percent, how many kanbans are needed for the wire lead process?

Solution:

Step 1:   Determine the given information.

Demand   = 800 staples per hour (100 frames per hour x 8 staples per frame)
Lead-time   = 45 min. (convert to hours – 45 min. / 60 min. in hr. = 0.75 hour)
Safety Stock   = 0.10 (800 x 0.75) = 60 – (safety factor* (demand x lead time))
Container Size = 150 staples

Step 2:   Calculate kanbans.

$$N = \frac{d * L + S}{C} = \frac{800 * 0.75 + 60}{150} = 4.4 \text{ kanbans}$$

Step 3:   Make your decision.

You can round either way, but rounding down to 4 kanbans would mean that you must improve the operations for the process.

1.   A JIT system uses kanban cards to authorize production and movement of materials. In one portion of the system, a workstation uses an average of 250 pieces per hour while running. The manager has assigned an efficiency factor of .25 to the center. Standard containers are designed to hold 80 parts each. The cycle time for parts containers is about 100 minutes. How many containers are needed?

2.   The Sport Racket produces a variety of athletic rackets. The manager wants to determine the number of containers to use for a kanban system to be installed in the spring. The process will have a usage rate of 85 pieces per hour. Because the process is new, the manager has assigned an efficiency factor of .45. Each container holds 60 pieces and takes an average of 80 minutes to complete a cycle. How many containers should be used? What would happen if the system improves to a .25 efficiency level?

3. The Dairy Mart uses large mixing containers to add the ingredients to its milk products. The additive containers hold 240 pounds each. The process adds 400 pounds of additives each shift (8 hour work day). The cycle time for the containers is an hour. The manager has assigned an efficiency level of .09 to the mixing process. How many additive containers will be used?

4. Lawn Specialty Inc., a manufacturer of fertilizer equipment, wants to use a JIT system with kanban cards to authorize production and movement of materials. The following table represents the workstations with the production rate, cycle times for the containers, and efficiency levels. Standard containers are designed to hold 50 parts each. How many containers are needed for each workstation per day?

Workstation	Production Rate Per Day	Cycle Time	Efficiency Level
1	1500	45 minutes	0.90
2	1200	60 minutes	0.80
3	1600	30 minutes	0.95

5. Laces With Style produces a variety of trendy shoelaces. The manager wants to determine the number of containers to use for a kanban system to be installed next month. The process of adding the plastic protective wrap will have a usage rate of 250 pieces per hour. The manager has assigned an efficiency factor of .85. Each container holds 160 pieces and takes an average of 30 minutes to complete a cycle. How many containers should be used?

6. Sparkle Pool Chemical uses special containers to mix the ingredients of its line of Sparkle Pool Chemicals. The vats of chemicals hold 50 gallons each. The process adds 200 gallons of special chemical each shift (8 hour work day). The cycle time for the containers is three hours. The manager has assigned an efficiency level of .95 to the mixing process. How many chemical vats will be used?

17

Maintenance and Reliability

I.   **The Strategic Importance of Maintenance and Reliability**

A. Maintenance includes all activities involved in keeping a system's equipment in working order.

B. Reliability is the probability that a machine part or product will function properly for a specified time under stated conditions.

C. The objective of maintenance and reliability is to maintain the capability of the system while controlling costs.

D. <u>4 tactics for improving reliability and maintenance</u>:
   1. Reliability tactics:
      a. Improving individual components.
      b. Providing redundancy.
   2. Maintenance tactics are:
      a. Implementing or improving preventive maintenance.
      b. Increasing repair capabilities or speed.

Lecture Key: *For a company to continue down the path to success, two important components needed are maintenance and reliability. For a system to be both maintained and reliable, it keeps the customers satisfied that their product will be of good quality. It also allows the company to keep its cost down because of so few repairs.*

II.   **Reliability**

A. Improving individual components
   1. Computing system reliability:
      $$R_s = R_1 \times R_2 \times R_3 \times \ldots \times R_n$$

Example: System Reliability

The National Bank of Greeley, Colorado, processes loan applications through three clerks set up in series:

If the clerks have reliabilities of .90, .80, .99, then the reliability of the loan process is

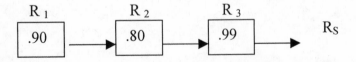

Solution:

$R_s = R_1 \times R_2 \times R_3 = (.90)(.80)(.99) = .713$ or 71.3%

    2. Product Failure Rate

        FR (%) = (# of failures / # of units tested FR (%)) x 100%

    3. Mean Time Between Failures

        MTBF = 1 / FR (N)

Example: Failure Rate and Mean Time Between Failures (MTBF)

Twenty air-conditioning systems designed for use by astronauts in NASA space shuttles were operated for 1,000 hours at NASA's Huntsville, Alabama, test facility. Two of the systems failed during the test—one after 200 hours and the other after 600 hours. To compute the percentage of failures, we use the following equation:

Solution:

FR (%)= (# of failures / # of units tested FR (%)) x 100%
     = (2 / 20) x 100% = 10%

Next we compute the number of failures per operating hour:

    FR (N) = # of failures / Operating time

Where:	Total time	$= (1000$ hr) (20 units) $= 20,000$ units-hr
	Nonoperating time	$= 800$ hours for 1st failure $+ 400$ hours for 2nd failure
		$= 1,200$ hours per unit
	Operating time	$=$ Total time $-$ Nonoperating time
	FR (N)	$= 2 / (20,000 - 1,200) = 0.000106$ failure /unit-hr

        and because

        MTBF = 1 / FR(N)
              = 1 / .000106 = 9,434 hr

If the typical space shuttle trip lasts 60 days, NASA may be interested in the failure rate per trip:

    Failure rate = (failures/unit-hr) (24 hr/day) (60 days/trip)
             = (.000106) (24) (60)
             = .152 failure/trip

Lecture Key: The system reliability is important because not only do you need to see how reliable each individual component is, but also, as a group, how reliable they are. As far as product failure rate, this is important because if the failure rate of a product is too high, the product then has to be reworked in some way to lower that rate. Lastly, mean time between failures, this is also important because if the product is continuously in the shop, maybe there is another alternative being that obviously this one is not working out as planned.

B. Providing Redundancy
    1. Redundancy is the use of components in parallel to raise reliabilities.
    2. They "back up" components with additional components to ensure that if one component fails, the system has a resource to another.
    3. $\left(\begin{array}{c} \text{Probability of} \\ \text{first component} \\ \text{working} \end{array} \right) + \left\{ \left(\begin{array}{c} \text{Probability of} \\ \text{second component} \\ \text{working} \end{array} \right) \times \left(\begin{array}{c} \text{Probability of} \\ \text{needing second} \\ \text{component} \end{array} \right) \right\}$

Example: System Reliability Using Parallel Components

The National Bank is disturbed that its loan application process has a reliability of only .713. The bank decides to provide redundancy for the least two reliable clerks.

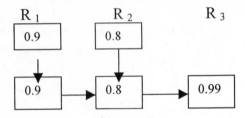

Solution:
$R_s = [(.90) + [.9 * (1 - .9)] * [(.80) + [.8 * (1 - .8)] * (.99)$
    $= (.99) * (.96) * (.99) = \ \ .94 \text{ or } 94\%$

By providing redundancy, the National Bank has increased the reliability of the loan process from .713 to .94.

Lecture Key: *Redundancy increases the reliability of the different components of the process by adding a back up if the first component fails. Example 3 shows the increase of reliability.*

III.   Maintenance

  A. Two types of maintenance:
    1. Preventative Maintenance involves performing routine inspections and servicing and keeping facilities in good repair.
    2. Breakdown Maintenance occurs when equipment fails and must be repaired on an emergency or priority basis.
    3. Implementing Preventative Maintenance
        a. Implies that we can determine when a system needs repair or service.
        b. Infant Mortality is a high initial failure rate that may exist for many products.
        c. Once the product, machine, or process has settled in, a study can be made of the MTBF (mean time between failure) distribution.
        d. We want to determine when preventative maintenance is economical.
          i. The more expensive the maintenance, the narrower the MTBF distribution (smaller standard deviation).
          ii. Preventative maintenance costs may be so incidental that it is appropriate even if MTFB distribution is flat.
    4. Firms can maintain records of individual processes, machines, or equipment so a profile can be developed of the kinds of maintenance required and the timing of the maintenance needed.

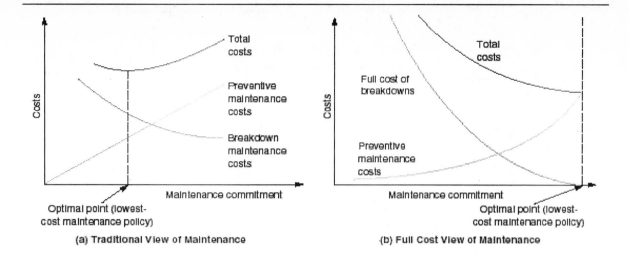

(a) Traditional View of Maintenance   (b) Full Cost View of Maintenance

5. Curves such as in Figure (a) seldom consider the full costs of a breakdown. Many costs are ignored because they are not directly related to the immediate breakdown.
6. Figure (b) may be a better representation of maintenance costs. In Figure (b), total costs are at a minimum when the system does not break down.

Lecture Key: *This is a traditional view of the relationship between preventive maintenance and breakdown maintenance. Operations managers consider a balance between the two costs. On the one hand, allocating more resources to preventive maintenance will reduce the number of breakdowns. At some point, however, the decrease in breakdown maintenance costs may be less than the increase in preventive maintenance costs. At this point, the total cost curve will begin to rise. Beyond this optimal point, the firm will be better off waiting for breakdowns to occur and repairing them when they do.*

Example: Preventive Maintenance Cost

A CPA firm, specializing in payroll preparation, has automated much of its work. The computerized approach has problems. Over the past 20 months, printers have broken down at the rate indicated in the table:

Number of Breakdowns	Number of Months Breakdowns Occur
0	2
1	8
2	6
3	4
	Total: 20

Solution:

Each time a printer breaks down, the firm loses an average of $300 in time and service expenses. One alternative is to purchase a preventative maintenance service contract. There will still be breakdowns *averaging* 1/month. The price is $150/month. Deciding whether firm will contract will require using a 4-step approach:

Step 1: Compute the *expected number* of breakdowns (past history) if firm continues without service contract.

Step 2: Compute the expected breakdown cost per month with no maintenance contract.

Step 3: Compute the cost of preventative maintenance.

Step 4: Compare the two options and select the one that costs less.

#1.

# of Breakdowns	Frequency	# of Breakdowns	Frequency
0	$2 / 20 = .1$	2	$6 / 20 = .3$
1	$8 / 20 = .4$	3	$4 / 20 = .2$

$$\begin{pmatrix} \text{Expected number} \\ \text{of breakdowns} \end{pmatrix} = \sum \left[\begin{array}{ccc} (\text{number of} & \times & (\text{corresponding} \\ \text{breakdowns}) & & \text{frequency)} \end{array} \right]$$

$$= (0)(.1) + (1)(.4) + (2)(.3) + (3)(.2)$$
$$= 0 + .4 + .6 + .6 = 1.6 \text{ breakdowns/month}$$

#2. Expected Breakdown Cost $= (\text{Expected \# of breakdowns}) \times (\$ \text{ per breakdown})$
$$= (1.6)(\$300) = \$480/\text{month}$$

#3. Preventative Maintenance \$ $= (\$ \text{ of expected breakdowns if contract is signed})$
$+ (\text{Cost of Service Contract})$
$= (1 \text{ breakdown/month})(\$300) + \$150/\text{month} = 450/\text{month}$

#4. Because it is less expensive overall to hire a maintenance service firm (\$450) than to not (\$480), the firm should sign the preventative maintenance contract.

7. Increasing Repair Capabilities
   a. Repair capability is important because reliability and preventive maintenance are not perfect.
   b. Six features required for a good maintenance facility:
      i. Well trained personnel
      ii. Adequate resources
      iii. Ability to establish a repair plan and priorities
      iv. Ability and authority to do material planning
      v. Ability to identify the cause of breakdowns
      vi. Ability to design
   c. Managers must determine how maintenance will be performed.

Lecture Key: *Preventative and breakdown maintenance both deal with keeping equipment in working order. The main difference between the two types of maintenance is whether the equipment has already failed. Many times less costs are incurred when maintenance is done on equipment before it actually fails. However, due to the infant mortality rate, it is difficult to evaluate when equipment is going to fail prior to it actually failing.*

IV. Total Productive Maintenance

A. Total Productive Maintenance – the concept of reducing variability through employee involvement and excellent maintenance records.

B. Total productive maintenance includes:
1. Designing machines that are reliable, easy to operate, and easy to maintain.
2. Emphasizing total cost of ownership when purchasing machines, so that service and maintenance are included in the cost.
3. Developing preventive maintenance plans that utilize the best practices of operators, maintenance departments, and depot service.
4. Training workers to operate and maintain their own machines.

Lecture Key: *Total productive maintenance is the practice of enabling employees to operate and maintain machinery in order to reduce costs.*

V. Techniques for Establishing Maintenance Policies

A. Simulation – Computer simulation is used to evaluate costs involved with maintenance decisions prior to the actual failure of machines.

B. Expert Systems – Managers use expert systems to assist staff in isolating and repairing faults in machinery and equipment.

Lecture Key: *Simulation and Expert systems allow managers to determine future costs and pinpoint faults when they do occur. Simulation allows managers to estimate the future deterioration of machinery.*

Reliability

S1.   Bailey's Bikes wants to determine the reliability of its newest bicycle. The company uses one vendor for all the necessary parts of this bike. Based on the reliabilities in the chart below, which of the three suppliers should Bailey's use? In other words, which has the best overall reliability?

Vendor	1	2	3	4
A	.99	.95	.96	.94
B	.97	.92	.99	.96
C	.94	.98	.97	.93

Solution:

This is an example of a straight series of operations. The reliability of the system is calculated by simply multiplying each part's reliability with the next part's reliability.

$$\text{Vendor:} \quad A = .99 \times .95 \times .96 \times .94 = 84.9$$
$$B = .97 \times .92 \times .99 \times .96 = 84.8$$
$$C = .94 \times .98 \times .97 \times .93 = 83.1$$

According to these reliabilities, Vendor A would be the best supplier.

S2.   The Hooley Dooley Restaurant will not open until certain standards are met. Most individuals have to prepare food and clean the restaurant. Each individual station has met the standard of 90%, but through the employees' work efforts, the manager realizes that to be efficient, the restaurant must have a reliability of at least 85%. If five employees are as follows in the below information, can the restaurant meet reliability standards?

Employee	Reliability
1	.90
2	.95
3	.92
4	.90
5	.90

Solution:

This is an example of a straight series of operations. The reliability of the system is calculated by simply multiplying each part's reliability with the next part's reliability.

$$\text{Reliability} = (.90) \times (.95) \times (.92) \times (.90) \times (.90) = .6371$$

S3.   The operating system of a marketing firm will not open until certain standards are met. Each salesperson has met the individual standard of 90%, but the senior partner of the firm also realizes that to be safe, the overall system must have a reliability of at least 85%. This includes number of sales, attention ratings, and customer satisfaction. If the 6 marketers are as follows in the table, can the firm meet its standards?

Marketer	Reliability
1	.95
2	.94
3	.96
4	.91
5	.93
6	.98

Solution:

This is an example of a straight series of operations. The reliability of the system is calculated by simply multiplying each part's reliability with the next part's reliability.

$$\text{Reliability} = .95 \times .94 \times .96 \times .91 \times .93 \times .98 = .7110 = 71.10\%$$

So, the marketing firm is not reliable.

S4.   EZ Rider Car Company makes automobiles with lap seat belts on the driver and passenger side. The car company must meet the safety standard of 90%. Since safety is so important, EZ Rider also includes airbags both on the driver and passenger side of the front seats.

a. Does EZ Rider achieve its 90% safety standard? Yes, they achieve well beyond 90% (97.12%).

Subsystem	Reliability – Main	Reliability – Backup
1	.99	.90
2	.98	--
3	.95	.92
4	.94	.93

Solution:
This is an example of a straight series of operations with backups (or parallel systems). The reliability of the system is calculated by the reliability of the main component (series) and the backup (parallel) together. You can then treat this reliability as the reliability of the subunit. Once you have calculated the reliability of the subunit, then treat as series of operations and multiply each subunit's reliability with the next subunit's reliability.

$$[.99 + [(1-.99)* .90)]] \;*\; [.98] \;*\; [.95 + [(1-.95) * .92]] \;*\; [.94 + [(1-.94) * .93] \;\; =$$
$$.999 \quad * \quad .98 \quad * \quad\quad .9960 \quad\quad * \quad\quad .996 \quad\quad = .9712$$

S5.   During tax season, printers are important. Before the next tax season comes, the company wants to back up some of their printers. They want to back up any printer with less than a 96% reliability value. All others stand alone. They want the overall reliability to be at least 90%.

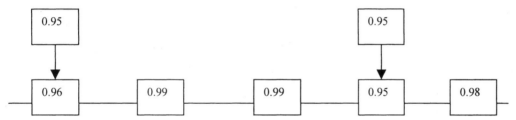

Solution:
This is an example of a straight series of operations with backups (or parallel systems). The reliability of the system is calculated by the reliability of the main component (series) and the backup (parallel) together. You can then treat this reliability as the reliability of the subunit. Once you have calculated the reliability of the subunit, then treat as series of operations and multiply each subunit's reliability with the next subunit's reliability.

$$[.96 + [(1-.96)* .95)]] \;*\; [.99] \;*\; [.99] \;*\; [.95 + [(1-.95) * .95]] \;*\; [.98] \;\; =$$
$$.998 \quad * \quad .99 \;*\; .99 \;*\; \quad .9975 \quad\quad * \quad .98 \quad = .9562 = 95.62\%$$

1.   The operating system of the local water control plant will not open the spillway until all the individual control values have met certain standards. Each station has met the individual standard of 90%, but the manager also realizes that to be safe, the overall system must have a reliability of at least 85%. If the five subsystems are as follows in the below table, can the spillway meet its reliability standards?

Subsystem	Reliability
1	.95
2	.99
3	.96
4	.95
5	.94

2.	Since the overall reliability is obviously important, the manager of the operating system of the local water control plant has decided to put backups on all the control values. Does the backup make a difference and increase the reliability to at least 85%? If the five subsystems are as follows in the below table, can the spillway meet the reliability standards necessary to open the spillway?

Subsystem	Reliability – Main	Reliability – Backup
1	.95	.94
2	.99	.99
3	.96	.90
4	.95	.93
5	.94	.90

3.	Bayou Gator Manufacturing has contracted three firms to design a new motor for their line of fishing boats. Due to the varying water compositions and changing weather, these motors must be put together very well. Before the company will buy the design from the winning firm, the prototype must achieve at least a 95% reliability rate on the company's test course, which contains all the "normal" conditions that the boat is designed to accept. The motor has 5 basic subassemblies that must be judged on reliability. Which firm should Bayou use?

Firm	1	2	3	4	5
A	.99	.94	.92	.98	.97
B	.94	.94	.95	.95	.94
C	.97	.96	.92	.94	.94

4.	What if Bayou Gator Manufacturing can buy each subassembly separately from the best firm? What is the highest reliability level that Bayou could hope for in this new motor? Use the previous problem's data.

5.	SuperBrakes wants to determine the reliability of its braking system for the latest large vehicles that car manufacturers are selling. It uses one vendor as a supplier for all brake parts. If the reliability for each part were listed in the following table, what would be the best supplier?

Vendor	PART #			
	1	2	3	4
A	.94	.95	.92	.94
B	.86	.99	.94	.97
C	.91	.94	.95	.96
D	.94	.97	.94	.92

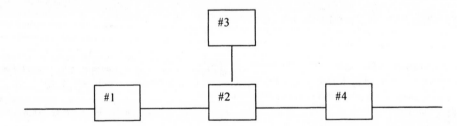

6. For its **Industrial Braking** Systems, SuperBrakes wants to determine the reliability of its braking system. It uses **the same vendors** as its supplier for all brake parts. The sequence changes slightly for this system. If the reliability for each part were listed in the following table, what would be the best supplier? Would that change your overall answer for #6?

Vendor	PART #			
	1	2	3	4
A	.94	.95	.92	.94
B	.86	.99	.94	.97
C	.91	.94	.95	.96
D	.94	.97	.94	.92

7. Robert runs a rehab clinic for physical injuries that require stabilization and strengthening in specific ranges of motion. He is analyzing different lines of equipment to replace his existing equipment. There has been a revolution in designs since Robert last had to buy a piece of equipment. Also, there is intense competition between competitors. With all the information and marketing campaigns in place, Robert doesn't know how to make a mistake. Since repetition and consistency are essential to successfully rehab patients, Robert knows that he has to count on the machines to work. He contacted some of the competitors' recent customers and asked about the reliability of five specialty pieces of equipment. The information is summarized below.

Machine	Supplier #1	Supplier #2	Supplier #3
Knee	.98	.94	.91
Elbow	.91	.95	.98
Ankle	.99	.94	.95
Shoulder	.90	.93	.93
Back	.99	.94	.94

From the information, calculate the reliability of the suppliers' machines. Which supplier should Robert use to purchase his new equipment? What other considerations or concerns might Robert have?

8. Calculate the following system's reliability.

a.

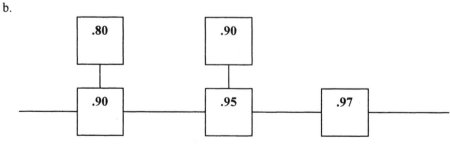

b.

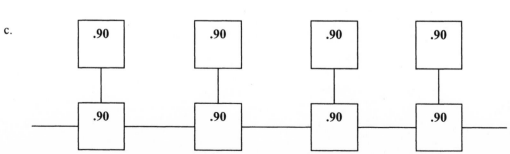

c.

9.   The Veggie Express is a new product that is composed of four parts. For the product to function as intended, all parts must work. Two of the parts have a .97 probability of working, and two have a .93 chance of working. What is the overall probability of the product working properly?

10.   A new detergent injector was developed to use with washing machines and dishwashers. It has three separate hoses with pumps attached that feed the different detergents to the washings. All three hoses are identical, but the detergents add varying wear to the hose and pumps. This explains the varying reliability rates for each component. The following information explains reliability rates for the three components.

Component	Reliability
Hose/Pump #1	.94
Hose/Pump #2	.97
Hose/Pump #3	.99

Module A
Decision-Making Tools

I.   The Decision Process in Operations

A. Managers must understand how decisions are made and know which decision-making tools to use to achieve the goals of their organizations.

B. Six steps to "good" decision making:
   1. Clearly define the problem and the factors that influence it.
   2. Develop specific and measurable objectives.
   3. Develop a model showing a relationship between objectives and variables.
   4. Evaluate each alternative solution based on its merits and drawbacks.
   5. Select the best alternative.
   6. Implement the decision and set a timetable for completion.

Lecture Key: *Operations managers are decision makers. Effective operations that will achieve the goals of an organization depend on careful decision making. "Good" decisions are based on logic and should consider all available data and possible alternatives.*

II.   Fundamentals of Decision Making

A. All decision makers are faced with alternatives and "states of nature."

B. Terms:
   1. Alternative—a course of action or strategy that may be chosen by a decision maker (for example, not carrying an umbrella tomorrow).
   2. State of nature—an occurrence or a situation over which the decision maker has little or no control (for example, tomorrow's weather).

C. Symbols used in a decision tree:
   1. □—decision node from which one of several alternatives may be selected.
   2. ○—a state-of-nature node out of which one state of nature will occur.

Lecture Key: *All decisions, no matter how simple or complex, involve alternatives and "states of nature." Managers can develop decision trees to create a visual representation of their decision alternatives. When constructing a decision tree, a manager must be sure that all alternatives and states of nature are in their correct and logical places and include all possible alternatives and states of nature.*

Example: Decision Tree

Getz Products Company is investigating the possibility of producing and marketing backyard storage sheds, requiring the construction of either a large or a small manufacturing plant. The market for the product produced (storage sheds) could be either favorable or unfavorable. Getz has the option of not developing the new product line at all.

A decision tree for this situation is presented below.

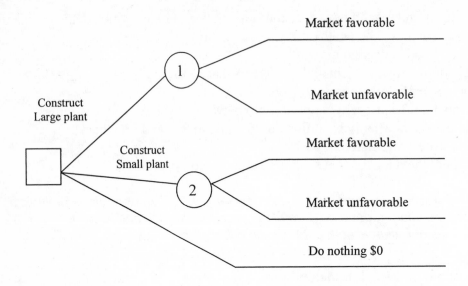

III. Decision Tables

A. Any alternative and a particular state of nature, there is a consequence or outcome.
B. The outcomes are expressed as a monetary value, called a conditional value.

Example

We construct a decision table for Getz Products (table below), including conditional values based on the following information. With a favorable market, a large facility would give Getz Products a net profit of $200,000. If the market is unfavorable, a $180,000 net loss would occur. A small plant would result in a net profit of $100,000 in a favorable market, but a net loss of $20,000 would be encountered if the market is unfavorable.

Decision Table for Getz Products		
	States of Nature	
Alternatives	**Favorable Market**	**Unfavorable Market**
Construct large plant	$200,000	-$180,000
Construct small plant	$100,000	-$20,000
Do nothing	$0	$0

C. Decision Making Under Uncertainty
  1. Maximax
     a. Finds an alternative that maximizes the maximum outcome for every alternative.
     b. Often called an "optimistic" decision criterion.
  2. Maximin
     a. Finds the alternative that maximizes the minimum outcome for every alternative.
     b. Often called a "pessimistic" decision criterion.
  3. Equally likely
     a. Finds the alternative with the highest average outcome.
     b. Assumes that each state of nature is equally likely to occur.

Lecture Key: *In order to help define their alternatives, managers may also develop a decision or payoff table, which is a tabular means of analyzing decision alternatives and states of nature. When there is complete uncertainty as to what probabilities will result for each possible outcome, we rely on three decision methods: maximax, maximin, and equally likely.*

Example: Decision Table

Given Getz's decision table above, determine the maximax, maximin, and equally likely decision criteria.

Solution:

Decision Table for Getz Products					
	States of Nature				
Alternatives	Fav. Market	Unfav. Market	Maximum in Row	Minimum in Row	Row Average
Construct large plant	$200,000	-$180,000	$200,000	-$180,000	$10,000
Construct small plant	$100,000	-$20,000	$100,000	-$20,000	$40,000
Do nothing	$0	$0	$0	$0	$0
			Maximax	Maximin	Equally likely

1.   The maximax choice is to construct a large plant. This is the maximum of the maximum number within each row, or alternative.

2.   The maximin choice is to do nothing. This is the maximum of the minimum number within each row, or alternative.

3.   The equally likely choice is to construct a small plant. This is the maximum of the average outcome of each alternative. This approach assumes that all outcomes for any alternative are equally likely.

D. Decision Making Under Risk
  1. Fundamentals
     a. Relies on probabilities.
     b. States of nature must be mutually exclusive and collectively exhaustive.
     c. States of nature probabilities must sum to 1.
  2. Expected Monetary Value (EMV)
     a. Sums the payoffs of the alternative, each weighted by the probability of that payoff occurring.
     b. Formula:
        EMV (Alternative i) = (Payoff of 1st state of nature)
                                   x (Probability of 1st state of nature)
                            + (Payoff of 2nd state of nature)
                                   x (Probability of 2nd state of nature)
                            +...+ (Payoff of last state of nature)
                                   x (Probability of last state of nature)

Lecture Key: *The more common task of decision making under risk, always follows certain criteria. Given a decision table with conditional values and probability assessments for all states of nature, a manager can determine the expected monetary value (EMV) for each alternative. This figure represents the expected value or mean return for each alternative if the manager could repeat the decision a large number of times.*

Example

Getz Products' operations manager believes that the probability of a favorable market is exactly the same as that of an unfavorable market; that is, each state of nature has a .50 chance of occurring. We can now determine the EMV for each alternative.

Solution:

1. EMV(A_1) = (.5)($200,000) + (.5)(-$180,000) = $10,000
2. EMV(A_2) = (.5)($100,000) + (.5)(-$20,000)   = $40,000
3. EMV(A_3) = (.5)($0) + (.5)($0)   = $0

The maximum EMV is seen in alternative A_2. Thus, according to the EMV decision criterion, we would build the small facility.

	States of Nature	
Alternatives	**Favorable Market**	**Unfavorable Market**
Construct large plant (A_1)	$200,000	-$180,000
Construct small plant (A_2)	$100,000	-$20,000
Do nothing (A_3)	$0	$0
Probabilities	.50	.50

E. Decision Making Under Certainty
    1. Expected Value of Perfect Information (EVPI)
        a. Determines difference between payoff under certainty and payoff under risk.
        b. Formula:
            EVPI = Expected value under certainty – Maximum EMV
    2. Expected Value Under Certainty
        a. Determines the expected (average) return if perfect information is available.
        b. Formula:
           Expected value under certainty = (Best outcome for 1st state of nature)
                x (Probability of 1st state of nature)
                  + (Best outcome for 2nd state of nature)
                x (Probability of 2nd state of nature)
                  +…+ (Best outcome for last state of nature)
                x (Probability of last state of nature)

Lecture Key: *If a manager were able to determine which state of nature would occur, then he or she would know which decision to make. Once a manager knows which decision to make, the payoff increases because the payoff is now a certainty, not a probability. Because the payoff will increase with knowledge of which state of nature will occur, this knowledge has value and is called expected value of perfect information (EVPI). In order to calculate the EVPI, the expected value under certainty must be determined.*

Example

By referring back to the table from the previous problem, the Getz operations manager can calculate the maximum that he would pay for information—that is, the expected value of perfect information, or EVPI. He follows a two-stage process. First, the expected value under certainty is computed. Then, using this information, EVPI is calculated. The procedure is outlined as follows:

Solution:
1.   The best outcome for the state of nature "favorable market" is "build a large facility" with a payoff of $200,000. The best outcome for the state of nature "unfavorable market" is "do nothing" with a payoff of $0. Expected value under certainty = ($200,000)(.50) + ($0)(.50) = $100,000. Thus, if we had perfect information, we would expect (on the average) $100,000 if the decision could be repeated many times.

2.   The maximum EMV is $40,000, which is the expected outcome without perfect information.

Thus:
        EVPI = Expected value under certainty – Maximum EMV
             = $100,000 – $40,000 = $60,000

In other words, the most Getz should be willing to pay for perfect information is $60,000. This conclusion, of course, is again based on the assumption that the probability of each state of nature is 0.50.

IV.   Decision Trees

A. Used when there are two or more sequential decisions and later decisions are based on the outcome of prior ones.

B. Graphic display of the decision process that indicates decision alternatives, states of nature and their respective probabilities, and payoffs for each combination of decision alternative and state of nature.

C. Analyzing problems with decision trees involves five steps:
1. Define the problem.
2. Structure or draw the decision tree.
3. Assign probabilities to the states of nature.
4. Estimate payoffs for each possible combination of decision alternatives and states of nature.
5. Solve the problem by computing expected monetary values (EMV) for each state-of-nature node.

Lecture Key: *Decisions that lend themselves to display in a decision table also lend themselves to display in a decision tree. A decision tree is a graphic display of the decision process that indicates decision alternatives, states of nature and their respective probabilities, and payoffs for each combination of decision alternative and state of nature. Expected monetary value (EMV) is the most commonly used criterion for decision tree analysis.*

Example

A completed and solved decision tree for Getz Products is presented in the figure below. Note that the payoffs are placed at the right-hand side of each of the tree's branches. The probabilities (first used by Getz in Example 3) are placed in parentheses next to each state of nature. The expected monetary values for each state of nature node are then calculated and placed by their respective nodes. The EMV of the first node is $10,000. This represents the branch from the decision node to "construct a large plant." The EMV for node 2, to "construct a small plant," is $40,000. The option of "doing nothing" has, of course, a payoff of $0. The branch leaving the decision node leading to the state of nature node with the highest EMV will be chosen. In Getz's case, a small plant should be built.

Solution:

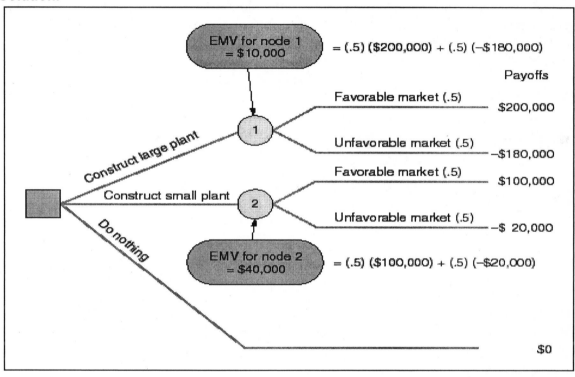

D. More Complex Decision Tree
1. Displays a sequence of decisions.
2. All possible outcomes and alternatives are included in their logical order.

Lecture Key: *When a sequence of decisions must be made, decision trees are much more powerful tools than decision tables. Providing all possible outcomes and alternatives in their logic sequence is one of the strengths of using decision trees. The manager is forced to examine all possible outcomes, including unfavorable ones. He or she is also forced to make decisions in a logical, sequential manner.*

Example

Examining the tree in the following figure, we see that Getz's first decision point is whether to conduct the $10,000 market survey. If it chooses not to do the study (the lower part of the tree), then it can either build a large plant, a small plant, or no plant. This is Getz's second decision point. If the decision is to build, the market will be either favorable (.50 probability) or unfavorable (also .50 probability). The payoffs for each of the possible consequences are listed along the right-hand side. As a matter of fact, this lower portion of Getz's tree is identical to the simpler decision tree shown in previous example.

Solution:

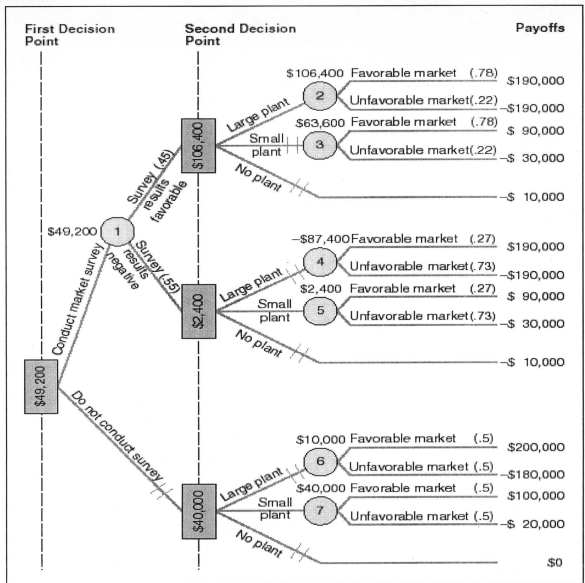

First Decision Point

Second Decision Point

Payoffs

$106,400 Favorable market (.78) $190,000
②   Unfavorable market(.22)   −$190,000

$63,600 Favorable market (.78) $90,000
Small plant ③   Unfavorable market(.22)   −$30,000

No plant   −$10,000

Large plant $106,400

Survey (.45) results favorable

$49,200 ①

Survey (.55) results negative

−$87,400 Favorable market (.27) $190,000
④   Unfavorable market(.73)   −$190,000

$2,400 Favorable market (.27) $90,000
Small plant ⑤   Unfavorable market(.73)   −$30,000

No plant   −$10,000

Large plant $2,400

Conduct market survey

$49,200

Do not conduct survey

$10,000 Favorable market (.5) $200,000
⑥   Unfavorable market (.5)   −$180,000

$40,000 Favorable market (.5) $100,000
Small plant ⑦   Unfavorable market (.5)   −$20,000

No plant $0

Large plant $40,000

Decision Making Criteria

S1.   Given the following payoff table (profits in $) and that no other information is known, determine the best decision using the following criteria. What is the best decision for the company with the following payoff information and decision criterias: Maximax, Maximin, and Equal likelihood?

Decision	States of Nature (in $1,000)			
	A	B	C	D
1	40	27	30	17
2	32	30	25	23
3	27	30	30	33

Solutions:
1.   Maximax:

Step 1:   Identify the largest possible profit in each decision row.

    Decision 1: $40
    Decision 2: $32
    Decision 3: $33

Step 2:   Pick the maximum of the maximum payoffs (or the maximum possible return of the largest possible for each individual decision). Decision 1 is the maximum of the three at $40, so it is the best alternative to maximize profits.

    Decision 1: $40,000

Step 3:   Analysis: This is the most optimistic decision criteria, especially since there are no probabilities for the states of nature.

2.   Maximin:

Step 1:   Identify the smallest possible profit in each decision row.

    Decision 1: $17
    Decision 2: $23
    Decision 3: $27

Step 2:   Pick the maximum of the minimum payoffs (or the maximum possible return of the smallest possible for each individual decision). Decision 3 is the maximum of the three at $27, so it is the best alternative to maximize profits.

    Decision 1: $27,000

Step 3:   Analysis: This is the most pessimistic decision criteria, especially since there are no probabilities for the states of nature. This criterion assumes the worst state of nature.

3.   Equal Likelihood:

Step 1:   Weight each state as equal and determine the expected value. The expected value is calculated by multiplying the profit under each State of Nature and by the weight. Since there are 4 States of Nature, to make them weighted equally, we give each 25% (1/4 = 0.25) of the emphasis.

    Decision 1: $40(0.25) + 27(0.25) + 30(0.25) + 17(0.25) = 28.5$
    Decision 2: $32(0.25) + 30(0.25) + 25(0.25) + 23(0.25) = 27.5$
    Decision 3: $27(0.25) + 30(0.25) + 30(0.25) + 33(0.25) = 30$

Step 2:   Pick the maximum of the expected values.

    Decision 3: $30,000

Analysis: When reviewing the decisions made using each of the criteria, decision 1 is picked two times, and decision 3 is picked two times. Either would be justified, but the decision would probably depend on how risk adverse the manager is when making decisions. If he/she is very optimistic, then the manager would probably choose decision 1.

S2.   Given the following payoff table (profits in $) and that no other information is known, determine the best decision using the following criteria. What is the best decision for the company with the following payoff information and decision criterias: Maximax, Maximin, and Equal likelihood?

Decision	States of Nature (in $100)	
	A	B
1	15	3
2	10	9
3	5	16

Solutions:
1.   Maximax:

Step 1:   Identify the largest possible profit in each decision row.

   Decision 1: $15
   Decision 2: $10
   Decision 3: $16

Step 2:   Pick the maximum of the maximum payoffs (or the maximum possible return of the largest possible for each individual decision). Decision 3 is the maximum of the three at $16, so it is the best alternative to maximize profits.

   Decision 3: $1600

Step 3:   Analysis: This is the most optimistic decision criteria, especially since there are no probabilities for the states of nature.

2.   Maximin:

Step 1:   Identify the smallest possible profit in each decision row.

   Decision 1: $3
   Decision 2: $9
   Decision 3: $5

Step 2:   Pick the maximum of the minimum payoffs (or the maximum possible return of the smallest possible for each individual decision). Decision 3 is the maximum of the three at $9, so it is the best alternative to maximize profits.

   Decision 2: $900

Step 3:   Analysis: This is the most pessimistic decision criteria, especially since there are no probabilities for the states of nature. This criterion assumes the worst state of nature.

3.   Equal Likelihood:

Step 1:   Weight each state as equal and determine the expected value. The expected value is calculated by multiplying the profit under each State of Nature and by the weight. Since there are 4 States of Nature, to make them weighted equally, we give each 25% (1/4 = 0.25) of the emphasis.

   Decision 1: $15(0.5) + 3(0.5) = 9.0$
   Decision 2: $10(0.5) + 9(0.5) = 9.5$
   Decision 3: $5(0.5) + 16(0.5) = 10.5$

Step 2: Pick the maximum of the expected values.

        Decision 3: $10,500

Analysis: When reviewing the decisions made using each of the criteria, decision 2 is picked once, and decision 3 is picked two times. The best alternative is decision 3, but the decision would probably depend on how risk adverse the manager is when making decisions. If he/she is very optimistic, then the manager would probably choose decision 1.

S3.   Given the following payoff table (cost in $) and that no other information is known, determine the best decision using the following criteria. What is the best decision for the company with the following payoff information and decision criterias: Maximax, Maximin, and Equal likelihood?

Decision	States of Nature (in $100)	
	A	B
1	100	80
2	100	100
3	125	90

Solutions:

It is important to remember that these values represent cost, not profit, so they are actually a negative value. This is important because the objective would be to minimize the cost or maximize savings.

1.   Maximax (since these are costs, maximize the smallest cost):

Step 1: Identify the smallest possible cost in each decision row.

        Decision 1: $80
        Decision 2: $100
        Decision 3: $90

Step 2: Pick the maximum of the maximum payoffs (or the smallest possible cost of the smallest possible for each individual decision). Decision 1 is the maximum savings of the three at $80, so it is the best alternative to maximize profits.

        Decision 1: $8000

Step 3: Analysis: This is the most optimistic decision criteria, especially since there are no probabilities for the states of nature.

2.   Maximin:

Step 1: Identify the largest possible cost in each decision row.

        Decision 1: $100
        Decision 2: $100
        Decision 3: $125

Step 2: Pick the maximum of the minimum payoffs (or the smallest possible cost of the largest possible for each individual decision). Decisions 1 and 2 are the smallest of the three at $100, either decision would be acceptable.

        Decisions 1 and 2: $10000

Step 3: Analysis: Upon further analysis, decision 1 would be the best considering that under State of Nature B the cost is lower ($80). This is the most pessimistic decision criterion, especially since there are no probabilities for the states of nature. This criterion assumes the worst state of nature.

3.   Equal Likelihood:

Step 1:   Weight each state as equal and determine the expected value. The expected value is calculated by multiplying the profit under each State of Nature and by the weight. Since there are 4 States of Nature, to make them weighted equally, we give each 25% (1/4 = 0.25) of the emphasis.

          Decision 1:   100(0.5) + 80(0.5) = 90
          Decision 2:   100(0.5) + 100(0.5) = 100
          Decision 3:   125(0.5) + 90(0.5) = 107.5

Step 2:   Pick the maximum of the expected values. Since this is cost, it means pick the largest savings or minimum cost.

          Decision 1: $9,000

Analysis: When reviewing the decisions made using each of the criteria, decision 1 is picked all three times. The best alternative is decision 1.

S4.   Given the following payoff table (profits in $) and the known probabilities for each state of nature, P(state of nature), determine the best decision using the following criteria. What are the expected values for each decision given that P(A) = 0.10, P(B) = 0.40, P(C) = 0.20, and P(D) = 0.30? What is the best decision based on the expected values? What is the expected value of perfect information?

Decision	States of Nature (in $1,000)			
	A	B	C	D
1	40	27	30	17
2	32	30	25	23
3	27	30	30	33

Solutions:

Step 1:   Calculate the expected value of each decision using the probabilities for each decision and the payoffs. The expected value equals the sum of the probabilities multiplied by the payoffs.

          EV (Decision 1) = 40 (.10) + 27 (.40) + 30 (.20) + 17 (.10) = $25.9
          EV (Decision 2) = 32 (.10) + 30 (.40) + 25 (.20) + 23 (.10) = $27.1
          EV (Decision 3) = 27 (.10) + 30 (.40) + 30 (.20) + 33 (.10) = $30.6

Step 2:   Determine the best decision for the expected values without perfect information. Since decision 3 has the highest value ($30.6), it would be the best alternative.

Step 3:   Calculate the expected value of having perfect information. Determine the maximum payoff under each state of nature and multiply the payoff by the probability of the state of nature occurring. The maximum of the payoff for each state of nature is:

	States of Nature (in $1,000)			
	A	B	C	D
Maximum	40	30	30	33
Probability	0.10	0.40	0.20	0.30
	4	12	6	9.9

Step 4:   Calculate the maximum value with perfect information. Sum the values above to get the expected value, which is 31.9.

Step 5:   Determine the value of perfect information. The expected value of perfect information (EVPI) is the value with perfect information (31.9) minus the value without perfect information (30.6). So,

          EVPI = EV with perfect information – EV without perfect information
               = $31.9 – 30.6 = $1.3 or $130

S5. Given the following payoff table (profits in $) and the known probabilities for each state of nature, P(state of nature), determine the best decision using the following criteria. What are the expected values for each decision given that P(A) = 0.10, P(B) = 0.40, P(C) = 0.20, and P(D) = 0.30? What is the best decision based on the expected values? What is the expected value of perfect information?

	States of Nature (in $100)	
Decision	**A**	**B**
1	15	3
2	10	9
3	5	16

Solutions:

Step 1: Calculate the expected value of each decision using the probabilities for each decision and the payoffs. The expected value equals the sum of the probabilities multiplied by the payoffs.

EV (Decision 1) = 15 (.55) + 3 (.45) = $9.6
EV (Decision 2) = 10 (.55) + 9 (.45) = $9.55
EV (Decision 3) = 5 (.55) + 16 (.45) = $9.95

Step 2: Determine the best decision for the expected values without perfect information. Since decision 3 has the highest value ($9.95), it would be the best alternative.

Step 3: Calculate the expected value of having perfect information. Determine the maximum payoff under each state of nature and multiply the payoff by the probability of the state of nature occurring. The maximum of the payoff for each state of nature is:

	States of Nature (in $100)	
	A	**B**
Maximum	15	16
Probability	.55	0.45
	8.25	7.2

Step 4: Calculate the maximum value with perfect information. Sum the values above to get the expected value, which is 15.45.

Step 5: Determine the value of perfect information. The expected value of perfect information (EVPI) is the value with perfect information (15.45) minus the value without perfect information (9.95). So,

EVPI = EV with perfect information − EV without perfect information
= $15.45 − 9.95 = $5.5 or $550

1. A manufacturer has developed a new line of electric toothbrushes for the upcoming Christmas season. The company will need to build a new plant to manufacture the new toothbrushes. Three sizes – small, medium, or large – are under consideration. Preliminary estimates of demand are low, average, or high demand. Some subcontracting is available, so it will be possible to meet some excess demand. The table below gives the estimated profits (in millions) for the various facility size–demand level combinations.

Facility Size	Low Demand	Average Demand	High Demand
Small	750	900	900
Medium	350	1,100	1,300
Large	(250)	600	2,000

a. Determine the best facility size using: Maximax, Minimax, and Equally Likely criteria.
b. The company's initial estimate of probabilities is: P(low) = .5; P(average) = .3; P(high) = .2. Determine the facility size that maximizes expected profits.
c. What is the expected value of perfect information?

2.   A construction company has the opportunity to bid on building a new office building. The manager estimates that the job will cost $500,000. The possible bids the contractor may make and her estimates of the probability of winning the contract at each bid level are:

Bid	Probability of Winning
$530,000	.90
$550,000	.75
$575,000	.50
$600,000	.25
$625,000	0

How much should the manager bid in order to maximize her expected profits?

3.   John has just received an inheritance of $10,000 from his aunt. She has four options for investing the money: stocks, bonds, commodities, or T-bills. The return for each will depend on the performance of the economy over the next year. The table below shows the gain (in $100s) for each investment for each performance level of the economy.

Investment Alternative	Recession	Stagnant	Growth
Stocks	(10)	0	80
Bonds	10	(10)	20
Commodities	(50)	5	50
T-bills	7	7	7

a. Determine the best investment strategy using: Maximax, Minimax, and Equally Likely criteria.
b Her estimate of the economy's performance is: P(recession) = .1; P(stagnant) = .6; P(growth) = .3. Determine the facility size that maximizes expected profits.
c. What is the expected value of perfect information?

4.   Barbara's Bakery bakes fresh muffins and pastries each morning for sale that day. A muffin costs $2 to make and sells for $4. Leftover cakes are sent to the day old bakery store where they are all sold for $1.50. Based upon past experience, the manager expects to sell 6 to 10 packages of muffins per day.

a. Construct a payoff table for the bakery's cake stocking problem.
b. Determine the number of cakes to bake using Maximax, Minimax, and Equally Likely criteria.
c. Based upon historical sales patterns, the estimated probabilities of the different demand levels are: P(6) = .1; P(7) = .2; P(8) = .4; P(9) = .2; P(10) = .1. How many packages should be baked to maximize expected profits?
d. What is the expected value of perfect information?

5.   The Pool Spec Company is going to introduce one of three new pool designs: the King, the Wave, or Fun & Splash. The market conditions (positive, neutral, or negative) will determine the profit or loss the company realizes, as shown in the following payoff table.

Product	MARKET CONDITIONS		
	Positive (0.2)	Neutral (0.7)	Negative (0.1)
King	120,000	70,000	-30,000
Wave	60,000	40,000	20,000
Fun & Splash	35,000	30,000	30,000

a. Compute the expected value for each decision and select the best one.
b. Determine how much the company would be willing to pay to a market research firm to gain better information about future market conditions.
c. Assume that the probabilities cannot be assigned to future market conditions, and determine the best decision using the maximax, maximin, and equal likelihood criteria.

6.   A local company has developed a new line of valves for the utility industry. The company will need to build a new plant to manufacture the new valves. Three sizes – small, medium, or large – are under consideration. Preliminary estimates of demand are low, average, or high demand. Some subcontracting is available, so it will be possible to meet some excess demand. The table below gives the estimated profits (in millions) for the various facility size–demand level combinations.

Facility Size	Low Demand	Average Demand	High Demand
Small	3750	4500	4500
Medium	1750	50,500	6050
Large	(2500)	3000	10,000

   a. Determine the best facility size using: Maximax, Minimax, and Equally Likely criteria.
   b. The company's initial estimate of probabilities is: P(low) = .4; P(average) = .35; P(high) = .25. Determine the facility size that maximizes expected profits.
   c. What is the expected value of perfect information?

7.   An accounting firm has the opportunity to take over three jobs for a local manufacturing company. The manager estimates that the jobs will cost $300,000. The accounting firm has developed a table with the possible bids they may make and the estimates of the probability of winning the contract for all three jobs at each bid level are:

Bid	Probability of Winning
$400,000	.90
$450,000	.75
$500,000	.50
$550,000	.25
$600,000	0

   How much should the manager bid in order to maximize her expected profits?

8.   Ken has just received a check for $10,000 for winning the lottery. He has three options for the money. He can invest the money, buy a house, or play the lottery again. The return for each will depend on the performance of the economy over the next year and Ken's luck. The table below shows the gain (in $100s) for each investment for each performance level of the economy.

Investment Alternative	Recession	Stagnant	Growth
Stock Market	(20)	0	100
Real Estate	10	10	50
Lottery	20	20	20

   a. Determine the best investment strategy using: Maximax, Minimax, and Equally Likely criteria.
   b. Her estimate of the economy's performance is: P(recession) = .2; P(stagnant) = .5; P(growth) = .3. Determine the facility size that maximizes expected profits.
   c. What is the expected value of perfect information?

9.   Barbara's Bakery bakes fresh bread each morning for sale that day. A loaf costs $0.50 to make and sells for $2.50. Leftover loaves are sent to the day old bakery store where they are all sold for $1.00. Based upon past experience, the manager expects to sell 16 to 20 loaves per day.

   a. Construct a payoff table for the bakery's cake stocking problem.
   b. Determine the number of cakes to bake using Maximax, Minimax, and Equally Likely criteria.
   c. Based upon historical sales patterns, the estimated probabilities of the different demand levels are: P(16) = .1; P(17) = .2; P(18) = .4; P(19) = .2; P(20) = .1. How many loaves should be baked to maximize expected profits?
   d. What is the expected value of perfect information?

10.   The Fad Spa is going to introduce one of three spa packages: the Queen, the In & Out, or the Pampered. The demand levels will determine the profit or loss the company realizes, as shown in the following payoff table.

Product	Low Demand	Average Demand	High Demand
Queen	50	45	45
In & Out	75	55	65
Pampered	(50)	30	100

a. Determine the best facility size using: Maximax, Minimax, and Equally Likely criteria.
b. The company's initial estimate of probabilities is: P(low) = .25; P(average) = .45; P(high) = .30. Determine the facility size that maximizes expected profits.
c. What is the expected value of perfect information?

Decision Tree

S1.   Kurt Wayne is interested in interviewing applicants for an open position in his company. From past experience, Kurt has determined that 90% of applicants are considered qualified (or good) and 10% are not qualified (or bad). He has also determined that if the applicant is qualified, he has a 90% chance of being successful. If the applicant is not qualified, then the applicant has only a 20% chance of being successful. What is the probability that a person will be successful if they are really not qualified? What is the probability that a person will not be successful if they are really qualified? What is the probability that the applicant will not be successful?

Solution:

Step 1:   The decision tree follows. It represents the series of sequential decision-making.

Step 2:   Calculate the expected values for each branch of the tree.

Branch 1: Probability (Qualified applicant) x Probability (successful given qualified)
EV = 0.90 x 0.90 or 0.81

Branch 2: Probability (Qualified applicant) x Probability (not successful given qualified)
EV = 0.90 x 0.10 or 0.09

Branch 3: Probability (Not Qualified applicant) x Probability (successful given not qualified)
EV = 0.10 x 0.20 or 0.02

Branch 4: Probability (Not Qualified applicant) x Probability (successful given not qualified)
EV = 0.10 x 0.80 or 0.08

Step 3:   Analysis:

What is the probability that a person will be successful if they are really not qualified?

Follow the branch for not qualified and successful (branch #3). The expected value is 0.02 or 2% will not be qualified and be successful anyway.

What is the probability that a person will not be successful if they are really qualified?

Follow the branch for qualified and not successful (branch #2). The expected value is 0.09 or 9% will be qualified and not successful.

What is the probability that the applicant will not be successful?

For this one, you have two branches to consider, qualified and not successful (branch #2) and not qualified and not successful (branch #4). Follow the branch for both and calculate the expected value as 0.09 or 9% (for branch #2) and 0.08 or 8% (for branch #4). To calculate the probability that the applicant will not be successful, add the individual probabilities for each branch together to get 17%.

P(not successful) = 9% + 8% = 17%

Decision Tree:

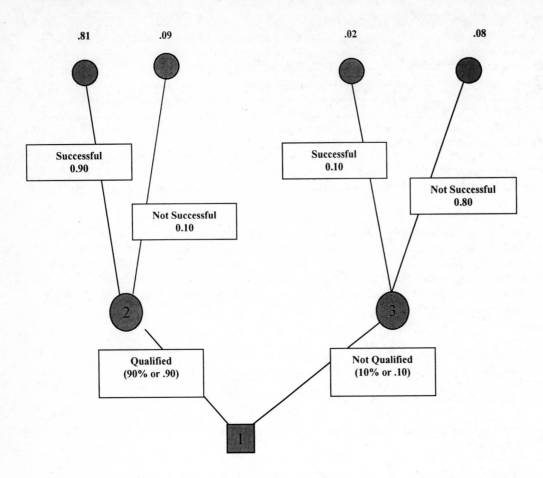

Decision Tree:

S1.   ComTech is bidding for a new state contract. The manager expects that his company has a 40% chance of getting the contract. The bidding process costs $50,000 (a cost that will be lost either way). If ComTech gets the contract, then they have two options (use current equipment and labor or buy new equipment). If they use current resources, then the cost is $40,000 (fixed) plus $20 per unit (variable). The new equipment and labor will cost $260,000 (fixed) plus $10 per unit (variable). The manager does have another concern if they use the current resources and that is what to do if demand changes. If other demand is light (only 10% of the time), the cost is $0 since it can be absorbed. If other demand is normal (only 70% of the time), the cost is $100,000. If other demand is heavy (only 20% of the time), the cost is $200,000. Should the manager go after the state bid?

Solution:

Step 1:   Draw the decision tree. The below table represents the series of sequential decision-making.

Step 2:   Calculate the expected values of the end nodes (6, 7, and 8). The analysis begins by calculating the expected values of nodes 6 and 7 (work backwards through the decision tree).

EV (node 6) = 0.20 ($200,000) = $40,000
EV (node 7) = 0.70 ($100,000) = $70,000
EV (node 8) = 0.10 ($0) = $0

Step 3:   Calculate the expected values for node 4 and node 5.

EV (node 4) = (Cost of production using the old resources)
            + [EV (node 6) + EV (node 7) + EV (node 8)]
          = (40,000 + 20x) + [40,000 + 70,000 + 0]
          = (40,000 + 20(10,000 units of production)) + [40,000 + 70,000 + 0]
          = −$350,000
EV (node 5) = 260,000 +10x = 260,000 + 10(10,000 units of production)
          = −$360,000

Step 4:   Make a decision for the value for node 2.

EV (node 4) = −$350,000
EV (node 5) = −$360,000

Since these are costs, you would want to choose node 4.
            (Use current resources at cost of $350,000.)

Step 5:   Calculate the expected cost of node 1 given the two states of nature.
            (get contract 40% of time and don't get contract 60% of the time)

Revenue from contract production = Revenue in $ x units of production
                                  = $50 x 10,000 units
                                  = $500,000
Cost of getting contract = Cost of bidding + Cost of production
                          = $50,000 + 350,000
                          = $400,000
EV (node 2) = Probability of getting contract
              x (Revenue from contract − Cost of getting contract)
          = .40 x ($500,000 − $400,000)
          = $40,000 in profit
EV (node 3) = Probability of not getting a contract x cost of bidding
          = 0.60 x −$50,000
          = −$30,000 in loss
EV (node 1) = EV (node 2) + EV (node 3)
          = $40,000 − 30,000 = $10,000

Step 6:   Analysis: Based on this decision tree, the manager expects to make $10,000 in profit. The recommendation would be to bid for the contract and produce using the current resources if the contract is received.

Decision Tree:

Expected Values

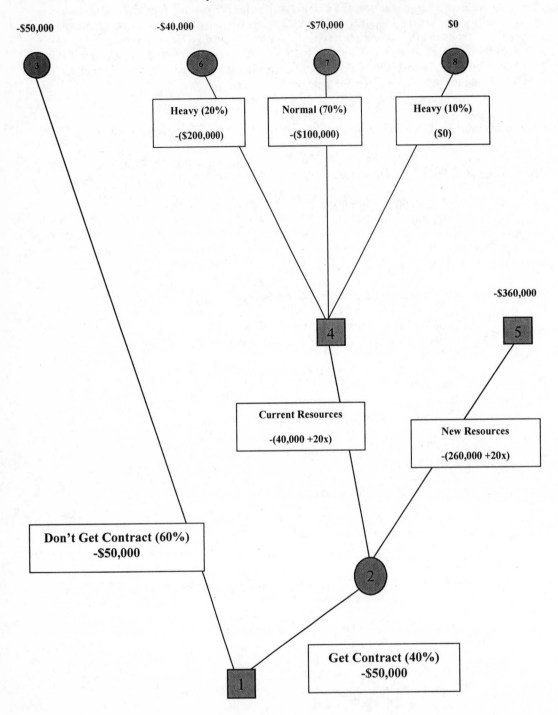

-$50,000

-$40,000

-$70,000

$0

3

6

7

8

Heavy (20%)

-($200,000)

Normal (70%)

-($100,000)

Heavy (10%)

($0)

-$360,000

4

5

Current Resources

-(40,000 +20x)

New Resources

-(260,000 +20x)

2

Don't Get Contract (60%)
-$50,000

Get Contract (40%)
-$50,000

1

1. Lower State University is being sued for damages as a result of injuries incurred during the university's 75th Anniversary celebration. The lawyers suggest taking a low/medium/high offer approach for settling the suits out of court. The city will initially offer $100,000, an amount that the lawyers feel has a 20% chance of being accepted. Alternatively, the city could offer $150,000, which the lawyers feel would have a 50–50 chance of being accepted, or they could offer $200,000, which would definitely be accepted.

   If the initial offer is not accepted, the city would make a second, higher offer of $175,000, which the lawyers feel would have a 50–50 chance of acceptance. If this were rejected, the city would have to offer $225,000 to guarantee acceptance. If the plaintiffs accepted neither offer, the lawyers felt that an offer of $250,000 would definitely be accepted.

   a. Draw a decision tree for this problem.
   b. What strategy should the city follow to minimize expected cost of settlement? That is, what should be the first offer, the second offer?
   c. If the probability of acceptance of the first offer changes to 30%, does this change the city's strategy?
   d. Determine the minimum probability of acceptance of an initial offer of $100,000 that would make the strategy starting with that amount optimal.

2. Kurt Wayne is the president of Factory Sheet Metal Company. Kurt is considering whether or not to build a manufacturing plant in New Orleans to supply the local petroleum plants. His decision is laid out in the following table:

Alternatives	Positive Market	Negative Market
Large Plant	$200,000	-$150,000
Small Plant	$40,000	-$5,000
Do Nothing	$0	$0
Market Probabilities	0.35	0.65

   a. Construct a decision tree.
   b. Determine the best strategy, using expected monetary value (EMV).
   c. What is the expected value of perfect information (EVPI)?

3. Lawn Trimmer Tractors buys batteries from two suppliers. The quality of the batteries from the suppliers is indicated below:

Percent Defective	Probability for Supplier #1	Probability for Supplier #2
1	.70	.30
3	.20	.40
5	.10	.30

   This means that the probability of getting a batch of batteries that are 1% defective from Supplier #1 is .70. This means that every time Lawn Trimmer makes an order of 1,000 batteries, then 10 will be defective. A defective battery can be repaired for $1.50. Although the quality of Supplier #2 is lower, it will sell an order of 1,000 for $37 less than Supplier #1.

   a. Develop a decision tree.
   b. Which supplier should Lawn Trimmer use?

4. Bonnie Hunt, manager of the Lake Arena that will be home to the new professional basketball team, wants to make plans for the gift shop needs for next season. She has developed a table of conditional values for the various alternatives (inventory for memorabilia) and states of nature (size of crowd).

Alternatives	STATES OF NATURE (size of crowd)		
	Large	Average	Small
Large force	$20,000	$10,000	$2,000
Average force	$15,000	$12,000	$6,000
Small force	$9,000	$6,000	$5,000

If the probabilities associated with the states of nature are 0.40 for a large crowd, 0.40 for an average crowd, and 0.20 for a small crowd, determine:

a. The alternative that provides the greatest expected monetary value (EMV).
b. The expected value of the perfect information (EVPI).

5. Shelia Rock is the Technology Manager for a local university. She is trying to determine whether to build a large annex on the Business Center. She has to determine if a large, small, or no annex is needed to meet the needs of the students and faculty. If the size of the university continues to grow, a large wing could return $500,000 in grant money and user fees each year. If the small annex were built, it would return $100,000 to the university each year if the population continues to grow. If the size of the university remains the same, the university would encounter a loss of $85,000 if the large annex were built. Furthermore, a loss of $45,000 would be realized if the small annex was constructed and the size remains the same. Unfortunately, Shelia does not have any information about the future size of the university.

a. Construct a decision tree.
b. Construct a decision table.
c. Using an equal likelihood criteria, determine the best alternative.
d. If the probabilities changed to: Growth = 0.60 and Remaining the Same = 0.40, what decision should Shelia make?

Module B
Linear Programming

I. Linear Programming

A. A mathematical technique designed to help operations managers plan and make decisions relative to the trade-offs necessary to allocate resources.

B. Successful applications of linear programming include:

1. Scheduling school buses to minimize the total distance traveled when carrying students.
2. Allocating police patrol units to high crime areas in order to minimize response time to 911 calls.
3. Scheduling tellers at banks so that needs are met during each hour of the day while minimizing the total cost of labor.
4. Selecting the product mix in a factory to make best use of machine- and labor-hours available while maximizing the firm's profit.
5. Picking blends of raw material in feed mills to produce finished feed combinations at minimum cost.
6. Determining the distribution system that will minimize total shipping cost from several warehouses to various market locations.
7. Developing a production schedule that will satisfy future demands for a firm's product and at the same time minimize total production and inventory costs.
8. Allocating space for a tenant mix in a new shopping mall so as to maximize revenues to the leasing company.

II. Requirements of a Linear Programming Problem

A. LP problems seek to maximize or minimize some quantity (usually profit or cost), which is also called an objective function.

B. The presence of restrictions, or constraints, limits the degree to which we can pursue our objective.

C. There must be alternative courses of action to choose from.

D. The objectives and constraints in linear programming problems must be expressed in terms of linear equations or inequalities.

Lecture Key: *In order to have a linear programming problem, there must be an objective. This could either be to maximize profits or to minimize cost. Linear programming is widely used to help operation managers plan and make the decisions to allocate resources. By doing so, the managers can make effective use of their resources.*

III. Formulating Linear Programming Problems

A. Product Mix problem is the most common linear programming.

1. Shader Electronics Example:

   a. The first step is the name the variables.

   x_1 = number of walkmans to be produced
   x_2 = number of watch TV's to be produced

   b. Now the LP objective functions can be created in terms of x and x':

   Maximize profits = $7x_1 + 5x_2$

c. The next step is to develop the mathematical relationships to describe the two constraints:

First constraint: electronic time used is $\leq$ electronic time available
$$4x_1 + 3x_2 \leq 240$$
Second constraint: assembly time used is < assembly time available
$$2x_1 + 1x_2 \leq 100$$

Lecture Key: *A company usually produces two or more products using limited resources. The company wants to know how many units of each product it should produce to maximize profits given its limited resources. The more units of one product being produced, the less it can produce of the other product. Having the constraints formula makes it easier to know the maximum amount of a product to produce.*

IV. **Graphical Solution to a Linear Programming Problem**

A. Graphical Representation of Constraints
   1. This approach can only be used when there are two decision variables.
   2. The first step in graphing the constraints is to convert them into equalities.

Constraint A: $4x_1 + 3x_2 = 240$

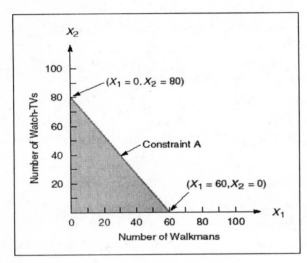

Constraint B: $2x_1 + 1x_2 = 100$

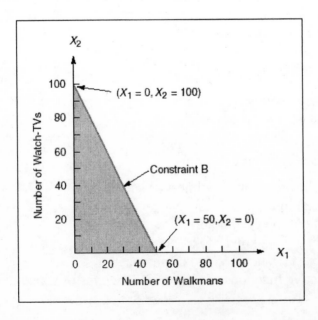

3. When putting the two constraints together, the feasible solution is the region where all the conditions are satisfied.

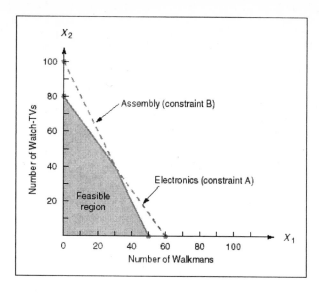

B. Iso-Profit Solution Method
   1. After the feasible region has been established, the iso-profit is the fastest way to solve for the optimal solution.
   2. In order to find the optimal solution, you can start by letting profits equal some small dollar amount.
      $$\$210 = 7x_1 + 5x_2$$
   3. The farther you move away from the origin, the higher your profit will be.

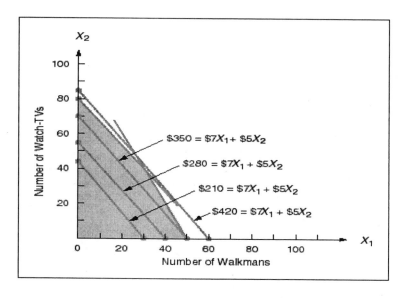

   4. The highest profit line that still touches the feasible region will pinpoint the optimal solution.

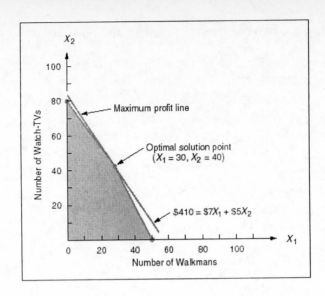

C. Corner-Point Solution Method
1. This second approach to solving LP problems is simpler than the iso-profit line approach.
2. The theory is that the maximum profit can be found at one of the corner points of the feasible region.

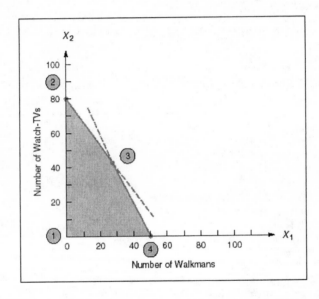

Lecture Key: *In order to find the best solution to a linear programming problem, the company must first plot the constraints on a graph to find the feasible region. The feasible region is the area that satisfies all constraints.*

V.   Sensitivity Analysis

A. Sensitivity analysis is an analysis that projects how much a solution might change if there were changes in the variables or input data.
1. There are two approaches to determine how sensitive an optimal solution is to change: the trial and error approach and the analytic postoptimality.
2. Trial and error usually requires a computer to resolve the entire problem.
3. The second approach is to determine a range of changes in problem parameters that will not affect the optimal solution or change the variable in the solution.

B. Sensitivity Report consists of two parts, the adjustable cells and the constraints.
1. What-if questions are answered through the sensitivity report.
2. The key assumption is that only a single input data value is changed.

C. Changes in the Resources or Right-Hand Side Values
1. The right-hand side values of the constraint represent the resources available to the firm.
2. If the size of the feasible region increases, the optimal objective function value could improve.
3. The shadow price for a constraint is the improvement in the objective function value that results from a one-unit increase in the right-hand side of the constraint.
4. The shadow price is valid as long as the change in the right-hand side is within the allowable increase and decrease values.

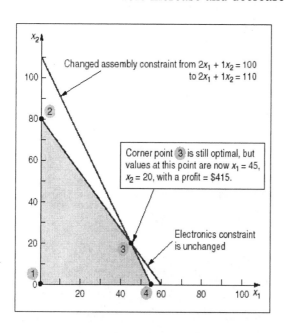

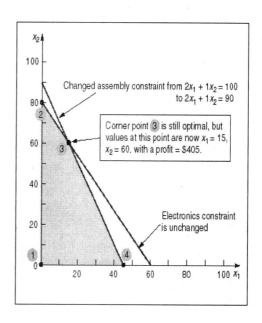

D. Changes in the Objective Function Coefficient
1. When the unit profit contribution changes, the slope of the iso-profit lines changes.
2. The location of the corner points remains the same.
3. The current optimal solutions remain optimal only with the allowable increase or decrease of the function coefficient.
4. A new corner point becomes an optimal if the objective function coefficient is decreased or increased too much.

Lecture Key: *Companies are interested in knowing more than the best solution. They also want to know what will happen if the parameters (numerical values in a problem) change. A sensitivity analysis tells a company how much a solution might change if there were changes in the variables or input data.*

VI. Solving Minimization Problems

A. Iso-cost is another approach to solving linear programming problems graphically.
B. This approach is similar to the iso-profit approach, but here it is to find the values that yield the minimal cost.
C. Minimizing problems are often unbounded outward.
D. The optimal solution is found at the point yielding the lowest total cost.

Example: Solving Minimization Problems

Cohen Chemicals, Inc., produces two types of photo-developing fluids. The first, a black-and-white picture chemical, costs Cohen $2,500 per ton to produce. The second, a color photo chemical, costs $3,000 per ton.

Based on an analysis of current inventory levels and outstanding orders, Cohen's production manager has specified that at least 30 tons of the black-and-white chemical and at least 20 tons of the color chemical must be produced during the next month. In addition, the manager notes that an existing inventory of a highly perishable raw material needed in both chemicals must be used within 30 days. In order to avoid wasting the expensive raw material, Cohen must produce a total of at least 60 tons of the photo chemicals in the next month.

We may formulate this information as a minimization LP problem. Let:
x_1 = number of tons of black-and-white picture chemical produced
x_2 = number of tons of color picture chemical produced

Subject to:
$$x_1 \geq 30 \text{ tons of black-and-white chemical}$$
$$x_2 \geq 20 \text{ tons of color chemical}$$
$$x_1 + x_2 \geq 60 \text{ tons total}$$
$$x_1, x_2 \geq \$0 \text{ nonnegativity requirements}$$

To solve the Cohen Chemicals problem graphically, we construct the problem's feasible region, shown in Figure B.9.

FIGURE B.9 ■

Cohen Chemicals'
Feasible Region

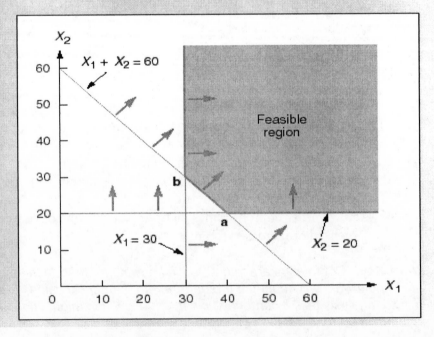

408

Solution:

Minimization problems are often unbounded outward (that is, on the right side and on the top), but this characteristic causes no problem in solving them. As long as they are bounded inward (on the left side and the bottom), we can establish corner points. The optimal solution will lie at one of the corners.

In this case, there are only two corner points, a and b, in the figure. It is easy to determine that at point a, $x_1 = 40$ and $x_2 = 20$, and that at point b, $x_1 = 30$ and $x_2 = 30$. The optimal solution is found at the point yielding the lowest total cost. Thus,

$$\text{Total cost at a} = 2,500x_1 + 3,000x_2 = 2,500(40) + 3,000(20) = \$160,000$$
$$\text{Total cost at b} = 2,500x_1 + 3,000x_2 = 2,500(30) + 3,000(30) = \$165,000$$

The lowest cost to Cohen Chemicals is at point a. Hence the operations manager should produce 40 tons of the black-and-white chemical and 20 tons of the color chemical.

Lecture Key: *Many linear programming problems involve minimizing a cost. By using this approach, the firms will be able to know how much of certain products to produce. Companies can use this method in all areas where they see fit in order to minimize shipping cost, labor cost, supply cost, etc.*

VII. Linear Programming Applications

A. Production-Mix Example: *see pg. 669 of text*
   Since the firm faces limited resources, the objective is to manufacture the selected products in such quantities that will maximize total profits.
B. Diet problem example: *see pg. 670 of text*
   1. This was originally used in hospital to figure out what the economical diet was for patients.
   2. This involves specifying a food or food ingredient combination that will satisfy stated nutritional requirements at a minimum cost level.
C. Production scheduling example: *see pg. 671 of text*
   1. One of the most important areas of linear programming application is production scheduling example.
   2. Solving production scheduling problems allows the production manager to set an efficient, low-cost production schedule for a product over several production periods.
   3. The objective is to either maximize profits or minimize the total cost.
D. Labor Scheduling Example: *see pg. 672 of text*
   1. Labor scheduling problems address staffing needs over a specific time period.
   2. They are useful when managers have some flexibility in assigning workers to jobs that require overlapping or interchangeable talents.

VIII. The Simplex Method of LP

A. Most real world linear programming problems have more than two variables and thus are too complex for a graphical solution.
B. Simplex method is actually an algorithm with which we examine corner points in a methodical fashion until arriving at the best solution – highest profit or lowest cost.

Lecture Key: *Due to the complexity of the problems, managers have to use certain software such as POM for Windows or Excel. The approach produces economic information such as the shadow price, or dual, and also provides sensitivity analysis on other inputs to the problem.*

MODULE B PROBLEMS

Linear Programming

1.   Discount Fabric is producing three types of patterns. The first print is very intricate, the second is moderate, and third is very simple. The 1ˢᵗ print requires 3 yards of material, the 2ⁿᵈ requires 2 yards of material, and the 3ʳᵈ requires 1 yard. The first design takes 12 hours per yard to complete, the second takes 8 hours per yard to complete, and the third takes 4 hours per yard to complete. The demand for the 1ˢᵗ is only 200 yards per month, the 2ⁿᵈ has a demand of 550 yards per month, and the 3ʳᵈ has a demand of 700 yards per month. Discount Fabric has a total of 5000 yards of material and 10,000 hours per month. Discount Fabric makes profits of $4.00 for the 1ˢᵗ design, $2.50 for the 2ⁿᵈ design, and $2.00 for the 3ʳᵈ. The manufacturer wants to know how many yards of each type of design to produce to maximize profit.

       a. Formulate a linear programming model for this problem.
       b. Solve this model using the graphical method.
       c. Solve this model using a computer.

Solve the following linear programming problems using the graphical method.

2.   Maximize $Z = x + 10y$
          Subject to: $4x + 2y \leq 40$
                  $3x + 4y \leq 36$
                      $y \geq 3$
                     $x, y \geq 0$

3.   Maximize $Z = 3x + 5y$
          Subject to: $4x + 4y \leq 48$
                  $1x + 2y \leq 20$
                      $y \geq 2$
                     $x, y \geq 0$

4.   Minimize $Z = 2x + 3y$
          Subject to: $8x + 5y \geq 200$
                $6x + 15y \geq 240$
              $12x + 4y \geq 180$
                      $y \geq 10$
                     $x, y \geq 0$

5.   Minimize $Z = 2x + 5y$
          Subject to: $2x + 4y \geq 20$
                  $6x + 2y \geq 18$
                  $2x + y \geq 12$
                     $x, y \geq 0$

Solve the following linear programming problems using a computer solution.

6.   Maximize $Z = 60x + 100y$
          Subject to: $20x + 20y \leq 240$
                 $5x + 10y \leq 100$
                      $y \geq 10$
                     $x, y \geq 0$

7.   Maximize $Z = 15x + 30y$
          Subject to: $16x + 18y \leq 58$
               $15x + 16y \leq 51$
                      $y \geq 15$
                     $x, y \geq 0$

8.   Minimize $Z = 80x + 120y$
                      Subject to: $80x + 50y \geq 2000$
                                $60x + 150y \geq 2400$
                    $120x + 40y \geq 1800$
                                      $y \geq 100$
                                  $x, y \geq 0$

9.   Minimize $Z = 15x + 25y$
                      Subject to: $12x + 40y \geq 200$
                              $16x + 20y \geq 180$
                              $20x + 10y \geq 120$
                                  $x, y \geq 0$

10.   Gator Spies packages and distributes Creole seasoning from south Louisiana. A normal shipment can be packaged in an AB crate, an LM crate, or a YZ crate. The following tables represent profit and shipping requirements. The manager must decide the optimal number of each type of crates to pack each week. He is bound by the resource limitations, but also decides that he must keep his six full-time packers employed all 240 hours (6 workers x 40 hours) each week.

Crate	Profit	RESOURCES NEEDED PER SHIPMENT	
		Shipping Material	Preparation Time
AB	5	4	2
LM	10	6	2
YZ	15	10	4
Total resources available/wk.		120 lbs.	240 hours

11.   Lawn Trimmer has 4 plants and 3 distribution warehouses. The table below represents the shipping costs between each factory and warehouse, the plant capacity, and the warehouse storage capacity. Using a computer linear programming solution, determine the optimal shipping routes and total cost.

From Plant:	To Warehouse:			
	Omaha	Sacramento	Atlanta	Production Capability
1	3	5	6	60
2	10	15	5	100
3	10	10	20	80
Capacity	70	120	50	

12.   Dairy Mart produces 4 types of milk products. The manager wants to determine how many containers of each product to produce this week to maximize profits using a computer linear programming method. The Dairy Mart has equal ingredients of the additives. Each product is produced in a one-gallon size. On hand there are 100 gallons of skim milk, 200 gallons of vitamin A/D milk, 400 gallons of 1% and 2% milk each. The manager wants the Vitamin Milk to be used no more than 30 percent of total production. Also, he wants the ratio of the number of gallons of 1% gallons to the number of 2% gallons to be at least 6 to 5. The following table will represent cost and the retail prices for each product.

Product	Cost	Retail Price
Skim Milk	$1.00	$3.00
Vitamin Milk	$1.50	$4.00
1% Milk	$.75	$2.75
2% Milk	$.75	$2.50

Module C
Transportation Models

I.   Transportation Modeling

   A. Transportation modeling finds the least-cost means of shipping supplies from several origins to several destinations.
   1. Origin points are factories, warehouses, car rental agencies, or any other points from which goods are shipped.
   2. Destinations are any points that receive goods.
   B. To be able to use the transportation model we need to know the following:
   1. The origin points and the capacity or supply per period at each.
   2. Destination points and demand per period at each.
   3. Cost of shipping one unit from each origin to each destination.
   C. The transportation model is actually a class of linear programming models to solve transportation problems.
   D. The first step in the modeling process is to set up a transportation matrix, which summarizes all relevant data and keeps track of algorithm computations.

Lecture Key: Although there is software, which can solve transportation problems, it is important to understand the background of the transportation model. Transportation modeling factors in supplies and demands associated with each origin and each destination and the cost of shipping to determine a way for manufacturers to deal with multiple factories being used to disperse their goods in the most cost effective way. It is very important for companies with distribution centers and outlets scattered throughout a territory.

II.   Developing an Initial Solution

   A. The Northwest-Corner Rule
   1. A procedure in the transportation model where one begins at the upper left-hand cell of a table (the northwest corner) and systematically allocates units to shipping routes. It is done as follows:
      a. Exhaust the supply (factory capacity of each row) before moving down to the next row.
      b. Exhaust the (warehouse) requirements of each column before moving to the next column on the right.
      c. Check to ensure that all supplies and demands are met.
   2. This method is easy to use, but totally ignores costs.

In the table below, we use the northwest-corner rule to find an initial feasible solution to the Arizona Plumbing problem. To make our initial shipping assignments, we need five steps:

1. Assign 100 tubs from Des Moines to Albuquerque (exhausting Des Moines's supply).
2. Assign 200 tubs from Evansville to Albuquerque (exhausting Albuquerque's demand).
3. Assign 100 tubs from Evansville to Boston (exhausting Evansville's supply).
4. Assign 100 tubs from Fort Lauderdale to Boston (exhausting Boston's demand).
5. Assign 200 tubs from Fort Lauderdale to Cleveland (exhausting Cleveland's demand and Fort Lauderdale's supply).

The total cost of this shipping assignment is $4,200.

FROM: \ TO:	(A) Albuquerque	(B) Boston	(C) Cleveland	Factory Capacity
(D) Des Moines	$5 / 100	$4	$3	100
(E) Evansville	$8 / 100	$4 / 100	$3	300
(F) Fort Lauderdale	$9 / 200	$7 / 100	$5 / 200	300
Warehouse requirement	300	200	200	700

Solution:

Computed Shipping Cost				
Route				
From	To	Tubs Shipped	Cost per Unit	Total Cost
D	A	100	$5	$500
E	A	200	8	1,600
E	B	100	4	400
F	B	100	7	700
F	C	200	5	$1,000
			Total:	$4,200

The solution given is feasible because it satisfies all demand and supply constraints.

B. The Intuitive Lowest-Cost Method
  1. A cost-based approach to finding an initial solution to a transportation problem based on the lowest cost. It uses the following steps:
    a. Identify the cell with the lowest cost. Break any ties for the lowest cost arbitrarily.
    b. Allocate as many units as possible to that cell without exceeding the supply or demand. Then cross out that row or column (or both) that is exhausted by this assignment.
    c. Find the cell with the lowest cost from the remaining (not crossed out) cells.
    d. Repeat steps 2 and 3 until all units have been allocated.

2. Although the likelihood of a minimum cost solution does improve with the intuitive method, this does not happen in all cases. These two approaches are only meant to provide us with a starting point and you may have to use an additional procedure to reach an optimal solution.

Example: Intuitive Lowest-Cost Method

When we use the intuitive approach on the data in the table below (rather than the northwest-corner rule) for our starting position, we obtain the solution seen in the following table.

The total cost of this approach is = $3(100) + $3(100) + $4(200) + $9(300) = $4,100
$\qquad\qquad\qquad\qquad\qquad$ (D to C)$\quad$ (E to C)$\quad$ (E to B)$\quad$ (F to A)

FROM: \ TO:	(A) Albuquerque	(B) Boston	(C) Cleveland	Factory Capacity
(D) Des Moines	$5	$4	$3	100
(E) Evansville	$8	$4	$3	300
(F) Fort Lauderdale	$9	$7	$5 200	300
Warehouse requirement	300	200	200	700

Solution:

FROM: \ TO:	(A) Albuquerque	(B) Boston	(C) Cleveland	Factory Capacity
(D) Des Moines	$5	$4	$3 100	100
(E) Evansville	$8	$4 200	$3 100	300
(F) Fort Lauderdale	$9 300	$7	$5 200	300
Warehouse requirement	300	200	200	700

Steps:

1. Cross out top row (D) after entering 100 units in $3 cell because row D is satisfied.

2. Cross out column C after entering 100 units in this $3 cell because column C is satisfied.

3. Cross out row E and column B after entering 200 units in this $4 cell because a total of 300 units satisfies row E.

4. Enter 300 units in the only remaining cell to complete the allocations.

Lecture Key: *The intuitive lowest-cost method and northwest-corner rule are important for providing us with a close estimate that is most useful as a starting point for employing additional procedures to reach an optimal solution.*

III. The Stepping Stone Method

A. This method helps move from an initial feasible solution to an optimal solution.

B. Stepping Stone Method is used to evaluate the cost effectiveness of shipping goods via transportation routes not currently in the solution.

C. Once this method is complete, we must then test to see if the solution is optimal or whether we can make any further improvements to help solve the problem.

D. Example on pg. 692 in the text.

Lecture Key: *Remember, the stepping stone method is used when evaluating the cost effectiveness of shipping goods through transportation route not currently being used in the solution. It also helps us move to an optimal solution in the transportation method.*

IV. Special Issues in Modeling

A. Demand Not Equal to Supply

1. Dummy sources can be used to solve these unbalanced problems, which are artificial shipping source points created in the transportation method when total demand is greater than total supply in order to effect a supply equal to the excess of demand over supply.

2. Dummy destinations are used if total supply is greater than total demand, and make demand exactly equal to the surplus by creating a dummy destination.

Example

Let's assume that Arizona Plumbing increases the production in its Des Moines factory to 250 bathtubs, thereby increasing supply over demand. To reformulate this unbalanced problem, we refer back to the data presented in the first example and present the new matrix in the table below. First, we use the northwest-corner rule to find the initial feasible solution. Then, once the problem is balanced, we can proceed to the solution in the normal way.

Solution:

Total cost $= 250(\$5) + 50(\$8) + 200(\$4) + 50(\$3) + 150(\$5) + 150(0) = \$3,350$

FROM: \ TO:	(A) Albuquerque	(B) Boston	(C) Cleveland	Dummy	Factory Capacity
(D) Des Moines	$5 250	$4	$3		250
(E) Evansville	$8 50	$4 200	$3 50		300
(F) Fort Lauderdale	$9	$7	$5 150	150	300
Warehouse requirement	300	200	200	150	850

B. Degeneracy

1. The number of occupied squares in any solution (initial or later) must be equal to the number of rows in the table plus the number of columns minus 1; solutions that do not satisfy this rule are called degenerate.

2. Degeneracy occurs when too few squares or shipping routes are being used; as a result, it becomes impossible to trace a closed path for one or more unused squares.

Martin Shipping Company has three warehouses from which it supplies its three major retail customers in San Jose. Martin's shipping costs, warehouse supplies, and customer demands are presented in the transportation table below. To make the initial shipping assignments in that table, we apply the northwest-corner rule.

The initial solution is degenerated because it violates the rule that the number of used squares must equal the number of rows plus the number of columns minus 1. To correct the problem, we may place a zero in the unused square that permits evaluation of all empty cells. Some experimenting may be needed because not every cell will allow tracing a closed path for the remaining cells. Also, we want to avoid placing the 0 in a cell that has the negative sign in a closed path. No reallocation will be possible if we do this.

For this example, we try the empty square that represents the shipping route from Warehouse 2 to Customer 1. Now we can close all stepping stone paths and compute improvement indices.

FROM: \ TO:	Customer 1	Customer 2	Customer 3	Warehouse Supply
Warehouse 1	$8	$2	$6	
	100			100
Warehouse 2	$10	$9	$9	
	0	100	20	120
Warehouse 3	$7	$10	$7	
		100	80	80
Customer Demand	100	100	100	300

Transportation Method

S1.   Ball bearing plants are located in three cities and can produce the following amounts.

Location	Weekly Production (Bins)
A. Alexandria	150
B. Savannah	320
C. Raleigh	210
	680

These plants supply regional motor plants located in four cities and have the following demand:

Location	Weekly Demand (Bins)
1. Birmingham	240
2. Nashville	130
3. Albany	70
4. Greenville	180
	620

Shipping Costs per bin of bearings are as follows:

From:	To:			
	1	2	3	4
A	14	9	16	18
B	11	8	7	16
C	16	12	10	22

What are the optimal shipments for these transportation routes?

Solution:

Shipper	Destination				Supply	Shipped
	1	2	3	4		
A	0	112	0	38	150	150
B	178	0	0	142	320	320
C	62	18	70	0	210	150
Demand	240	130	70	180	680	
Bins Shipped	240	130	70	180		
Cost	$7830					

What happens if the route from Alexandria to Nashville is unavailable? *Set the cost of that route to a high number so that the route won't be used.*

Shipper	Local Warehouses				Supply	Shipped	Excess Supply
	1	2	3	4			
A	0	0	0	150	150	150	150
B	240	50	0	30	320	320	320
C	0	80	70	0	210	150	150
Demand	240	130	70	180	680		
Bins Shipped	240	130	70	180			
Cost	$7880						

S2.   Ceiling fan plants are located in three cities and can produce the following amounts.

Location	Monthly Production (crates)
A. Waco	150
B. Little Rock	320
C. San Angelo	210
	680

These plants supply regional warehouses located in four cities and have the following demand:

Location	Monthly Demand (crates)
1. Montgomery	240
2. Decatur	130
3. Albuquerque	130
4. Rapid City	180
	680

Shipping Costs per crates of bearings are as follows:

From:	To:			
	1	2	3	4
A	140	90	160	180
B	110	80	70	160
C	160	120	100	220

What are the optimal shipments for these transportation routes?

Solution:

Sources	Destinations				Supply	Shipped	Excess Supply
	1	2	3	4			
A	0	50	0	100	150	150	0
B	240	0	0	80	320	320	0
C	0	80	130	0	210	210	0
Demand	240	130	130	180	680		
Bins Shipped	240	130	130	180			
Cost	84300						

1.   Fruit Orchards are located in three cities and can produce the following amounts.

Location	Monthly Production (bushels)
A. Port Charlotte	1500
B. Jacksonville	2100
C. Fresno	3800
	6800

These plants supply regional rail warehouses located in four cities that ship throughout the country. Each has a different demand level as follows:

Location	Monthly Demand (crates)
1. Waycross	1600
2. Pensacola	1000
3. Huntsville	1200
4. Bakersfield	3000
	6800

Shipping Costs per crates of bearings are as follows:

	To:			
From:	1	2	3	4
A	25	20	90	120
B	10	30	70	80
C	600	200	105	20

What are the optimal shipments for these transportation routes?

2.   Christmas Tree Farms are located in three cities and can produce the following amounts.

Location	Yearly Production (trees in 1,000s)
A. Bend	100
B. Salem	200
C. Spokane	250
	550

These farms supply regional nurseries located in four cities and have the following demand:

Location	Yearly Demand (trees in 1,000s)
1. San Jose	100
2. Billings	75
3. Flagstaff	70
4. Salt Lake	280
	620

Shipping Costs per shipment of bearings are as follows:

	To:			
From:	1	2	3	4
A	140	140	160	110
B	110	150	170	120
C	190	90	260	225

What are the optimal shipments for these transportation routes?

3.   Drilling platforms are located in three sites in gulf and can produce the following amounts of crude oil.

Location	Weekly Production (Barrels)
A	8000
B	32000
C	19000
	59000

These platforms supply refineries located in four cities and have the following demand:

Location	Weekly Demand (Barrels)
1	6000
2	12000
3	26000
4	11000
	55000

Shipping Costs per barrel are as follows:

	To:			
From:	1	2	3	4
A	4	1	6	8
B	1	2	3	6
C	6	2	4	2

What are the optimal shipments for these transportation routes?

4.   If Refinery #1 increases production, their demand will increase to 10,000 barrels. How does this change your optimal levels?

5.   If the bridge that connects platform B to Refinery 2 is destroyed in a hurricane, how does this change your decision?

6.   A group of small engine plants are located in four cities and can produce the following amounts.

Location	Weekly Production
A. Lansing	350
B. Sioux Falls	150
C. Raleigh	100
D. Lubbock	250
	850

These plants supply lawn mower production plants located in five cities and have the following demand:

Location	Weekly Demand
1. Detroit	250
2. Ashville	70
3. Springfield	150
4. Prescott	175
5. Memphis	205
	850

Shipping Costs per shipment are as follows:

From:	To:				
	1	2	3	4	5
A	2	6	5	25	6
B	7	15	4	9	8
C	20	1	6	28	5
D	24	22	8	4	7

What are the optimal shipments for these transportation routes?

7. The plant located in Ashville is rumored to be closing. How would that loss of demand affect how you shipped your small engines?

8. A new interstate will be completed within the month that would connect Prescott and Sioux Falls. This would reduce the shipping cost between these two locations to $2 per engine. Does this change your decisions in problem 6?

9. A new production facility is being considered in Louisville. This site would take over Ashville's production plus take 50 of the units normally produced in Memphis. The only two routes that can supply this facility are Sioux Falls ($4 /engine) and Raleigh ($3/engine). How would this new information change your answer?

10. A clothing manufacturer has six plants with locations in three cities (2 per city) and can produce the following amounts.

Location	Weekly Production (Boxes)
A-1	10
A-2	5
B-1	25
B-2	8
C-1	12
C-2	28
	88

The manufacturer wants to minimize the cost associated with shipping to its largest outlets. The outlets have the following demand:

Location	Weekly Demand (Boxes)
1. Portland	15
2. Tucson	8
3. Biloxi	20
4. Jacksonville	18
5. Minneapolis	27
	88

Shipping Costs per box are as follows:

From:	To:				
	1	2	3	4	5
A-1	5	10	3	4	7
A-2	6	11	3	6	8
B-1	4	15	4	7	11
B-2	5	16	4	8	13
C-1	9	6	5	12	3
C-2	8	5	5	10	2

What are the optimal shipments for these transportation routes?

Module D
Waiting-Line Models

I. **Characteristics of a Waiting-Line System**

A. Arrivals or inputs to the system. Characteristics such as:
   1. Population size
   2. Behavior
   3. Statistical distribution
B. Queue discipline, or the waiting line itself. Characteristics include:
   1. Whether it is limited or unlimited in length.
   2. Discipline of people or items in it.
C. The service facility. Its characteristics include its design and the statistical distribution of service times.

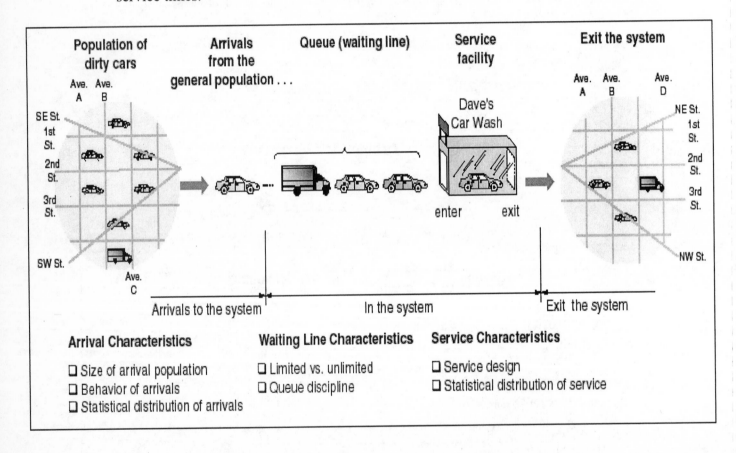

D. Arrival characteristics
   1. Size of the arrival population
      a. Unlimited/Infinite
         i. The number of customers or arrivals on hand at any given moment is just a small portion of all potential arrivals.
         ii. Example: Students arriving to register for classes at a large university.
      b. Limited/Finite
         i. A limited number of potential users of this service.
         ii. Example: Population is found in a copying shop that has eight copy machines; each copier is a potential "customer" that might break down and require service.
   2. Pattern of arrivals at the queuing system
      a. Schedule
         i. Customers arrive at a service facility at a specific time.
         ii. Example: One patient is scheduled every fifteen minutes.
      b. Random
         i. Customers are independent of one another and their occurrence cannot be predicted exactly.
         ii. Follows the Poisson Distribution and uses the formula below.
         iii. Example: Customers per hour can arrive at any time.

$$P(x) = \frac{e^{-\lambda}\lambda^x}{x!}$$

Where: $P(x)$ = probability of x arrivals
       x = number of arrivals per unit of time
       λ = average arrival rate
       e = 2.7183 (which is the base of the natural log)

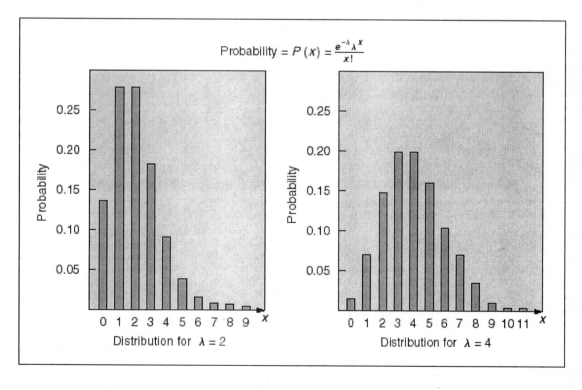

423

3. Behavior of arrivals
    a. Balk – example such as: Customer refuses to join the waiting line because it is too long to suit their needs or interests.
    b. Reneging – example such as: Customers who become impatient and leave without completing their transactions.

Lecture Key: *The input source that generates arrivals for customers for a service system contains these three characteristics: size, pattern, and behavior. It is important to understand the arrival characteristics so that you can fulfill the wants and needs of your customers in order to have a successful business.*

E. Waiting-line characteristics
    1. Length of the line
        a. Limited
            i. Cannot, either by law or because of physical restrictions, increase to an infinite length.
            ii. Ex: A small barber shop will have only a limited number of waiting chairs.
        b. Unlimited
            i. Size is unrestricted.
            ii. Example: Toll booth serving arriving automobiles.
    2. Queue discipline
        a. FIFO (First In, First Out)
        b. The rule by which the customers in the line are to receive service.
        c. Example: In a supermarket, the first in line are the first checked out.

Lecture Key: *The waiting-line itself is the second component of the queuing system. Successful operations are contingent upon customer satisfaction, loyalty, and patience. Because most customers have strong feelings about waiting in lines, which can have an effect on their satisfaction, managers must be aware of the waiting-line characteristics.*

F. Service characteristics
    1. Design of the service system
        a. Single-channel queuing system
            i. A service system with one line and one server.
            ii. Example: Drive-in bank with only one open teller.
        b. Multiple-channel queuing system
            i. A service system with one waiting line, but with several servers.
            ii. Example: A bank with several tellers on duty, and each customer waiting in one common line for the first available teller.
        c. Single-phase system
            i. A system in which the customer receives service from only one station, and then exits the system.
            ii. Example: A fast-food restaurant in which the person takes your order also brings your food and takes your money.
        d. Multiphase system
            i. A system in which the customer receives services from several stations before exiting the system.
            ii. Example: The restaurant requires you to place the order at one station, pay at a second, and pick up your food at a third.

2. Distribution of service time
   a. Constant
      i. It takes the same amount of time to take care of each customer.
      ii. Example: A machine performing a service such as an automatic car wash.
   b. Random
      i. Negative exponential probability distribution.
      ii. A continuous probability often used to describe the service time in a queuing system.
      iii. Example: When an average service time is 20 minutes, it is unlikely a customer will require more than 90 minutes in the service facility.

Lecture Key: *The third part of any queuing system is the service characteristics. Design of the service system and the distribution of service time are the two basic properties. A manager must determine which one of these systems is best suited for the company's business operations.*

G. Measuring the queue's performance
   1. Queuing models – Help managers make decisions that balance service costs with waiting-line costs.
   2. Queuing analysis – Can obtain many measures of waiting-line system's performance including:
      a. Average time that each customer or object spends in the queue.
      b. Average queue length.
      c. Average time that each customer spends in the system (waiting time plus service time).
      d. Average number of customers in the system.
      e. Probability that the service facility will be idle.
      f. Utilization factor for the system.
      g. Probability of a specific number of customers in the system.

Lecture Key: *To measure the performance, use the average time each customer spends in the queue, queue length, time that each customer spends in the system, and number of customers in the system. Also use the probability that the service facility will be idle, utilization factor for the system, and the probability of a specific number of customers in the system.*

II. **Queuing Costs – Trade-off between waiting costs and service costs**
   A. Method of evaluating a service facility
      Total expected costs = $\sum$(expected service costs plus expected waiting costs)
   B. Service costs:
      1. Costs increase as level of service increases. Example: In grocery stores, managers and stock clerks can open extra checkout counters.
      2. Waiting time decreases as level of service improves.
         a. The costs of long waiting lines may be intolerably high.
         b. Example: Emergency ambulance service.

Lecture Key: *Different organizations clearly place different values on their customers' time. For instance, the Department of Motor Vehicles places minimal costs on waiting time, which makes customers often wait hours for service. This again can greatly affect customer satisfaction and loyalty.*

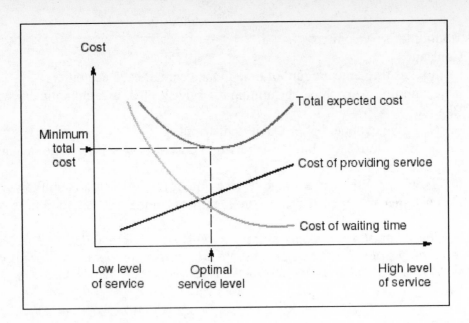

III. The Variety of Queuing Models

A. Three common characteristics for all four queuing models:
1. Poisson distribution arrivals
2. FIFO discipline
3. A single service phase
B. Four most widely used models
C. Model A: Single-Channel Queuing Model with Poisson Arrivals
1. Exponential Service Times
2. Arrivals form a single line to be serviced by a single station.
    Example: Information counter at a department store.

Equations for M/M/1 Model:

λ = mean number of arrivals per time period

μ = mean number of people or items served per time period

L_s = average number of units (customers) in the system (waiting and being served)
  = $\lambda / (\mu - \lambda)$

W_s = average time a unit spends in the system (waiting time plus service time)
  = $1 / (\mu - \lambda)$

L_q = average number of units waiting in the queue
  = $\lambda^2 / \mu (\mu - \lambda)$

W_q = average time a unit spends waiting in the queue
  = $\lambda / \mu (\mu - \lambda)$

ρ = utilization factor for the system
  = λ / μ

P_0 = probability of 0 units in the system (that is, the service unit is idle)
  = $1 - (\lambda / \mu)$

$P_{n>k}$ = probability of more than k units in the system, where n is the number of units in the system
  = $(\lambda / \mu)^{k+1}$

Example

Tom Jones, the mechanic at Golden Muffler Shop, is able to install new mufflers at an average rate of 3 per hour (or about 1 every 20 minutes), according to a negative exponential distribution. Customers seeking this service arrive at the shop on the average of 2 per hour, following distribution. They are served on a first-in, first-out basis and come from a very large (almost infinite) population of possible buyers.

Solution:

From this description, we are able to obtain the operating characteristics of Golden Muffler's queuing system: $\lambda = 2$ cars arriving per hour $\mu = 3$ cars serviced per hour

L_s $= \lambda / (\mu - \lambda) = 2 / (3 - 2) = 2$ cars in the system on avg.

W_s $= 1 / (\mu - \lambda) = 1 / (3 - 2) = 1$-hr. average waiting time in the system

L_q $= \lambda^2 / \mu (\mu - \lambda) = $ $2^2 / 3(3 - 2) = 1.33$ cars waiting in line on average

W_q $= \lambda / \mu (\mu - \lambda) = 2 / 3(3 - 2) = 40$-minute avg. waiting time per car

ρ $= \lambda / \mu = 2 / 3 = 66.6\%$ of time mechanic is busy

P_0 $= 1 - (\lambda / \mu) = 1 - (2 / 3) = .33$ probability there are 0 cars in the system

Probability of More Than k Cars in the System	
k	$P_{n>k} = (\lambda / \mu)^{k+1} = (2 / 3)^{k+1}$
0	.667 (This is equal to $1 - P_0 = 1 - .33 = .667$.)
1	.44
2	.296
3	.198 (Implies that there is a 19.8% chance that more than 3 cars are in system.)
4	.132
5	.088
6	.058
7	.039

Example

The owner of the Golden Muffler Shop estimates that the cost of customer waiting time, in terms of customer dissatisfaction and lost goodwill, is $10 per hour of time spent waiting in line. Because the average car has a 2/3-hour wait (W_q) and because there are approximately 16 cars serviced per day (2 arrivals per hour times 8 working hours per day), the total number of hours that customers spend waiting each day for mufflers to be installed is:

$(2 / 3)(16) =$ 10.66 hour

Solution:

Hence, in this case,

Customer waiting-time cost   = $10 (10.66 hr.) = $107 per day

The only other major cost that Golden's owner can identify in the queuing situation is the salary of Jones, the mechanic, who earns $7 per hour, or $56 per day. Thus:

Total expected costs   = $107 + $56   = $163 per day

D. Model B: Multiple-Channel Queuing Model
   1. Two or more servers or channels are available to handle arriving customers.
   2. Example: Airline ticket counter.

Equations for M/M/S Model:

M = # of channels open λ = avg. arrival rate μ = avg. service rate at each channel

P_0 = probability of 0 customers in the system

$$= \frac{1}{\sum [(1/n!)(\lambda / \mu)^n] + [(1/M!)(\lambda / \mu)^M (M\mu / (M\mu - \lambda))]}$$

L_s = average number of people or units in the system

$$= \left(\frac{\lambda\mu \ (\lambda / \mu)^M}{(M-1)! \ (M\mu - \lambda)^2} \right) P_0 \ + \ \frac{\lambda}{\mu}$$

W_s = average time a unit spends in the system (waiting time plus service time)
   = L_s / λ

L_q = average number of units waiting in the queue
   = $L_s - (\lambda / \mu)$

W_q = average time a unit spends waiting in the queue
   = L_q / λ

The Golden Muffler Shop has decided to open a second garage bay and hire a second mechanic to handle installations. Customers, who arrive at the rate of about $\lambda = 2$ per hour, will wait in a single line until 1 of the 2 mechanics is free. Each mechanic installs mufflers at the rate of about $\mu = 3$ per hour.

To find out how this system compares to the old single-channel waiting-line system, we will compute several operating characteristics for the M = 2 channel system and compare the results with those found in first example:

Solution:

$\lambda = 2$ customers per hour
$\mu = 3$ mufflers per hour
M = 2 mechanics

Using the multiple-server model formulas, we can compute the following operating characteristics for the service department:

$$P_0 = \frac{1}{[\Sigma[(1/n!)\,(\lambda/\mu)^n\,]] \;+\; [1/M!(\lambda/\mu)^M\,(\,M\mu\,/\,M\mu - \lambda)]}$$

$$= \frac{1}{1 + (2/3) + (1/2)(4/9)\,[6/(6-2)]} = 0.5 \text{ probability that no cars in the system}$$

Then,

$L_s = .75$ average number of cars in the system

$W_s = L_s / \lambda = (3/4) / 2 = 22.5$ minutes average time a car spends in the system

$L_q = L_s - (\lambda / \mu) = (3/4) - (2/3) = .083$ average number of cars in the queue

$W_q = L_q / \lambda = .083 / 2 = 0.0415$ hours or 2.5 minutes average time a car spends in queue

We can summarize the characteristics of this 2-channel model and compare them to those of the single-channel model as follows:

	Single Channel	Two Channels
P_o	.33	.5
L_s	2 cars	.75 cars
W_s	60 minutes	22.5 minutes
L_q	1.33 cars	.083 cars
W_q	40 minutes	2.5 minutes

The increased service has a dramatic effect on almost all characteristics. In particular, time spent waiting in line drops from 40 minutes to only 2.5 minutes.

E. Model C: Constant Service Time Model
  1. Customers or equipment are processed according to a fixed cycle.
  2. Example: Amusement park ride.

Equations for M/D/1 Model:

L_q = average number of units waiting in the queue

$\quad = \lambda^2 / 2\mu(\mu - \lambda)$

W_q = average time a unit spends waiting in the queue

$\quad = \lambda / 2\mu(\mu - \lambda)$

L_s = average number of people or units in the system

$\quad = L_q + (\lambda / \mu)$

W_s = average time a unit spends in the system (waiting time plus service time)

$\quad = W_q + (1 + \mu)$

Example

Garcia-Golding Recycling, Inc., collects and compacts aluminum cans and glass bottles in New York City. Its truck drivers currently wait an average of 15 minutes before emptying their loads for recycling. The cost of driver and truck time while they are in queues is valued at $60 per hour. A new automated compactor can be purchased to process truckloads at a constant rate of 12 trucks per hour (that is, 5 minutes per truck). Trucks arrive according to a Poisson distribution at an average rate of 8 per hour. If the new compactor is put in use, the cost will be amortized at a rate of $3 per truck unloaded. The firm hires a summer college intern, who conducts the following analysis to evaluate the costs versus benefits of the purchase:

Solution:
Current waiting cost / trip = (1/4 hr. waiting now)($60/hr. cost) = $15 / trip

New system: λ = 8 trucks/hr. arriving $\quad \mu$ = 12 trucks / hr. served

Average waiting time in queue = $\lambda / 2\mu(\mu - \lambda)$ = 8 / 2(12)(12 − 8) = 1 / 12 hr.

Waiting cost / trip with new compactor = (1 / 12 hr. wait)($60 / hr. cost) = $5 / trip

Savings with new equipment = $15(current system) − $5(new system) = $10 / trip

Cost of new equipment amortized: = $3 / trip

Net savings: = $7 / trip

F. Model D: Limited Population Model
   1. Limited population of potential customers for a service facility.
   2. Example: A hospital ward that has 20 beds.

Equations for Limited Population Model:

Service factor: $X = T / (T + U)$

Average number waiting: $L = N(1 - F)$

Average waiting time: $W = T(1 - F) / XF$

Average number running: $J = NF(1 - X)$

Average number being serviced: $H = FNX$

Number of population: $N = J + L + H$

Where:

D = prob. that a unit will have to wait in queue

F = efficiency factor

H = average number of units being served

J = avg. number of units not in queue or in service bay

L = avg. number of units waiting for service

U = avg. time between unit service requirements

N = number of potential customers

T = avg. service time

W = avg. time a unit waits in line

M = number of service channels

X = service factor

Example

Past records indicate that each of the 5 laser computer printers at the U.S. Department of Energy in Washington, D.C., needs repair after about 20 hours of use. Breakdowns have been determined to be Poisson-distributed. The one technician on duty can service a printer in an average of 2 hours, following an exponential distribution. Printer downtime costs $120 per hour. Technicians are paid $25 per hour. Should the DOE hire a second technician?

Assuming the second technician can repair a printer in an average of 2 hours, we can use Table D.7 on pg. 721 of the text (because there are $N = 5$ machines in this limited population) to compare the costs of 1 versus 2 technicians.

Solution:
1. First, we note that $T = 2$ hours and $U = 20$ hours.
2. Then, $X = T / (T + U) = 2 / (2 + 20) = .091$ (close to .090).
3. For $M = 1$ server, $D = .350$ and $F = .960$.
4. For $M = 2$ server, $D = .044$ and $F = .998$.
5. The average number of printers working is $J = NF(1 - U)$.
   For $M = 1$, this is $J = (5)(.960)(1 - .091) = 4.36$.
   For $M = 2$, this is $J = (5)(.998)(1 - .091) = 4.54$.
6. The cost analysis follows:

# of Technicians	Avg. # Printers Down (N – J)	Avg. Cost /Hr. for Downtime (N – J)($120/hr.)	Cost/Hr. for Technicians (at $25/hr.)	Total Cost / Hr.
1	.64	$76.80	$25.00	$101.80
2	.46	$55.20	$50.00	$105.20

This analysis suggests that having only one technician on duty will save a few dollars per hour ($105.20 − $101.80 = $3.40).

Lecture Key: Although all four models have those three characteristics listed in common, they all describe service systems that operate under steady, ongoing conditions, and they differ in the number of channels, service time pattern, and population size. Visit a bank or a drive-through restaurant and see what kind of distribution they might reflect.

IV. Other Queuing Approaches

A. Variation of the four mathematical models often are present in an analysis.
B. Normal probability distribution instead of the exponential.
   Example: Service times in an automobile repair shop.
C. First-come, first-served model with a preemptive priority queue discipline.
   Example: Using a college registration system in which seniors have first choice of classes and hours over other students.

MODULE D PROBLEMS

Single Server Model

S1.   Ships arrive at the Customs dock (one dock) at an average rate of one every 2 hours (interarrival times are exponentially distributed) and the mean service rate is 1 customer per hour (exponentially distributed). If all ships coming into the port must go through Customs before continuing to their port, then the other ships form a waiting line. What are the operating characteristics (such as the probability of no customers in the system, the average number of customers in the queuing system, etc.) for this waiting line system?

Solution:

Step 1:   Analysis: Identify this as a single server model since there is one dock and one waiting line.

Step 2:   Identify the mean arrival rate. The problem reads 1 every 2 hours, or $\lambda = 0.5$. Putting the arrival rate in fraction form and simplifying, determine the arrival rate.

$\lambda = 1$ customer / 2 hours = 0.5 customers per hour

Step 3:   Identify the mean service rate. The problem reads 1 customer per hour, or $\mu = 1$. Putting the arrival rate in fraction form and simplifying, determine the arrival rate.

$\mu = 1$ customer / hour = 1 customers per hour

Step 4:   Determine the operating characteristics.

Probability of no customers in the system:
$$P_o = [1 - (\lambda / \mu)]$$
$$= [1 - (0.5 / 1)] = 0.50 \text{ probability of no customers in system}$$

Number of customers in the queuing system:
$$L = \lambda / (\mu - \lambda)$$
$$= 0.5 / (1 - 0.5) = 1 \text{ customer on the average in the queuing system}$$

Number of customers on average in the waiting line:
$$L_q = \lambda^2 / [\mu (\mu - \lambda)]$$
$$= (0.5)^2 / [1(1 - 0.5)] = 0.005 \text{ customers on the average in the waiting line}$$

Average time in the system (waiting line and being serviced):
$$W = 1 / (\mu - \lambda) \text{ or } W = L / \lambda$$
$$= 1 / (1 - 0.5) = 2 \text{ hours average time in the system per customer}$$

Average time in the waiting line per customer:
$$W_q = \lambda / [\mu (\mu - \lambda)]$$
$$= 0.5 / [1 (1 - 0.5)] = 1 \text{ hour average time in the waiting line per customer}$$

Probability the server (dock) will be busy and the customer (ship) must wait:
$$\rho = \lambda / \mu$$
$$= 0.5 / 1 = 0.50 \text{ probability that the server will be busy and the customer must wait}$$

Probability that the server will be idle and customer can be served immediately:
$$I = 1 - \rho$$
$$= 1 - .50 = 0.50 \text{ probability that the server will be idle and customer is served}$$

S2.   Students arrive at the University counselor (one counselor) at an average rate of 64 during a typical 8-hour day during registration (assuming a Poisson distribution) and the mean service rate is 10 students per hour (exponentially distributed). If all students that want to register must see the counselor before continuing with registration, then the other students form a waiting line. What are the operating characteristics (such as the probability of no customers in the system, the average number of customers in the queuing system, etc.) for this waiting line system?

Solution:

Step 1:   Analysis: This is a single server model since there is one counselor and one waiting line.

Step 2:   Identify the mean arrival rate. The problem reads 64 students during 8-hour period, or $\lambda = 8$. Putting the arrival rate in fraction form and simplifying, determine the arrival rate.

$$\lambda = 64 \text{ customer} / 8 \text{ hours} = 8 \text{ customers per hour}$$

Step 3:   Identify the mean service rate. The problem reads 10 customers per hour, or $\mu = 10$. Putting the arrival rate in fraction form and simplifying, determine the arrival rate.

$$\mu = 10 \text{ customers} / \text{hour} = 10 \text{ customers per hour}$$

Step 4:   Determine the operating characteristics.

Probability of no customers in the system:
$$P_o = [1 - (\lambda / \mu)]$$
$$= [1 - (8 / 10)] = 0.20 \text{ probability of no students in system}$$

Number of customers in the queuing system:
$$L = \lambda / (\mu - \lambda)$$
$$= 8 / (10 - 8) = 4 \text{ students on the average in the queuing system}$$

Number of customers on average in the waiting line:
$$L_q = \lambda^2 / [\mu (\mu - \lambda)]$$
$$= (8)^2 / [10 (10 - 8)] = 3.2 \text{ students on the average in the waiting line}$$

Average time in the system (waiting line and being serviced):
$$W = 1 / (\mu - \lambda) \text{ or } W = L / \lambda$$
$$= 1 / (10 - 8) = 0.5 \text{ hour average time in the system per student}$$

Average time in the waiting line per customer:
$$W_q = \lambda / [\mu (\mu - \lambda)]$$
$$= 8 / [10(10 - 8)] = 0.4 \text{ hour average time in the waiting line per student}$$

Probability the counselor will be busy and the customer (student) must wait:
$$\rho = \lambda / \mu$$
$$= 8 / 10 = 0.80 \text{ probability that the server will be busy and the student must wait}$$

Probability that the counselor will be idle and student can be served immediately:
$$P_o = 1 - \rho$$
$$= 1 - .80 = 0.20 \text{ probability that the server will be idle and customer is served}$$

1. A secretary at a local engineering firm has to type 20 letters a day on the average (assume a Poisson distribution). It takes her approximately 20 minutes to type each letter (assume an exponential distribution). Assuming the secretary works eight hours a day:

    a. What is the secretary's utilization rate?
    b. What is the average waiting time before the secretary types a letter?
    c. What is the average number of letters waiting to be typed?
    d. What is the probability that the secretary has more than five letters to type?

2. Ben is a physical therapist working in an office by himself. Ben can work with a person every 10 minutes. It is estimated that the people will arrive independently and randomly throughout the day at a rate of one dog every twenty minutes according to a Poisson distribution. Also assume that Ben's service times are exponentially distributed. Determine the:

    a. Probability that Ben is idle.
    b. Proportion of the time that Ben is busy.
    c. Average number of people being serviced and waiting to be serviced.
    d. Average number of people waiting to be serviced.
    e. Average time a person waits before service.
    f. Average amount (mean) of time a person spends between waiting in line and getting serviced.

3. The Milk Shake Express has a drive-up window that can service customers. If customers arrive every minute and it takes a minute to service them (exponentially distributed), then what percentage of customers will have to wait to receive service? On average, how long is the line and how long will a customer spend at the drive-up window?

4. The handyman is a contracted repairman for the local appliance manufacturer. The average job requires an average of two hours per call. The jobs arrive at a mean rate of 3.5 per 8-hour day (Poisson distribution). What are the operating characteristics?

5. Lower State University has been approached about building a new basketball court for the students' residential halls. Based on interest, an average of 11 groups per 15-hour day will want to use the facility. The residents proposed a 1.5-hour playing limit. It is expected that groups would use their entire 1.5 hours. Determine the percentage of court utilization, the average number of groups waiting to use the court, and the average length of time a group will have to wait.

6. Tire World has a single mechanic available to work on customer's cars. Rotating the tires of a car takes on average 45 minutes and a standard deviation of 30 minutes. If customers arrive at a rate of one per hour, then determine the percentage of time the mechanic is busy, the average number of cars waiting for service, and the average time a car spends at the service station.

7. The On The Corner Deli has one counter server who takes the order, fills the orders, and checks people out. The customers who line up at the counter to pay for their selections form the waiting line. Customers arrive at a rate of 45 per hour according to a Poisson distribution ($\lambda=45$), and service times are exponentially distributed, with a mean rate of 55 customers per hour ($\mu = 55$). The deli manager wants to determine the operating characteristics for this waiting line system. Evaluate alternatives such as: 1. an additional server to help the counter server (increase the service rate to 65 per hour at a cost of $6 per hour), and 2. adding an additional counter with cash register and server (increase in service rate to 85 per hour at a cost of $100 per hour). The deli is open for 8 hours per day. The average customer spends $5 and the loss of business is estimated at $20 per hour.

Waiting Line Cost Analysis

S1.   Ships arrive at the Customs dock (one dock) at an average rate of one every 2 hours (interarrival times are exponentially distributed) and the mean service rate is 1 customer per hour (exponentially distributed). If all ships coming into the port must go through Customs before continuing to their port, then the other ships form a waiting line. For safety reasons, the port has concern about ships waiting in line at the beginning of the port. The port manager wants to know the effect of adding another customs port. Using the operating characteristics (such as the probability of no customers in the system, the average number of customers in the queuing system, etc.), help the manager evaluate the proposal for the waiting line system.

The manager estimates that the additional dock will cost the port $1500 per week. With the port's risk manager helping, the manager has determined that for each 10-minute period that the ship's waiting time is reduced, the port avoids an insurance premium of $800 per week.

If the new dock is put in place, ships can be served in less time – the service rate, the number of customers served per time period, will increase. The service rate with one dock is $\mu = 1$ ship served per hour. The service rate with two docks will be $\mu = 1.2$ ships served per hour. We assume the arrival rate will remain the same ($\lambda = 0.5$ per hour), since the increased service rate will not increase arrivals but will minimize the premiums that have to be paid.

Solution:

Step 1:   Analysis: Identify this as a single server model since there is one dock and one waiting line.

Step 2:   Identify the mean arrival rate. $\lambda = 1$ customer / 2 hours = 0.5 customers per hour

Step 3:   Identify the mean service rates. With 1 dock, it is 1 ship per hour, or $\mu = 1$. With 2 docks, it is 1.2 ships per hour, or $\mu = 1$.

Step 4:   Determine the operating characteristics of both systems.

1 Dock (with $\lambda = 0.5$ and $\mu = 1.0$):

Probability of no customers in the system:
$$P_o = [1 - (\lambda / \mu)] = [1 - (0.5 / 1)] = 0.50 \text{ probability of no customers in system}$$

Number of customers in the queuing system:
$$L = \lambda / (\mu - \lambda) = 0.5 / (1 - 0.5) = 1 \text{ customer on the average in the queuing system}$$

Number of customers on average in the waiting line:
$$L_q = \lambda^2 / [\mu (\mu - \lambda)] = (0.5)^2 / [1(1 - 0.5)] = 0.005 \text{ customers on the average in the waiting line}$$

Average time in the system (waiting line and being serviced):
$$W = 1 / (\mu - \lambda) \text{ or } W = L / \lambda = 1 / (1 - 0.5) = 2 \text{ hours average time in the system per customer}$$

Average time in the waiting line per customer:
$$W_q = \lambda / [\mu (\mu - \lambda)] = 0.5 / [1 (1 - 0.5)] = 1 \text{ hour average time in the waiting line per customer}$$

Probability the server (dock) will be busy and the customer (ship) must wait:
$$\rho = \lambda / \mu = 0.5 / 1 = 0.50 \text{ probability that the server will be busy and the customer must wait}$$

Probability that the server will be idle and customer can be served immediately:
$$P_o = 1 - \rho = 1 - .50 = 0.50 \text{ probability that the server will be idle and customer is served}$$

2 Docks (with $\lambda = 0.5$ and $\mu = 1.2$):

Probability of no customers in the system:
$Po = [1 - (\lambda / \mu)] = [1 - (0.5 / 1.2)] = 0.5833$ probability of no ships in system

Number of customers in the queuing system:
$L = \lambda / (\mu - \lambda) = 0.5 / (1.2 - 0.5) = 0.714$ ships on the average in the queuing system

Number of customers on average in the waiting line:
$L_q = \lambda^2 / [\mu (\mu - \lambda)] = (0.5)^2 / [1.2(1.2 - 0.5)] = 0.297$ ships on the average in the waiting line

Average time in the system (waiting line and being serviced):
$W = 1 / (\mu - \lambda)$ or $W = L / \lambda = 1 / (1.2 - 0.5) = 1.43$ hours average time in the system per ship

Average time in the waiting line per customer:
$W_q = \lambda / [\mu (\mu - \lambda)] = 0.5 / [1.2 (1.2 - 0.5)] = 0.60$ hours average time in the waiting line per ship

Probability the server (dock) will be busy and the customer (ship) must wait:
$\rho = \lambda / \mu = 0.5 / 1.2 = 0.416$ probability that the dock will be busy and the ship must wait

Probability that the server will be idle and customer can be served immediately:
$Po = 1 - \rho = 1 - .416 = 0.583$ probability that the dock will be idle and ship is served

Step 5: Calculate the savings for the decrease in waiting times. The average waiting time per ship has been reduced from 2 hours to 1.43 hours. The savings (that is, the decrease in premiums) is computed as:

2 hours – 1.43 hours = 0.57 hours (or 34.2 minutes)

34.2 minutes / 10 minute periods = 3.42

3.42 ten minute periods x $800/week = $2736 per week

Step 6: Calculate the total savings to the system. Taking the total savings from the additional dock minus any cost incurred computes the total savings. The extra dock costs the port $1500 per week, the total savings will be:

$2736 – 1500 = $1236 per week

Step 7: Analysis: This would make good sense to add the additional dock at a savings of $1236 per week. If the port is in operation 52 weeks a year, it would mean a savings of $64,272. Other considerations would be things such as: does the port have an additional space for the dock and any initial improvements that may have to be made to get the space operational?

1. At Super Discount Mart, the arrival rate of 30 customers per hour means that, on the average, a customer arrives about every 2.0 minutes (i.e., 1/30 x 60 minutes). This indicates the store is busy. The manager believes that it is unacceptable for a customer to wait 8 minutes and spend a total of 10 minutes in the queuing system (not including the actual shopping time). The manager wants to test several alternatives for reducing customer-waiting time: 1.) another employee to pack up the purchases; and 2.) another checkout counter. The additional employee will cost the market $200 per week. Also, the manager believes that he can avoid $100 in lost sales for every minute that he is able to reduce the waiting time. The following table represents the service times.

Number of employees	Service rate
1	30 per hour
2	40 per hour

Another checkout counter would cost $6,000, plus an extra $200 per week for an additional cashier. The arrival time would be adjusted to 15 customers per hour, but the service time would remain constant at 30 customers per hour. Which alternative is best?

2.   The dollar store has a single checkout line. The cashier can check a customer out in 5 minutes (exponentially distributed), and the customers arrive at the cashier every 7 minutes. The manager is worried that if the customers have to wait too long, then they may stop buying from the store. He has estimated that customers waiting cost him $18 per hour in lost sales. The manager is thinking of hiring a bagger to help the cashier. The bagger will make $5 per hour. The bagger will speed the checkout time for the cashier by 1.5 minutes. Should the bagger be hired?

3.   The manager of DL Hunt Department Store is analyzing the need for loading docks. The manager has determined that each truck can be expressed as a cost of $500 per day and that each dock with crew costs $1,300 per day. How many docks would be optimal if trucks arrive at the rate of five per day and each dock can service 6 trucks per day (both rates are Poisson distribution)? A second alternative to increasing dock space is to improve the equipment being used to unload the trucks. The new equipment would speed up the loading rate to 7 trucks per day. The equipment would cost $125 per day for each dock. Should the manager use the new equipment for the docks?

Single Server Model with Constant Service Time

S1.   The Juice Bar is an automatic vending machine that can distribute a variety of different types of juices into an 8 oz cup. The bar can accommodate one customer at a time, and it requires a constant time of 1.75 minutes to fill a customer's cup. Customers arrive at the bar at an average rate of 25 per hour (Poisson distributed). The owner wants to determine the average length of the waiting line and the average waiting time at the bar to see if additional machines should be added around the building.

Solution:

Step 1:   Identify this model as a single server (1 bar) with a constant service time (1.75 min. to fill cup).

Step 2:   Determine arrival rate, λ. The problem reads that 25 customers arrive per hour, so:

$\lambda = 25$ customers per hour

Step 3:   Determine arrival rate, μ. The problem reads that the service time is constant at 1.75 minutes, so:

$\mu = 60$ minutes in an hour / 1.75 minutes to service = 34.3 customers per hour

Step 4:   Determine the average length of the waiting line, L_q. Given the above arrival rates and service times, use the formula below to compute the length.

$L_q = \lambda^2 / [2\mu (\mu - \lambda)] = 25^2 / [2(34.3) (34.3 - 25)] = 0.98$ customers waiting

Step 5:   Determine the average length of the waiting line, W_q. Given the above arrival rates and service times, use the formula below compute the length.

$W_q = L_q / \lambda = 0.98 / 25 = 0.0392$ hour (x 60 minutes in hour = 2.352 minutes) waiting in line

Step 6:   Analysis: Since the goal of these types of operations is quick and convenient service, the owner should look at adding additional machines to avoid the loss of customers.

1.   Bayou Mart has operated a car wash behind the market for 20 years. Recently, they converted a terminal to an automatic car wash. The car wash can accommodate one car at a time, and it requires a constant time of 3.0 minutes for a wash. Cars arrive at the car wash at an average rate of 12 per hour (Poisson distributed). The manager wants to determine the average length of the waiting line and the average waiting time at the car wash.

2.   Customers arrive at an automated spring water machine at a rate of four per minute, following a Poisson distribution. The coffee machine dispenses a cup of coffee at a constant rate of 10 seconds.

   a. What is the average number of customers waiting in line?
   b. What is the average number in the system?
   c. How long does the average person wait in line before receiving service?

3.   A vending machine for hot chocolate is located in the lobby of the university dorm. The machine has a constant service time of 25 seconds. On average, 80 customers per hour want hot chocolate. What is the average number of customers waiting in line? What is the average time that customers spend in the system? What is the average number in the system?

4.   Customers of the local Savings & Loan use the automatic bank machine to conduct transactions. The customers use the machine for after hour banking and convenience. Each customer transaction takes an average of 2 minutes to complete, and the customers arrive at the machine one every 3 minutes. (Assume the distributions are exponential.) What is the average time that customers spend at the machine either waiting or making a transaction? What is the probability that a customer will not have to wait upon arriving at the banking machine?

Single-Server Model with Finite Queue

S1.   Spiral Manufacturing produces wire-binding material. The company uses one process engineer to make adjustments to their 5 machines. The setups usually take an average of 15 minutes per machine (exponentially distributed). The machines operate for an average of 60 minutes (exponentially distributed) before any adjustments are needed. If more than 2 machines need adjusting, Spiral will outsource to another department to avoid large down time (this means 1 being fixed and 1 waiting). While operating, each machine can turn out 60 pieces per hour. Determine the operating characteristics of the system.

   Slick's Quick Lube is a one-bay service facility next to a busy highway. The facility has space for only one vehicle in service and three vehicles lined up to wait for service. There is no space for cars to line up on the busy adjacent highway, so if the waiting line is full (3 cars), prospective customers must drive on.

   The mean time between arrivals for customers seeking lube service is 3 minutes. The mean time required to perform the lube operation is 2 minutes. Both the interarrival times and service times are exponentially distributed. The maximum number of vehicles in the system is four. Determine the average waiting time, the average queue length, and the probability that a customer will have to drive on.

Solution:

Step 1:   Identify the model type. This is a single server waiting line since it is assumed that one engineer is needed per machine. Also, there is one queue for each machine, but only 5 (finite queue) machines, waiting for the engineers.

Step 2:   Identify and compute the average arrival time λ and service time μ. The arrival and service times are given exponentially as $(1/\lambda)$ and $(1/\mu)$. This has to be converted to number of customers arriving per hour. So, divide the minutes per hour (60 minutes) by the time between arriving machines (60 minutes). This gives you 60 / 60, or 1 machines per hour.

   $\lambda = 1$ machine per hour

Step 3: Compute the average service time, μ. The service time is given exponentially as $(1/\mu)$. This has to be converted to number of machines serviced per hour. So, divide the minutes per hour (60 minutes) by the average service time per machine (15 minutes). This gives you

60 / 15, or 4 machines per hour

μ = 4 machines per hour

The number of machines possible in queue is: M = 2 machines

Step 4: Compute the probability that the system is full and the machine must be outsourced, P_M. However, this first requires the determination of P_O, as follows:

$$P_O = [1 - (\lambda / \mu)] / [1 - (\lambda / \mu)^{M+1}]$$
$$= [1 - (1 / 4)] / [1 - (1 / 4)^3] = 0.76 \text{ probability of no machines}$$

Calculate the system being full using the formula:

$$P_M = P_O (\lambda / \mu)^n = (0.76)(1/4)^3$$
$$= 0.0118 \text{ probability that 2 machines need adjusting and another engineer is outsourced}$$

Step 5: Compute the average number in the system, L. The average number of machines in the system must be computed as follows:

$$L = \left[\frac{(\lambda / \mu)}{1 - (\lambda / \mu)} \right] - \left[\frac{(M+1)(\lambda / \mu)^{M+1}}{1 - (\lambda / \mu)^{M+1}} \right]$$

$$= \left[\frac{(1 / 4)}{1 - (1 / 4)} \right] - \left[\frac{(2+1)*(1/4)^3}{1 - (1/4)^3} \right] = 0.29 \text{ machines in the system}$$

Step 6: Compute the average queue length, L. The average number of machines in the queue must be computed as follows:

$$L_q = L - [(\lambda(1 - P_M)) / \mu]$$
$$= 0.29 - [(1*(1 - 0.0118))/4] = 0.043 \text{ machines waiting}$$

Step 7: Compute the average time in the system, W.

$$W = L / (\lambda(1 - P_M))$$
$$= 0.29 / (1*(1 - 0.0118)) = 0.293 \text{ hours (17.60 min.) in the system}$$

Step 8: Compute the average waiting time, W_q.

$$W_q = W - (1 / \mu)$$
$$= 0.293 - (1 / 4) = 0.043 \text{ hours (2.58 min.) waiting in line}$$

S1.   Quick Cuts is a one-chair barbershop with limited waiting space. The shop has space for only two chairs waiting for service. If the waiting line is full (2 chairs), prospective customers will leave. The mean time between arrivals for customers seeking lube service is 18 minutes. The mean time required to perform the hair cut is 12 minutes. Both the interarrival times and service times are exponentially distributed. The maximum number of customers in the system is three. Determine the average waiting time, the average queue length, and the probability that a customer will have to leave.

Solution:

Step 1:   Identify the model type. This is a single server waiting line since it is one barber with one queue for the barber. There are only 2 (finite queue) chairs waiting for the barber.

Step 2:   Identify and compute the average arrival time λ and service time μ. The arrival and service time are given exponentially as $(1/\lambda)$ and $(1/\mu)$. This has to be converted to number of customers arriving per hour. So, divide the minutes per hour (60 minutes) by the time between arriving customers (18 minutes). This gives you 60 / 18, or 3.34 customers per hour.

λ = 3.34 customers per hour

Step 3:   Compute the average service time, μ. The service time is given exponentially as $(1/\mu)$. This has to be converted to number of customers serviced per hour. So, divide the minutes per hour (60 minutes) by the average service time per customer (15 minutes). This gives you

60 / 12, or 5 customers per hour

μ = 5 customers per hour

The number of customers possible in queue is: M = 2

Step 4:   Compute the probability that the system is full and the customers must be leave, P_M. However, this first requires the determination of P_O, as follows:

$$Po = [1 - (\lambda / \mu)] / [1 - (\lambda / \mu)^{M+1}]$$
$$= [1 - (3.34 / 5)] / [1 - (3.34 / 5)^3] = 0.4729 \text{ probability of no machines}$$

Calculate the system being full using the formula:

$$P_M = Po (\lambda / \mu)^n = (0.4729) * (3.34/5)^3$$
$$= 0.141 \text{ probability that 3 chairs (1 barber chair + 2 waiting chairs) are full}$$

Step 5:   Compute the average number in the system, L. The average number of customers in the system must be computed as follows:

$$L = \left[\frac{(\lambda / \mu)}{1 - (\lambda / \mu)} \right] - \left[\frac{(M+1)(\lambda / \mu)^{M+1}}{1 - (\lambda / \mu)^{M+1}} \right]$$

$$= \left[\frac{(3.34 / 5)}{1 - (3.34 / 5)} \right] - \left[\frac{(2+1) * (3.34 / 5)^3}{1 - (3.34 / 5)^3} \right] = 0.738 \text{ customers in the system}$$

Step 6:   Compute the average queue length, L. The average number of customers in the queue must be computed as follows:

$$L_q = L - [(\lambda (1 - P_M)) / \mu]$$
$$= 0.738 - [(3.34 * (1 - 0.141)) / 5] = 0.164 \text{ customers waiting}$$

Step 7:   Compute the average time in the system, W.
$$W = L / (\lambda(1 - P_M))$$
$$= 0.738 / (3.34 * (1 - 0.141)) = 0.257 \text{ hours (15.43 min.) in the system}$$

Step 8:   Compute the average waiting time, W_q.
$$W_q = W - (1 / \mu)$$
$$= 0.738 - (1 / 5) = 0.538 \text{ hours (32.28 min.) waiting in line}$$

1.   Big D's is a drive through restaurant that has limited space for customers since it is located next to a busy highway. The restaurant has space for only one vehicle at the window and four vehicles lined up to wait for service. There is no space for cars to line up on the busy adjacent highway, so if the waiting line is full (4 cars), prospective customers must drive on.

   The mean time between arrivals for customers seeking food is 2 minutes. The mean time required to perform the lube operation is 1.5 minutes. Both the interarrival times and service times are exponentially distributed. The maximum number of vehicles in the system is five. Determine the average waiting time, the average queue length, and the probability that a customer will have to drive on.

2.   Bryant's Computer Repair averages five computers to repair per 8-hour day. The service manager would like a service time of 3.5 days. If Bryant's can only accommodate up to 20 computers at a time, what is the probability that the number of computers on hand (under repair and waiting for service) will exceed the shop capacity?

3.   Tim paints cars in his spare time. Since this is his second job, Tim works out of his home garage. He can only have 5 cars in his shop or yard at a time. The paint jobs take on average 3 days to complete due to preparation, painting, and allowing for curing. Tim also realized that the customer will not be able to pick his car up until the next weekend, so the actual time from drop off to pick up is on average 7 days. Paint jobs are requested at 1 every 10 days. Tim wants to know what the probability is that the number of jobs in the system will exceed the shop's capacity. How might he use this information to help the business?

Single-Server Model with Finite Calling Population
Use the computer software to help with these problems.

1.   KidCo operates a manufacturing plant for producing children's toys. The company has 10 machine areas. Due to the type of work performed in the plant, the machines require frequent repair and maintenance. When a machine within an area breaks down, the entire area is shut down with the date of breakdown noted. The company has one senior repairperson, with an assistant, who repairs the machines based on an oldest-date-of-breakdown rule (i.e., a FIFO queue discipline). Each machine operates an average of 600 hours before breaking down, and the mean repair time is 5.8 hours. The breakdown rate is Poisson distributed and the service times are exponentially distributed. The company would like an analysis performed of machine idle time due to breakdowns in order to determine if the present repair staff is sufficient.

2.   Hudson Valley Books is a small independent publisher of fiction and nonfiction books. Each week the publisher receives an average of seven unsolicited manuscripts to review (Poisson distributed). The publisher has 12 freelance reviewers in the area that read and evaluate manuscripts. It takes a reviewer an average of 10 days (exponentially distributed) to read a manuscript and write a brief synopsis. (Reviewers work on their own, 7 days a week). Determine how long the publisher must wait on average to receive a reviewer's manuscript evaluation, how many manuscripts are waiting to be reviewed, and how busy the reviewers are.

3.   A retail catalog operation employs a bank of six telephone operators, who process orders using computer terminals. When a terminal breaks down, it must be disconnected and taken to a nearby electronics repair shop, where it is repaired. The mean time between terminal breakdowns is 6 working days, and the mean time required to repair a terminal is 2 working days (both exponentially distributed). As a result of lost sales, it costs the mail-order operation an estimated $50 per day in lost profits each day a terminal is out for repair. The company pays the electronic repair shop $3,000 per year on a service agreement with another electronics repair shop that will provide substitute terminals while the broken ones are at the repair shop. However, the new service agreement would cost the mail-order operation $15,000 per year. Assuming that there are 250 working days in a year, determine what the mail-order operation should do.

4.	Bayou Seasoning operates 5 filling machines that are identical. The machines carry out their operations automatically. However, they occasionally will stop up with seasoning ingredients. This happens on average of once every 6 minutes per machine, following a Poisson process. Clearing a jammed machine is usually fast, taking an average of 35 seconds (exponentially distributed). Each machine operates in a different production line with one operator responsible. What is the average number of machines not in production (stopped up and either being cleared or waiting) at any given moment? What is the average amount of time a stopped up machine must wait to be cleared? What are the other operating characteristics for the line?

5.	Jason Lewis, a computer technician, is responsible for 5 clients. Customers request assistance at an average (Poisson) rate of once every five working days. Jason can service an average (Poisson) of 1.5 calls per day. What are the operation characteristics for this model?

6.	Ryan and Kurt, two electricians for a local power plant, are responsible for 12 machines. To fix general maintenance problems, the average time is 13 minutes per machine. The machines operate for an average of 2.0 hours between servicing. What are the operating characteristics for system?

Multiple-Server Waiting Line System
S1.	The Student Federal Credit Union has three tellers to service customers. Computer logs show that an average of 20 customers arrive per hour (according to a Poisson distribution), and an average service time of 6 minutes per customer (exponentially distributed). Customers enter the credit union and form a single waiting line. The customers are treated on a first-come, first-served basis. The manager wants to know the operating characteristics of the system.

Solution:
Step 1:	Identify the model type. This is a multiple server waiting line since there is one queue that the customers enter. They are waiting for 1 of 3 tellers to become available to serve them.

Step 2:	Identify and compute the average arrival time λ, service time μ, number of servers (s), and average number of customers serviced by the system (sμ).

$\lambda = 20$ customers per hour

The service time is given exponentially ($1/\mu$) as a time per customer. This has to be converted to number of customers per hour. So, divide the minutes per hour (60 minutes) by the time needed to service a customer (6 minutes). This gives you 60 / 6, or 10 customers per hour.

$\mu = 10$ customers per hour per teller

$s = 3$ tellers

We can determine the total number of customers being served by the system by multiplying the number of tellers (s) by the average number of customers serviced per hour (10 customers). So, s$\mu = 3 * 10 = 30$ (>$\lambda = 20$).

Step 3:	Determine the operating system characteristics. Using the multiple server model formulas, we can compute the following operating characteristics for the credit union:

Probability that there are no customers in the system:

$$Po = \frac{1}{[\Sigma[(1/n!)\,(\lambda/\mu)^n\,]]\ +\ [1/M!(\lambda/\mu)^M\,(\,M\mu\,/\,M\mu - \lambda)]}$$

$$= \frac{1}{[\Sigma[(0/0!)\,(20/10)^0 + (1/1!)\,(20/10)^1 + (1/2!)\,(20/10)^2]] + [(1/3!)(20/10)^3\,(3*10\,/\,((3*10) - 20))]}$$

$$= \frac{1}{[\Sigma[0 + 2 + 2]] + [(1.33)\,(30\,/\,10)]}$$

$=$	0.125 probability that no customers are in the service department

443

Step 4: Determine average number of customers in the system using the formula below.

$$L = \frac{\lambda\mu(\lambda/\mu)^M}{(M-1)!\,(M\mu-\lambda)^2} * Po + \frac{\lambda}{\mu}$$

$$= \left[\frac{20*10*(20/10)^3}{(3-1)!\,(3*10-20)^2}\right] * (0.125) + \left[\frac{20}{10}\right] = 3 \text{ customers in the service department}$$

Step 5: Determine average time a customer spends in the system using the formula below.

$$W = L/\lambda = 3 \text{ customers} / 20 \text{ arrivals} = 0.15 \text{ hours (9 min.) in the system}$$

Step 6: Determine average number of customers in the queue using the formula below.

$$L_q = L - (\lambda/\mu) = 3 - (20/10) = 1 \text{ customer waiting to be served}$$

Step 7: Determine average waiting time a customer spends in the queue using the formula below.

$$W_q = L_q/\lambda = 1/20 = 0.05 \text{ hours (3 min.) waiting in line}$$

Step 8: Determine the probability that a customer will have to wait in the system using the formula below.

$$P_W = \left[\frac{1}{M!}\right]\left[\frac{\lambda}{\mu}\right]^M \left[\frac{M\mu}{M\mu\lambda}\right] Po$$

$$= \left[\frac{1}{3!}\right]\left[\frac{20}{10}\right]^3 \left[\frac{3*10}{3(10)-20}\right] * (.125)$$

$$= (0.166) * (8) * (3) * (0.125) = 0.498 \text{ probability that a customer must wait}$$

S2. The Student Medical Center has a waiting room in which chairs are placed along a wall, forming a single waiting line. Students with regular medical conditions are treated on a first-come, first-served basis. Students arrive at an average of 5 minutes between arrivals (mean interarrival time is exponentially distributed). This means that $\lambda = 60$ minutes per hour / 5 minutes between arrivals = 12 students per hour (according to a Poisson distribution), and an average of 7.5 students can be served per hour by a doctor (Poisson distributed). The center has 2 doctors on staff to examine students.

Step 1: Identify the model type. This is a multiple server waiting line since there is one queue that the students enter. They are waiting for 1 of 2 doctors to become available to serve them.

Step 2: Identify and compute the average arrival time λ, service time μ, number of servers (s), and average number of customers serviced by the system (sμ). The service time is given exponentially (1/λ) as a time between arrivals. This has to be converted to number of customers arriving per hour. So, divide the minutes per hour (60 minutes) by the time between arriving customers (5 minutes). This gives you 60 / 5, or 12 customers per hour.

$\lambda = 12$ customers per hour

The service time is given as a Poisson distribution for how many students can be serviced by one of the doctors per hour.

$\mu = 7.5$ students per hour per doctor

s = 2 doctors

We can determine the total number of students being served by the system by multiplying the number of doctors (s) by the average number of students serviced per hour (7.5 students). So, s$\mu = 2 * 7.5 = 15$ (>λ = 12).

Step 3: Determine the operating system characteristics. Using the multiple server model formulas, we can compute the following operating characteristics for the medical center:

Probability that there are no customers in the system:

$$P_0 = \cfrac{1}{[\sum[(1/n!)\,(\lambda/\mu)^n\,]] + [1/M!(\lambda/\mu)^M\,(\,M\mu\,/\,M\mu - \lambda)]}$$

$$= \cfrac{1}{[\sum[(0/0!)\,(12/7.5)^0 + (1/1!)\,(12/7.5)^1]] + [(1/2!)(12/7.5)^2*(2*7.5\,/\,((2*7.5) - 12))]}$$

$$= \cfrac{1}{[\sum[0 + 1.6]] + [(1.28)*(15\,/\,12)]}$$

$$= 0.125 \text{ probability that no customers are in the service department}$$

Step 4: Determine average number of customers in the system using the formula below.

$$L = \cfrac{\lambda\mu(\lambda/\mu)^M}{(M-1)!\,(M\,\mu - \lambda)^2} * P_0 + \cfrac{\lambda}{\mu}$$

$$= \left[\cfrac{12*7.5*(12/7.5)^2}{(2-1)!\,((2*7.5) - 12)^2}\right] * (0.125) + \left[\cfrac{12}{7.5}\right]$$

$$= (25.6)*(0.125) + (1.6) = 4.8 \text{ students in the center}$$

Step 5: Determine average time a student spends in the system using the formula below.

$$W = L/\lambda = 4.8 \text{ students} / 12 \text{ arrivals} = 0.4 \text{ hours (24 min.) in the system}$$

Step 6: Determine average number of students in the queue using the formula below.

$$L_q = L - (\lambda/\mu) = 4.8 - (12/7.5) = 3.2 \text{ students waiting to be served}$$

Step 7: Determine average waiting time a student spends in the queue using the formula below.

$$W_q = L_q/\lambda = 3.2/12 = 0.266 \text{ hours (16 min.) waiting in line}$$

Step 8: Determine the probability that a student will have to wait in the system using the formula below.

$$P_W = \left[\cfrac{1}{M!}\right]\left[\cfrac{\lambda}{\mu}\right]^M \left[\cfrac{M\mu}{M\mu\lambda}\right] P_0$$

$$= \left[\cfrac{1}{2!}\right]\left[\cfrac{12}{7.5}\right]^2 \left[\cfrac{2*7.5}{2(7.5)-12}\right] * (.125)$$

$$= (0.5)*(2.56)*(5)*(0.125) = 0.80 \text{ probability that a customer must wait.}$$

1. The portrait studio at DL Hunt Department Store has a waiting area in which chairs are placed along a wall, forming a single waiting line. Customers come with questions, wait for a portrait session, or to see proofs. Three photographers, each located in a different room, service the customers. The customers are treated on a first-come, first-served basis. The manager wants to analyze this queuing system because excessive waiting times can irritate customers to the point that they will go to another store. A study of the studio for a 6-month period shows that an average of 5 customers arrive per hour (according to a Poisson distribution), and an average of 3 customers can be served per hour by a photographer (Poisson distributed).

2. Heaven on Earth Body Spa is a popular salon and spa near the campus of the local university. Three beauticians work full-time and spend an average of 25 minutes on each customer. Customers arrive all day long at an average rate of 10 per hour. Arrivals tend to follow the Poisson distribution, and service times are exponentially distributed.

    a. What is the probability that the salon is empty?
    b. What is the average number of customers in the spa?
    c. What is the average time spent in the salon?
    d. What is the average time that a customer waits to be called to be serviced?
    e. What is the average number waiting to be served?
    f. What is the salon's utilization factor?
    g. The manager is thinking of adding a fourth beautician. How will this affect the utilization rate?

3. Heaven on Earth Body Spa also has 2 massage therapists working full-time, who spend an average of 30 minutes on each customer. Customers arrive all day long at an average rate of 1.75 per hour. Arrivals tend to follow the Poisson distribution, and service times are exponentially distributed.

    a. What is the probability that the salon is empty?
    b. What is the average number of customers in the salon?
    c. What is the average time spent in the salon?
    d. What is the average time that a customer waits to be served?
    e. What is the average number waiting to be served?

4. The Patient Services Supervisor at the local hospital wants to ensure the best possible service for its patients. The Supervisor is especially worried about Saturdays since they are heavy days. She estimates that the patients arrive one every 10 minutes. She also knows that it usually requires 25 minutes to see each patient (exponentially distributed). The first available doctor sees patients on a first-come, first-served basis. How many doctors should be on duty on Saturdays if the Supervisor wants patients to wait 20 minutes or less on average to be seen by a doctor?

5. The Patient Services Supervisor at the local hospital wants to ensure the best possible service for its patients. Patients arrive at different rates during the day. There are four doctors available to treat patients when needed. If not needed, they can be assigned to other responsibilities (for example, lab tests, reports, x-ray diagnoses) or else rescheduled to work at other hours.

    The Supervisor wants the patients to not have to sit in the waiting area for more than five minutes before being seen by a doctor. Patients are treated on a first-come, first-served basis and see the first available doctor after waiting in the queue. The arrival pattern for a typical day is:

Time	Arrival rate
9 am – 3 pm	6 patients / hour
3 pm – 8 pm	4 patients / hour
8 pm – midnight	12 patients / hour

    These arrivals follow a Poisson distribution, and treatment times, 12 minutes on the average, follow the exponential pattern. How many doctors should be on duty during each period in order to maintain the level of patient care expected? You will need to use computer software to help you.

6.   DL Hunt Department Store has approximately 200 customers shopping in its store between 10 am and 6
       pm on Saturdays. The manager wants to determine how many cash registers to keep open each Saturday.
       The manager considers two factors: customer waiting time (and the associated waiting cost) and the
       service cost of employing additional checkout clerks. Checkout clerks are paid an average of $5 per hour.
       When only one is on duty, the waiting time per customer is about 10 minutes (or 1/6 of an hour); when
       two clerks are on duty, the average checkout time is 6 minutes per person; 4 minutes when three clerks are
       working; and 3 minutes when four clerks are on duty.

       The manager has conducted customer satisfaction surveys and has been able to estimate that the store
       suffers approximately $5 in lost sales and goodwill for every hour of customer time spent waiting in
       checkout lines. Using the information provided, determine the optimal number of clerks to have on duty
       each Saturday in order to minimize the store's total expected cost.

7.   The x-ray technicians at the local hospital have patients arrive at a rate of 14 per hour (Poisson distributed)
       during normal working hours (8am to 4 pm). An average of eight x-rays per hour can be processed by the
       two lab technicians working the lab (exponentially distributed). What percentage of time are the
       technicians busy? What is the probability that both technicians are idle at the same time and the average
       number of x-ray patients are waiting? What is the average amount of time a patient waits to be processed
       and the average time a patient spends at the lab?

8.   For the previous problem, determine how many x-ray technicians are needed if the patients need to be
       processed (time from when the patient reaches the waiting room and service time) within 45 minutes.

Module E
Learning Curves

I. Learning Curves

   A. Most organizations learn and improve over time.

   B. They learn how to perform more efficiently, so task times and costs decrease.

   C. Based on the premise that people and organizations become better at their tasks as the tasks are repeated.

   D. Learning curves are based on a doubling of production.

      1. When production doubles, the decrease in time per unit affects the rate of the learning curve.

      2. If the learning curve is an 80% rate, the second unit takes 80% of the time of the first unit, the fourth unit takes 80% of the time of the second unit.

      3. Calculated with the following formula:

$$T \times L^n = \text{Time required for the nth unit}$$

        Where: T = unit cost or unit time of the first unit

                      L = learning curve rate

                      n = number of times T is doubled

II. Learning Curves in Services and Manufacturing

   A. The rate of learning varies depending of the quality of management and the potential of the process and product.

   B. Any changes in the process, product, or personnel disrupt the learning curve.

   C. The lower the number (say 70% compared to 90%), the steeper the slope and the faster the drop in costs.

   D. Other uses include:

      1. Internal: labor forecasting, scheduling, establishing costs and budgets.

      2. External: supply chain negotiations.

      3. Strategic: evaluation of company and industry performance, including costs and pricing.

III. Applying the Learning Curve

   A. A mathematical relationship enables us to express the time required to produce a certain unit.

   B. Function of how many units have been produced before the unit in question and how long it took to produce them.

   C. Arithmetic Approach – the simplest approach to learning-curve problems.

   D. Logarithmic Approach – allows us to determine labor for any unit, T_N, using the formula:

$$T_N = T_1(N^b)$$

        Where: T_N = time for the Nth unit

                     T_1 = hours to produce the first unit

                     b = (log of the learning rate) / (log 2) = slope of the learning curve

E. Learning-Curve Coefficient Approach
$$T_N = T_1(C)$$

Where: T_N = number of labor-hours required to produce the Nth unit
T_1 = number of labor-hours required to produce the first unit
C = learning-curve coefficient found in Table E.3 on pg. 737 of the text

Example

It took a Korean shipyard 125,000 labor-hours to produce the first of several tugboats that you expect to purchase for your shipping company. Great Lakes, Inc. boats 2 and 3 have been produced by the Koreans with a learning factor of 85%. At $40 per hour, what should you, as purchasing agent, expect to pay for the fourth unit?

Solution:
First, search Table E.3 for the fourth unit and a learning factor of 85%. The learning-curve coefficient, C, is .723. To purchase the fourth unit, then, takes

$$T_N = T_1(C)$$
$$T_4 = (125,000)(.723) = 90,375 \text{ hours}$$

To find the cost, multiply by $40:

  90,375 hours x $40 per hour = $3,615,000

How long will all four coats require?

Solution:
Looking this time at the "total time" column in Table E.3 on pg. 737 of the text, we find that the cumulative coefficient is 3.345. Thus, the time required is:

$$T_N = T_1(C)$$
$$T_4 = (125,000)(3.345) = 418,125 \text{ hours in total for all 4 boats}$$

Great Lakes, Inc. believes that unusual circumstances in producing the first boat imply that the time estimate of 125,000 hours is not as valid a base as the time required to produce the third boat. Boat number 3 was completed in 100,000 hours.

Solution:
To solve for the revised estimate for boat number 1, we return to Table E.3 on pg. 737, with a unit value of N = 3 and a learning-curve coefficient of C = .773 in the 85% column. To find the revised estimate, we divide the actual time for boat number 3, 100,000 hours, by C = .733.

  Revised = 100,000 hours / .733 = 129,366 hours for number 1

IV. Limitations of Learning Curve

A. Because learning curves differ from company to company, as well as industry to industry, estimates for each organization should be developed rather than applying someone else's.

B. Learning curves are often based on the time necessary to complete the early units; therefore, those times must be accurate. As current information becomes available, reevaluation is appropriate.

C. Any changes in personnel, design, or procedure can be expected to alter the learning curve. And the curve may spike up for a short time even if it is going to drop in the long run.

D. While workers and processes may improve, the same learning curves do not always apply to indirect labor and material.

E. The culture of the workplace, as well as resource availability and changes in the process, may alter the learning curve. For instance, as a project nears its end, worker interest and effort may drop, curtailing progress down the curve.

MODULE E PROBLEMS

Learning Curve

S1.   The manager is interested in determining the amount of time to complete the construction of 20 bookcases. Since the first is the most difficult and takes 90 minutes to complete, the manager expects his workers to improve the completion time of the following bookcases. He expects that the learning curve between bookcases is 88%. What amount of time do you expect bookcase numbers 5, 10, and 15 to take to complete?

Solution:

Step 1:   Determine the information needed.

Time to complete the first bookcase: t_1 = 90 minutes

Formula: $t_n = t_1 * n^b$

n is the repetition that you are to calculate the time for completion.

Learning curve: 88%

$b = \ln(\text{Learning Curve}) / \ln 2 = \ln(.88) / \ln 2 = -0.1844$

Step 2:   Calculate the time required for the 5th, 10th, and 15th repetitions:

The time required for the 5th unit is computed using the learning curve formula:

$t_n = t_1 * n^b$
$t_9 = 90 * 5^{\ln(0.88)/\ln 2}$
$t_9 = 90 * 5^{-0.1844}$ = 66.88 minutes

The time required for the 10th unit is computed using the learning curve formula:

$t_n = t_1 * n^b$
$t_9 = 90 * 10^{\ln(0.88)/\ln 2}$
$t_9 = 90 * 10^{-0.1844}$ = 58.86 minutes

The time required for the 15th unit is computed using the learning curve formula:

$t_n = t_1 * n^b$
$t_9 = 90 * 15^{\ln(0.88)/\ln 2}$
$t_9 = 90 * 15^{-0.1844}$ = 54.62 minutes

S2.   Barb's YumYum Bakery is baking cakes for a Mardi Gras ball. An order for 5 large cakes (10 ft. long) is taken on Friday morning (6:30 am). The cakes are needed for the ball at 9 pm on Friday, and it will take an hour to deliver the cakes to the ball. Since the bakery has other customers, the manager is only willing to allocate one worker and one oven to the cakes. The first cake takes 3 hours to make. The manager estimates that the worker will have an 85% learning curve. What is the earliest that the cakes can be ready given the time requirement and learning curve for the five cakes? Can the cake be delivered in time for the party? If the cakes can be delivered by 8:15 pm on Friday, the bakery will get a bonus of $100 plus the $75 per cake. The manager estimates the cost of each cake to be $45 per hour in direct labor (regular time and overtime) plus materials. Do you think that it was wise for the manager to accept an order?

Solution:

Step 1: Determine the information needed.

Time to complete the first bookcase: $t_1 = 180$ minutes   Formula: $t_n = t_1 * n^b$

n is the repetition that you are to calculate the time for completion.

$b = \ln(\text{Learning Curve}) / \ln 2 = \ln(.85) / \ln 2 = -0.2345$ Learning curve: 85%

Step 2: Calculate the time required for each cake:

The time required for the 1st cake is: 180 minutes (from the write up)

The time required for the 2nd cake is computed using the learning curve formula:

$t_n = t_1 * n^b$
$t_2 = 180 * 2^{\ln(0.85) / \ln 2}$
$t_2 = 180 * 2^{-0.2345} = 153$ minutes

The time required for the 3rd unit is computed using the learning curve formula:

$t_n = t_1 * n^b$
$t_3 = 180 * 3^{\ln(0.85) / \ln 2}$
$t_3 = 180 * 3^{-0.2345} = 139.1$ minutes

The time required for the 4th unit is computed using the learning curve formula:

$t_n = t_1 * n^b$
$t_4 = 180 * 4^{\ln(0.85) / \ln 2}$
$t_4 = 180 * 4^{-0.2345} = 130$ minutes

The time required for the 5th unit is computed using the learning curve formula:

$t_n = t_1 * n^b$
$t_5 = 180 * 5^{\ln(0.85) / \ln 2}$
$t_5 = 180 * 5^{-0.2345} = 123.4$ minutes

Step 3: Calculate the total time to complete the 5 cakes. Add the time for the five cakes to determine the total time.

Total baking time $= 180 + 153 + 139.1 + 130 + 123.4 = 725.5$

Step 4: Convert to hours. Divide the total time in minutes by the 60 (minutes in an hour).

Hours $= 725.5 / 60 = 12.09$ hours or 12 hours 6 minutes.

Step 5: Analysis: Yes, if the order is started immediately at 6:30 am and it takes 12 hours and 6 minutes to complete the order, it will be completed at 6:36 pm. The manager then will have to deliver the cakes an hour away, so the cake could be at the ball by 7:36 pm.

If the cakes can be delivered by 8:15 pm on Friday, the bakery will get a bonus of $100 plus the $75 per cake. The manager estimates the cost of each cake to be $45 per hour in direct labor (regular time and overtime) plus materials. Do you think that it was wise for the manager to accept an order?

Step 6: Determine the cost and revenue. Based on the cost of the cakes per hour ($45 per hr.) multiplied by the time required to produce the cakes (12.09), the cost is $544.05. The revenue is determined by the price per cake ($75) multiplied by the number of cakes (5), or $375, plus the $100 bonus for delivery before the ball. The total revenue is $475. At these levels, the bakery would lose $69.05 on this order, so the manager should not have taken the order.

1.   Given that it takes 25 hours to complete the first unit of production and that the learning curve is 80%, how much time is needed to complete units 4 and 5?

2.   Given that it takes 1.5 hours to complete the first unit of production and that the learning curve is 75%, how much time is needed to complete units 5 and 15?

3.   Given that it takes 8 hours to complete the first unit of production and that the learning curve is 89%, how much time is needed to complete units 10 and 25?

4.   Given that it takes 40 minutes to complete the first unit of production and that the learning curve is 95%, how much time is needed to complete units 3 and 6?

5.   Now, Barb's YumYum Bakery has received another order for 15 large cakes (10 ft. long) on Thursday afternoon (12:30 pm). The cakes are needed for the ball at 1 pm on Saturday, and it will take an hour to deliver the cakes to the ball. Since the Bakery has other customers, the manager is only willing to allocate one worker and oven to the cakes. The first cake takes 3 hours to make. The manager estimates that the worker will have an 85% learning curve. The manager will stop production at 6 pm on Thursday and Friday to avoid extra cost. What is the earliest that the cakes can be ready given the time requirement and learning curve for the 15 cakes? Can the cake be delivered in time for the party? If the cakes can be delivered by 8:15 pm on Friday, the bakery will get a bonus of $100 plus the $75 per cake. The manager estimates the cost of each cake to be $45 per hour in direct labor (regular time and overtime) plus materials. Do you think that it was wise for the manager to accept an order?

Module F
Simulation

I. What is Simulation?

A. The attempt to duplicate the features, appearance, and characteristics of a real system.

B. Used to estimate the effects of various actions.

C. Reasons for using simulation:
1. To imitate a real-world simulation mathematically,
2. Then to study its properties and operating characteristics, and
3. Finally to draw conclusions and make action decisions based on the results of the simulation.

D. Steps to using simulation:
1. Define the problem.
2. Introduce the important variables associated with the problem.
3. Construct a numerical model.
4. Set up possible courses of action for testing.
5. Run the experiment.
6. Consider the results (possibly modifying the model or changing data inputs).
7. Decide what course of action to take.

II. Advantages and Disadvantages of Simulation

A. Advantages:
1. Simulation is relatively straightforward and flexible.
2. It can be used to analyze large and complex real-world situations that cannot be solved by conventional operations management models.
3. Real-world complications can be included that most OM models cannot permit. For example, simulation can use any probability distribution the user defines; it does not require standard distributions.
4. "Time compression" is possible. The effects of OM policies over many months or years can be obtained by computer simulation in a short time.
5. Simulation allows "what-if" types of questions. Managers like to know in advance what options will be most attractive. With a computerized model, a manager can try out several policy decisions within a matter of minutes.
6. Simulations do not interfere with real-world systems. It may be too disruptive, for example, to experiment physically with new policies or ideas in a hospital or manufacturing plant.
7. Simulation can study the interactive effects of individual components or variables in order to determine which ones are important.

B. Disadvantages:
1. Good simulation models can be very expensive; they may take many months to develop.
2. It is a trial-and-error approach that may produce different solutions in repeated runs. It does not generate optimal solutions to problems.

3. Managers must generate all of the conditions and constraints for solutions that they want to examine. The simulation model does not produce answers without adequate, realistic input.
4. Each simulation model is unique. Its solutions and inferences are not usually transferable to other problems.

III. **Monte Carlo Simulation**

A. Simulation of systems that exhibit chance (or probabilistic) behaviors.
B. Uses a random sampling experimentation.
C. Steps of the technique:
1. Establishing probability distributions
2. Building a cumulative probability distribution for each variable
3. Setting random-number intervals
4. Generating random numbers
5. Simulating the experiment

Example

Let's illustrate the concept of random numbers by simulating 10 days of demand for radial tires at Barry's Auto Tire (see table below). We select the random numbers needed from Table F.4 on pg. 751 of the text, starting in the upper left corner and continuing down the first column:

Barry's Auto Tire			
Daily Demand	Cumulative Probability	Interval of Probability	Random Numbers
0	.05	.05	01 through 05
1	.10	.15	06 through 15
2	.20	.35	16 through 35
3	.30	.65	36 through 65
4	.20	.85	66 through 85
5	.15	1.00	86 through 00

Solution:

Day Number	Random Number	Simulated Daily Demand
1	52	3
2	37	3
3	82	4
4	69	4
5	98	5
6	96	5
7	33	2
8	50	3
9	88	5
10	90	5
	Total 10-day demand:	39

Tires Average Daily Demand = 39 / 10 days = 3.9 tires per day

It is interesting to note that the average demand of 3.9 tires in this 10-day simulation differs substantially from the expected daily demand, which we may calculate from the data in the first table:

$$\text{Expected demand} = \Sigma \, (\text{probability of } i \text{ units}) \times (\text{demand of } i \text{ units})$$
$$= (.05)(0) + (.10)(1) + (.20)(2) + (.30)(3) + (.20)(4) + (.15)(5)$$
$$= 2.95 \text{ tires}$$

However, if this simulation were repeated hundreds of thousands of times, the average simulated demand would be nearly the same as the expected demand.

IV. Simulation of a Queuing Problem

Example

Following long trips down the Mississippi River from industrial midwestern cities, fully loaded barges arrive at night in New Orleans. The number of barges docking on any given night ranges from 0 to 5. The probabilities of 0, 1, 2, 3, 4, and 5 arrivals is displayed in the table below. In the same table, we establish cumulative probabilities and corresponding random-number intervals for each possible value.

Overnight Barge Arrival Rates and Random-Number Intervals			
Number of Arrivals	Probability	Cumulative Probability	Random-Number Interval
0	.13	.13	01 through 13
1	.17	.30	14 through 30
2	.15	.45	31 through 45
3	.25	.70	46 through 70
4	.20	.90	71 through 90
5	.10	1.00	91 through 00
	1.00		

A study by the dock superintendent reveals that the number of barges unloaded also tends to vary from day to day. In the table below, the superintendent provides information from which we can create a probability distribution for the variable daily unloading rate. As we just did for the arrival variable, we can set up an interval of random numbers for the unloading rates.

Unloading Rates and Random-Number Intervals			
Daily Unloading Rates	Probability	Cumulative Probability	Random-Number Interval
1	.05	.05	01 through 05
2	.15	.20	06 through 20
3	.50	.70	21 through 70
4	.20	.90	71 through 90
5	.10	1.00	91 through 00
	1.00		

Barges are unloaded on a first-in, first-out basis. Any barges not unloaded on the day of arrival must wait until the following day. However, tying up barges in dock is an expensive proposition, and the superintendent cannot ignore the angry phone calls from barge owners reminding him that "time is money!" He decides that, before going to the Port of New Orleans controller to request additional unloading crews, he should conduct a simulation study of arrivals, unloadings, and delays. A 100-day simulation would be ideal, but for purposes of illustration, the superintendent begins with a shorter 15-day analysis. Random numbers are drawn from the top row of Table F.4 on pg. 751 of the text to generate daily arrival rates. To create daily unloading rates, they are drawn from the second row of Table F.4. The table below shows the day-to-day port simulation.

	Queuing Simulation of Port of N.O. Barge Unloadings					
(1) Day	(2) # Delayed From Previous Day	(3) Random Number	(4) # of Nightly Arrivals	(5) Total to Be Unloaded	(6) Random Number	(7) Number Unloaded
1	---	52	3	3	37	3
2	0	06	0	0	63	0
3	0	50	3	3	28	3
4	0	88	4	4	02	1
5	3	53	3	6	74	4
6	2	30	1	3	35	3
7	0	10	0	0	24	0
8	0	47	3	3	03	1
9	2	99	5	7	29	3
10	4	37	2	6	60	3
11	3	66	3	6	74	4
12	2	91	5	7	85	4
13	3	35	2	5	90	4
14	1	32	2	3	73	3
15	0	00	5	5	59	3
	20		41			39
	Total delays		Total arrivals			Total unloadings

The superintendent will likely be interested in at least three useful and important pieces of information:

Avg. Number of Barges Delayed to the Next Day   =   20 delays / 15 days
    =   1.33 barges delayed per day

Avg. Number of Nightly Arrivals   =   41 arrivals / 15 days
    =   2.73 arrivals per night

Avg. Number of Barges Unloaded Each Day   =   39 unloadings / 15 days
    =   2.60 unloadings per day

V.   Simulation and Inventory Analysis

Example

Simkin's Hardware sells the Ace model electric drill. Daily demand for the drill is relatively low but subject to some variability. Over the past 300 days, Simkin has observed the sales shown in column 3 of the table below. He converts this historical frequency into a probability distribution for the variable daily demand (column 3). A cumulative probability distribution is formed in column 4. Finally, Simkin establishes an interval of random numbers to represent each possible daily demand (column 5).

Probabilities and Random-Number Intervals for Daily Ace Drill Demand				
(1) Demand for Ace Drill	(2) Frequency	(3) Probability	(4) Cumulative Probability	(5) Interval of Random Numbers
0	15	.05	.05	01 through 05
1	30	.10	.15	06 through 15
2	60	.20	.35	16 through 35
3	120	.40	.75	36 through 75
4	45	.15	.90	76 through 90
5	30	.10	1.00	91 through 00
	300 days	1.00		

When Simkin places an order to replenish his inventory of drills, there is a delivery lag of 1 to 3 days. This means that lead-time may also be considered a probabilistic variable. The number of days that it took to receive the past 50 orders is presented in the table below. In a fashion similar to the creation of the demand variable, Simkin establishes a probability distribution for the lead-time variable (column 3 of table below), computes the cumulative distribution (column 4), and assigns random-number intervals for each possible time (column 5).

Probabilities and Random-Number Intervals for Reorder Lead-Time				
(1) Lead Time (Days)	(2) Frequency	(3) Probability	(4) Cumulative Probability	(5) Interval of Random Numbers
1	10	.20	.20	01 through 20
2	25	.50	.70	21 through 70
3	15	.30	1.00	71 through 00
	50 orders	1.00		

The first inventory policy that Simkin wants to simulate is an order quantity of 10 with a reorder point of 5. That is, every time the on-hand inventory level at the end of the day is 5 or less, Simkin will call his supplier that evening and place an order for 10 more drills. Note that if the lead-time is 1 day, the order will not arrive the next morning, but rather at the beginning of the following workday.

The entire process is simulated in the next table for a 10-day period. We assume that beginning inventory (column 3) is 10 units on day 1. We took the random numbers (column 4) from column 2 of Table F.4 on pg. 751 in the text.

The next table was filled in by proceeding 1 day (or line) at a time, working from left to right. It is a four-step process:

1. Begin each simulated day by checking to see whether any ordered inventory has just arrived. If it has, increase current inventory by the quantity ordered (10 units, in this case).

2. Generate a daily demand from the demand probability distribution by selecting a random number.

3. Compute: ending inventory = beginning inventory minus demand. If on-hand inventory is insufficient to meet the day's demand, satisfy as much demand as possible and note the number of lost sales.

4. Determine whether the day's ending inventory has reached the reorder point (5 units). If it has, and if there are no outstanding orders, place an order. Lead-time for a new order is simulated by choosing a random number and using the distribution in the "Probabilities and Random-Number Intervals for Reorder Lead-Time" table.

Simkin Hardware's First Inventory Simulation. Order Quantity = 10 Units; Reorder Pt. = 5									
(1) Day	(2) Units Received	(3) Beg. Inventory	(4) Random Number	(5) Demand	(6) End. Inventory	(7) Lost Sales	(8) Order?	(9) Random Number	(10) Lead Time
1	---	10	06	1	9	0	No		
2	0	9	63	3	6	0	No		
3	0	6	57	3	3	0	Yes	02	1
4	0	3	94	5	0	2	No		
5	10	10	52	3	7	0	No		
6	0	7	69	3	4	0	Yes	33	2
7	0	4	32	2	2	0	No		
8	0	2	30	2	0	0	No		
9	10	10	48	3	7	0	No		
10	0	7	88	4	3	0	Yes	14	
					41	2			

Simkin's first inventory simulation yields some interesting results. The average daily ending inventory is:

Average ending inventory   =   41 total units / 10 days
                            =   4.1 units / day

We also note the average lost sales and number of orders placed per day:

Average lost sales   =   2 sales lost / 10 days
                            =   .2 units / day
Average number of orders placed = 3 total units / 10 days
                            =   .3 orders / day

Example

Simkin estimates that the cost of placing each order for Ace drills is $10, the holding cost per drill held at the end of each day is $.50, and the cost of each lost sale is $8. This information enables us to compute the total daily inventory cost for the simulated policy in the previous example. Let's examine the three cost components:

Solution:

Daily order cost = (cost of placing 1 order) x (# of orders placed per day)
= $10 per order x .3 orders per day = $3

Daily holding cost = (cost of holding 1 unit for 1 day) x (avg. ending inventory)
= $.50 per unit per day x 4.1 units per day = $2.05

Daily stockout cost = (cost per lost sale) x (avg. # of lost sales per day)
= $8 per lost sale x .2 lost sales per day = $1.60

Total daily inventory cost = Daily order cost + Daily holding cost + Daily stockout cost
= $6.65